RULERS AND REBELS

A PEOPLE'S HISTORY OF EARLY CALIFORNIA, 1769–1901

LAURENCE H. SHOUP

IUNIVERSE, INC.
NEW YORK   BLOOMINGTON

Rulers and Rebels
A People's History of Early California, 1769–1901

iUniverse books may be ordered through booksellers or by contacting:

iUniverse
1663 Liberty Drive
Bloomington, IN 47403
www.iuniverse.com
1-800-Authors (1-800-288-4677)

Because of the dynamic nature of the Internet, any Web addresses or links contained in this book may have changed since publication and may no longer be valid.

ISBN: 978-1-4502-5590-5 (sc)
ISBN: 978-1-4502-5592-9 (dj)
ISBN: 978-1-4502-5591-2 (ebk)

Library of Congress Control Number: 2010914500

Printed in the United States of America

iUniverse rev. date: 11/5/2010

This book is dedicated to my mother, Edna Jaenke Shoup, and my wife, Suzanne Baker. Their lives have been characterized by empathy, generosity, solidarity, and the promotion of social justice.

CONTENTS

MAPS

ILLUSTRATIONS

PREFACE

I was born in Los Angeles during the Second World War. My parents had moved to Southern California early in the war, and my father found a job as a tool-and-die maker at Lockheed Aircraft Company, making P-38 fighters. He was a member of the Machinists Union. Later he established a small jewelry sales and repairing business with a one-store retail outlet. My mother was a housewife, taking care of the family, house, and garden, as well as being active in the Methodist Church.

While growing up in a semi-rural section of postwar Los Angeles, my recreational activities included a varied menu of reading, as well as the usual outdoor play with friends and three brothers. From an early date, my intellectual interests included biography and the history of the western United States, especially my home state of California. This included the California Gold Rush as a special interest, but also extended to other historic eras and the ethnohistory and archaeology of the native peoples of my state. As a youth, I always looked forward to family trips to museums, archaeological sites, and historic locations, such as missions and ghost towns.

Soon after entering college in 1961, I decided to major in history and eventually earned both masters and doctorate degrees. My first two books, *Imperial Brain Trust, The Council on Foreign*

Relations and United States Foreign Policy (coauthored with William Minter) and *The Carter Presidency and Beyond, Power and Politics in the 1980s,* both focused on aspects of the United States' power structure, especially how the American ruling class operates on both national and international levels.

Following several years teaching United States history at a university, in 1978 I embarked upon a second career as senior historian for Archaeological/Historical Consultants, a cultural-resources-management partnership. In this capacity, during the past thirty-two years, I have researched and authored or coauthored over two hundred reports on California history for a variety of private and governmental clients.

This work often required in-depth research, not only in historic texts but also in primary, documentary-source materials, such as historic maps and photographs, manuscript collections, old newspapers, magazines, city and county directories, property deeds, and interviews with surviving "old-timers."

These efforts allowed me to discover a hidden history of early California—an epic marked by control by a series of ruling classes and exciting, but largely forgotten, episodes of class and ethnic conflict, as well as rank-and-file rebellion. These confrontations, together with their resulting victories and defeats, triumphs and tragedies, have been central in making my state what it is today. Encouraged by my long time friend, Professor S. Daniel Schwartz, I decided to bring the most dramatic, interesting, and important incidents of rebellion into a book that would also offer a framework for understanding the entire early history of the region. You now hold that book in your hands.

It is a pleasure to be able to acknowledge and formally thank the people who have been especially helpful in the preparation of this book. My wife and partner, Suzanne Baker, has been a constant source of support and assistance, as well as a challenging editor and critic. The book is much improved because of her input, probing questions, and insightful suggestions.

Our son, Dr. Daniel D. Shoup, has also been very supportive of this project. He has made a number of useful comments and suggestions along the way, and he, along with Jen Angel, helped me with the website, rulersandrebels.com. Geoff Goodman spent many hours helping with editing and preparing the detailed index. Tammara Norton developed the maps. Their assistance has been invaluable.

Howard Zinn, the author of the original "people's history," generously encouraged my efforts to produce a people's history of California. He set a wonderful example of what it means to be an engaged scholar in solidarity with the peoples' movements. He passed away just before I finished the manuscript for this book. We will miss him.

The staff of the Bancroft Library of the University of California at Berkeley, especially David Kessler and Susan Snyder, were, over the many years that it took to research this book, unfailingly helpful in my seemingly never-ending requests for books, manuscripts, maps, and photos from the library's rich collections.

The staffs of the California State Library and the California State Archives, in Sacramento, have also always been of assistance in accessing their valuable primary and secondary material.

Thanks also go to the San Francisco Bay Area *LaborFest*, especially Steve Zeltzer. This annual event was a place where I was able to share some of my results and try out ideas before audiences of labor activists. I also appreciate the Institute for the Critical Study of Society at the Niebyl-Proctor Library in Oakland, where I was also able to present concepts, gain a hearing, and receive helpful suggestions.

Laurence H. Shoup
Oakland, California
June 2010

INTRODUCTION

History is not everything, but it is a starting point.
History is a clock that people use to tell their political
and cultural time of day. It is a compass they use to
find themselves on the map of human geography. It
tells them where they are, but more importantly,
what they must be and where they still must go.
—John Henrik Clarke

At this writing, early in the twenty-first century, California is one of the most influential regions in the entire world. With nearly forty million people and production levels that make it one of the ten largest economies in the world, California is the most populous and arguably the most powerful state in the United States economically, politically, socially, and culturally. Considering that the nation is still the strongest on a shrinking globe, its future is often written in California, which is commonly on the cutting edge of environmental, economic, demographic, cultural, and political change.

As it has been for over 150 years, today's California is also a place of hope and high expectations, the focus of both dreams and future national trends. Its own future is, like all places, linked to its past. So to understand California history, its dynamic evolution and sharp contradictions, is to understand not only the history of the most important state in the United States, but also much of the history and meaning of the United States of America. Key aspects of this history and meaning include hierarchical domination from the top of the society, creating alienation and periodic disruption of this dominance by the rebellion of the rank–and–file and their communities. By its very nature, such rebellion aims at participation, empowerment, and self-actualization of this class of people.

The stories told in this book focus on the fundamentals from the perspective of those at the bottom of society—the rebels. The rulers range from military men representing the Spanish ruling class to early-day capitalists organizing industrial production in the post-Gold Rush/Civil War era, to the banking, commercial, and railroad robber barons of the late nineteenth century. These male, European American rulers created—and tried to preserve—a status quo favorable to their short-term and long-term interests. The rebels of early California history, on the other hand, are a much more diverse group.

The first rebels were the original inhabitants, Native Americans resisting dispossession—invaders were taking their land, their culture, and their very lives. Later rebel groups included African Americans, Irish American and Chinese American immigrants, and working-class unionists all fighting for personal and collective self-realization and against alienation and exploitation.

The rebels portrayed in this book—largely unknown figures, from the Native American Charquin to the union leader Furuseth—had the revolutionary courage to resist the rulers' corrupt schemes and try, often against all odds, to create justice and to expand equality and human rights. They created a hidden culture of solidarity and resistance that periodically erupted in volcanic and seemingly spontaneous rebellion.

While the twin objectives of these community rebellions were always to protest against the injustices that the people faced and to reassert their own humanity and power, the underlying goal was always to change the conditions that had taken over their lives. Their aim was to end all such situations that disenfranchised the people from the decisions that impacted their lives and alienated them from nature and their fellow humans. Such estrangement from one's human potential can lead to revolutionary collective action, a fight for a full and meaningful life, for the opportunity for self-realization free from the massive commoditization and alienation that was—and arguably still is—characteristic of capitalism.

Understanding the rich but largely hidden history of peoples' struggles in the key state of California can be both inspiring and a beginning to the development of popular consciousness and an organized alternative to an increasingly unacceptable status quo. California workers have been always been combative. What has often been missing from their contentiousness with employers and those in authority is the ability to generalize about their experiences, build power, and organize resistance for the long term.

What is common to peoples' stories of resistance and rebellion, then and now, is that they have been excluded from the orthodox histories, the standard textbooks, and the most powerful media outlets. However, they are central to this book, one that makes clear that any "rights" that citizens possess do not accrue from lawmakers or the courts. They exist only due to the past struggles of the rank-and-file, and today only become real and alive when we engage in direct action powerful enough to assert our rights anew.

In this respect, the history of the rebellion and resistance of the majority in many ways reflects the voice of a people in the process of growing, of becoming—our real voices. It releases us from feelings of powerlessness and self-blame, while at the same time challenging us to continue the struggle for a more substantial and advanced democracy, free from alienation and with real equality, solidarity, and social justice. The numerous organized and unorganized rebellions, refusals, desertions, disruptions, demonstrations, boycotts, protests, walkouts, strikes, and insurrections of the people have often altered history. They show us that building power through organization and direct action is the main way forward. This is the way that a real, participatory, and protagonist democracy has been and will continue to be made alive.

PART ONE

PRE-CAPITALIST CALIFORNIA: THE MISSION AND RANCHO ERAS

From 1769 until 1846, military rulers and Catholic missionaries dominated California. The workforce consisted of Native Americans, initially living as semi-slaves in missions and later as peons on ranches. It was the rebellion of these Indian workers that ended the mission system and undermined the semi-feudal, pastoral, *ranchero* system that followed it.

1

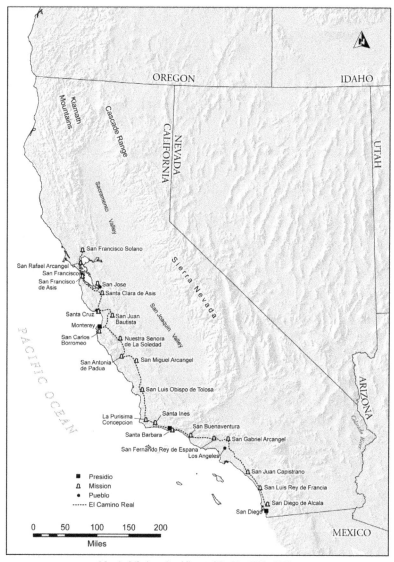

Map 1. Missions, Presidios, and Pueblos 1769 - 1830.

Map 1: Missions, Presidios, and Pueblos 1769–1830

1

MILITARISTS, MISSIONARIES AND
NATIVE RESISTANCE 1769–1830

In 1769, Spain began to systematically impose colonialism on the Native Americans of California, whom the Spanish called "Indios." Colonialism was one of the creators of our modern world, and its effects in California were as horrific as in the rest of the Americas.

The history of the first six decades of the European colonization of California is characterized by the conflicting relationships between the exploiting Spanish and, after 1821, Mexican military leaders and missionaries on the one hand, and the native Californian resistance on the other. There are four primary keys to understanding this history,

1. The nature of the original native economy and society in California
2. The semi-enslavement of these original inhabitants in the colonial social structure of the presidio, mission, and pueblo
3. Native California resistance and rebellion, both in its early and later manifestations

4. The responses to that resistance and rebellion by the Spanish/Mexican ruling class that eventually resulted in the creation of a new and different social formation.

THE POLITICAL ECONOMY OF NATIVE CALIFORNIA

Before the arrival of Spanish colonialism, there were four major culture areas, dozens of major tribal groups, and many more, smaller subdivisions, making California one of the most diverse regions of ancient North America. Native California had no fewer than twenty-three language families and language isolates, making up ninety distinct languages and even more dialects (Moratto et al. 1984, 530). The various Indian groups had a variety of ways of making a living and governing themselves. Those located on the northwestern coast were, for example, very different from those who lived along the southern borders of the state. A brief, general statement about dominant Native patterns is nevertheless possible. (See also Moratto et al. 1984; Kroeber 1925; and Heizer 1978).

The Native California political economy commonly had two central aspects, a political structure consisting of tiny nations called "tribelets," together with a hunting-and-gathering economy. The tribelets were autonomous clusters of different families (usually about two hundred to four hundred people total) forming independent, cooperative landholding communities that conducted religious ceremonies together. Each tribelet controlled an area a dozen or so miles in diameter, forming a small national unit with its own separate and mostly egalitarian political structure. Political leadership was often in the hands of elders—male leaders, called *jefes* (captains) by the Spanish, and occasionally female chiefs. Women were also often organizers of the ritual dances that were a central part of their religion (Grant 1978, 511). When the Spanish government requested that Mission San Jose priest Narciso Duran characterize native political organization, he described an egalitarian structure guided by religious leaders:

They recognize neither distinction nor superiority
at all. Only in war do they obey the most valiant or
the luckiest, and in acts of superstition they obey the
sorcerers and witch-doctors. Outside of these they
do not recognize any subordination, either civil or
political. (McCarthy 1958, 274)

This approach was common throughout aboriginal North America, where politics was intermixed with religious ritual. Land and water were generally held in common for the use of all members of the community, although specific resources like some oak groves (for acorns), seed patches, and fishing spots might be held by a family group. Moreover, Native Californians had a deep attachment to place and felt that they *belonged to* the land more than they owned the land.

The complex hunting and gathering economy of the Native Californians was technologically relatively simple but very efficient, relying on naturally produced food, both plant and animal. Seeds, acorns, fish, and a multitude of animals were the main foods. Burning was used to stimulate an increase in naturally growing seeds. Except along the Colorado River in the southeastern borderlands of the state, there was no real agriculture in "prehistoric" California. Yet, due to the richness of California's benign climate and naturally fertile environment, along with moderate population and consumption levels, native people had a relatively high level of individual free time and independence.

A mainly gender- and age-based division of labor existed, with the men hunting animal resources and the women gathering plant resources. This division of labor was not rigid, however, and men provided labor during the harvest and women would sometimes drive game into traps set by the men. Extensive trade networks existed to transfer goods like obsidian, which might not have been available locally. Shell money was widely used. Native Californian men were skilled at working stone and fashioning hunting and trapping gear. The basket making of the women was outstanding, and California baskets rank among the best in the world.

The Chumash of the Santa Barbara coast, the Yokuts and Miwok of the Sacramento delta area, and the Yurok of the northwest coast were relatively advanced economically and politically. These tribes and their locations have therefore been called the climax regions and cultures of native California:

> *With concomitant exploitation of acorn and marine resources, cultural climax regions, characterized by elaborations in technology and art, developed along the Santa Barbara coast and the San Francisco Bay-Sacramento-San Joaquin delta regions. Later, it appears that essentially riverine-coastal cultures, exemplified by the ethnographic Yurok, also experienced a climax; again, marine exploitation seems to have played a contributing part. (Elsasser 1978, 57)*

The social, economic, and technological complexity of the Chumash is illustrated by the fact that some of their villages had as many as one thousand residents, making them the largest settlements in the aboriginal Far West. Their economic, political, and social structures were as elaborate as any of the world's numerous hunting and gathering societies (Moratto et al. 1984, 118–119). The Yokuts were also a very successful group; their eighteenth century population may have numbered as much as 41,000, the largest ethnic group in prehistoric California. While speaking different dialects, these dialects were remarkably homogeneous, giving this group a greater potential for unity and collective action (Moratto et al. 1984, 173; Silverstein 1978, 446).

MILITARISTS AND MISSIONARIES, COLONIAL SOCIAL FORMATION AND POWER STRUCTURE

The viceroy of Mexico, who was the direct agent of the Spanish king, sent the Spanish colonists who arrived in Southern California at the end of the 1760s. The king and viceroy were pursuing traditional imperial goals: to develop a colony, seize, control, and exploit the land and labor of the local Native California population, and to prevent rival nations (Russia and England especially) from taking over California and threatening Mexico's northern frontier. California's great economic potential was as yet unknown; these more general imperial goals were, therefore, in the forefront of policy makers' minds.

In the process of seizing power and expropriating the native lands of coastal California, Spanish goals and tactics had to take account of demographic realities. Spanish manpower available for colonization was very limited; therefore, the natives themselves had to be converted and used as the labor force for the new colony. This need for labor heavily influenced the careful strategy the Spanish followed.

The new colonists had several factors working in their favor. One was their technological superiority in the military field. They had guns, swords, lances, horses, as well as both leather and sheepskin armor, making the Spanish soldier on horseback the most formidable fighting man of that time and place. A second was their centralized leadership and unity of command. A third was the Machiavellian attitude and consequent actions of their leaders. Large-scale duplicity was used to achieve hidden goals destructive to the colonized peoples—using missionaries as the point men in the colonization scheme was useful, since it hid the real aim, which was controlling land, resources, and people for the king; that is, for the secular authorities. A final factor was the array of material culture they commanded, including the animals and seeds they brought for food, the beads and clothing they wore, and the buildings they conceived and built. This material culture dazzled the native people and was a key factor in attracting them to the missions. As one missionary expressed it:

> *They can be conquered first only by their interest in being fed and clothed, and afterwards they gradually acquire knowledge of what is spiritually good and evil. If the missionaries had nothing to give them, they could not be won over. (Palou 1786, quoted in Milliken 1995, 82–83)*

The Spanish and later the Mexican colonial system had a three-part power structure, the presidio and mission being the most important. The weakest part of the Spanish and early-Mexican era power structure was the civilian, agricultural pueblo. There were three pueblos: at San Jose, Los Angeles, and Santa Cruz.

THE PRESIDIOS

In contrast to the weakness of the pueblos, the presidio was at the heart of state power. It was the political, military, and administrative center, commanded by the military governor housed in the Presidio of Monterey. Three other presidios also existed—at San Francisco, Santa Barbara, and San Diego. The soldiers at the presidios made up the police and military force.

The governor, appointed by the Spanish king, was an absolute ruler, commanding the military and sanctioning the use of state violence. He also controlled all government functions, administrative, legislative, and judicial. Land ownership, very important in this agricultural colony, was also under the purview of the governor, who enforced the "right" of the King of Spain to "own" virtually all of California, which was land seized by force from the Indians. This political system was, therefore, an absolutist state and extremely hierarchical, unlike the one created by Native Californians.

THE MISSIONS

The missions made up the second part of the power structure of Spanish and Mexican California into the 1830s. The missions were a type of totalitarian, religious commune in which the Catholic priests or "fathers" ruled over the Indian "neophytes," who were seen as perpetual children. As the main economic institution of the epoch, the missions were where the bulk of the production needed to sustain the colony took place.

Native Californians made up the labor force necessary to sustain the twenty-one missions and the entire colonial enterprise known today as the Catholic California Mission. Indians did all the planting, harvesting, cooking, animal husbandry, weaving, construction, woodcutting, and other economic activities at the missions (Webb 1952, 84; Forbes 1982, 41).

Priests of the Franciscan order organized the missions, which were located along the coastal strip from San Diego in the south to Sonoma in the north. So long as production was assured, the governor gave the priests significant independence in handling the Indians. The missions bartered some of their surplus production with the California governor for items that they could not produce (certain tools, iron, cloth, glass beads), and as time went on, increasingly for worthless promises to pay from the military officials who ruled the colony. Soon the entire colony came to depend upon the missions and Indian labor to produce the necessities of survival on this frontier. During the sixty years from 1769 to 1829, this production system developed into a powerful economic institution. At their peak, the twenty-one missions housed about 30,000 Indians, controlled about eight million acres of land, had extensive field crops (especially wheat and corn) and as many as 420,000 cattle, 320,000 sheep, and over 60,000 horses and mules (T. Hittell 1885, 2:207; Hornbeck 1983, 56–57).

Laurence H. Shoup

Native Americans Dancing at Mission Dolores
Dances were a key expression of community life for the Indians of
California. This early painting shows them dancing in front of the San
Francisco Mission. [Courtesy of the Bancroft Library, University of
California, Berkeley.]

The Indians, whose options were restricted when the Spanish
colonialists seized their land and resources to use for grazing
Spanish livestock and raising Spanish crops, were attracted to
the missions with a combination of goods (food, beads, cloth),
promises of security (including security from Spanish violence),
and spiritual salvation. In exchange, the Indians lost their freedom
and, once baptized by the priests, could not leave except with
permission. Their lives were totally controlled and regulated
twenty-four hours a day for their entire lives. The only exception
was once a year (or so) when they were given permission and a pass
to return to their villages for a few weeks' holiday. Running away
and numerous other disciplinary infractions, both minor and
major, were punished by solitary confinement, flogging, branding,
the stocks, hobbles (chaining to weights), and other humiliations
(Cook 1976, 91–101; Jackson and Castillo 1995, 44; Jackson

1994, 126, 165–166; Castillo 1978, 101). As one contemporary observer later recalled:

> *Indians belonging to the missions could not leave them without special permission, and this was seldom granted. Frequently they were sent to work in the towns or the presidios under contract. They were not paid for the work they did ... I do not know whether or not the padres sometimes exceeded their authority in delivering punishments. I do know that they frequently castigated the Indians who had committed faults with lashes, confinement, and chains. On some occasions, I saw Indians working in chains ... and I also saw them in stocks. (Lugo [1877] 1950, 226–227).*

Since Indians were at the bottom of a caste system from which there was no legal escape, and because their labor was forced, the system has been labeled by both contemporary observers and many scholars as "slavery" or "practical slavery" (Bannon 1964, 191; Archibald 1978, 181; T. Hittell 1885, 3:59, 77, 210; Caughey 1940, 193; Harlow 1982, 20). For example, Jean F. La Perouse, a French visitor to the missions in the 1780s, concluded that even by this early date the California missions were all too much like the slave plantations of Santo Domingo ([1786] 1989, 41, 81). The 1997 *Historical Encyclopedia of World Slavery* pointed out that mission Indians were held in "virtual slavery ... were tied to the mission lands ... and had every aspect of their lives controlled by the priests" (Rodriguez 1997, 605).

The Indians were, however, not bought and sold, as African slaves were in the United Sates, so the concept of *peonage* is also needed to fully understand the organization of work in the missions. When the Indians joined these missions, they incurred a religious rather than monetary debt. James A. Sandos argues that the Indians in the mission system had therefore the status of spiritual-debt peons (Sandos 2004, 178–179). This forced-labor

11

system, a combination of slavery and peonage, was the dominant type of labor system in Spanish and Mexican California until the 1830s.

In addition, the missions were very unhealthy places, rife with disease, poor sanitation, and unlivable conditions. The Indians, not surprisingly, were alienated and very depressed living there and their immune systems reduced; they often could not resist the new diseases introduced by Europeans. The problem of disease was immensely worsened by the practice of systematic rape of native women by Spanish soldiers, which introduced syphilis into the population on a massive scale. Colonial officials spoke against the common practice of soldiers assaulting Indian women, that the scholar Sherburne Cook called "notorious," but they never instituted effective deterrents (Cook 1976, 24–25). The California Missions founder, Father Junipero Serra, himself stated that some of the Spanish soldiers were so evil that sometimes "even the children who came to the mission were not safe from their baseness ... " (Tibesar 1955, 362–363).

Cook concluded,

> *[It is] clear that from the time the Spanish first set foot in California, there was ample opportunity for the introduction of syphilis to the native population, not at one but at many places. Indeed, since there were soldiers stationed at every mission, since the troops were continually moving around from one place to another, and since this military group was itself generously infected, the introduction may be regarded as wholesale and substantially universal. (Cook 1976, 25)*

Beginning in 1793, the reports of Spanish officials frequently mention syphilis as a serious health problem. As time went on and the mission population was increasingly saturated with chronic venereal disease, the Indians easily succumbed to the maladies that arrived all too regularly—measles, dysentery, typhoid, tuberculosis, typhus, and pneumonia. Since huge numbers were dying of disease at the missions and others were running away, the missionaries, Christian Indians, and soldiers constantly had to recruit new groups of "gentile" or free Indians into the mission system. Otherwise, the high death rate would have spelled the end of the missions.

About 85,000 Indians were baptized in the missions during 1769–1834, but so many died or ran away that there were only 15,000 left in the mission system in 1834 (Hornbeck 1983, 48–49). As the free Indians near the missions became scarce, the Spanish had to go farther and farther east, into the interior of California, the central valley, and the Sierra foothills to bring in enough Indians to do the work at the missions. Indians in places remote from the missions had more options and were thus more reluctant to come to live in a distant and alien institution, which had attractions (different animals and foods, new goods, and powerful people), but also the negatives of exploitation by forced labor, violence, sickness, and constant death.

As time went on, Native Californian resistance increased, and the Spanish and later the Mexicans had to increasingly use military power to maintain their labor force. The authorities gave excuses about capturing runaway neophytes and suppressing rebellion, but the process was more accurately characterized as the destruction of normal village life and food sources so that the natives had to go into the missions both as a refuge and a means of survival (T. Hittell 1885, 3:116; Cook 1976, 73–84). A related factor was the need for repression to keep the Indians at the missions, because there were immense areas of land to the east of coastal California that the Spanish did not control. Indians who came from these distant areas could escape from the missions and return to their homelands.

One direct effect of cheap Indian slave labor was the almost total lack of technological advances during this entire era. Even though windmills and water-powered mills were well known to the Spanish and Mexicans, these labor-saving devices were almost entirely missing from the early California economy. As was the case for other slave economies in the historical past, there was simply no incentive for technological innovation.

The mission system was thus an extreme form of class exploitation that the rulers tried to morally justify in two key ways. The first was as a paternalism under which the Indian was seen as a perpetual child, who always needed the assistance of the white "people of reason." Under this paternalism, the forced labor of Indian slaves was viewed as a fair exchange for the mission's protection and direction, as well as for the new goods and foods it offered. This paternalism represented an attempt to overcome one of the fundamental contradictions of the mission system—the impossibility of the mission Indian slave to ever become what he or she was supposed to become—an independent citizen equal to a "person of reason." As a perpetual child and peon, the Indian never had this chance so long as he or she stayed in the mission and obeyed its strictures, as so many did.

A second justification was that mission lands and property were supposedly being held in trust as a community asset for all the Indians. While many of the priests were undoubtedly sincere, this concept was essentially a dead letter, since it was the king and later the Mexican state that actually held title. This left the way open to expropriate and distribute all mission property to leading official families during the 1830s, as will be discussed in chapter two. A precedent had been set during the earlier period (1769–1832) when the governor and political authorities gave fifty provisional land grants to retired military men and their families (Hornbeck 1983, 58).

THE PUEBLOS

The pueblos, which were always small and dependent upon Indian labor, were eventually supposed to take over the economic functions of the missions, which would then devolve into parish churches. Some believed they could do so as Christianized Native Californians became sufficiently acculturated and trained in western ways to join the pueblos as equal members. This never happened, in no small part due to the resistance and rebellion of the natives themselves.

Given the above facts, the mission labor system, a key part of the colonial social formation during this era, which set the tone for the life of early California, can be characterized as a type of forced labor system, a combination of slavery and debt peonage where surplus value was coercively extracted from the primary producer. This system operated within the context of a rigidly hierarchical caste system where colonial domination, racism, violence, and military force were constants. The two office-holding groups—the ruling class of military officers and the priests—directly benefited from the labor of tens of thousands of Indian peons, who were born, lived, worked, and died in the missions, presidios, and pueblos of early California. These peons were not always passive, however, despite facing a technologically far superior and better-organized enemy. They also resisted and fought back on a massive scale. Their resistance and rebellion was thus a main theme of the entire 1769–1830.

NATIVE CALIFORNIA RESISTANCE

The Spanish and subsequently Mexican colonial ruling class was tiny, made up of several dozen military and clerical officials, supported by relatively small numbers of mid-level presidio soldiers and pueblo farmers. In contrast, there were large numbers of exploited native California Indian laborers at the bottom of the social structure. From the beginning of the colonization, these central facts dictated Spanish colonial strategy. Above all, Spanish unity and regional military security had to be maintained. Conversely, Native Californians had to be kept divided, and the development of any overall unity among them prevented. The decentralized, tribelet political form and frequent warfare among Indian groups made the task of the Spanish and Mexicans easier.

Because they were acutely aware of their limited numbers and the potential for over-extension and defeat, the Spanish were from the beginning vigilant and responded with swift violence to suppress any threat near their presidios, missions, and pueblos. At the same time, they were much more careful and prudent when these threats were more distant. This gradually changed as they became stronger and the natives weaker. Eventually, Spanish power was extended east of the coastal settlements at least a hundred miles.

Spanish policy also specifically targeted the Native California leadership and any transgressors of Spanish law and rules, making a negative example of such individuals by killing, imprisoning, whipping, or beating them. This loss of leadership and organization weakened the resistance that nevertheless continued throughout the entire 1769–1830 period.

SAN DIEGO AND SAN GABRIEL, 1769–1776

Native Californians resisted the very first expedition to establish a colony at San Diego in 1769, attacking the Spanish camp on August 15, 1769. At San Gabriel, a mission founded in 1771 near today's Los Angeles, local Indians attacked the mission twice. The Spanish soldiers killed one of the local native leaders, cutting off and putting the chief's head on a pole as an example for the other Indians. The source of the conflict was reportedly the soldiers' frequent rape of native women as well as the destruction of the food supplies of the local people (Jackson and Castillo 1995, 74–75). Father Junipero Serra described the behavior of the soldiers and the responses of the natives *(gentiles)* as follows:

> *At one of these Indian villages near this mission of San Diego ... the gentiles ... many times have been on the point of coming here to kill us all, and the reason for this is that some soldiers went there and raped their women, and other soldiers ... turned their animals into their fields and ... ate up their*

crops. Three other Indian villages have reported the same thing to me several times ... six or more soldiers would set out together ... on horseback, and go to the distant rancherias ... [T]he soldiers, clever as they are at lassoing cows and mules, would catch Indian women with their lassos to become prey for their unbridled lust. At times, some Indian men would try to defend their wives, only to be shot down with bullets. (Serra in Tibesar 1955, 1:362–363)

Spanish abuses created a measure of native unity and violent rebellion. Two native resistance leaders—Francisco of Cuiamac village and Zegotay of Matamo village—organized a coalition of about eight hundred men from a number of villages. On the night of November 5, 1775, the coalition attacked and burned the San Diego Mission, killing two soldiers and one priest (Bean 1973, 43; Jackson and Castillo 1995, 75; Castillo 1978, 103; Luomala 1978, 595; Castillo 1989, 385). One of the native leaders later explained that they wanted to destroy the missions "in order to live as they did before" (Cook 1976, 66). Although the infant mission was destroyed, the revolt was later crushed and the mission rebuilt. When resistance continued, four village leaders were tried, convicted, and sentenced to death by a Spanish military court. The four—Aachil, Taguagui, Aalcurin and Aaaran—were shot by a firing squad on March 11, 1778. This was the first public execution in California history (Castillo 1989, 386).

THE SAN FRANCISCO BAY AREA, INITIAL RESISTANCE, 1776–1777

Within months of the Spanish arrival into their territory, the Native Californians of the Bay Area began to resist foreign domination. In December 1776, in the new settlement of San Francisco, a group of the more courageous natives began firing arrows, acting in a threatening manner, and robbing the invaders. In response, Spanish soldiers captured a leader of the group and flogged him. Such punishment was unknown in native society, and hearing the victim's cries of pain, two of his comrades tried to free him, but were driven off by Spanish musket fire. The next day, the soldiers went after those who had resisted their "right" to whip any native. A group of Indians shot arrows at them, wounding a horse and one soldier. The Spanish responded with their ultimate weapon, the musket, killing one native and wounding another. The Indians then surrendered, and two were punished by whippings and threatened with death (Milliken 1995, 64-65).

Another violent incident took place a few weeks later near the newly founded Mission Santa Clara, about fifty miles south of San Francisco. The missionaries and their soldier-protectors had brought with them a menagerie of tamed animals, including cattle, horses, mules, sheep, goats, pigs, and chickens. These animals were turned loose to graze upon the fields that supplied the local people with greens, seeds, and roots, as well as wild animals. The natives then saw the colonists' animals as fair game. A group of local men killed a few mules and were roasting them to eat, when the soldiers came to arrest and punish them. The priest, Francisco Palou, described the ensuing confrontation:

> *The Lieutenant of the Presidio attempted to capture them, and they hid themselves in the brush of a grove. The soldiers followed them, and seeing that they were firing arrows, they had to kill three, and with this example, they stopped. They took some of the leaders to the mission and flogged them. (Palou {1786} 1913, 161; Miliken 1995, 67)*

Again, those who had the courage and leadership qualities to resist Spanish control were either killed by gunfire or whipped. Despite this, Palou reported that theft continued to be common, although less openly. More covert resistance like running away from the missions gradually became the norm. Nonetheless, overt resistance also continued as the Spanish recruited new tribal groups from areas more distant from the newly established missions.

COLORADO RIVER REBELLION, 1781

The biggest native victory over Spanish imperialism in California came in 1781 on the Colorado River, along the state's southeastern borderlands. Two Spanish settlements had been established among the Quechan people in 1780 along the river, because of its strategic position on the land route between Mexico and California. This settlement was a hybrid of the mission, presidio, and pueblo, and the Spanish, with their seizures of land and floggings, soon alienated the Quechans and their leaders. In June 1781, a group of Spanish soldiers on their way to the California coast stopped on the Colorado River. About half of the group went on, but the remainder decided to rest. Their cattle soon destroyed part of the Indians' food supply of mesquite beans, adding to the already existing tensions. Led by Salvador Palma, the Quechans, on July 17, attacked and destroyed both missions. They then surprised and killed the remaining group of soldiers.

One estimate put Spanish-Mexican dead at fifty-five (four priests, thirty-one soldiers, twenty settlers), with sixty-seven soldiers, settlers, women, and children captured and enslaved (Castillo 1989, 386; Bean 1973, 48; Forbes 1982, 45; Rice et al. 1988, 90–91). Although the Spanish authorities tried to reconquer the area, they failed and had to give up. Land communication between California and Mexico was virtually cut off until the 1820s. The Quechan struggle for freedom had temporarily succeeded, and they would live for many decades without outside interference.

CHARQUIN AND THE QUIROSTE RESISTANCE, 1791–1795

In November of 1791, a young Indian from the San Mateo coast named Charquin was baptized at the San Pedro outstation of the Mission San Francisco, located south of the mission. He was from the Quiroste tribelet, which lived in the Point Año Nuevo area about thirty miles farther down the coast. Charquin quickly came to hate the semi-slavery characteristic of mission life and stayed there only about a week before escaping and returning to his homeland in the mountains above Point Año Nuevo.

Charquin's village soon became a haven for mission runaways and a center of resistance to Spanish colonialism with its dispossession and exploitation. This made it a serious long-term threat to the new system, since it threatened the withdrawal of the labor upon which the entire colonial enterprise was built. Running away from the missions and returning to their homelands was to become a ubiquitous resistance pattern for Native Californians. To deal with the runaways, the Spanish power structure would typically respond in a step-by-step manner, to try to isolate leaders for punishment and break down the resistance. That way, long-term control over the labor force could be asserted with a minimum of conflict. Therefore, missionized Indians were initially sent to try to capture Charquin and reduce the size of his group. These expeditions all failed, and by early 1793, the Spanish ruling class had resolved to use their own soldiers to defeat Charquin.

Surviving reports from the period state that the missionaries and officers had decided that ...

> *Charquin had finally given them enough to endure. The commander of the Presidio of San Francisco concluded that he ... would no longer allow such excesses ... He desires to go under cover of darkness to capture this Indian and give him what he deserves, regardless of the obstacles presented by the impregnable reaches of the mountains in which he pulls together his forces. (Milliken 1995, 117)*

No reports of the attack on Charquin and his followers are known to have survived, but indirect evidence indicates that his village was defeated and he was captured in the spring of 1793. The Quiroste resistance continued, however, and this group attacked Mission Santa Cruz in mid-December 1793. Two Spanish soldiers were wounded, and the roofs of two buildings were set afire before the Quiroste withdrew. Mission Indians were dispatched in response and successfully captured five Christian Indians and a "large number" of non-Christian Indians, sending them all to the Monterey Presidio for punishment. Charquin, a resistance leader who the Spanish ruling class continued to see as a dangerous threat, spent the rest of his life in presidio dungeons, eventually serving time at all four of California's presidios. His actions included an escape from the Santa Barbara Presidio on June 10, 1795. Recaptured, he was sent far from his homeland to the San Diego Presidio dungeon, where he died under unknown circumstances in the spring of 1798.

Soon after the defeat of Charquin's Quiroste resistance, there was a serious drought and loss of seed crops (1794–1795). The mission priests saw the opportunity and adopted a more aggressive approach to converting the natives in order to take advantage of the new situation. As the commander of the San Francisco Presidio wrote to the governor in late November of 1794:

> *[T]he Reverend Fathers believe it to be an opportune moment, because the pagans are without food, having lost their harvest due to the severity of the drought, which facilitates drawing them in.... (Milliken 1995, 132)*

As a result of the drought, the year 1795 saw the largest mass conversion of Native Californians to Christianity and migration to the missions in the history of the Bay Area. This was, of course, in no sense "voluntary"; it was the direct result of the destruction of all alternatives.

THE SACLAN RESISTANCE, 1795–1800

Following the mass conversion of 1794–1795, the San Francisco Bay Area mission system faced another crisis during the mid-1795 to fall 1800 period. Very few Indian people moved to area missions during these years, and many ran away. This created a demographic and economic challenge to the system, since deaths and runaways were greatly exceeding births. California missions had annual death rates that reached as high as 16 percent; some of the highest ever recorded for an ongoing institution. Without a steady supply of new Indian recruits, the missions and, indeed, the entire colony ran the risk of collapsing due to the lack of a labor force in less than a decade. This also meant that the very existence of resistance movements was a mortal threat to the Spanish colonial enterprise.

During this period, one such resistance movement was led by the Saclan tribelet, which lived in the mountains of north central Contra Costa County. This group also had ties to other tribelets to the south, as well as to the north across the Carquinez Strait in southern Napa County, giving them a geographical reach and strength in numbers not matched by most other tribal groups.

Active resistance began when a group of new Saclan converts left Mission San Francisco on sanctioned leave to visit their former homeland in mid-1795. After they failed to return after two weeks, the priests sent a group of fourteen other mission Indians, led by both of their *alcaldes* (Indian leaders at the mission), with "short ropes" to tie up the runaways and return them for punishment and renewed forced labor (Milliken 1995, 138–139). The posse found the escapees attending a dance with hundreds of other people in the lower Napa River region. Governor Diego de Borica later summarized the statement of one of the survivors who described what happened:

> *Upon their arrival, men armed with bows and arrows emerged from the dance house with such force that they broke down its walls. They began at once to fire arrows, yelling, "These men are our enemies." Faced with such violence, the alcaldes tried to calm them down … They paid no attention, but continued to fire arrows until they killed… seven. (Milliken 1995, 140)*

Those killed included the two *alcaldes*; the remaining seven men escaped and fled back to Mission San Francisco. At this point, the Spanish military felt stretched too thin to respond to this defeat. The successful resistance, therefore, stimulated more mission Indians to rebel and run away from Mission San Francisco in large numbers. By the end of the summer of 1795, at least 280 had fled, a high enough percentage of the total population to threaten the survival of the institution. To save the situation, the governor decided he had to act on two levels: first, by sending a raiding party out to defeat the Saclan resistance and capture its leaders; second, by launching an inquiry into the causes of the mass flight from Mission San Francisco.

On July 10, 1797, the governor directed his sergeant, Pedro Amador, to gather both regular and veteran retired soldiers from Pueblo San Jose to go:

> *... to the village of the Sacalan (sic), fall upon them at daybreak, and capture the ring-leaders of those who participated in the deaths of the seven Mission San Francisco Christians in 1795. He should bring them, as well as any runaway Christians found among them, back to San Jose. In this expedition, he is to avoid any loss of blood. Only if the pagans take up arms against our people in a way that risks wounding someone will gunfire or lances be used, and then only to the minimum extent necessary to achieve control. (Milliken 1995, 157)*

At dawn on July 15, 1797, Amador and his mounted soldiers attacked the Saclan village of Jussent, located in the Moraga/Lafayette area of central Contra Costa County. Borica later reported to the viceroy on this action:

> *Amador ... told them several times that he did not want to fight, but only to take away the Christians. But he was unable to persuade them to turn them*

over. On the contrary, sheltered by some steep-walled wells and trenches which they had prepared in their village with defense in mind, they began shooting arrows at our men … They managed to kill a horse and injure two others. Amador, seeing their stubbornness, used his arms … At last they gave up after seven Indians had died. He arrested over thirty Christians that they found there, and then continued on through two other villages … On the nineteenth, Amador arrived at the new mission of San Jose, bringing along eighty-three Christians of all types and ages from the Mission of San Francisco, as well as nine pagan leaders and culprits in the aforementioned deaths and beatings. The first were turned over to their Father ministers. The second group were given punishment according to the part they had played … We will work at converting them through kindness into the pale of our sacred religion. (Milliken 1995, 307–308)

The captured "pagan leaders and culprits" were then questioned, tried, and many of them convicted. The main Saclan resistance leader was Portroy, who had been baptized in 1795 and apparently escaped that same year. Under questioning, he admitted that he had helped kill the seven Christians because he believed that they were coming to his village to convert the non-Christians. Portroy was sentenced to receive seventy-five lashes apportioned over three distinct occasions, one year in shackles on rations, and then returned to the semi-slavery of the mission, well cautioned not to run away or misbehave, on pain of even more severe punishment. The other main resistance leaders were each sentenced to a lesser number of lashes and months in shackles.

The second part of the governor's program, the inquiry into the causes of mass escapes from the mission, took testimony in August 1797 from recaptured runaways, who therefore can still speak to us directly about the oppressive conditions and the violence which led them to reject and rebel against the mission:

> *Tiburcio: After his wife and daughter died, on five separate occasions Father Dante ordered him whipped because he was crying.*

> *Macario: His wife and child had died.*

> *Magin: His hunger and because they had put him in the stocks when he was sick.*

> *Ostano: His wife, one child, and two brothers had all died; also he quarreled with another Indian who was directing their work group.*

> *Roman: His wife and son had fled, because of the many whippings.*

> *Claudio: He was continually fighting with his brother-in-law, and because the alcalde was frequently clubbing him and forcing him to work when sick.*

> *Jose Manuel: When he refused an order, he was hit with a heavy cane, rendering one hand useless.*

> *Homobono: When his brother died and he cried for him they whipped him; also the alcalde hit him with a heavy cane when he went to look for mussels for food.*

> *Liborato: His mother, two brothers, and three nephews all died of hunger, and he was afraid he would as well.*

> *Timoteo: The alcalde whipped him when he was sick, then Father Antonio hit him with a heavy cane.*

Otolon: His wife had sinned with the vaquero Salvador; then would not bring him food. Father Antonio blamed him and ordered him whipped.

Milan: He worked all day in the tannery without food for himself, his wife, or child. Then he was whipped by Father Dante when he went to gather clams to feed his family.

Patabo: His wife and children died, and he had no one to take care of him.

Orencio: Father Danti refused him his ration of meat, always hitting him with a cudgel; later his niece died of hunger.

Toribio: He was always very hungry and escaped with his uncle.

Lopez: Went to the presidio to look for something to eat, and upon returning, Father Danti refused him his ration.

Magno: His son was sick, and he could not go to work because he had to care for him. As a result, he was given no ration, and his son died of hunger.

Prospero: He had gone one night to hunt ducks for food, and for this, Father Dante had ordered him stretched out and beaten. A week later, he was whipped for going out on a pass. (Milliken 1995, 299–303; Beebe and Senkewicz 2001, 266–269)

The repeated statements about violence, hunger, death, and conflicts relating to injustice around work as motives for escape indicate that this mission was in a serious economic crisis. Short of food and short of manpower, the mission's power structures used violence and denial of food to try to increase discipline and production. This fomented rebellion and increased the number of escapes plaguing the mission. Another important factor was that the Native Californians still had their traditional way of life available as an alternative to the colonial system. As the Spaniards succeeded in crushing this alternative, the people had no choice but to resume flooding into the mission.

THE LUECHA RESISTANCE, 1805

In January of 1805, a small group of Indians and Spaniards, led by Father Cueva, set out from Mission San Jose. Their destination was the mountainous territory southeast of today's Livermore, in eastern Alameda County. A new and inexperienced missionary, Cueva apparently wanted to proselytize in this area to bring in more natives to replace those constantly dying at the missions. When they reached an Indian village on their route, they were attacked by members of the Luecha tribelet, part of the numerous Yokuts people. The Luecha were able to kill Ygnacio Higuera, the *mayordomo* or steward of the mission, and three Christian Indians. Father Cueva was also wounded, along with another Spaniard.

Later that same month, the San Jose Mission sent out a raiding party to punish the resisters. The soldiers killed at least eleven Indians and captured a smaller number. Two more major raids followed to punish the Luechas and adjacent tribelets in the same area. Spanish soldiers swept through a seventy-five-mile long corridor in May–June 1805, disrupting tribal life and terrorizing the local people. Leaderless and frightened of the Spanish military—and also perhaps other Indian groups farther to the east—Indians poured into the Bay Area missions during June, July, and August of 1805, fleeing to a place of relative security.

THE SUISUN RESISTANCE, 1804–1811

At almost the same time that the Luechas and adjacent tribelets were being reduced by Spanish military attacks, another tribelet to the north also began to resist Spanish colonialism. This was the Suisun group, located in today's Solano County. In 1804, this group killed eleven Christianized Indians, but due to the Luecha revolt and the technological and logistical problems posed by mounting a major expedition northward across the Carquinez Strait, the Spanish military did not respond right away.

A measles epidemic struck Bay Area missions in 1806, peaking at Mission San Francisco in May. This epidemic alone killed almost half of the adult women of this mission, along with 20 percent of the men, every single girl under the age of five, and 70 percent of infant boys (Milliken 1995, 200). Other mission Indians ran away to escape from the spreading plague, intensifying the Indian labor crisis at this mission. In early 1807, a large party of neophyte men was dispatched to Suisun lands to bring back the runaways who had fled there. The reason for the expedition was ostensibly to recover the wife of one of the San Francisco Mission Indians, but the larger goal of recovering runaways was obviously also operative (Milliken 1995, 204–207).

The mission posse, reportedly consisting of over a hundred men, stopped along the way to gather up the runaways. One of the San Francisco Mission priests, Father Abella, later reported that several runaways …

> took the lead in firing arrows and [urged] the pagans to do the same. Even the old women were waiting with sticks when they arrived. Nevertheless, they still brought the village under control. But soon men joined in from neighboring rancherias, particularly from one called Suio Suiu … and began firing arrows. Then the neophytes took off running."
> (Milliken 1995, 315)

Twelve neophytes were killed in this episode, again including both *alcaldes* of the Mission San Francisco. Abella also stated in his report to the governor that an expedition of Spanish troops would need to be undertaken to suppress the Suisun resistance.

Otherwise, he concluded, "all is finished here, because the runaways will never return … Many will now flee …" (Milliken 1995, 315–316).

Nothing was done until May of 1810, when, following another incident in which three San Francisco Mission Indians were killed by the Suisuns, the San Francisco Presidio sent out an expedition of Spanish soldiers and Christian Indians to attack the main resistance village. The Suisuns fought fiercely, wounding a number of soldiers, but a large number were killed by the soldiers, including a group burned alive when their grass house was set on fire.

Between 1811 and 1816, large numbers of Suisuns and related tribelets moved to the San Francisco Mission, helping that institution temporarily avert the demographic crisis it faced, repeating a well-established pattern of divide and conquer— dividing the native peoples from their lands to conquer their spiritual culture.

The Spanish were demonstrating by example that violence, especially military violence, was the decisive means for dominance—or deliverance. Furthermore, the Spanish gave the Indians no other option. Organized violent rebellion was the only alternative to sure cultural and bodily destruction in the missions. In the 1820s, this form would become the dominant mode of resistance.

MISSION REBELLIONS, 1820S

The nature of the colonial system and missions figured largely in the California Indian rebellions of 1824 and 1828–1829. There had been a change of tone in the colony after Mexican independence. The missions, exempt from taxation during the Spanish era, became heavily taxed in food and goods to maintain the colony, as most outside aid was cut off during the independence war years (1810–1821). Then, following Mexico's victory, these levies were increased (Hackel 1998, 128–130; Engelhardt 1913, 3:187–195). Following strong protests from several mission priests, Governor

Luis Arguello (the first *Californio,* or California-born, military governor), supported the taxes and ordered the missionaries to stop complaining. This led to the following response to the governor from the father president of the missions, suggesting that many of the priests wanted to quit, since their Indians were being exploited to the absolute maximum:

> *I have to say in return that those mentioned in your letter are not the only ones who have expressed themselves in such bitter terms with regard to the bad spirit of the new regulations. There are others who ask for permission to retire, who want to renounce a service which they cannot exercise without subjecting the neophytes to hard slavery, or to a condition even worse than that; for slavery does not deny the necessary food at least to human beings. (Engelhardt 1913, 3:187–188)*

As another padre expressed it, the Native Americans, "bitterly complained that they had to work so that the soldiers might eat, and that nothing was paid them for their toil and labor" (Engelhardt 1913, 3:195).

Thus, what the religious scholar Engelhardt called the "heartless calculation" of the ruling class "aroused the Indians to turn upon their tormentors ..." (Engelhardt 1913, 3:194). The resulting gross exploitation led to major, open rebellion beginning in 1824. Smaller-scale uprisings, such as the one led by Chief Marin and Pomponio against the San Rafael Mission 1822–1824 also took place, but the large rebellions were in the Santa Barbara area and San Jose/Santa Clara/Central Valley region, and these will be focused on here (see Goerke 2007 for information on Marin and Pomponio).

If the immediate cause of the 1824 revolt was the increased exploitation of the Indians, background causes included the mission semi-slave system itself and the strong desire to be free by destroying it (Osio [1851] 1996, 268n2). During the prior four decades, Native American resistance to the system in the southern part of California had manifested itself mainly in running away and other individualistic acts of rebellion, such as faking illness and a few hit-and-run raids. But it was only during the 1820s that the development of class relations at the missions had reached a crisis point, and that substantial numbers of Indians were ready to rebel.

The significance of these instances of mass insurrection lies not in their frequency or success, but in their very existence as the ultimate manifestation of class struggle and the aspirations of the people for freedom and human rights under the most unfavorable of conditions. It should be pointed out that these native people came out of a non-authoritarian society and had little experience with organized warfare, military discipline, or strong, decisive leaders. Furthermore, the soldiers they faced were trained in the military arts, were obedient to command, and had greatly superior arms. Those who led and participated in these violent rebellions were thus unusually courageous and resourceful people. As we shall see, many suffered and died for their failure against what were, in reality, long odds.

The 1824 rebellion took place in Chumash territory, along the southern sector of California's central coast region. It was set off by the flogging of a neophyte by soldiers at the Santa Ines Mission. The Indians of three missions (Santa Ines, La Purisima, and Santa Barbara) then conspired and organized a rebellion to attack and kill the soldiers and some priests and destroy the missions. It began on February 21, 1824, at Santa Ines when, using bows and arrows, the Indians attacked the soldiers guarding the mission and set fires which burned a "large part" of the mission (Bancroft 1886, 2:528; Engelhardt 1913, 3:195).

Two Chumash were reportedly killed in the fighting. Due to the arrival of Mexican re-enforcements, the rebels retreated to Mission La Purisima, where that mission's Indians were also in rebellion. At Purisima, Corporal Tapia of the Mission Guard, together with a few other men, held out through the first night, but surrendered when their ammunition ran out. The Indians then allowed them and their families, and one of the padres, Orday, to retire to Santa Ines, while the other padre, Rodriguez, was allowed to stay with the rebels. The Native Americans, in Bancroft's words, "showed no disposition to molest him" (Bancroft 1886, 2:529). Thus, the Indians, in a battle for their lives, and even after having some of their people killed, were still willing to let the priests and the soldiers and their families leave and live peacefully.

On the other hand, during this battle at La Purisima, four Mexican Californios were killed. They were reportedly travelers on their way to Los Angeles, and it is unknown exactly how or why the Indians killed them. On the Indian side, at least seven were buried at the mission during the following two days, probably killed in the struggle or dying of wounds (Bancroft 1886, 2:529; Osio [1851] 1996, 55–56). The Chumash Indians held La Purisima for almost a month, drilling, erecting palisade foundations, cutting loopholes for shooting through the church walls, mounting an old cannon they had captured, and generally laying preparations for the attack they knew would come.

During this period, according to Richard Street in *Beasts of the Field,* the "entire population" of Indians of Mission Santa Barbara also revolted and armed themselves, apparently seizing some guns from the soldiers' stores (2004, 60). The Santa Barbara rebels promised the padre they would do no harm if the soldiers retreated, but wounded two soldiers who refused to leave without their weapons. Since the Santa Barbara Presidio was close by, however, the Californios, led by the military officer Pablo de la Guerra, whose family later became leading landowners in this region, were able to quickly launch a counter-attack.

After a fight of several hours, interrupted by a lunch break called by de la Guerra, the Indians took what property they could carry and retreated to the nearby hills. Several rebels had been killed, and there were wounded on both sides. In his takeover of the mission, de la Guerra's troops reportedly killed at least one Indian straggler, who was trying to flee riding a mule while carrying a blanket filled with grain. Within a couple of days, the soldiers sacked Indian houses in the area and killed other stragglers and at least four peaceful Indians who happened by chance into the area (Engelhardt 1913, 3:199–201; Bancroft 1886, 2:530). Messages were passed between the rebels and the padres, (who typically acted as intermediaries between the Indians and soldiers), but the rebels refused to surrender. Instead, they retreated further to the east, toward the Tulares, a wild region in the southern part of the San Joaquin Valley, and set up independent settlements there. At least twelve Indian victims of the rebellion were buried at Santa Barbara by the end of February 1824.

Santa Barbara Mission, Founded in 1786
One of the sites of the massive Chumash rebellion of 1824, suppressed by force by the colonial military. [Courtesy of the Bancroft Library, University of California, Berkeley.]

Meanwhile, Governor Arguello, having heard about the rebellion, sent a force of over a hundred soldiers, including infantry, cavalry, and artillery, to La Purisima under the command of Mariano Estrada. On March 16, 1824, this small army reached Purisima and soon was bombarding the Indians with musket bullets and rounds from a four-pound artillery piece. The Indians, reportedly about four hundred strong, returned the fire, but since they were untrained in the use of firearms, failed to have much effect. The soldiers were better shots and had superior weapons. Soon sixteen Indians were dead, and a large number wounded. As many as five soldiers were reportedly killed, and many wounded (Castillo 1978, 103).

Many Native Americans were also captured while attempting to flee. Depositions of prisoners were taken in order to single out the leaders for more serious punishment. As a result, seven Indian leaders were condemned to death and shot by Estrada and de la Guerra (who had arrived on the scene). Twelve others were sentenced to eight to ten years' hard labor at the Presidio of Santa Barbara. The soldiers were then sent after the Indians who had fled to the Tulares. They killed additional Indians during a battle in this region, but the padres were able to convince the governor to pardon the remaining Indians if they would return to their missions.

Once this was accomplished, many of the remaining rebels returned and the revolt was mostly over (Bancroft 1886, 2:531–536; Englehardt 1913, 3:205–206). At least fifty Indians (and probably many more, since records are fragmentary) had been killed, along with as many as nine Californios. There were a large number of wounded on both sides. Some refused to return, however, and the Tulares area continued to be inhabited by escaped Indians. A decade or so later, a party of US trappers found a rebel Chumash sanctuary in the Kern River area of today's northeast Kern County. They estimated that the settlement had as many as seven or eight hundred people growing crops, raising horses, and trading with other Indian groups (Castillo 1989, 391; Phillips 1993, 68).

The great Indian rebellion of 1824 had only been over for a few years when another epic, resistance struggle took place, this time at two northern missions. This became known as the Estanislao Rebellion, after its most famous leader. The first sign of mass Indian dissatisfaction came in May of 1827, when Padre

Narciso Duran of Mission San Jose reported to Ignacio Martinez, the San Francisco Presidio commander, that about four hundred Yokuts Indians had escaped from this mission and returned to their home villages in the San Joaquin Valley (Sullivan 1936, 99–102). Since their villages were far removed from the missions, it was difficult to capture and force the Yokuts to return.

In late 1828, another mass breakout from Mission San Jose took place. This time, an Indian leader emerged to guide the struggle against the Mexican *Californio* ruling class. The priests of Mission San Jose had named this man Estanislao. He was from a Yokuts tribelet called the Lakisamne. He had been a *vaquero* (cowboy), mule trainer, and Indian leader (*alcalde*) at Mission San Jose (Phillips 1993, 78). At the same time, another group of Yokuts, led by a man called Cipriano, launched a mass escape from nearby Mission Santa Clara. The two Indian groups united and established a large, fortified camp along today's Stanislaus River in the San Joaquin Valley (Shoup and Milliken 1999, 89–90). Estanislao and Cipriano then sent a message to Padre Duran that their people no longer feared the soldiers and were rising in revolt. In response, Duran notified Commander Martinez that groups of Yokuts had rebelled and had good leadership. Recognizing the importance of this leadership, Duran maintained, ominously, that "everything depends upon capturing dead or alive the Indian Estanislao from San Jose and another from Santa Clara called Cipriano" (Phillips 1993, 78).

Three military expeditions were necessary to eventually defeat this Indian rebellion. The Indians easily turned back the first one, in early 1829. The second expedition brought a cannon to dislodge the rebels from the stockade and trenches they had built. In the battle that followed, at least two soldiers were killed, along with eight Yokuts. There were also wounded on both sides. The Californios again failed to defeat the rebels and had to retreat, leaving behind a prisoner in the hands of the Indians. This man, Andres Mesa, was then publicly executed by the Indians. He was reportedly hanged by one foot from the branch of a tree and shot with arrows until dead. His body was then burned (Phillips 1993, 79).

The Indian victory and loss of *Californio* lives outraged the military, resulting in the organization of a third and larger expedition. This was the most powerful one yet, consisting of over a hundred soldiers and mobilized civilians, along with about fifty Indian auxiliaries from Missions San Jose and Santa Clara (Indian auxiliaries were loyal to the missions or were from other Native American groups who were traditional enemies and thus hostile to the Yokuts tribelets). Their commander was Mariano Guadalupe Vallejo, who left San Jose on May 26, 1829.

Vallejo's command had the most advanced weapons then available in California, including at least one cannon. The cannon was the decisive factor; it was something against which the Indian rebels had no defense. The cannon was used to break the Indian fortifications, while the woods in the area were also set on fire. Exposed to musket and cannon fire, the Indians were defeated, and a number of them were seized and summarily executed by Vallejo's troops. After Vallejo gave permission, at least one of these captured Indians was killed, as Mesa had been, by a group shooting arrows into him. A *Californio* officer completed the ritual execution with a shot to the head (Hurtado 1988, 44; Phillips 1993, 80–81). An unknown number of Indian rebels were killed during the Vallejo expedition, but it is known that at least fourteen of those who died were from Mission Santa Clara (Shoup and Milliken 1999, 92–93; Phillips 1993, 81). Most of these fourteen rebels had lived in the mission for many years—they knew the institution well and decided to risk their lives to rebel against it, a damning indictment of the mission system.

The rebellions of 1824 and 1828–1829 were a disaster for the mission system. Recruitment of gentiles to replace those who died or ran away was now more difficult than ever. The result was that mission population began to drop rapidly. Production of field crops was also in serious decline. The rebellions were a key factor, which laid the basis for the overthrow of what was now a dying institution (Hornbeck 1983, 46, 52–53).

RULING CLASS RESPONSES

Large-scale class struggle from below calls forth not only repression from the powers-that-be, but also change, the amelioration of the material and other conditions which lead to rebellion. The Indian struggles of the 1820s bore witness both to the Indians' courage and the growing limits of European American domination. Moreover, their rebellion began the train of events that led to the eventual destruction of the deadly and hated mission system.

When the 1824 rebellion took place, the governor was Luis Antonio Arguello, who had been the commander of the Presidio of San Francisco. Arguello wrote a report to his superiors in Mexico City that included statements critical of the treatment of the Indians (for example pointing out the injustice of keeping them in a state akin to slavery), but he was replaced in early 1825, even before his report got to Mexico City (T. Hittell 1885, 2:77–78).

The new governor was Lieutenant Colonel of Engineers Jose Maria de Echeandia. Echeandia recognized the need for reform, but also the true object of reform: the prevention of a fundamental change in colonialist rule. His orders from the Mexican government included investigation to see what could be done to ameliorate the conditions of the mission Indians. At first, Echeandia was only willing to take three cautious steps. The first was to plan the establishment of a model Indian pueblo north of Los Angeles, a plan that was never implemented. The second was to limit the number of lashes that could be laid on an Indian by a missionary to fifteen, which was hardly much of a "reform." The third allowed the emancipation from semi-slavery of those mission Indians within three areas of California (San Diego, Santa Barbara, and Monterey) found to be qualified to become

Mexican citizens. Unfortunately, only a few Indians were found to be so qualified (T. Hittell 1885, 2:91–93).

Following the 1828–1829 rebellion, however, the California governor developed a more radical and detailed plan that represented the first great step toward secularizing the missions. This plan provided that all but two of the missions should be converted into civilian pueblos—as rapidly as possible and certainly within five years. This plan proposed to give the Indians—and Mexican Californios who chose to join them—land, tools, and animals, presumably to be taken from mission stocks (T. Hittell 1885, 2:93–96). In October 1829, the governor ordered all Indian children who had been enslaved outside the missions as a result of military expeditions against the gentile Indians to be released and restored to their parents. In a bitterly ironic twist, he also ordered that, if the children's parents could not be located, these Indians were to be delivered to the nearest mission (T. Hittell 1885, 2:116).

The often-shifting struggle for power in Mexico City soon resulted in the replacement of Echeandia as governor, however, and one Manuel Victoria took his place. Just prior to leaving office in January 1831, however, Echeandia issued a lengthy proclamation ordering that his secularization plan be put into effect. His successor countermanded this order immediately upon assuming office (T. Hittell 1885, 2:123–124). It soon became clear that Governor Manuel Victoria, an extreme conservative, was anxious to preserve the status quo. Those who wanted the missions to immediately give up their lands, livestock, and other property to selected mission Indians and Mexican Californios would have to wait.

As it happened, that wait would not be for long. Another revolt was brewing among a new socioeconomic group, which was soon to become the new ruling class of California.

2

CALIFORNIOS, PEONS, AND INDIAN RAIDERS, 1831–1846

During the early and mid 1830s, California underwent a revolution. The combination of disease, leading to very high mortality rates, and native resistance had seriously weakened the missions, the central economic institution of the colony. Although it was Indian resistance that decisively undermined the exploitative mission system, Indians were not the ones to benefit from the end of this system. Instead, the power void created by the decline of the missions was filled by a new political and economic ruling class—California-born Spanish and Mexican families. These newly dominant families have been labeled "Californios" to distinguish them from the original Spanish and Mexican settlers.

A NEW CALIFORNIO RULING CLASS

Two fundamental developments led to the creation of this new Californio ruling class. The first was demographic. Many members of the Spanish officer corps that had entered California in the last third of the eighteenth century had married and created large families. The children of these official families, born late in the eighteenth or at the beginning of the nineteenth century, came of age in the 1815–1830 period. They lived mainly in the relatively cramped presidios and the larger, but still restricted, spaces of the pueblos. A few had also been given provisional land grants for adjacent lands. The military was the normal calling for the men, and family life occupied the women.

The second generation also married and had large families, and their economic livelihood within the mission economy had become increasingly problematic. The European American population of the presidios and pueblos grew by 65 percent between 1815 and 1830 (from 2,334 to 3,851), the largest increase during the entire 1800–1845 period (Hornbeck 1983, 50–51).

The second development was economic. During the 1820s, the world trade system began to connect more closely with the Mexican colony. After an independent Mexico loosened trade restrictions, British and American trading houses sent merchant agents to California to establish trade relations. The industrial expansion of a rising capitalism in both England and New England had, by the early 1820s, created a large demand for leather, especially for shoe and boot manufacturing. A demand for tallow or rendered cow fat also existed for soap, candle making, and other uses (Hackel 1998, 130–133). With its vast mission-owned cattle herds, California was in an excellent position to supply some of this demand. English and American agents made contracts with the missionaries to exchange cattle hides and tallow for such manufactured goods as iron, tools, dyes, clothes, kitchen equipment, and similar articles. This trade was successful for both the foreign traders and the Mexican ruling class, but not for the exploited Indians. During their last years, the missions were transformed from self-sufficient communities to large commercial ranches focused on increasing their output of cattle (Hornbeck 1983:56–57).

By the 1830s, the leading Californio families had been intermarrying for a number of decades. Most, if not all, of these marriages were planned and arranged by the older male members

of each family, at least in part to cement the family's connections
to other leading families. As Richard Henry Dana characterized
the ruling class of the time, "Those who are of pure Spanish
blood … form the aristocracy; intermarrying, and keeping up an
exclusive system in every respect" (quoted in Kowelskwi 1997, 8).
Thus socioeconomic factors and the clannishness of an emerging
upper class prevented marriages across class lines. Military
weddings were common, with the officers marrying into other
military families (Miranda 1981:89). The result of this process
by the 1830s was a dense network of family kinship ties, which
were the interlocking directorates of the era. One contemporary
observer, discussing Southern California during the early 1850s,
but reflecting the reality of the earlier era as well, noted:

> *[T]he old wealthy and intelligent Spanish families
> had formed a strictly exclusive class. They meant
> to make up the aristocracy of the country, and
> dispensed a liberal hospitality that did honor to
> them as a people, as well as to the more favored
> class of Americans who were so fortunate as to gain
> admission to their circles. (Bell 1881, 88)*

In late 1852, this same observer went to a ball at the home of
Don Jose' Antonio Carrillo, whose family was among the most
important of the time:

> *The ball was the first of the season, and was attended
> by the elite of the country from San Diego to Monterey.
> The dancing hall was large, with a floor as polished
> as a bowling saloon. The music was excellent—
> one splendid performer on an immense harp. The
> assembled company was not only elegant—it was …
> brilliant. The dresses of both ladies and gentlemen
> could not be surpassed in expensive elegance … the
> dancing on that occasion was something more than
> elegant, it was wonderful, while the most dignified*

41

> *and staid decorum was observed to the end of the*
> *festivities. (Bell 1881, 88–89)*

A small group of intermarried landowning families made up the core of the new Californio ranching ruling class, often called the "rancheros." It had matured during the 1820s and, by 1831, was ready to assume a decisive political and economic role, thus moving from being a class *in* itself to a class *for* itself. They were in the process of achieving political power and at the same time privately expropriating eight million acres of mission lands, along with hundreds of thousands of cattle, sheep, horses, and other livestock. Thousands of mission-trained and exploitable Indian laborers went along with the land, since most had nowhere else they could go.

THE THIRTEEN FAMILIES

By the early 1830s, there were at least thirteen families of great importance—these were the key ruling class families who ran California from the early 1830s to the mid-1840s.

The first and most important was the Carrillo family, led by three brothers—Jose Antonio, Carlos, and Anastasio—who were active in California political, military, social, and economic life. It was also a large clan, related by blood or marriage to many of the other leading Californio families. If intermarriages were the interlocking directorates of this period, then the Carrillos had the most interlocks. They were directly related to the Pico, Bandini, Castro, Vallejo, de la Guerra, Ortega, and Lugo families and indirectly connected to many more.

The second key family was the Picos. Pio and Andres were the two most active members of the Pico family during this era. Pio was the last Mexican Californio governor of California. He and his brother were directly related to the Carrillos through the marriage of three male members of the Carrillo family to three female Picos. One of these marriages, in 1823, united Jose Antonio Carrillo with Maria E. Pico, a sister of Pio and Andres. When she died, Jose Antonio married another Pico sister (Northrop 1976, 1:100–101, 1984, 2:213–214). Besides the Carrillos, the Picos also intermarried with the Alvarado, Ortega, Bernal, and Arguello families.

The third most significant family was the Vallejos. Two male members of the Vallejo family, Mariano de Guadalupe and Jose de Jesus Vallejo, were military, political, social, and economic leaders during this era. The mother of these two men and the mother of the Carrillo brothers were sisters (both were Lugos), making the two leading Vallejos and the three leading Carrillos cousins. Mariano de Guadalupe Vallejo, the military commander who defeated the Estanislao-Cipriano rebellion of 1828–1829, and another of his brothers also married members of the Carrillo family (Northrop 1976, 1:100–101, 210–211, 350–351). The Vallejo brothers' older sister married Jose Francisco Alvarado in 1808 and was the mother of Governor Juan B. Alvarado, who was therefore a nephew of the Vallejo brothers. Governor from 1836 to 1837 and from 1839–1842, Juan B. Alvarado was the key member of his family. His mother was Maria Josefa Vallejo and he married Martina Castro (Northrop 1976, 1:103–104)

Merchant capitalist Juan Bandini of Los Angeles was the senior member of the Bandini family. He married twice, and his two wives were Dolores Estudillo and Refugio Arguello, both from prominent families. One of his daughters married one of Carlos Carrillo's sons. The Castro family had a number of branches, but the most important was headed by Jose' Tiburcio Castro and his son Jose'. Carlos Carrillo married Maria J. Castro in 1808 (Northrop 1976, 1:100–101). The Castros also intermarried with the Alvarado, Estrada, Vallejo, and Bernal families.

The de la Guerra family was the leading family of Santa Barbara, headed by Jose' Antonio de la Guerra during this era. He was the military commander who suppressed the Chumash rebels in 1824. In 1804 Jose' married Maria Antonia Carrillo, an elder sister of the three Carrillo brothers (Northrop 1984, 2:101, 119–120). Joseph Dario Arguello headed the Arguello family;

he was a presidio commander and was also acting-governor of California in 1814–1815. His son, Luis Antonio Arguello, became the commander of the Presidio of San Francisco, then the first California-born governor from 1822 to 1825. Luis Antonio married twice, to women from the Sal and Ortega families. Other Arguellos married into the Estrada, Bernal, Estudillo, Bandini, Lugo, and Pico families (Northrop 1976, 1:45–51).

Jose Maria Estudillo, a military officer in Monterey and San Diego, headed the Estudillo family. His daughters married into the Bandini and Arguello families (Northrop 1984, 2:84–85).

The Lugo family, intermarried with the Carrillo, Ortega, Vallejo, and Verdugo families, were early grantees of several Southern California ranches. Maria Antonia Lugo married Ignacio Vallejo and was the mother of Mariano de Guadalupe Vallejo and all his brothers and sisters (Lugo [1877] 1950, 187). The Yorba family intermarried with both the Carrillo and Lugo families. It became one of the largest Southern California landowners (Northrop 1976, 1:363–366).

One member of the Ortega family, Jose Joaquin Ortega, was important during this era. He married a sister of Pio and Andres Pico, and one of his sisters wed a son of Carlos Carrillo. One of his daughters later married a member of the de la Guerra family. Two of his sisters also married into the Arguello family (Northrop 1987, 1:246–252).

Two brothers, Jose' Mariano Estrada and Jose Raymundo Estrada, were prominent members of the Estrada family during this period. Jose' Mariano married a member of the Arguello family, and one son married into the Castro family. Jose' Raymundo wed an older sister of the Vallejo brothers (Northrop 1984, 2:1, 77–80).

MARRIAGES TO FOREIGNERS

Beginning in the 1820s and increasing throughout the 1830s and 1840s, prominent Californio families married their daughters to the foreign merchants and others who increasingly settled in California. These unions included a daughter of Jose Raymundo Estrada, who wed the Mexican Jose Abrego, an important merchant. Juan Bandini's daughter Arcadia married New Englander Abel Stearns, one of the richest merchants of the era.

In 1825, the prominent English merchant William Hartnell wed Maria T. de la Guerra, a daughter of Jose' Antonio de la Guerra and his wife, Maria Antonia Carrillo. William G. Dana, a native of Boston and relative of Richard Henry Dana, married a daughter of Carlos A. Carrillo. Jacob Leese, from Ohio, married a sister of the Vallejo brothers. Englishman John Forster wed a sister of the Pico brothers.

The marriages with foreign merchants solidified the growing commercial ties between the Californio ruling class and prominent foreigners, linking the Californios into the rising capitalist world trade system. These foreigners were also from the same racial group and perceived to be from the same social class as well. This was important in a caste society where racial background and light skin color were important. These were not everything, however, since a dark skinned person could and sometimes did rise to a position of power in Mexican California.

POLITICS, SECULARIZATION PLANS, AND A COUP

In early 1822, in the wake of Mexican independence from Spain, Pablo Vicente de Sola, the last Spanish appointed governor, called together a council or junta composed of leading Californio military officers and the two top Franciscan missionaries. The purpose of the meeting was to swear loyalty to Mexico and discuss the new political situation (T. Hittell 1885, 2:44). New regulations had come from Mexico City that allowed California to have its own provincial legislature and to send one of its members to the supreme legislative body in Mexico City. Accordingly, in 1822 Sola's council choose a provincial legislature, called the *diputacion*. Over the next decade or so, its dominant members were the three

Carrillo brothers mentioned above, three members of the Castro family, three Ortegas, along with Pio Pico, Juan Bandini, Jose de la Guerra, Mariano G. Vallejo, and members of the Estudillo, Arguello, and Estrada families (T. Hittell 1885, 2:45, 50, 89, 96, 122, 224–228; Osio [1851] 1996, 113). Thus by mid-1831, many of the leading male members of these major families had completed almost a decade of political involvement.

The successful suppression of the Indian resistance of the mid- and late-1820s, combined with the demographic pressures and the commercial possibilities of cattle ranching, created a strong constituency for what was called "secularization," the expropriation of the vast mission acreage and livestock and their distribution to the leading Californio families. Only by removing the missions and the seizure and redistribution of their lands, could the Californios directly participate in the lucrative hide and tallow trade.

They agitated for secularization because they planned to confiscate the land and livestock involved. The mission Indians would also be freed from bondage to the church and therefore available as a cheap and skilled labor supply. The demand for secularization and redistribution therefore grew stronger throughout the 1820s, culminating in Governor Echeandia's plan of 1829–1830, discussed above in chapter 1. When Governor Victoria came to power in early 1831 and reversed Echeandia's plan, the new generation of Californios objected most strenuously, since they expected to be the main beneficiaries of the secularization process.

When Governor Victoria entered office, he not only reversed plans for secularization, he also refused to call the local legislature into session. He ruled in a dictatorial fashion and also instituted and carried out the death penalty for minor offenses (Rice et al. 1988, 117; Osio [1851] 1996, 108–110). This offended the colony's increasingly powerful families, which made up the new ruling class. When Victoria ordered both Abel Stearns and Jose Antonio Carrillo into exile, many were ready to rebel. Stearns refused to go into exile, but Carrillo, whose brother was now California's representative to Mexico City, decided to pretend to go into exile while actively plotting a revolution. Carrillo simply went over the border into Baja California briefly and then returned to San Diego. He met with Juan Bandini, Pio Pico, Abel Stearns, and a few others, developing a plan to violently overthrow Victoria's government.

On the evening of November 29, 1831, the conspirators armed themselves, surprised the guard at the San Diego Presidio, and took possession of this military base with all its arms, cannons, ammunition, and soldiers. Other officers were later captured at their homes and converted to the rebellion. Following a proclamation to the effect that Victoria was a tyrant who had to be overthrown, the rebels proceeded to capture Los Angeles (T. Hittell 1885, 2:123–139; Bell 1881:64–66). By this time, Victoria had organized a counterattack out of his Monterey headquarters and had a small army, which he soon brought overland to the Los Angeles area. Carrillo, Pico, and Bandini had a much larger army, however, and the support of more of the key leaders, including members of the Ortega, Castro, and Vallejo families (Osio [1851] 1996, 106–113).

There was a skirmish in December 1831 in which only two men were killed, one on each side. But Governor Victoria was himself seriously wounded in the fight, souring him on California. He soon resigned his position as governor and left the province in January 1832. Henceforth, the new Californio ruling class always had a major role in how they were to be ruled, even when the governor was sent from Mexico City. Conflict was frequent, however, developing out of what could be called the fragmentation of sovereignty characteristic of the socioeconomic system as it developed over the following few years. This fragmentation took place because the system was very decentralized, with private landholding and wealth separated from any public responsibility, replacing the former absolute state with a form of feudalism.

The result was a very weak, divided government, with constant struggles for power between members of the leading families.

THE SECOND GREAT EXPROPRIATION, RANCHEROS AND PEONS

The expropriation or "secularization" of the missions by the new Californio ruling class was a key first step towards creating an entirely new economy and society in coastal California. The Mexican Congress passed the necessary enabling legislation in August of 1833, and a plan to actually carry out the expropriation, the "emancipation" of the Indians, and the redistribution of mission property was in place by August of 1834 (T. Hittell 1885, 2:188). The governor appointed men from Californio families to carry out the actual process of inventorying and distributing the properties at each individual mission. The entire process was extremely corrupt. As one early day scholar wrote:

> *[T]he great mass of the commissioners and other officials, whose duty it became to administer the properties of the missions and especially their great numbers of horses, cattle, sheep and other animals, thought of little else and accomplished little else than enriching themselves. It cannot be said that the spoliation was immediate; but it was certainly very rapid. A few years sufficed to strip the establishments of everything of value and leave the Indians, who were, in contemplation of law the beneficiaries of secularization, a shivering crowd of naked and, so to speak, homeless wanderers ... the mission properties ... soon began to find their way into the hands of private individuals; and the commissioners and officials in general began to grow rich. (T. Hittell 1885, 2:206–207, 209)*

Some Indians did get land and livestock from the missions; others got a few horses or cows, but most got nothing. On the other hand, the leading ruling class families, who had mainly been military officers and officials up to the early 1830s, got the bulk of the mission wealth. They were able to seize vast landed estates along with most of the animals and Indians residing there (see Shoup and Milliken 1999, 110–126). For example, Mariano G. Vallejo, one of the commissioners of the San Francisco Solono Mission north of San Francisco, was able to claim 300,000 acres in land grants, largely from that mission's property. Members of the de la Guerra family soon had at least 326,000 acres; Pio and Andres Pico got over 532,000 acres; Yorba family members received over 235,000 acres; and Abel Stearns soon owned 200,000 acres and thousands of head of cattle. Other individuals and families got lesser amounts but still substantial amounts as follows:

- Carrillos over 165,000 acres
- Juan Bandini over 130,000 acres
- Castros over 120,000 acres
- Arguellos over 116,000 acres
- Lugos over 100,000 acres
- Estradas over 66,000 acres
- Ortegas over 44,000 acres
- Estudillos over 35,000 acres

Sources: T. Hittell 1885, 2:209, 753; Monroy 1998, 182; Dunlap 1982, 192; Cowan 1956, 20–112.

This great transfer of land and resources—by far the greatest since the Spanish had seized the land from the Indians beginning in 1769 and amounting to California's second great expropriation—created an extensive system of private ranchos as the dominant economic unit reinforcing the rule of the new Californio ruling class, the rancheros (Hackel 1998, 132; Monroy 1998, 180).

The ranchero system was unique to its time and place—California during the 1830s and 1840s. Since the large estates were the dominant economic and social units, their labor system defined the social formation. First of all, native people remained the overwhelmingly dominant labor source. The Indians continued to do almost all the hard work needed to sustain a frontier economy based on cattle raising. As one contemporary later wrote:

> *Some of the great ranchos of the country were baronial in their extent and surroundings. Their proprietors being great dignitaries, maintaining large numbers of vassals—for such they were, mostly Indians who, under Mexican majordomos, did all of the labor for the ranch. (Bell 1881, 288)*

In the big houses of the landowners, there were large numbers of female Indian servants. Señora Vallejo recounted:

> *Each child (of whom there were sixteen) has a personal attendant, while I have two for my own needs; four or five are occupied in grinding corn for tortillas, for so many visitors come here that three grinders do not suffice; six or seven serve in the kitchen, and five or six are always washing clothes for the children or other servants; and finally, nearly a dozen are employed at sewing and spinning. (quoted in Caughey and Caughey 1976, 105)*

Second, while there was some variability in labor systems during this era—there were small numbers of both wage laborers and Indian slaves—the most common situation was a type of peonage personal dependence on a master (Cook 1976, 302–306; Pitt 1966, 15–16; Castillo 1978, 105; Hurtado 1988, 55–71; Hackel 1998, 134). Central to such a system were reciprocal obligations. The Indian peon typically received food, clothing, some land use rights, and basic supplies from the master ("Don") in exchange for his and his family's labor. Ranchero Salvador Vallejo (Mariano's brother) justified the relationship in a typical colonialist fashion, stressing how well treated and loved the hard working and largely powerless peons were:

Many of the rich men of the country had from twenty to sixty Indian servants whom they dressed and fed ... our friendly Indians tilled our soil, pastured our cattle, sheared our sheep, cut our lumber, built our houses, paddled our boats, made tiles for our homes, ground our grain, slaughtered our cattle, dressed their hides for market, and made our unburnt bricks; while the Indian women made excellent servants, took good care of our children, made every one of our meals ... Those people we considered as members of our families. We loved them and they loved us. (quoted in Cook 1976, 305)

In many cases, emancipated mission Indians who had lived in an area for all their lives simply transferred allegiance from the mission to the new lord and master and became peons. This was the case, for example, at both Mariano G. Vallejo's, and Pio Pico's vast estates (Gonzalez 1998, 165). Some of these operations were quite substantial; Vallejo reportedly had hundreds of Indian peons, and Pico's ranch had over 100 (Silliman 2004, xii; Cook 1976, 457; Hackel 1998, 134). The system was very hierarchical, and caste-like, since racial differences between Europeans and Indians were involved. The white male head of family was also in almost total control of both his own family and "his" Indian laborers. William A. Streeter, an early American settler who visited the Jose' de la Guerra family often in the 1840s, reported that Don José:

was esteemed and respected by all, both Californians and foreigners, and among the simple minded natives he was venerated next to the Mission Fathers. While he was living, few Californians thought of passing before his house without taking off their hats. (Streeter [1878] 1939, 169)

This kind of respect extended to his own family. Streeter also reported that after the required late afternoon prayers at the de la Guerra house, "the old man remained at the head of the table, the sons and daughters retiring, and kissing their father's hand as they filed past" (Streeter [1878] 1939, 170).

This strict paternalistic and hierarchical control applied even more to the Indians. One white resident at the Rancho Petaluma said that Mariano G. Vallejo's "will was law" at the place, and no one dared contradict it (Silliman 2004, 197). A US military officer commented that Vallejo held the lives of "wild" Indian to be very cheap, "The value of an Indian's life in the eye of the rulers scarcely exceeds that of the wild cattle. The commandant-general is frequently said to hunt them" (quoted in Silliman 2004, 3).

In such a system of reciprocal demands and expectations, the paternalism of the master was a key factor, since the peons were not tied to the institution in the same way that labor was under either the mission system or in European style feudalism. The Indian peons had to see the master as somehow necessary for survival and be in a real sense a willing participant in their own exploitation and alienation from control over the means of life. But a lack of other options also entered into the calculation. As the missions disintegrated and their land and animals were expropriated, the mission Indians were cast adrift and had to find ways to survive. Becoming a peon on a Californio's ranch was often, depending upon the nature of the don, the more viable and attractive option.

Mariano G. Vallejo's large Rancho Petaluma had four different groups of Indian workers. The largest group was debt peons, Native Americans who had "invested" their few cattle into the hands of Vallejo, who kept them on his land in exchange for their labor. This group came from the missions and was culturally and politically closer to the Californios. Such Indians would have had more skills in farming and construction, and so would have been more likely to be used as supervisors of other Indians, as well as servants, cooks, and artisans.

A second group was composed of workers who Vallejo captured in raids into the adjacent interior. Vallejo's relationship with them was more oppressive, and the Indians more like slaves, used for the hardest physical labor. A third group of Indian workers was sent at Vallejo's request by his Indian ally Chief Solano. Some had also been captured in wars. Finally, there were Indians who used the Petaluma Rancho as a part of their family or group survival strategy, as a part of a seasonal round. They would visit the ranch and exchange work for food and shelter for part of the year, and then move on (Silliman 2004, 55–58).

These Indians took advantage of the fact that the peonage system of the rancho was less coercive than the mission. They could thus move from one ranch to another. Emancipated Indians from the missions could also run away and return to their homelands, which, in the case of the Sierra Miwok, Central Valley Yokuts, and other groups was a hundred or more miles away. Consequently, a segment of the Indian population during this period was "extremely mobile" (Jackson and Castillo 1995, 94). This mobility, combined with the injustice of both the mission expropriation process and the oppression of the peonage system, soon began to directly impact the Californio ranchos.

REBELLION

Every social formation has its own unique constellation of strengths, contradictions, and vulnerabilities. The lack of options for many of the mission Indians supplied a largely docile and inexpensive labor force, strengthening ruling-class rule. But California's ranchero system of the 1830s and 1840s was vulnerable because of the very mobility of groups of dissatisfied Indians who were from more-distant places and who had not been pacified by the mission system. In the 1830s and 1840s, these were most commonly Plains Miwok and Central Valley Yokuts. The Plains Miwok had come to the missions and later the ranchos from the area south and southeast of today's Sacramento and the Central

Valley Yokuts from the plain of the San Joaquin Valley (Levy 1978, 400; Wallace 1978, 468–469).

By the early 1830s, these native people had been in close contact with the Europeans for several decades and many had become proficient with horses while herding cattle. As the missions disintegrated under the impact of rebellion and secularization, these Indians had the option of returning to their villages or working on the ranchos. Some worked on the ranchos, some returned to their villages, and some did both at different times. The effect was to establish a network of information about the location of ranchos and their herds, routes to and from these places from the central valley, and the presence or absence of armed opposition. Another factor at work was the knowledge of and desire for European foods, beef, mutton, and horseflesh. Cook recounted the origins of this situation as follows:

> *Very early in mission history, outlying heathen began to slip in and run off stock. As the years went on, they learned two things … They learned that with the correct technique such raids were very easy to carry out, and that they were highly irritating to the white men. Furthermore, the acquisition of horses enabled the Indians to improve their methods by providing fast transportation. As the great herds of cattle and horses spread out from the coastal ranches, the opportunities increased, until by 1835 stock raiding was universal. (Cook 1976, 34)*

Resistance and class struggle from below took the form of Indian raids on rancho settlements during this period (Monroy 1998, 191). Raiding was also the easiest way to get favored food items. Raiding was both very common and often intense, and since the response of the Californios was to organize relatively small, ad hoc expeditions to try to chase down and punish the stock thieves, records of every incident do not exist.

The desire to capture a cheap labor force to serve as peons was also often a part of the Californio's armed response. As Cook expressed it: "punishing stock thieves and capturing farm labor became almost the same in method" (Cook 1976, 201).

This warfare was also quite bloody, with intense hatred expressed on both sides. The Californios commonly cut off the heads, ears, and even the genitalia of their Indian enemies, and were also known to drag them to death with horses and ropes (Rice et al. 1988, 94).

The Californios perpetuated many massacres, one of the most notorious being the 1837 Mesa-Amador expedition against the Miwok. The expedition went out from Mission San Jose, captured an entire Indian rancheria, then "butchered 100 in cold blood ... then massacred a second hundred" (Cook 1976, 250). Jose Maria Amador later recounted in chilling detail how many of these Indians were terrorized and murdered:

> *At every half mile or mile, we put six of them on their knees to say their prayers, making them understand that they were about to die. Each one was shot with four arrows, two in front and two in the back. Those who refused to die immediately were killed with spears.* (quoted in Rice et al, 1988, 94)

Although we will never have accurate figures, Cook estimates that at least 2,245 Native Americans were slaughtered on such expeditions during the 1831–1841 period alone (Cook 1976, 202–206).

Indians had inferior weapons and were much less bloodthirsty, so inflicted fewer losses on the Californios. Reportedly, the most sensational episode took place in 1837 at Rancho Jamul, Southern California home of the mother of Pio and Andres Pico. Indian attackers killed Mayordomo Leiva and several other defenders, kidnapping the mayordomo's two daughters, who were never heard from again (Monroy 1998, 192). A Californio's eyewitness report called the event an Indian uprising:

> *[A]ll of a sudden they fell upon servants at the ranch,
> who were the majordomo, Juan Leiva, his son Jose
> Antonio, a youth ... Molina, and another from
> Lower California named Comancho. They killed all
> at the cornfield except Juan Leiva, who broke away
> toward the house to defend his family. When he went
> toward the gun room, an Indian cleaning woman of
> the house who had locked that room and put the key
> in her pocket mockingly showed him the key, saying
> that there were no hopes in that direction. Leiva ran
> to the kitchen and defended himself with coals of fire
> for a while; but at the end they killed him and threw
> his body into the hall of the house.*
>
> *Afterward they overcame his wife, Dona Maria,
> a little son named Claro, and his two daughters,
> Tomasa and Ramona (fifteen and twelve years old,
> respectively). The Indians were going to kill Dona
> Maria and the boy, when supplications of Dona
> Tomasa made them desist. They took off all the
> woman's clothes and those of the boy, and in spite of
> the screams and moans of all the family, they carried
> off the two girls toward the Colorado River. Before
> starting they removed everything from the ranch,
> taking with them horses, cattle, and all other things
> of value, and burned the houses ... All the efforts
> that were made to recover the lost property and ...
> ransom the kidnapped girls were useless. To this
> day, what was the fate of those unhappy creatures is
> unknown. (quoted in Bebee and Senkewicz 2001,
> 415–416)*

Details about several other incidents among many will serve
to illustrate the techniques and results common during this era.

In August 1838, fifty Indian horse raiders crossed the
Sacramento River and appeared at Soscol with a band of tame

horses, the idea apparently being to stampede the horses at nearby Sonoma. General Vallejo's men discovered this threat, attacked, and killed thirty-four Indians. Their chief, Cumuchi, was later shot at Sonoma for this and other raids (Bancroft 1886, 4:73).

In 1839, an Indian leader named Yoscolo led several raiding parties into the Santa Clara Valley, hitting ranches around San Jose, as well as Mission Santa Clara itself. On one of their raids, the Indian group was chased into the Santa Cruz Mountains where they were all killed, along with two Californios. Yoscolo's head was reportedly cut off, stuck on a lance, and paraded around San Jose. The head was then taken to the mission and nailed to a pole next to a large cross in front of the church where it was left for two or three months as a warning to all thieves and rebels (Phillips 1993, 112–113; Bancroft 1886, 4:75–76).

That same year (1839), Governor Alvarado received a letter from one of the leaders of Los Angeles, which stated, "the number of Indians who have run away to take up criminal pursuits is so great that the entire southern district is paralyzed" (Monroy 1998, 191).

In 1838, Indians killed several rancheros near Monterey, and in 1841, Mission San Juan Bautista was under siege. At San Luis Obispo, more than a thousand head of stock were lost in a single raid (Beck and Haase 1974, 23).

In 1846, a group of Indians killed three Californios near San Diego. José del Carmen Lugo then organized a counterattack together with Indian allies under the control of a chief called Juan Antonio. Lugo's group ambushed the Indians, and as Lugo later recounted,

> *[They] made a great slaughter, and falling upon them from the rear killed many of them ... eighteen or twenty of them turned back and gave up their arms. They were made prisoners and placed in charge of Chief Juan Antonio ... On reaching Aguanga we amused ourselves killing some three Indians who*

> *continued fighting ... After terminating the affair,*
> *in which perhaps a hundred Indians perished,*
> *we went back to Juan Antonio and found that he*
> *had killed all the prisoners ... The booty that was*
> *collected amounted to no more than a few sarapes,*
> *arrows, lances and other trifles. (Lugo [1877] 1950,*
> *208–209)*

Despite such counterattacks, by the early 1840s, Indian raids had put the Californios on the defensive, and the governor proposed that a fort be built on Pacheco Pass, which raiders used as one of the main transportation routes from the San Joaquin Valley to the coast. The fort was never built, but the proposal showed how serious things had become (Beck and Haase 1974, 23; Cook 1976, 231–232). Cook summed up the situation:

> *The acquisition of horses and the practice derived*
> *from years of experience wrought a further extension*
> *of their warfare, for it is but a short step from the*
> *quick dash to cut away stock to the serious armed*
> *cavalry assault on a fixed point, such as a ranch*
> *house or settlement. These developments follow*
> *rather naturally ... Thus from a race of slow,*
> *unwarlike, sedentary seed-gatherers, these tribes were*
> *evolving rapidly into a group of fast, shifty, quite*
> *clever cavalrymen. This was a physical response, an*
> *adaptation to new conditions of the first order of*
> *magnitude. As a result of this process, by 1845 the*
> *valley Indians had made inland expeditions and*
> *invasions very costly and dangerous, but, more*
> *important, they had also actually begun to drive in*
> *the Spanish frontier. (Cook 1976, 230–231)*

The Californio ruling class had, during the early and mid-1830s, expropriated the mission properties, accumulated land and livestock, and created their own unique system for the exploitation of the California environment and Indian labor. By the late 1830s, this unjust system had engendered intense resistance on the part of two large Native Californian groups: the Miwok and Central Valley Yokuts. These Indian groups had been less centrally involved in the mission and rancho social-formations than were the coastal Indian groups, who, in any case, had almost completely died off due to conditions at the missions. This put the Miwok and Yokuts in a position to know these systems but to stand apart from them and rebel against the new system. That they were able to put the Californios on the defensive and even begin to raise doubts about the viability of the entire rancho peonage system was quite an achievement. But their increasing success was cut short by the influx into California of a different set of European Americans who were arriving in larger and larger numbers as the 1840s progressed.

These were the Anglo Americans. Their aggressively imperialistic attitudes and policies, their rush for gold, their technological superiority, and their vast numbers soon overwhelmed both the Indians and the Californio ranchero ruling class. Most of the Californio landowners were soon to be defeated and their land expropriated or sold to the newcomers. Native Californians, who had made up the labor force for the first seventy-five years of the European settlement of California, were also soon to be completely pushed aside by the rush of a new and vast wave of humanity.

PART TWO

THE TRANSITION TO CAPITALISM, 1846–1860s

The United States' war to annex Mexico's northern territories, together with the rush for gold, the conquest of the Native Americans, the rise of hard-rock mining, and the advent of industrial capitalism and Republicanism in San Francisco created a new California that was increasingly characterized by capitalist economic, social, and political relationships.

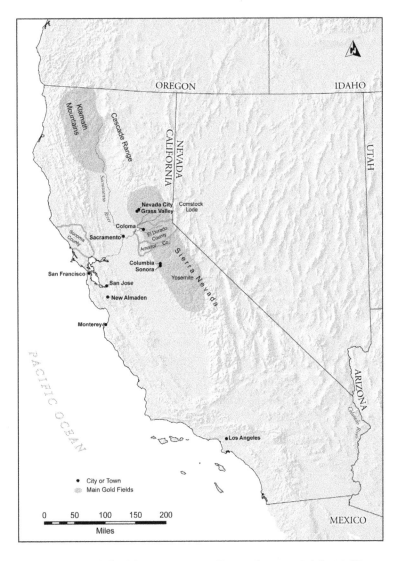

OREGON

IDAHO

Klamath
Mountains

Cascade Range

NEVADA

CALIFORNIA

UTAH

Sacramento River

Nevada City
Grass Valley

Comstock
Lode

Coloma

El Dorado
County

Sonoma
County

Sacramento

Amador Co.

Sierra Nevada

Columbia
Sonora

Yosemite

San Francisco

San Jose

New Almaden

Monterey

PACIFIC OCEAN

ARIZONA

Colorado River

Los Angeles

● City or Town
Main Gold Fields

0   50   100   150   200
Miles

MEXICO

Map 2: The Transition to Capitalism, 1846–1860s

3

WAR, GOLD RUSH, AND CONQUEST, 1846–1856

In 1845, on the eve of the war between the United States and Mexico, the population of California consisted of about 100,000 individuals, approximately 80,000 unassimilated Native Americans, 10,000 assimilated (Christianized) Indians, 7,000 Californios, 680 Americans, and 200 Europeans (Cook 1976, 4–5; Caughey 1940, 260; St. Clair 1998–99, 185). In the eventful decade that followed, several hundred thousand people—mostly young male adventurers—invaded California. They came to try to make their fortunes during one of the greatest and most democratic mineral rushes in world history. They originated from all over the world, but mainly from the United States, Mexico, China, Europe, and South America. The basis for the future development of the state was laid by the rapid socioeconomic and political transformations that soon followed.

WAR

During the ranchero era, the United States was a rising imperial power that began to see California as a prize. US citizens had begun to settle in California in the 1820s, and by the mid-1840s, hundreds called it home. Their political and economic leaders wanted California because of its potential importance for accessing the trade and resources of the Far East. The harbor at San Francisco was especially valuable. As early as 1818, American officials expressed interest in this port, one US agent noting that the Bay of San Francisco was the "most convenient, extensive, and safe in the world," adding ominously that it was "wholly without defense" (Harlow 1982, 48). By 1835, top U.S. officials strongly desired acquisition of California and began energetically pursuing this goal (Harlow 1982, 48). At least by 1842, US Navy commanders in the Pacific had standing instructions to seize California by force should a state of war develop between Mexico and the United States. Thus, in October of 1842, Thomas ap Catesby Jones,[1] the commander of American naval forces in the Pacific, landed at and captured Monterey, the capital of Mexican California. Jones was under the misapprehension that war between the two countries existed and so carried out his orders, as he understood them. Since no war had begun, Jones issued an apology, exited California, and sailed south (Caughey 1940, 265–266).

By the mid-1840s, the push was on to acquire the territory by any means necessary. US leaders had tried to purchase California, but Mexican officials always refused to sell. During the mid-1840s, three different but interrelated strategic plans were therefore developed. The first of these, operative in 1845, could be called the *peaceful annexation plan*. It relied on persuading key members of the Californio-ranchero ruling class, which was in full control of the de facto independent state of California, to favor the voluntary annexation of California to the United States.

The American representative in California, Monterey merchant Thomas O. Larkin, was instructed to begin to carry out the peaceful annexation plan in 1845. Toward this end, Larkin developed a list of the most prominent men of California, along

---

1   Note: "ap" is a Welsh indication for "son of," akin to van, del, and so on.

with an evaluation of their personal history, net worth, character, and political leanings. He forwarded this list to the United States Secretary of State to be used by US officials. Larkin's analysis was that four powerful families were able to influence politics in all of California—the Carrillos and Picos in Southern California and the Alvarados and Castros in the north (Larkin [1846] 1863, 153). Larkin also noted the most prominent foreign-born individuals residing in California, along with their political leanings and roles (Larkin [1846] 1863, 148–159).

The problem with the peaceful annexation plan was that the Californio ruling class was divided, with the balance of power strongly against annexation. The Picos, Carrillos, Castros, and de la Guerras were all against the United States and held most of the key governmental posts (in 1846, for example, Pio Pico was governor and Jose Castro was overall military commander). The Alvarados, Vallejos, and Bandinis were pro-US, but were in much weaker political positions (Harlow 1982, 99, 107–108, 143–144, 147–149, 161, 174, 182, 241). Certainly, there were serious divisions within the anti-American faction of the Californio ruling class (for example, Governor Pico and Commander Castro were in almost constant conflict), a concrete political result of the disunity inherent in the division of sovereignty characteristic of the rancho political economy. Unfortunately for Larkin, however, the weaker, pro-US faction was unable to take advantage of this, so the entire original annexation plan and policy for acquiring California (short of war) soon collapsed.

A second track to annexation was based on what was bluntly called "the Texas game." As had happened in Texas only a decade before, during the 1830s, this plan projected that US citizens in California, most of them recent arrivals in the state, would organize themselves, form an army, and seize power. Once in control of the government, they could declare their independence from Mexico and, like Texas, join the United States. Since the Californio armed forces were quite weak and Mexican armed forces virtually nonexistent in California, a few hundred well-armed and well-led men had a real chance to seize power.

For over a century, American frontier settlers had been in the habit of forming their own government wherever they went. Therefore, it was not hard to convince them to act. All that was needed was decisive leadership, and this was supplied by a US Army officer, Captain John C. Fremont, and his men. Fremont headed up an elite force of about sixty heavily armed soldiers. In late 1845 and early 1846 they were technically on a "mapping expedition" in the undefended northern territories of Mexico, a military activity undertaken without the permission of the Mexican authorities. Obviously, conducting an armed "mapping expedition" into another country's territory without permission was an aggressive action, but it was meant to be provocative. The expedition's horses pulled artillery, the heavy weapons of the period, throughout Mexico's land, which lay to "the west" of the United States.

After attempting and failing to provoke the Californios into a battle at Gavilan Peak near today's San Juan Bautista, Fremont headed north on the way out of California in the spring of 1846. Near the Oregon border, he was overtaken by a US Marine officer named Archibald H. Gillespie who gave Fremont verbal instructions from President Polk, Secretary of State Buchanan, and Secretary of the Navy Bancroft. The messages were more than six months old, but Gillespie had traveled overland through Mexico on the way to California, and he believed that war between the United States and Mexico was imminent.

After meeting with Gillespie and hearing the verbal orders from United States leaders, Fremont turned around and returned to central California to organize the "Bear Flag Revolt" of June–July 1846 (Rosenus 1995, 79–103; Harlow 1982, 80–114). This revolt brought together Fremont's troops and American settlers in California in an attempt to seize state power by force of arms, with the aim of joining the United States. Fremont later stated that his "private" instructions were to carry into California a war of conquest against Mexico, an action designed to assure that California would be annexed to the United States and not to Britain. He added that, when he made the decision to act, it "was the first step in the conquest of California" (quoted in Harlow 1982, 85). Fremont always accepted personal responsibility for the actions that led to the Bear Flag Revolt (Harlow 1982, 98). Perhaps deliberately, the first Californio official that Fremont and his "Bears" captured and imprisoned was also one of those Californios most favorable to American annexation, General Mariano G. Vallejo (Harlow 1982, 102; Rosenus 1995, 109–142).

During June of 1846, Fremont continued to build his force, which reached 224 armed men by early July 1846. Fremont and his men were also busy carrying out armed actions to undermine Californio control when word arrived in mid-July 1846 that war had been declared and the US Navy, under Commodore John D. Sloat, had forcibly seized Monterey.

The US capture of Monterey represented the implementation of the third strategic alternative, outright war on Mexico to capture and annex her northern territories, including California. President Polk and his cabinet had apparently decided upon this course of action in January of 1846 when the president ordered General Zachary Taylor and his army into disputed territory along the Mexico–Texas border. Polk had evidently grown impatient with the other options. The slow communications characteristic of the time resulted in Larkin and Fremont still pursuing the first two plans for another six months.

Provoking a war with Mexico took some time to set in motion. General Taylor had to get into position, and he was slow in doing so. Polk again became impatient and prepared a war message for Congress even before fighting broke out between American and Mexican forces in the disputed territory. Polk's original message called for war to be declared on Mexico based on unpaid US claims, Mexico's refusal to receive a US envoy, and other supposed grievances (Harlow 1982, 57). Just before Polk was scheduled to present his very weak case for war to Congress, however, word came at last that fighting had started, giving Polk the excuse he needed. Polk asked for war based on what he called a fact: "American blood had been shed on American soil."

Congress passed a declaration of war, but not before a young congressman from Illinois named Abraham Lincoln had introduced the "spot resolution," asking the president to identify the exact spot where "American blood had been shed on American soil." Lincoln's position was that the territory where the conflict originated was disputed and not part of the United States.

The war on Mexico was a successful national war of conquest, one that technically brought a very large piece of territory into the United States, including all or parts of Upper California, Arizona, New Mexico, and Colorado. The annexation was only technical, however, because much of California, along with huge sections of the remaining territory, was actually controlled by Native Americans. These Indian people would have to be displaced or destroyed to make any US claim effective. Compounding the problem were the claims of the Californios, who were promised in the February 1848 Treaty of Guadalupe Hidalgo, which ended the war, that their property rights would be respected. At first, US leaders expected a long process to sort out the conflicting claims. But then the unexpected discovery of gold in California achieved the rapid displacement of both the Native Americans and Californios and a consolidation of American power.

THE GOLD RUSH AND A NEW SOCIAL FORMATION

While working on building a sawmill for John A. Sutter on the South Fork of the American River in the foothills of the Sierra Nevada, John Marshall discovered gold in January 1848, only a few weeks before the signing of the peace treaty between the United States and Mexico. Word of the find soon spread and "the blacksmith dropped his hammer, the carpenter his plane, the mason his trowel, the farmer his sickle, the baker his loaf, and the tapster his bottle. All were off for the mines, some on horses, some on carts ... some on crutches, and one went in a litter" (Colton 1850, 247).

People rapidly arrived on the South Fork in search of the valuable yellow metal. Although Marshall was a millwright and had never been a miner, many saw him nevertheless as a knowledgeable gold miner, and they came to his headquarters at Coloma to ask advice. Not realizing how widespread the gold deposits of California really were, and wanting to rid himself of these unwanted pests, Marshall sent the new arrivals off in all directions, saying there was plenty of gold if they would only take the trouble to look for it. Marshall's attempt to send people on a wild goose chase did not work, because there really were large gold deposits in every direction (Marshall in Kowalewski [1891] 1997, 49). Soon word of extensive deposits reached beyond the local audience to adjacent territories, then to the rest of the United States, and finally to the remainder of the world. President Polk, wanting to rapidly solidify his hold on California, announced in December of 1848 that extensive gold deposits existed in the territory, encouraging a rush (Caughey 1940, 293). Meanwhile in California, Colonel Mason, the military governor, stated that, although all miners were technically trespassing on public (i.e., US government) land and taking gold and other resources that belonged to the government, he would not interfere, because the government benefited from the mining (Sherman [1875] in Kowalewski 1997, 149). Thus began one of the strangest and most colorful chapters in world history.

Gold, universal symbol of power, beauty, wealth, and success, is the stuff of dreams. In all of previous history, it was the kings, the large landowners, and rich merchants who had monopolized possession of gold and ownership of gold mines and other precious mineral sources. Here was a case where the gold was free for the taking; all you had to do was get to California and be willing to work hard and brave the elements in the mining regions— including heat, cold, isolation, lack of food, wild animals, Indians, and other miners. Over 200,000 people, mainly single, young men, flooded into California during the 1848–1852, creating a new political and socioeconomic formation. It was an egalitarian social order created by strong, young men, most of whom hated class privilege. As Mark Twain later wrote,

> *It was a driving, vigorous, restless population in those days. It was a curious population. It was the only population of the kind the world has ever seen gathered together, and it is not likely that the world will ever see its like again. For observe, it was an assemblage of two hundred thousand young men— not simpering, dainty, kid-gloved weaklings, but stalwart, muscular, dauntless young braves, brim full of push and energy … No women, no children, no gray and stooping veterans … They cooked their own bacon and beans, sewed on their own buttons, washed their own shirts—blue woolen ones; and if a man wanted a fight on his hands without any annoying delay, all he had to do was to appear in public in a white shirt or a stove-pipe hat, and he would be accommodated. For those people hated aristocrats. They had a particular and malignant animosity toward what they called a "biled shirt."* (quoted [1872] in Kowalewski 1997, 361–362)

These Gold Rush miners soon created self-governing mining camps and small towns. Twain described a prototypical one:

> *[A] fiercely-flourishing little city, of two thousand or three thousand souls, with its newspaper, fire company, brass band, volunteer militia, bank, hotels, noisy Fourth of July processions and speeches, gambling hells crammed with tobacco smoke, profanity, and rough-bearded men of all nations and colors, with tables heaped with gold dust sufficient*

for the revenues of a German principality—streets
crowded and rife with business—town lots worth
four hundred dollars a front foot—labor, laughter,
music, dancing, swearing, fighting, shooting,
stabbing—a bloody inquest and a man for breakfast
every morning—everything that delights and adorns
existence—all the appointments and appurtenances
of a thriving and prosperous and promising young
city. (quoted [1872] in Kowalewski 1997, 361)

At the core of the new social formation was the existence of widespread surface deposits of gold and the right of an individual or partnership to own a mining claim. The individual miner was the base of the new system; it was his work—in the form of simple, small-scale commodity production, using his own labor and simple tools—that built the new society. His gold was sold on the capitalist world market, to pay for the vast amounts of supplies shipped into the instant city of San Francisco and on to the mines. The world market regulated the economy, and although the miners had gold, they had little control over this world market or the prices merchants charged for the food, tools, and other items they required. Most had little or no non-market access to any means of subsistence, such as a self-sufficient farm. They had to try to accumulate wealth, often conflicting with each other and always impacting the ecological basis of life. They were, however, independent of the political and economic control characteristic of previous social formations in California and also free of the exploitation of the owning class, slavery, wage labor, and the factory.

California Gold Diggers, 1849
This painting illustrates the typical mode of work, dress, tools, and lodgings of the early gold miners. [Courtesy of the Bancroft Library, University of California, Berkeley.]

By moving away from the relative self-sufficiency of the earlier era of California and towards market dependency, the state and its new population had taken a big step in the direction of creating a fully capitalist system. But it was not yet full-scale capitalism, because most miners owned their own means of production and were not engaged in wage labor. The formerly dominant labor systems of California, semi-slavery and peonage, still existed in parts of the state, especially the south, but were soon greatly overshadowed by small-scale commodity production of gold. The 1850 federal census, while not complete (some returns were lost), is nevertheless instructive. This census recorded 57,797 miners in California, who were fully 74.5 percent of the working population. Thus, the division of labor characteristic of a more fully developed economy did not exist in 1850 or for a number of years thereafter.

Some of the Gold Rush miners recognized the unusual nature of the resulting society. As one remarked in an 1854 letter home,

> *A labouring man in this country is a different thing from one in any other. Here he is what he should be, the world over. Here, he is exempt from the slavery imposed by capital. Here, there is no necessity for cringing to it for the privilege of earning a bare subsistence. Here, the labourer is the corner stone of society ... wherever he strikes his pick, if he has even the poorest kind of fortune, he can earn not only a living, but a good one. (Marks [1854] 1997, 328)*

This miner added that, as a result, there was no hierarchy, plutocracy, or oligarchy, only a real democracy by the mass of "hardy, toilsome miners" (Marks [1854] 1997, 328).

This basic egalitarianism was meant, however, only for white males. Both women and racial minorities were excluded. The concept of "democracy" for white men only needs to be understood to fully account for the nature of the new system developed by the gold miners of 1849 and subsequent years. In order to prevent competition and justify the exclusion of minority racial groups from access to the gold fields, "white" European Americans began a process of *racialization* of other peoples. It resulted in the imposition of a racist, white supremacist framework upon the new and developing Gold Rush society. The dominant European Americans oppressed Native Americans, African Americans, Asian Americans, and Latin Americans. White males were socialized to feel—and act—superior, and to control these other groups by any means necessary, including violence and terror. This reinforced a class structure brought from the United States that ranked all whites above all people of color. Violence and exclusion fostered a level of social cohesion within white society—overcoming, to some degree, class divisions (see Martinot 2003).

Whites as a collective considered themselves above all people of color. At the same time, the miners feared that the rich and powerful and these subordinate, "servile" groups, would collude to benefit the capitalists and hurt the independent producers. A tyranny was therefore imposed on these minority groups, with democratic rights like voting, sitting on juries, and testifying in court restricted to white males. Similarly, men as a collective considered themselves above all women. Women, as was the case all over the United States and the rest of the "civilized" world, were excluded from most democratic rights, but women were relatively scarce in Gold Rush California, especially in the mining regions.

The racial discrimination and violence that developed in California during the 1850s had its origins outside the state. These origins can be traced to cultural traditions that came out of the slave system of the South, including the Democratic Party's white-supremacy philosophy of the time and place. Thus, the material interests of white men combined with existing American racial ideologies constructed a system of white and gender supremacy in California early on (see Almaguer 1994).

The resulting society had both romantic and tragic elements. The fabulous quantity of golden wealth available to the hardworking immigrant miners, the long and dangerous treks needed to bring them to California, the conflicts between individuals and groups in a setting often without effective law and order, and the hardships required to live and work in remote mountainous locations all strengthened the romance. Consequently, the Gold Rush continues to hold an important place in American folklore and the American psyche. But there was also a darker, more tragic side to the Gold Rush story. Most miners suffered frequent disappointments and were in sharp competition with each other. They led unsettled and transient lives filled with conflict, loneliness, and lack of community feeling. They were also often at the mercy of speculators, gamblers, and merchants and subject to the frequent violence that developed out of their circumstances.

One contemporary observer found California a dreadful place, characterized by ...

> *thousands of penniless vagabonds who wander about in misery and dejection ... an astounding number of suicides and murders ... incessant brawls and tumults ... arbitrary doing of mobs ... the supremacy of lynch-law ... frauds and stratagems practiced in almost every transaction. (Helper [1855] 1949, 156–157)*

> *[W]e know of no country in which there is so much corruption, villainy, outlawry, intemperance, licentiousness, and every variety of crime, folly, and meanness. (Helper [1855] in Kowalewski 1997, 311)*

The social consequences were often tragic. Transient groups of disconnected, wealth-seeking young men, trained to view different races with hostility, were bound to resent their competition and would sometimes react violently out of frustration. Aggression and social conflict were thus a central part of the experience of being a Gold Rush miner. White miners tended to blame Native Americans and Californios as the most frequent barriers to success.

RACIAL WAR AND THE SUPPRESSION OF THE NATIVE AMERICANS

During their almost eight decades in control of California, the Spanish and the Californios had only fully occupied the states' central and southern coastal strips. In 1848, the eastern and northern parts of California were controlled by a large number of independent Indian groups. Many of these areas had rich *placer* gold deposits—the gold found in sandbanks and riverbeds—and a massive wave of miners invaded, in effect expropriating Indian land and setting off a war over who would control this land. During the initial phase of invasion (1848 until the summer of 1849), there were ample gold-mining sites for all, and Indians, Californios, and new arrivals from Latin America were able to peacefully work alongside Anglo Americans. Indians were at first hired by Anglos, but soon many mined on their own.

As more European Americans arrived during the second half of 1849 and throughout the early 1850s, however, conflict increased. The newcomers wanted the mines and land for themselves and did not want to compete against or work with non-whites. This was, at least initially, partly because non-whites were seen as "servile" and working for a pittance; the European Americans thought that undermined their ability to make a good living. Later the desire to acquire Indian land became the basis for racial war.

Many European Americans came out of the direct action component of the frontier tradition, which generally refused to respect the land ownership and other rights of either native people or other people of color. In addition, many of the new arrivals settled in remote parts of the gold country and tried to live off the land to the extent that they could, killing deer and other animals for food. This and the environmental destruction the miners wrought (for example, ruining salmon runs by polluting the streams), soon created a food crisis for many Indian groups. As a result, refusal to respect native rights was followed by native resistance to the loss of their tribal lands and means of livelihood. As a result, innumerable small but very violent episodes of war and massacre broke out between Native Americans and the newly arrived European Americans throughout this period and extending well into the 1860s and even 1870s, with heavy losses on the Indian side (Forbes 1982, 69).

In the early 1850s, the California state government officially encouraged settler wars of extermination against the native peoples and received federal appropriations to pay for this mass murder. (Gottesman 1999, 79). Early California writer Joaquin Miller well described one of the common dynamics involved, played out

with small variations again and again during the Gold Rush and
subsequent decades:

> *There was a tribe of Indians camped down on the
> rapid, rocky Klamat river ... The snow, unusually
> deep this winter, had driven them all down from
> the mountains, and they were compelled to camp
> on the river. The game, too, had been driven down
> along with the Indians, but it was of but little use to
> them. Their bows and arrows did poor competition
> with the rifles of the whites in the killing of the game.
> The whites fairly filled the cabins with deer and
> elk, got the lion's share, and left the Indians almost
> destitute.*
>
> *Another thing that made it rather more hard on
> the Indians than anything else was the utter failure
> of the annual run of salmon the summer before, on
> account of the muddy water. The Klamat, which
> had poured from the mountain lakes to the sea as
> clear as glass, was now made muddy and turbid
> from the miners washing for gold ... Mine? It was
> all a mystery to these Indians as long as they were
> permitted to live ... I have seen them gather in
> groups on the bank above the mines and watch in
> silence for hours as if endeavoring to make it out ...
> Why we should tear up the earth, toil like gnomes
> from sun-up to sun-down, rain or sun, destroy the
> forests, and pollute the rivers was to them more than
> a mystery—it was a terror. I believe they accepted it
> as a curse, the work of evil spirits, and so bowed to
> it in sublime silence ...*
>
> *[W]hat made matters worse, there was a [group]
> of men, low men, loafers, and of the lowest type,
> who would hang around those lodges at night, give*

the Indians whiskey of the vilest sort, debauch their women, and cheat the men out of their skins and bows and arrows. There was not a saloon, not a gambling den in camp that did not have a sheaf of feathered, flint-headed arrows in an otter quiver, and a yew bow hanging behind the bar. Perhaps there was a grim sort of philosophy in the red man so disposing of his bow and arrows now that the game was gone ... sold them for bread for his starving babes maybe. How many tragedies are hidden there?

In this condition of things, about mid-winter ... there was a murder. The Indians had broken out! The prophesied massacre had begun! Killed by Indians! It swept like a telegram through the camp ... gathered force and form as the tale flew on from tongue to tongue, until it assumed a frightful shape. A man had been killed by the Indians down at the rancheria. Not much of a man, it is true. A ... hanger-on about the lowest gambling dens. Killed, too, down in the Indian camp when he should have been in bed, or at home ... All this made the miners hesitate a bit as they hurriedly gathered in at The Forks, with their long Kentucky rifles, their pistols capped and primed, and bowie knives in their belts.

But as the gathering storm that was to sweep the Indians from the earth took shape and form, these honest men stood out in little knots, leaning on their rifles in the streets, and gravely questioned whether, all things considered, the death of the "Chicken," for that was the dead man's name, was sufficient cause for interference. To their eternal credit, these men mainly decided that it was not, and two-by-two they turned away, went back to their cabins, hung their rifles up on the rack, and turned their thoughts to their own affairs. But the hangers-on about the town were terribly enraged. "A man has been killed!" they proclaimed aloud. "A man has been murdered by the savages!!"

In one of the saloons where men were wont to meet at night, have stag-dances, and drink lightning, a short, important man, with the print of a glass-tumbler cut above his eye, arose and made a speech ..." Fellow miners, a man has been kilt by the treacherous savages—kilt in cold blood! ... Range around me. Rally to the bar and take a drink, every man of you ..." This was the beginning; they passed from saloon to saloon, the mob gathering force and arms as it went, then wild with drink and excitement, moving down upon the Indians, some miles away on the bank of the river ...

We followed not far behind the crowd of fifty or sixty men armed with pistols, rifles, knives, and hatchets. The trail led to a little point overlooking the bar on which the Indians were huddled ... They were out in the extreme curve of a horse-shoe made by the river, and we advanced ... They were in a net. They had only a choice of deaths: death by drowning, or death at the hands of their ... foe ... The crowd advanced to within half a pistol shot, and gave a shout as they drew and leveled their arms. Old squaws came out—bang! bang! bang! shot after shot, and they were pierced and fell, or turned to run. Some men sprung up, wounded, but fell the instant; for the whites, yelling, howling, screaming, were among the lodges, shooting down at arm's length man, woman, or child. (quoted in Kowalewski 1997, 366–370)

Laurence H. Shoup

In 1869, John S. Hittell reported on another common pattern:

The Indians were driven from their hunting grounds and fishing places by the whites, and they stole cattle for food; and to punish and prevent them from stealing, the whites made war on them ... Such has been the origin of most of the Indian wars which have raged. (J. Hittell 1869, 388)

These wars of terror and massacre were usually small in scale because Native American society was decentralized. Indians typically could not unite across group lines, often lacked any firearms, and had women and children to protect. Despite unfavorable odds, they did resist white encroachment in many places. One example was the Garra rebellion of 1851–52 in Southern California.

Antonio Garra had been a mission Indian at San Luis Rey Mission. He urged all the scattered Southern California Indian groups to unite under his leadership and rise up together to drive out the European Americans. Garra was joined by people from the Quechan, Chemehuevi Paiute, Luiseno, Kamia, southern Cahuilla, and Hamakhava tribelets, to wage rebellion , capturing large areas of the river and desert county along the Colorado River and in San Diego County. A counterattack, however, largely wiped out Indian resistance, and another Indian leader betrayed Garra. He was then tried by a military court-martial, condemned, and executed by firing squad (Forbes 1982, 74–75; Hudson n.d., 154–159).

At about the same time that Garra was leading his rebellion in the south, Indians in the Sierra foothills were also resisting the white invasion. In response, James D. Savage and a group of armed settlers organized the "Mariposa Battalion." While chasing and capturing groups of Yosemite and Chowchilla Indians led by Chief Tenaya, Savage and his men rediscovered Yosemite, which became one of the showplaces of the new state.

A more successful example of Native American resistance was a five-year war waged by Hupa, Whilkut, and others, beginning about 1858. Due to the crisis of the Civil War, these Indians were granted a part of their ancestral land on the Trinity River in 1864, what is now known as the Hoopa Reservation, the largest tract of land with Indian sovereignty in California (Forbes 1982, 75, 84; Eargle 2000, 93).

A final example of Native American rebellion was the "Modoc War" of 1872–1873, when the US Army was sent to defeat the Modoc people of northeastern California led by Kentipoos, also known as Captain Jack, and relocate them to a reservation. Under constant attack by a vastly larger, better armed and supplied military force, they held out courageously in their rough, lava-bed fortress for over three months, but were eventually defeated and forced onto the reservation (Caughey 1940, 384–386; Forbes 1982, 75).

Over the decades of the 1850s and 1860s especially, Indian rebellion continued in many areas of California. The Indians, however, suffered from a general lack of unity and low numbers, a shortage of firearms and, because of their family and tribelet structure, a lack of mobility. These facts doomed their often-brave attempts to repel the invaders of their lands and rights. They were killed by the thousands and had to flee to ever more remote and inhospitable places. If not killed outright, captured groups were often driven on "death marches" to reservations where overcrowding, disease, demoralization, and lack of food would kill still more. The overall result was the genocide of some groups and the near-extermination of others. There was broad participation by the newly arrived white population in this genocide, and government at all levels cooperated. These facts, in the opinion of one leading scholar, "makes the sequence of events all the more distressing, since it serves to indict not a group of cruel leaders, or a few squads of rough soldiers but, in effect, an entire people; for the conquest of the Native Californian was above all else a popular, mass enterprise" (Forbes 1982, 69).

The nineteenth-century historian H.H. Bancroft also observed:

> *The California valley cannot grace her annals with a single Indian war bordering on respectability. It can boast, however, a hundred or two of as brutal butcherings, on the part of our honest miners and brave pioneers, as any area of equal extent in our republic. (quoted in Caughey 1940, 381)*

A RACIALIZED LEGAL AND POLITICAL PROCESS

The expenditure of the sum of $1.51 million, a huge sum for the 1850s, was authorized for the "suppression of Indian hostilities," aimed at developing a racialized legal and political process, promoting disempowerment, enslavement, and genocide. A series of 1850s and early 1860s laws passed the California state legislature and were backed up by court decisions. These laws resulted in heavy consequences for California Indians. They prevented Indians from testifying in court, becoming citizens, serving on juries, or attending school. The transfer of firearms or ammunition to Indians was prohibited.

New laws also imposed a heavy monetary fine and up to twenty-five lashes as the penalty for any Indian convicted of stealing a horse, cow, or mule. Whites won the right to obtain and control Indian children as "servants" and the right to contract for the labor of any Indian convicted of a crime. Any Indian found "strolling or loitering, begging or leading a profligate life" could be arrested and sentenced to four months of forced labor. The legislation authorized the indenture to whites of any "vagrant" Indian for "employment and training" up to the age of forty for men and thirty-five for women Exploitation was assured through a bidding system—the Indian leased to the highest bidder (Heizer and Almquist 1971, 39–64; Almaguer 1994, 132–138).

These laws allowed the enslavement of Indians all over California during the 1850s and 1860s, a practice which included women and men and extended to children. Anthropologist and historian Sherburne Cook estimated that between three and four thousand Indian children were kidnapped and sold during the 1852–1867 years alone along with an unknown number of Indian men seized for labor and women taken and sold for labor, concubinage, and prostitution (Cook 1976, 315). During the rancho era, raiding had also taken place to kidnap Indians to use as servant peons, but since demand was relatively low, sale was usually not the motivating force.

Among the adults, women were especially at risk. Historian Tomás Almaguer points out:

> *In the early 1850s, Indian women were routinely captured and either held as concubines by their kidnappers or sold to other white men for their personal use. One Anglo pioneer in Trinity County reported that traffickers of Indian women had even devised a system which classified them into "fair, middling, inferior, [and] refuse" categories of merchandise. (Almaguer 1994, 120)*

After detailed study of white-settler kidnapping and rape of Indian women, Cook concluded, "There can be no question that crimes of violence perpetrated on Indian women by white men were numbered … very likely by thousands … Indeed, it would not be overstating the situation to say that during the decade 1850–1860 no single squaw in northern California could consider herself absolutely safe from violence at the hands of white men" (Cook 1976, 87, and 87n140).

The clear result of white attacks on Indian women was that by 1860 there were substantially fewer Indian women than men in every age group. As Albert Hurtado concludes, "All Indians were at risk during the tumultuous 1850s, but women's chances for survival were measurably worse than men's. Brutal assaults, deadly diseases, and general privation killed women and left their communities' reproductive potential in doubt" (Hurtado 1988, 188).

Nor did Indian children escape the oppressive, racialized system created for them by the invading whites. All over California, Indian children were captured and enslaved on a large scale during the 1850s and 1860s (Almaguer 1994, 130–150). One example of how this was done is from an 1853 report authored by the district attorney of Contra Costa County, complaining of the sale of Indian slaves in his county:

> *Ramon Briones, Mesa, Quiera, and Beryessa of Napa County, are in the habit of Kidnapping Indians in the mountains near Clear Lake, and in their capture several have been murdered in cold blood. There have been Indians to the number of one hundred and thirty-six thus captured and brought into this county, and held here in servitude adverse to their will. These Indians are now to be in the possession of Briones, Mesa, and sundry other persons who have purchased them in this county. It is also a notorious fact that these Indians are treated inhumanly, being neither fed nor clothed; and from such treatment many have already died. (Heizer and Almquist 1971, 40)*

Another example of the enslavement of Indians was the Los Angeles slave mart of the 1850s as reported by early settler Horace Bell:

> *These Indians were Christians, docile even to servility, and the best of laborers. Then came the Americans ... and the ruin of those once happy and useful people commenced. The cultivators of vineyards commenced paying their Indians with aguardiente, a veritable firewater and no mistake. The consequence was*

that on being paid off on Saturday evening, they would meet ... and pass the night in gambling, drunkenness and debauchery ... By four o'clock on Sunday afternoon Los Angeles street ... [and] Aliso street from Los Angeles to Alameda ... would be crowded with a mass of drunken Indians, yelling and fighting. Men and women, boys and girls, tooth and nail ... frequently with knives, but always in a manner that would strike the beholder with awe and horror.

About sundown the pompous marshal, with his Indian special deputies, who had been kept in jail all day to keep them sober, would drive and drag the herd to a big corral in the rear of the Downey Block, where they would sleep away their intoxication, and in the morning they would be exposed for sale, as slaves for the week. Los Angeles had its slave mart ... only the slave at Los Angeles was sold fifty-two times a year as long as he lived, which did not generally exceed one, two, or three years ... Those thousands of honest, useful people were absolutely destroyed in this way ... (Bell [1881] in Caughey and Caughey 1976, 124–125)

As a result of this displacement, genocide, and enslavement, as well as disease, the population of Indian people dropped by approximately 60,000 between 1846 and 1870, from something over 90,000 living in the state in 1846, to only about 30,000 in 1870 (Bean 1973, 169). By 1900, it is estimated that 95 percent of the original indigenous population of California had been wiped out (Gottesman 1999, 77–79).

A SQUATTERS' WAR OVERTHROWS THE CALIFORNIO/RANCHERO RULING CLASS

In 1846, a small number of Californio families ruled coastal California politically and economically, owning hundreds of thousands of cattle, millions of acres of the world's most productive land, and controlling many thousands of peon Indian laborers (Bean 1973, 70–72, 154, 203). Under different circumstances, such a system could have been perpetuated for many decades, even centuries, as indeed it has been in many Latin American countries. But in most cases and in most places in California, the real power of the old Californio ruling class would be destroyed within a decade.

The main technique for breaking ranchero control and seizing their land was class struggle from below, "direct action" by tens of thousands of people. Legal, political, economic, and ideological attacks also at times played important roles, but confrontation, especially in the form of settling on (or "squatting" on) Californio land was central. As was the case with the destruction of the Native Americans, it was numerous small skirmishes rather than fewer large battles that achieved the end result. Seizing and settling on land was, by 1850, a long-standing American frontier tradition. The government had long encouraged the settlement of "vacant" (i.e., occupied "only" by Indians) "public land" on the frontier. Laws were passed, such as the preemption law of 1841, which encouraged claiming and settling unsurveyed public lands, which could be paid for at a later date.

The problem in California was that public land had not yet been fully separated from private land, and the Californio ruling class held much of the best land under Spanish and especially Mexican grants. The land making up these grants often appeared to be unoccupied and unused, which raised a question of the validity of the land grants in the minds of those who were also interested in seizing such lands. The peace treaty settling the 1846–1848 war between Mexico and the United States said that all Spanish and Mexican claims were legal and valid. To be sure, the Treaty of Guadalupe Hidalgo established a peace by and for the victor, but the United States did commit to fully respecting property rights of "every kind" held by Mexicans and Californios.

The federal government had little interest in enforcing these provisions, however, and much more interest in the rapid settlement of California. It therefore encouraged the rush for gold. As immigrants arrived in California and eventually began turning from mining to farming, they found, often to their surprise, that millions of acres of the best land were already claimed and unavailable for preemption.

Furthermore, large-scale land speculation had already begun. For example, at an early date, merchant Thomas O. Larkin purchased several large land grants amounting to almost 200,000 acres (Bean 1973, 154). Such giant landholdings, especially those of the Californios, soon became targets, particularly in Northern California where the new, Gold Rush–inspired immigrant population was so much larger than in the south. Many of the newly arrived Americans considered the Californios an inferior race and a defeated people, who were not, in any case, putting the land to its full and best use.

As gold became less abundant and harder to find, some of the new arrivals squatted on Californio land. Calling themselves "settlers" and forming "settlers' leagues" and other similar organizations, they soon formed a potent political, social, and economic force in northern California (*Daily Alta California* June 16, 1855, 2). The Sacramento County Settlers' League, in an 1853 broadside, expressed what was at stake against the "Spanish Claims." It called upon all settlers to unite and fight for their rights, pointing out that the large Californio land claims would reestablish the "old Feudal System" of "landed monopoly" in California. This in turn would create the danger that "the homes of American freemen will become the huts of tenants and serfs." The old "aristocracies," "monopolies," and "monarchical tyranny" had to be "humbled" and "pulled down," and republican institutions erected upon their ruins (Sacramento Settlers' League 1853). Gold Rush conditions, together with the American frontiersman political and ideological perspective, led to a flourishing popular movement of squatterism during the 1850s.

Those whose ownership interests were threatened by the squatter movement launched counterattacks, and the resulting conflicts caused many deaths and injuries. The first such serious conflict took place in the city of Sacramento during the summer of 1850.

John A. Sutter had claimed, under a Mexican grant, vast sections of the Sacramento Valley, including the location of the city of Sacramento. In 1849, as the city was established and began a period of rapid expansion, Sutter's agents sold town lots, many of which had apparently been purchased for speculative purposes and were not developed. During the first six months of 1850, thousands of settlers squatted on these vacant lots, conveniently claiming the land on the grounds that Sutter's Mexican grant was illegal. Some settlers put up fences and began to build houses. Sacramento's new establishment and its courts soon stood against the squatters, asserting private property rights even if the land was currently unused.

The conflict escalated in August of 1850 when police and armed "law-and-order" squads, organized by speculator forces, began to seize the disputed pieces of property from the squatters, destroying houses and fences. The settlers resisted and some were arrested. An armed group of squatters tried to release those captured and were opposed by a law-and-order group led by the mayor and city assessor.

In the resulting shootout, three squatters and the city assessor were killed, and the mayor and three others were wounded. The next day, the Sacramento sheriff was killed as he led a raid on a roadhouse frequented by squatters. His men killed two of the squatters and arrested four more. The fighting ended only after 130 militia and volunteer firemen arrived from San Francisco to reinforce the local government, which then successfully asserted private property rights against the squatters (Bean 1973, 154–155; Jackson 1980, 292–293).

The serious conflict over the validity of Californio land titles and mass popular pressure to overthrow these grants soon resulted in a piece of federal legislation designed to definitively settle the question. The Democratic Party took the lead on the issue.

A Democrat leader, David C. Broderick of San Francisco, defended the squatters and advocated for a federal homestead act to facilitate settlement of public land. Another Democrat leader, Senator William Gwin, then carried the bill in the US Senate (Pitt 1966, 89–90; Saxton 1990, 209–210; *Daily Alta California* July 22, 1853, 2). The resulting law, called the 1851 Land Act, set up a three-judge panel to hear evidence and rule on the validity of each of the more than eight hundred Spanish and Mexican claims. This established a system whereby Californio claims were assumed to be fraudulent until proven otherwise. Since appeals to the US District Court and US Supreme Court were possible, a claimant might have to prove his title a number of times over a period of many years and at great legal expense (Pitt 1966, 89–90; 1971, 85–95; Caughey 1940, 364–368). In fact, one authority has asserted that the *average* length of time required to prove ownership was fully seventeen years (Bean 1973, 157).

Only a small percentage of claims were actually determined to be fraudulent, although it was common for leading Californio families to claim several different grants (Leach 1917, 102–105). Often all or part of the land in question would have to be sold to hire the lawyers needed to hold on to even part of the grant. The first phase of this legal struggle over land titles continued until 1856, when the three-judge panel concluded its work. The conflict then continued in the courts for a number of years more. At the end of the process, an estimated 25 percent of ranchero wealth had been lost during the process of litigation alone (Pitt 1966, 94).

While this litigation was ongoing, squatters' actions also continued. Throughout Northern California especially, the settlers/squatters engaged in what was, in effect, guerrilla warfare to seize land that was now in dispute. Squatters would seize, fence, and build on a piece of land, then take a bit more. It was difficult to force them off, since violence was a constant possibility, and effective law enforcement was frequently nonexistent. By 1853, every rancho reportedly had its squatters (Pitt 1966, 95).

The difficulties involved were exemplified by the situation of Mariano G. Vallejo, who had to sell or mortgage much of his land, while thieves tore down his fences and stole his cattle. Vallejo complained that if he took the thieves to court, he would "lose the suit and moreover will pay for it" (Rosenus 1995, 213).

This in turn was the result of the political power of the squatter movement. As the *Daily Alta California* put it in mid-1853:

> *It is an undeniable fact that one of the most important and powerful elements of politics in California ... has been the particular interest known as Squatterism ... This interest, in one form or another, has been steadily gaining strength and growing in extent, until it has come to be more courted by politicians ... than any other in the State.* (Daily Alta California *June 26, 1853, 2)*

A second way in which the Californios, along with recent Latino immigrants, were affected was through the passage of discriminatory laws. The first of these was the confiscatory Foreign Miners' Tax of 1850, authored by a state legislator who was a former slaveholder from Texas. It imposed the prohibitive tax of twenty dollars a month upon "foreign" miners, and was especially aimed at the Latin American miners who were numerically a very large group in the southern mines.

The real reason for this law was, of course, to eliminate competitors in the hunt for gold. The enforcement of the tax soon resulted in serious conflict in the Sonora–Columbia area of

Tuolumne County, where large numbers of Latin American, as well as French, miners lived and worked. On Sunday, May 19, 1850, an estimated three thousand to five thousand armed foreign miners gathered outside Sonora to protest the new law. They sent a delegation into town, requesting that the tax be overturned, offering to pay a more-reasonable four or five dollars a month instead. The Anglo Americans quickly sent out alarms to adjacent mining camps, and by evening, they had more than five hundred armed men who were reinforced the next day. Not wanting a war, which could quickly escalate, the foreigners quietly dispersed and large numbers left for their homelands. So many left, in fact, that the merchants who lived off selling goods to the miners protested to the governor that their losses outweighed any possible gains from the unreasonable tax. The tax was then reduced, later repealed, and finally re-imposed at a much lower rate, but by then a majority of foreign miners had left the state. Estimates put the number leaving the southern mines alone at about ten thousand (Cornford 1998/99, 86; Jackson 1980, 266–267; Ellison 1950, 126–127).

Many of those who were unfairly targeted were embittered, and some became outlaws, robbing and killing to get what they felt was due them. This in turn reinforced the anti-Latin prejudices held by some miners, who responded with more violence, often aimed at innocent people. This vicious spiral continued throughout the first half of the 1850s, when numerous small-scale conflicts resulted in the killing and expulsion of more Latin Americans.

Events in Amador County during the summer of 1855 may be seen as an example of the worst of such conflicts. A band of nine bandits, almost all of them Latin Americans, carried out a number of robberies in Amador County, against business establishments like saloons and against groups of miners, such as the Chinese on Dry Creek. These bandits would sometimes use extreme violence; for example, killing five men in a saloon they were robbing in the village of Rancheria in August of 1855 (*Daily Alta California* August 11, 1855, 2).

The response of the US settler population to these outrages was also extreme, and a general reign of terror was launched against all Mexicans and men from Chile, called Chilenos, irrespective of guilt or innocence. At least sixteen Mexicans and Chilenos were caught and hanged; every Mexican home in the town of Sutter Creek was torn down, and the entire Mexican population expelled. All Mexicans in Rancheria were also ordered out of town (*Daily Alta California* August 11, 1855, 2). A few days after these events, the *Alta* editorialized on the mob violence, blaming a general lack of confidence in the law, courts, and judges:

> *The … spirit of mob law is widely at work in the country. The horrible massacre at Rancheria, Amador County, has inflamed the public mind against the Mexican population, and a war cry of extermination is going on against them. No inquiry is made as to the guilt of one of the proscribed race, but they are hanged as unceremoniously as the huntsman shoots down the deer or the coyote. Nearly every man in that region is under arms and ready to level on the first unfortunate greaser that comes across his track … This is a dreadful picture, but the half is not told. The people have no confidence in the law as an engine of punishment and protection … Men do not rely on the courts for protection, but mad anarchy prevails. The times are out of joint. (Daily Alta California August 13, 1855, 2)*

These out-of-joint times were at least partly the result of the decline of the supply of easy-to-get gold and the subsequent economic depression around the state, a downturn that was at its worse in 1855–1856, signifying the end of the Gold Rush.

In Southern California, discrimination and violence against Latin Americans led to the organization of bandit gangs who, according to one scholar, had "vaguely political motives" (Pitt 1966, 168). In 1857, one of these groups, the "Flores gang," led by

Juan Flores and Poncho Daniel, consisted of over fifty horsemen and apparently had significant support among the Latino population. When the sheriff tried to kill or capture the gang with a small posse, the bandits defeated the law in a galloping twelve-mile long shootout that killed the sheriff and two of his deputies. A much larger Anglo vigilante group converged on the outlaws, eventually capturing and hanging eleven men without a trial. Flores and Daniel met the same fate, lynched by a white mob after they were captured (Pitt 1966, 167–173).

The outlaw Tiburcio Vasquez was a similar "social bandit," a rebel with political overtones, a type described by Eric Hobsbawm in his classic book *Primitive Rebels* (1959). Born in Monterey County, Vasquez's horse stealing and other criminal activities were motivated by feelings of injustice done to himself and his people. As he expressed it, "I believed we were being unjustly deprived of the social rights that belonged to us" (Dunlap 1982, 210). Vasquez escaped capture for many years but was eventually apprehended and executed after a trial (Dunlap 1982, 210–211).

One of the legal discriminations imposed upon the old Californio ruling class was a revenue system that heavily taxed real property such as Californio land, which was more concentrated in Southern California, and only very lightly taxed the mining and personal property of the north (Jelinek 1998–99, 235). Table 1 graphically shows the unfair results of this tax system.

Table 1, Results of California Tax System—1852			
Locations	Population	Property Taxes	Poll Taxes
Rural Southern Counties	6,000	$42,000	$4,000
Urban and Mining Northern Counties	120,000	$21,000	$3,500

Source: Caughey 1940, 336

The establishment of this tax system was the product of the electoral system introduced in 1849 and the influence of a state legislature largely elected by miners and merchants who lived off the miners. Because the rancheros were relatively wealthy during the early years of the Gold Rush due to cattle sales, the impact of this discriminatory taxation was not severe at first. Later, when prices declined, squatters seized land, and drought killed large numbers of cattle, these higher taxes severely affected the wealth and social power of most Californio landowners.

The overall result of the squatters, the unfair taxes and laws, and the violence against Latin people was the sharp decline of the old Californio ruling class. By the mid-1850s, the overthrow of Californio ranchero power was a fact in Northern California, by far the most populated part of the state. While areas of Southern California would remain under Californio control for some years more, their statewide power was effectively destroyed by 1856. Leonard Pitt summed up the situation as follows:

> *In the north of California, then, the basis of landownership had changed drastically by 1856. Through armed struggle, legislation, litigation, financial manipulation, outright purchase, and innumerable other tactics, Yankees had obtained a good deal of interest in the land ... In the eyes of the Californios ... the results of the land transfers amounted to something akin to social revolution ... Of the forty-five Californios representing the twenty-five families whom Thomas Oliver Larkin had enumerated in 1846 as the "principal men" of the old regime, the vast majority went to their graves embittered. Indeed, the gentry ... were a ruling class militarily conquered, bereft of national sovereignty and a constitutional framework, and alienated from their land, homes, civil rights, and honor. (Pitt 1966, 103, 278)*

The old Californios had resisted those who wanted to accumulate land at their expense. But they had failed, and their land often went into the hands of Anglo speculators and large

94

owners, the new accumulators. Even squatters who were able to successfully seize some land often had to sell out during periods of economic downturn.

The overthrow of the Californio ruling class created a temporary opening for more democratic forces to rule the state, and as long as the readily available gold lasted and self-employed miners owning their own means of production were in the majority, California lacked a powerful ruling class. A system of commodity production based on small-scale mining was more conducive to the rule by the many and not by the few. The amount of gold available to the pick-and-pan miner was finite, however, and was bound to decline, forcing miners to give up their claims and find other ways to survive.

THE DECLINE OF THE PLACERS AND THE END OF THE GOLD RUSH

Gold production reached its peak in 1851 ($75.9 million) and 1852 ($81.3 million). By 1853 and 1854, output had dropped to 83 percent and 85 percent of the 1852 figure, and it dropped still further in 1855 and 1856 (to 68 percent and 71 percent of the peak, respectively) (Rice et al. 1988, 185). This decline reflected the depletion of easy-to-mine placer gold, and its impact began to be felt statewide. Bancroft called the change that took place in the mid-1850s a gradual "revolution":

> *The diggings were declining ... mining was passing largely into the hands of companies and employers, to the exclusion of a host of humble miners, who were cast adrift to swell the labor market, and lower incomes in every direction. (Bancroft 1890, 7:173)*

Wages, for those engaged in wage labor, were, in effect, pegged to the ease in finding gold, so they dropped from about five dollars a day on average in 1853–1855 to a little over three dollars a day in 1856 (Paul 1947, 120). Cattle prices, reflecting both supply and demand, dropped from seventy dollars to ninety dollars a head at the height of gold output in 1852 to only sixteen dollars a head in 1856 (Rosenus 1995, 213).

The last big year of river mining was in 1856 (Paul 1947, 129, 240). Sharp declines then followed. In September 1856, the *Sacramento Weekly Union* reported:

> *As a general rule, but few places can now be found in the mines where, without the expenditure of considerable capital, individuals, or even companies, can make three dollars a day. (Quoted in Paul 1947, 171)*

Early in 1857, one miner who had spent most of the prior seven years working in the southern mines, talked to a number of other miners in the area and observed:

> *They had told me that everywhere, on the placers they knew, people were shoving and elbowing each other; everywhere there was a great number of people who did not find enough to pay for their labor, who did not earn enough, often, to pay for the supplies they consumed. They saw some, they said, who were working for a dollar a day. This gave me something to think about ... Under these conditions, the miner ceased to be a man pursuing a fortune, and was no more than a laborer seeking work ... Everything was changing on the placers; companies raised on shares exploited them on a large scale ... in order to have gold, it would be necessary to begin by having much silver ... The isolated worker could not struggle against the capitalists, from the moment that they intervened. (Perlot [1897] 1985, 300–301)*

This miner and his friends collectively agreed that the time had come to give up mining and find another profession:

We were agreed in saying that the situation was profoundly changed in California, as the placers were exhausted, the immigrants increasing; one had to dig hard now to find a little gold ... there was nothing better to do than to throw away pick and shovel, and to seek another employment for one's activity and one's intelligence. From then on it was necessary to turn to commerce or industry ... it was successively proposed that we become farmers, butchers, brick makers, milkmen, sawyers, café owners, grocers, hotel keepers, to say nothing of business agents ... We ended by deciding to go, provisionally, to reflect on all this in San Francisco. (Perlot [1897] 1985, 311–312)

The growing signs of the exhaustion of the placers caused a general business decline statewide. In the mining regions, there was a "depressed state of business and a scarcity of money" (*San Francisco Bulletin* August 23, 1856, 3). Large numbers of water ditch companies went bankrupt (Sherman [1875] 1990, 150–154). In San Francisco, by far the biggest city in California and the West, some banks failed and hundreds of businesses went bankrupt (Sherman [1875] 1990, 150–151; Colville 1856, xxxiv-xxxv; Klein1908, 60). In 1855 and 1856, almost 250 insolvent firms had debts of almost $12 million, with assets of only a little over $2 million (J. Hittell 1869, 334). The economic depression marked an era coming to a close; henceforth, "dead labor"—accumulated capital—would be as necessary as living labor to successfully mine gold. Capital-intensive quartz mining was the wave of the future in mining, and this required both better machinery and laws favorable to capital. In May of 1856, *Daily Alta California* reflected:

There was a time in California ... when labor, physical strength, assumed a lofty position above the crushing power of capital, and asked no aid from it.

> *But that time is rapidly passing away in California—and we fear that for a successful development of our immense mineral resources something more than labor is now required; that capital, which like a galvanic current gives life and vitality to labor, is also needed ... It is now very generally conceded that the permanent mineral wealth of California exists in her veins of gold-bearing quartz ... But these require the investment of capital.* (Daily Alta California May 1, 1856, 2)

As independent small-scale commodity-production of gold declined, a new system—full-blown capitalism, based on the extraction of surplus value through the exploitation of wage labor—arose. Some of the miners had done well and were now able to become owners of productive property (as merchants, farmers, or industrialists). But most ex-miners became wage laborers, not because they wanted to, but because they had to in order to survive. Their labor power was soon commodified, and economic life rapidly transformed under the impact of an increasingly dominant market.

Vast changes were created by the California Gold Rush. The changes included statehood, a new constitution and government, a population explosion of people from many races and cultures, mushrooming cities, new trade, transportation and communications systems, and the beginnings of agriculture and industry. Just as important was a set of less-tangible mental attitudes that grew out of the Gold Rush experience and, over time, became typically Californian: materialism and individualism, innovation and experimentation, confidence and great expectations, impatience and futuristic thinking. The exploitation characteristic of a class system in which one group of owners holds the means of life in the form of productive property while others have to work for these owners to survive was also part of the new California, as was the racialization and frequent exclusion of people of color. While having its own distinct characteristics, California was not and is not a place apart from the rest of the country. Rather, it represents an intensification of the nature of the United States—like the rest of the nation, only more so (McWilliams 1968, 5).

The placer miners and their gold had provided the accumulated wealth—the capital—needed to begin to unlock California's great natural and human potential. The early center of this accumulation was San Francisco, the place where fully developed capitalism first made its appearance in California. The political element in its foundation was laid in 1856 in conjunction with the violent seizure of power by a group of businessmen, most of whom were leading merchant capitalists. To establish their political goals, they engaged in insurrection, risking a civil war.

4

THE RISE OF INDUSTRIAL CAPITALISM
1856–1865

THE EARLY DEVELOPMENT OF INDUSTRIAL CAPITALISM IN CALIFORNIA

The initial development of industrial capitalism in California had a number of key characteristics that distinguish the reign of capital from the prior modes of production discussed in the previous chapters.

Most fundamental was the change from a rural, Gold Rush type of economy and society where the majority owned some productive property, to an urban system where the great majority owned no means of production and survived by working for wages. Key factors in this shift were both the decline of the placers and the California industrial revolution itself. Industrial capitalism has always been built on the tomb of smaller producers. The owners of small-scale productive property like placer mines disappear; they are bankrupted and must begin to sell their labor power to survive.

The small producers of California had usually lived at least partly outside of the market; they had use-rights, such as mining claims, and the ability to take water, forest products, and wild animals from the public domain. Industrial capitalism gradually transformed this situation to make most people dependent on the labor market and wages. The resulting full commodification of labor was an aspect of this process.

Second, and alongside the above change, was the rise of a class of owners of industrial, agrarian, and financial capital, families who owned the main means of production—the factories, banks, railroads, insurance companies, mines, big farms and commercial businesses—which made up the living heart of the new industrial economy of California. The new system created the market in commodified labor by enabling these new owners to hire the now propertyless workers at the lowest possible cost. The market in human labor becomes a central aspect of the industrial capitalist economy.

The division between owners and workers created an intensified class system with new classes, the majority working class—fragmented into many different subgroups—and a small minority, the owning or capitalist class, further subdivided into larger and smaller capitalists. Each class and subclass came to have common experiences, and a social consciousness developed as a result of their collective experiences. Minority racial and national groups—mainly Chinese, Latin Americans, Irish, and Indians—were racialized and gradually integrated into the new class system as the most exploited workers, which were then used to force down the wages of all workers. These racial and national minorities represented the poorest and most oppressed sector of the working class, forcing them into a caste apart from the new and developing class system. This special role helped the ruling class divide the workforce against itself since "white" workers were also disadvantaged by their presence.

Third, the new system, in California and elsewhere, was more productive than any system in the entire history of humanity.

This both accumulated capital at a rapid rate and allowed a higher standard of living, especially for those at the higher levels of society.

Fourth, private accumulation of capital was the central goal of the resulting system, and was achieved by the private economic appropriation of human-produced surplus value together with the dispossession of many, especially Native Americans, and the exploitation of the environment. Everything, even human beings, soon became commodities with a market price.

Fifth, governmental structures were in the hands of the capitalist class, a new ruling class that used government mainly for their own purposes and not for the welfare of the whole population.

Sixth, stock exchanges, finance capital, monopoly, and speculation rapidly developed once capitalism took hold. The result was both fantastic economic growth and appalling human and environmental devastation. Living human labor came to be dominated by capital and the drive for accumulation; the earth, with its resources and living things, was increasingly seen only as something to exploit to accumulate wealth.

Finally, the system created alienation within the population and resistance to aspects of the system, mini-wars within and among California's class, racial, and nationality groups—historical struggles that will be discussed in detail below.

IMPERIAL SAN FRANCISCO AND THE RISE OF INDUSTRIAL CAPITALISM

The city of San Francisco rose to importance in 1849–1850 and was initially ruled by merchant capital. But with industrial capitalism's rise in San Francisco, it became the dominant force in the state. Just as the massive growth of London during the eighteenth and early nineteenth centuries was a product of and represented the emergence of industrial capitalism in England, so the gigantic growth of San Francisco during the 1850s and

1860s was emblematic of the capitalist industrial revolution in California. San Francisco's rapidly expanding population already stood at about 35,000 in 1852, and by 1870 had reached over 149,000, making it by far the leading city in the western United States. By all measures, San Francisco dwarfed the rest of the state and region. It had 15 percent of California's total population in the 1850s—a figure that jumped to over 25 percent in the 1860s. Sacramento, the second largest city of the 1850s with less than 4 percent of the state's population, dropped below 3 percent in the 1860s.

One unified, integrated, and initially competitive market was created in San Francisco during the 1850s, a market soon brought under the control of a class of exploitive industrial, commercial, and financial capitalists extracting surplus value from commodified wage labor. Beginning in the mid-1850s and continuing into the twentieth century, San Francisco was the dominant capitalist city lying at the epicenter of the California economy. San Francisco had everything that was most advanced and most diversified. It was a super city, the place where modern California's commerce and industry were born. It was where people, news, merchandise, credit, capital, and industry were concentrated and circulated. It was a variegated place characterized by diverse races, classes, languages, cultures, religions, and modes of dress. As the capitalist market expanded, the super city developed a surrounding archipelago of towns that acted in a cooperative but subordinate role. These were essentially colonies with which an imperial San Francisco engaged in unequal market-exchange relations, allowing the super city to drain the wealth of the less advanced areas.

Closest to San Francisco in size and importance stood a middle group of developing cities—Oakland, Sacramento, Marysville, Stockton, and Virginia City, Nevada—that had some of the same advantages as San Francisco. Outside these places lay a vast and varied periphery of smaller towns, villages, and rural regions with more scattered and less educated populations, more primitive living conditions, and general backwardness. The super city sent investment capital to these peripheral areas to exploit the mineral deposits, forests, agricultural land, water, and other resources.

The smaller-scale capitalists or commercial farmers operating in these locations received capital, supplies, machinery, and direction from San Francisco, sending their products back to "the city," setting up and reinforcing unequal exchanges. In this way, the metropolis benefited from the more extensive environmental destruction and brutal labor systems characteristic of these outlying areas. Wherever market imperatives regulated the economy and governed society, there could be no escape from the dispossession and exploitation of the wage-labor system, along with varied forms of colonialism, environmental destruction, and class, race, gender, and ethnic conflicts.

The ruthless competition of the market was the usual means by which the accumulation of capital through class and environmental exploitation took place, but the racialization and violent dispossession of the Indians, Chinese, and Latin American peoples was ongoing, reinforcing their subordinate, caste-like status.

MERCHANT CAPITALIST COUP D'ETAT, SAN FRANCISCO'S 1856 COMMITTEE OF VIGILANCE

In 1856, San Francisco saw a revolution that ushered in new leaders and the new age of industrial capitalism under the auspices of a group of upper class businessmen called the Committee of Vigilance. The Committee of Vigilance of 1856 had political goals, but their actions had important economic implications as well. The political and economic context of San Francisco in 1856 was characterized by rapid, almost chaotic change. There were four political parties operating in San Francisco at the time, led by the dominant Democrats. The American (also known as the Know Nothing Party) and the Whig parties were both in deadly decline. The Republicans, although only just established, were growing rapidly.

The Democrats were divided into two factions: the first being the pro-slavery "Chivalry" group, led mainly by men of Southern birth and Southern principles. The Chivalry was described by one early-day Republican as a "crowd of brandy-drinking, pistol-shooting, swearing, swaggering gentry, who turn up their noses at all honest labor" (quoted in Phillips 1929, 89). While not politically dominant in San Francisco, the Chivalry was powerful in other parts of California, and were represented by William Gwin (originally from Mississippi), in the US Senate.

The second Democratic Party faction was called the "Broderick Machine," after David Broderick, the political leader of San Francisco's Irish Americans. Broderick was a working-class politico from New York; his thinking had a radical democratic edge, and he belonged, heart, soul, and upbringing, to the working class. He felt that workers submitted too tamely to oppression and he wanted to abolish slavery. He was the first Irish American working-class hero of San Francisco (see Quinn, 1997).

Economically, California was still clearly pre-industrial and pre-capitalist in 1856, but moving rapidly toward both. As discussed above, one of the bases of this change was the decline of placer mining and the movement of the mining population to the cities and agricultural valleys. Another, of course, was the accumulation of capital by merchants, many of whom realized that much of this capital should be invested in industry—the factory system, wage labor, steam power, foundries, gas lighting, and the greater efficiencies possible with an ever finer division of labor.

Merchant capitalists were traders who, as their predecessors had for many generations, simply bought cheap and sold dear. They were, however, quickly transforming themselves into industrial capitalists who produced commodities by employing wage laborers in factories lit by gaslights and powered by steam engines. As the economic system went into crisis due to a decline in placer mining in 1855 and 1856, the businessmen who wanted to move toward industrial development believed that a number of factors were mitigating against the success of industrial capitalism. These included the current political structure, with its yearly elections and patronage-based machine politics fueled by Irish American immigrant votes, as well as by a general lack of industrial discipline.

The political and economic crisis of the mid-1850s caused many businesses to fail, and some individuals lost vast sums of capital almost overnight. One of these was an aspiring capitalist named James King of William. The "of William" was a pretentious way of distinguishing himself from the many other James Kings then in California. King had been a banker, reportedly worth $125,000 in 1851 and $250,000 by 1854, but he lost almost everything in the depression and market crashes of 1854–1855 (Senkewicz 1985, 157; Scherer 1939, 142). Using his contacts among the merchants and bankers of San Francisco, he was able to raise enough money to start a crusading newspaper, the *San Francisco Evening Bulletin,* in October 1855.

The tone and content of King's newspaper focused on a few key themes. The first was the supposed political corruption (ballot-box fraud and misallocation of funds) of Broderick's dominant Democratic Party machine in San Francisco, which relied on immigrant votes. A second theme was the need to suppress crime and vice (and thus promote both the security of property and an industrial work ethic on the part of the population). A third focus was the promotion of a transcontinental railroad to more closely connect California with the rest of the country. These editorial and news themes soon marked the *Bulletin* as the organ of the rising Anglo American capitalist class of the city, which naturally assumed that the rich should rule.

King strongly attacked the Democratic Party, its leaders like David Broderick, and their business allies, such as the banking firm of Palmer, Cook and Company, largely putting the blame on them for the business depression and resulting crisis of the system. King and the *Bulletin* soon became very popular and influential among the higher circles of San Francisco.

In late 1855 and early 1856, King's attacks on the political and economic status quo in San Francisco came together around the cases of two men, one accused of murder and the other of political corruption. The first was Charles Cora, an immigrant gambler who lived with a well-known prostitute named Belle; the second was James P. Casey, an Irish American Democratic party politician, who had recently been elected a San Francisco supervisor.

In November of 1855, a personal conflict led to the shooting death of a US Marshall named Richardson at Cora's hands. King recounted his view of the incident in the *Bulletin* shortly after it occurred, agitating against Cora and pointing out that the excitement of a segment of the people reminded him of an 1851 Vigilance Committee, which had temporarily seized power in the city, executed four people, and exiled many more:

> *The cowardly-like assassination on Saturday of the U.S. Marshall, General Richardson, on one of our public thoroughfares and within a few yards of Montgomery street, calls for some expression of opinion from us. We are told by those who knew the deceased that he was a good citizen and an efficient officer, ever diligent in the discharge of his duties. Cora was an Italian assassin and gambler. The excitement on Saturday night was immense, and strongly reminded us of the old Vigilance Committee times. We passed through those times and scenes when an incensed and outraged people, having no faith in the corrupt ministers of the law, took the administration of public justice in their own hands and inflicted merited punishment on the heads of some of the murderers of those days ... Thus acted the Vigilance Committee. If he be guilty, he must be hung! ... we want to know why the laws in this State against gambling are not enforced? ... Let this*

man Cora, and the gamblers generally with their disreputable houses, meet their deserts (sic), and there will be no need of immigration meetings. The honest and industrious from every land will flock to our shores. (San Francisco Evening Bulletin *November 19, 1855, 2)*

The next day, King and his paper again agitated for a Vigilance Committee to seize power and forcibly solve the sociopolitical and economic problems of San Francisco, pointing out that the Democratic Party politicians elected in 1855 were not suitable, and strongly condemning individuals such as the Democratic sheriff and Democratic party political operative Billy Mulligan, who was the keeper of the county jail:

What we do want is a respectable sheriff. And that we have not. We want a good Deputy to keep the County jail, and that we have not. We want good officers of the law to break up the gambling dens and move the houses of prostitution from their present localities, and these we have not. We want a bolder and more efficient Mayor and Common Council, who whether elected next year or not, will, whilst in office, do their duty, and these we have not. Now what we propose is this: If the jury which tries Cora is packed, either hang the Sheriff, or drum him out of town, and make him resign. If Billy Mulligan lets his friend Cora escape, hang Billy Mulligan, or drive him into banishment. The receiver is as bad as the thief, and in this case the man who lets Cora loose to murder another victim, should suffer in his place… Extreme cases require severe remedies. Now is the time to give warning to these parties to avoid the necessity of a Vigilance Committee. And if the above authorities do not act rightly now, we believe such *an organization will be resorted to. (*San Francisco Evening Bulletin *November 20, 1855, 2)*

Cora was tried for the murder of Richardson, but he had a good legal defense team and the trial resulted in a hung jury in January 1856. King and the *Bulletin* both expressed anger and also increased the stakes by blaming corruption, lawyers, officers of the law, and the law itself:

Rejoice ye gamblers and harlots! … Your triumph is great—oh, how you have triumphed! Triumphed over everything that is holy, and virtuous, and good, and triumphed legally—yes, legally! Your money can accomplish anything in San Francisco …

Talk of safety in the law! It is a humbug, the verist humbug in existence is the present system of jury trials … Rail at the Vigilance Committee, and call it an illegal tribunal? What scoundrel lost his life by their action who did not most richly deserve it? Men complain of Vigilance Committees and say we ought to leave criminals to be dealt with by law! Dealt with by law indeed!

*We want no Vigilance Committee if it can be avoided, but we do want to see the murderer punished for his crimes. If we remember rightly, one article in the Constitution of the Vigilance Committee was that no lawyer could become a member! Peter the Great, when he was in Paris once, said he had but three lawyers in his Empire, and he intended hanging two of them immediately on his return. What purpose does the law serve but to bind honest men and let loose the vile and guilty? (*San Francisco Evening Bulletin *January 17, 1856, 2)*

The reason for the lack of conviction may have been the self-defense argument (reportedly, both Cora and Richardson had guns drawn, were ready to shoot, and Cora shot first) or the excellence of Cora's legal team, or some bias on the part of the jury (Gordan 1987, 9). It was reported that Belle, Cora's lover, had enough money to hire expensive and gifted lawyers, among them Col. E. D. Baker, who may have been able to sway at least one member of the jury (*San Francisco Evening Bulletin* March 12, 1856, 2).

King's outspoken style included strong attacks on the Democratic Party, whose leaders included an Irish American county supervisor, James P. Casey. King and his newspaper attacked Casey in mid-May, accusing him of engaging in election fraud and also pointing out that:

> *The fact that Casey has been an inmate of Sing-Sing prison in New York is no offense against the laws of this state; nor is the fact of his having stuffed himself through the ballot-box as elected to the Board of Supervisors from a district where it is said he was not even a candidate. (San Francisco Evening Bulletin May 14, 1856, 2)*

Casey had apparently been an inmate in Sing Sing, but ballot fraud was harder to prove. But the facts and accusations printed in a newspaper hostile to the Democratic Party, made Casey violently angry. The very next day, he visited King at the *Bulletin* and, following a verbal altercation, lay in wait and assassinated King on the street outside King's office. The newspaper reported as follows on the assassination:

> *About four o'clock yesterday afternoon ... Casey called at the editorial room of the paper and saw King, who was seated alone in the apartment ... Casey was apparently much excited and spoke as if short of breath. He asked King what he meant by the*

article in the Bulletin just issued. King asked him what article he had reference to; when Casey replied, "To that which says I was a former inmate of Sing-Sing Prison." King answered, "Is not that true?" Casey replied, "That is not the question. I don't wish my past acts raked up; on that point I am sensitive." King then said, "Are you done? There's the door—go! Never show your face here again." Casey, slapping his hand on his breast, then said, "If necessary, I shall defend myself." Casey immediately went down stairs, without saying another word.

*At a few minutes past five o'clock, Mr. King left his office, as usual, for dinner. He walked on the pavement in front of Montgomery Block, going northward. At the Bank Exchange, he crossed the street diagonally towards the Pacific Express office. Casey, who had been previously observed walking on the west side of Montgomery street, opposite Montgomery Block, as if watching for King's appearance, was at this time on the pavement before the Express office. He was observed to step into the street as King crossed, and suddenly throwing off a short cloak which he wore, presented a revolver at King's person, when he and King were only a few feet apart, and fired. The shot took effect in King's breast and passed through his body. (*San Francisco Evening Bulletin *May 15, 1856, 2)*

The effect of King's shooting was electrifying. Almost immediately, an angry crowd gathered at the jail where Casey had been taken for his own safety. The mayor and sheriff appealed for calm. Just as quickly, reportedly within a few hours of the shooting, a group of merchants and former members of the 1851 Vigilance Committee began to meet to decide if they wanted to use this incident as a pretext to take control of the city.

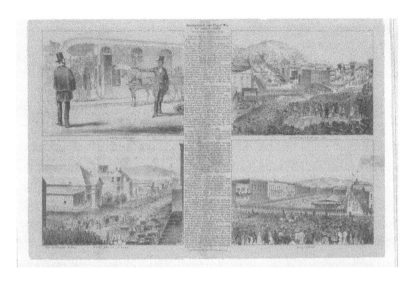

The Vigilance Committee of San Francisco, 1856
This letter sheet illustrates the assassination of King, the seizing of the jail, and the execution of Casey and Cora. [Courtesy of the Bancroft Library, University of California, Berkeley.]

The decision was soon made to launch what can only be labeled a revolution, a military seizure of political power in San Francisco, to solve the twin questions of who should rule and what political and economic programs would be implemented. This coup d'etat was to be commanded by a small group of white, Protestant Anglo Americans, called the Executive Committee, operating in a strictly hierarchical, military style. Everyone who wanted to join the 1856 Vigilance Committee (and was subsequently selected for membership) had to swear obedience to this Executive Committee. There are lists of this several-dozen-member body (Colville 1856, 226; Bancroft 1887, 113; Tays 1936, 15). It was led by an upper-class commission merchant (a large scale importer and exporter of goods) named William T. Coleman and consisted of representatives from most of San Francisco's largest importers and merchants, along with bankers, brokers, corporation directors, and industrialists. The key members of the Executive Committee included:

WILLIAM T. COLEMAN, PRESIDENT

Born on the family estate in Kentucky, Coleman's ancestors had come from England in 1635, and his grandfather was a "Virginia gentleman." Many of his other relatives were Southern plantation owners, and as a young adult, he had worked as an overseer of slaves on his uncle's Louisiana plantation. Family or personal friends included Senator Henry Clay of Kentucky and San Francisco lawyer/businessman Lloyd Tevis, who later became president of Wells Fargo Bank.

Coleman arrived in San Francisco in 1850 and was a leader of the 1851 Vigilance Committee, but also spent much time in New York, developing an extensive business there, as well as in San Francisco. As was the case for a number of other Vigilance Committee leaders, his business included acting as commission agent for a number of San Francisco manufacturers, helping them buy supplies and sell their product in the east. This linked him closely to the rising industrialists (Decker 1978, 188). In 1852, he married Carrie M. Page in Boston. Miss Page was the daughter of the founder of the banking firm of Page & Bacon and was a direct descendant of a Mayflower pioneer (Scherer 1939, 18–65, 131–133, 147; Tays 1936, 13).

CLANCEY DEMPSTER, VICE PRESIDENT

Dempster was a partner in D. L. Ross and Company, commission merchants, and an officer in the San Francisco Chamber of Commerce (Colville 1856, 55; Baggett, Joseph & Company 1856, 80).

THOMAS J. L. SMILEY, VICE PRESIDENT

A partner in Smiley, Yerkes and Company, auction and commission merchants (Colville 1856, 203), Smiley had been a leader of the

1851 Vigilance Committee, and by 1860 was a leader of the local Republican Party (Tays 1936, 13; *Daily Alta California* August 17, 1860, 1).

CAPTAIN J. D. FARWELL, VICE PRESIDENT

Farwell was a ship chandler, who had also been a member of the 1851 Vigilance Committee (Colville 1856, 68; Tays 1936, 13).

WILLIAM ARRINGTON, VICE PRESIDENT

He was a partner in Arrington and Company, wholesale grocers, and also a director of the Pioneer Society of California (Colville 1856, 5, 176). Arrington, too, had been involved in the 1851 Vigilance Committee (Tays 1936, 13).

ISAAC BLUXOME JR., SECRETARY

Bluxome was a merchandise broker, who had also been a member of the 1851 Committee (Langley 1858b, 68; Scherer 1939, 115–120). He was later a strong Union man in the Civil War, and one biographer called him "a Republican of pronounced type" (Phelps 1881, 270).

MYERS F. TRUETT

Said to be "among the leading merchants of the city," Truett was a partner in Truett and Jones, imported- and wholesale-liquor merchants (Bancroft 1887, 97–107, 125). He owned the building at Sacramento and Front Streets, called "Fort Gunnybags," which became the headquarters of the Vigilance Committee.

RICHARD M. JESSUP

A director of the largest California corporation of the time, the California Steam Navigation Company, which had a capital stock of $2.2 million in 1856. Jessup was also a commission merchant and a key figure in the Broadway Wharf Company (Colville 1856, 30–31, 109; Langley 1858b, 387).

JAMES DOWS, TREASURER

A distiller of liquor and thus part of the growing industrial capitalist class, Dows had been a leader of the 1851 Vigilance Committee (Colville 1856, 59; Scherer 1939, 115–120).

J. W. BRITTAN

Brittan had begun as an importer and dealer of stoves and hardware but was soon also manufacturing these items (Colville 1856, 23; Decker 1978, 187).

EDWARD P. FLINT

Partner in Flint, Peabody and Company, commission merchants, and a prominent early Republican party leader. Flint was a director of California's first railroad, the Sacramento Valley Railroad, and an investor in early San Francisco manufacturing (Colville 1856, 73; *Daily Alta California* May 1, 1856, 2; *Sacramento Daily Union* November 14, 1855, 2).

A. L. TUBBS

Tubbs was a main owner of Tubbs and Company, importers and dealers in ship-chandlery (Colville 1856, 221; Decker 1978, 187). Together with E. P. Flint, he later owned and operated the ropewalk in the Potrero District, which manufactured rope for many purposes.

E. B. GODDARD

Goddard owned the Pacific Foundry, which employed 50–80 wage workers in 1856, doing an average annual business of $240,000 (Colville 1856, 82, 166).

GEORGE R. WARD

Ward was a broker and land agent (Colville 1858, 277).

Besides the executive committee members listed above, others who were known to be prominent or active in the work of the Vigilance Committee included:

WILLIAM C. RALSTON

A banker with the firm Garrison, Fritz and Ralston, Ralston reportedly joined the vigilance movement the day after King was shot. His firm gave the upper floor of its bank building at Clay and Battery for an armory. Ralston biographer David Lavender stated that Ralston was very active in the committee (Lavender 1975, 99–106).

THOMAS H. SELBY

A merchant and importer of metals, Selby later became an important manufacturer, the owner of Selby's Smelter and mayor of San Francisco (Colville 1856, 197).

JOHN O. EARL

Earl was a merchant and later the president of the Gould and Curry Mine, the richest early hard-rock mine on Nevada's Comstock lode (Phelps 1882, 311–313).

SAMUEL SOULE

A director of the California Steam Navigation Company, Soule was an early Republican Party leader and member of the Republican State Central Committee in 1856 (Colville 1856, 30; Davis 1893, 66; *San Francisco Evening Bulletin* August 29, 1856, 3).

LELAND STANFORD

Stanford was a merchant, later a railroad mogul. He became a Republican Party leader, was Republican candidate for state treasurer in 1857, and was elected Republican governor in 1862, and later US senator. Stanford traveled from his home base in Sacramento to join the Vigilance Committee in mid-June 1856, indicating his strong support for its approach (Senkewicz 1985, 195).

C. P. HUNTINGTON, CHARLES CROCKER, AND MARK HOPKINS

These three merchants, who later joined Stanford to make up the "Big Four" owners of the Central Pacific and Southern Pacific railroads, all petitioned the governor of California in favor of the Vigilance Committee in June of 1856 (Florcken 1936, 76).

IRA P. RANKIN

A merchant (Rankin and Company), Rankin later became part owner of the Pacific Foundry. He was also active in the chamber of commerce and was appointed collector of customs (Decker 1978, 112). During the month of August 1856, he chaired a key vigilance subcommittee and later became the Republican Party's nominee for one of California's two congressional seats (*San Francisco Evening Bulletin* August 29, 1856, 3; T. Hittell 1898, 3:637–638).

GEORGE H. HOWARD

A member of a wealthy land owning family, Howard was a real estate proprietor in 1856 and dispossessed Native Americans off of their land (Baggett, Joseph and Company 1856, 191).

SIDNEY P. WEBB

Webb was elected mayor as the anti-Catholic Know Nothing (American) Party candidate in 1854, but lost to the Democrats in the election of 1855 (Decker 1978, 128).

JOHN PARROTT

A leading San Francisco banker, Parrott supported the Committee by donating money to the cause (T. Hittell 1898, 3:500–501).

ANNIS MERRILL

A strong supporter of the Vigilance Committee, Merrill was reportedly the organizer of the first Republican Party club in California. He also was a member of the Republican State Central Committee in 1856 (Merrill 1878, 8–10; Davis 1893, 61).

In sum, the 1856 Vigilance Committee was made up of very prominent and wealthy men. Two separate studies found that at least 70 percent of the leaders were high-status importers, merchants, bankers, manufacturers, brokers, or professionals (Decker 1978, 140; Senkewicz 1985, 170). Coleman himself stated, "The largest element of the Committee was of northern and western men, chiefly representing the mercantile, manufacturing, and vested interests" (Scherer 1939, 218). Philosopher-historian Josiah Royce called it "that unique historical occurrence, a Business Man's Revolution," led by the "most prominent merchants" (Royce [1886] 1970, 346–347).

Interestingly enough, no lawyers were involved in prominent positions. This was undoubtedly due to the fact that lawyers would be more likely to respect the Constitution and existing bodies of laws, and therefore might question the seizure of government power by military force, as well as extralegal trials, executions, and banishments. The committee's own constitution, in fact, stressed the need to be freed from the "quibbles of law" (Senkewicz 1985, 170–171).

The Vigilance Committee was very popular among the upper strata of San Francisco's population. Although it formally banned Chinese and African Americans from membership and apparently, de facto, banned Irish Americans, whose Democratic Party political organization was a main committee target, it still was able to enroll thousands of people in active roles (Ellison 1950, 240). An estimated six to eight thousand people quickly joined the committee, making it the largest such body in the long history of the extra-legal United States vigilante movements (Senkewicz 1985, 8; Decker 1978, 125).

Popular excitement among Anglo Americans, stimulated by King's newspaper writings and his demise, was intense, and the committee's leadership took full advantage of it. Circumstantial evidence indicates that these men had been preparing to act even before King's death. First of all, King's newspaper articles during the first months of 1856 repeatedly mentioned the possible need for another Vigilance Committee and, given King's close connections to the business community and the leading role of the *Bulletin*, it is very likely that discussions of this possibility were widespread in leading business circles. Second, one businessman supporter just happened to have several thousand muskets on hand and gave them to the committee to arm its members. The committee also had access to several cannons (*The San Francisco Herald* August 19, 1856, 2; Scherer 1939, 166). Third, the committee was able to organize, arm, and train twenty-six hundred men within three days of King's murder, an amazing feat and one unlikely to be achieved without at least some advance planning (Ellison 1950, 245). While no one could have anticipated the assassination, the actions of the Vigilance Committee of 1856 showed that their goals were long term, amounting to a political transformation that, in turn, set the stage for an economic transformation of California's key city, San Francisco.

On May 18, 1856, three days after Casey shot King, fifteen hundred armed Vigilance Committee troops marched to the county jail, hauling a cannon with them. Training the cannon on the jail door, their commander demanded custody of both James P. Casey and Charles Cora, who was still incarcerated awaiting a new trial. The sheriff had only thirty men and decided to yield under protest to superior numbers, and the committee took the two men to their headquarters (Ellison 1950, 245; *San Francisco Evening Bulletin* May 19, 1856, 2). When King died of his wounds on May 20, Casey and Cora were rapidly tried and condemned by the Vigilance Executive Committee. They were executed by hanging in front of Fort Gunnybags on May 22, the same day that King's funeral took place.

Prior to his execution, Cora was married by a Catholic priest to Arabella Ryan, his "Belle" (*San Francisco Evening Bulletin* May 23, 1856, 2). Meanwhile, King was buried. His pallbearers included Samuel J. Hensley, president of the California Steam Navigation Company, former US Consul Thomas O. Larkin, president of the Pioneer Society and a leader of the new Republican Party, and wealthy banker John Parrott, one of the few Catholics in the entire vigilance leadership. His ties, however, were to Latin American and not Irish American Catholicism *(San Francisco Evening Bulletin* May 23, 1856, 2; Colville 1856, 30, 97, 124).

After the execution of Casey and Cora, the Vigilance Committee leaders focused their attention on terrorizing and smashing the Democratic Party in general and the political machine of David Broderick specifically:

> *In short order, a number of Broderick's political operatives found themselves surrounded on the streets by squads of armed vigilantes and hustled to the waiting executive committee. They were tried for a variety of offenses, mostly relating to political fraud and ballot box stuffing. After conviction, which was virtually automatic, they were hurried off for deportation on ships. (Senkewicz 1985, 172–173)*

Those deported, who included at least two other San Francisco supervisors, McLean and Mosgrove, were forbidden to return to California on pain of death. Another vigilante target, an Irish American named "Yankee" Sullivan, ostensibly committed suicide while in the committee's custody before he could be deported. Later, the committee issued, and then rescinded, an order for the arrest of David Broderick himself, deciding only to ask him to appear and answer questions. Broderick refused and escaped the city to Sacramento. Hundreds of others also fled the city in fear (Senkewicz 1985, 173; Gordan 1987, 14; Ellison 1950, 249; J. Hittell 1883, 25–26; T. Hittell 1898, 3:618).

The frontal attack on the Democratic Party of San Francisco was obvious to all who wanted to see it. Under the guise of assuring security of life and property, preventing ballot-box fraud and punishing crime, a recognized and powerful political party, and especially the Irish American sector of this party, was temporarily crushed. While Irish American political power was the special object of attack, one Democratic journal said at the time that the committee "has declared war on the Democratic Party" (quoted in Bancroft 1887, 625).

The next stage in the drama came when the state authorities decided to get more seriously involved in opposing the illegal seizure of power. On June 3, Governor Johnson, who was also the leader of the American or Know Nothing Party, issued a "Proclamation against the Vigilance Committee," stating that they were leading an illegal insurrection against the constitution and laws of the state and requesting various state militia units to report to Major General William T. Sherman, commander of the Second Division of the California Militia (*San Francisco Herald* August 26, 1856, 4). This order was not successful, however—most militiamen were with or sympathetic to the committee. Some responded, but the "law and order" group, as it was called, made up mainly of leading Democrats, especially Southerners, was much smaller and weaker than the committee and had significantly fewer weapons (Ellison 1950, 251–257; Atherton 1914, 202).

Having successfully outmaneuvered the state government, the committee captured, tried, and executed two more men accused of murder, one of which had been involved in earlier squatter conflicts. The background to this latter execution is traceable to 1853 and 1854, when several men were killed in land disputes. Both a "Settlers' Association" and an opposing "Association for the Protection of Property and the Maintenance of Order" had been formed in 1854 (Drummond Jr. 1952, 72; Koford 1938, 19). The Settlers' Association opposed the "land monopolists," and at least some of their supporters spoke of the "plunder of the poor" by the rich (Drummond Jr. 1952, 77, 83). The Protection of

Property group set up an organization of special police supervised by some of the most prominent men of San Francisco, including two land speculators, Thomas O. Larkin and Dr. Samuel Merritt, as well as prominent business leaders like William Sharon and Louis McLane (Drummond Jr. 1952, 73; Koford 1938, 9, 11, 16, 17).

During this period of San Francisco history, settler/squatter interests often had influence on city government through the Broderick faction of the Democratic Party. They opposed "superseding the laws ... by force and violence" and so were against the special police and propertied group (Drummond Jr. 1952, 83). In mid-1853, the *Daily Alta California* had argued that some of the Broderick Democrats advocated for the view that all real estate in California was common property and every individual had a natural right to it, thereby helping to cause squatterism. The *Alta* added that a "combination of capitalists" was ultimately responsible in San Francisco, because they encouraged the squatters to seize property, and then purchase and resell it at a profit. In the words of the *Alta*:

> *The course of events in this city during the last few days has assumed a serious turn and induced people to look upon squatterism as something more than a mere thoughtless, irregular attempt of a few individuals to gain a temporary advantage by seizing upon unoccupied and unimproved lots here and there in the city ... It is a well known fact that a large and powerful political party of the State has, for more than two years past, advocated and defended, at least imperfectly, the general doctrine that all real estate in California is common property, to which every individual has a natural right, without regard to ownership, and that lawful title is no barrier to forcible possession. This is perhaps the primary influence which has given rise to squatterism in the*

> *agricultural districts, and made it an element of our political system. But there are additional causes to which squatterism in this city must be attributed.*
>
> *We are satisfied from such investigation as we have been able to make, that there is a combination of capitalists here who have organized the band of squatters whose proceedings have been so prominent lately, and who are immediately responsible for the outrages that have been committed ... we wish to hint to them in the most quiet manner that they will serve their own interests by confining themselves to their legitimate business and desisting from further participation in an unlawful and unjust enterprise.*
> (Daily Alta California *July 22, 1853, 2*)

The conflicts over land in San Francisco in 1853 and 1854 previewed the rise of the extralegal Vigilance Committee a few years later. Joseph Hetherington, involved in an 1853 squatter-related shootout over land in which another man was killed, was tried and executed for this shootout by the committee in the summer of 1856 (Drummond Jr. 1952 54; *Daily Alta California* August 2, 1853, 2; October 15, 1853, 2). A jury had failed to convict Hetherington, a common occurrence since the juries of the time were frequently influenced by settler/squatter views.

The Vigilance Committee then planned their official "grand" farewell parade, which took place in mid-August 1856. It was a great military parade, with thousands of armed men marching along with cannons, bands, cavalry, citizens on horseback, and even a kind of a float, a representation of Fort Gunnybags (J. Hittell 1878, 259–260). A critical newspaper called it a "grand funeral procession," and under the headline "2740 Traitors Under Arms," said the Vigilance Committee's "past career is written in lines of blood, and the pen of the honest historian will hand them down to posterity with ... shame and infamy" (*The San Francisco Herald* August 19, 1856, 2).

Before officially disbanding, the committee organized a new, local political party, the "People's Reform Party." They secretly maintained their organization to choose and promote the candidates for this party and also kept a "small police force" to protect themselves. The executive committee was also, reportedly, still meeting in 1859 (*San Francisco Evening Bulletin* August 27, 1856, 1; Ellison 1950, 264–265; Scherer 1939, 224). One committee member even reported that as late as 1886 the organization was still "in perfect organization and could resume active service at the shortest possible notice" (Ayres 1886, 166).

The new People's Reform Party, ostensibly "non-partisan" but controlled by Vigilance Committee members, was in fact increasingly allied with the new Republican Party, which was also the political party of rising industrial capitalism. The California branch of the Republican Party had been founded in Sacramento in April 1856, only a month before King's assassination. One hundred and twenty five delegates from thirteen California counties attended, but over half of the delegates came from San Francisco and Sacramento counties, marking the initial stage of Republican Party organization as strongly urban and industrial-capitalist in nature. The key resolutions adopted included opposition to both the slave-owning planter class (called the "slave power" by the Republicans), the further expansion of slave territory, a welcome to immigrants (for their cheap labor), support for the speedy construction of a transcontinental railroad, and a rapid settlement of land-title disputes (Severson 1973, 134).

The vice president representing San Francisco at this Republican convention was merchant Edward P. Flint, soon to be a member of the executive committee of the Vigilance Committee (*Daily Alta California* May 1, 1856, 2). When the Republican State Convention met in August of 1856, two Republicans who had been active in the committee were voted into important positions: Samuel Soule became the San Francisco representative on the State Central Committee and Ira P. Rankin became one of the two party nominees for Congress (*San Francisco Evening Bulletin*

August 29, 1856, 3; T. Hittell 1898, 3:637–638; Davis 1893, 64–66). Other members of the committee who were also leaders of the Republican Party included the future Republican governor Leland Stanford and Annis Merrill. Conversely, Democratic and Know Nothing/American Party leaders were not part of the vigilance leadership of 1856, although some rank-and-file members of both parties undoubtedly were (Colville 1856, 226; Davis 1893, 57–59, 67–68, 77). Newspapers of the time recognized the connections between the Vigilance Committee and the Republican Party. As one Democratic newspaper stated in August 1857:

> It is worthy of remark, that not only in San Francisco, but throughout the State, the same feeling has widely prevailed, which, in San Francisco broke out in a Vigilance Committee; and that wherever the reformatory spirit has been found, it has exhibited strong affinities for Republicanism. Not that every Republican is a Vigilance Committee man, or that every Vigilance Committee man is a Republican. Such is not the fact. Yet such are the affinities between this reformatory feeling and the principles and dispositions of the Republican party, that ultimately the reformers of the State will, of necessity, find themselves in the Republican Party. (The San Francisco Herald August 6, 1857, 2)

A final step in the growing unity among the Vigilance Committee, its "People's Reform Party," and the new Republican Party was the endorsement by the Republicans of all of the local candidates of the People's Reform Party in the November 1856 election. In at least two cases, the People's Reform and Republican Parties united and fielded joint, local candidates. Finally, the Republicans ran candidates for state and federal offices, but the People's Reform did not. This was part of a plan to separate local government from more general party politics (Bancroft 1887, 652–653). The result was a virtual sweep for the Republicans and People's Reform candidates in San Francisco. The only loss was in the presidential contest, where the Republican Fremont narrowly lost to the Democrat Buchanan in San Francisco (*San Francisco Evening Bulletin* November 8, 1856, 3; T. Hittell 1885, 2:638). Every other race from congressional to justice of the peace in this key election was won by the Republican/People's Reform alliance.

In the wake of the successful vigilance war on the Democratic Party, politics had been transformed in the dominant city of California, and the Democrats, Whigs, and American/Know Nothings were on the outs. This transformation of political life lasted for over a decade; the Know Nothings collapsed, and Democrats were out of power in San Francisco until 1867. During this decade-long period, San Francisco became a stronghold of both industrial capitalism and the Republican Party. In 1860, for example, when Abraham Lincoln won California and the nation in a close, four-way race for the presidency, he won only about 32 percent of the statewide vote, just a few hundred votes ahead of the Democrat Douglas. In San Francisco, however, Lincoln won with 47.9 percent of the vote (2,879 votes ahead of Douglas, who was second with 27.9 percent) (*Daily Alta California* November 17, 1860, 1). San Francisco was thus clearly a key to Lincoln's narrow victory in California.

The Vigilance Committee's military seizure of political power and the three-month reign of terror it imposed on the Democratic Party political machine thus had very important ramifications for the political future of the entire state: the decisive empowerment of the Republican Party, the party of industrial capitalism and the rise of a new ruling class consisting mainly of the largest merchants, who were accumulating capital and beginning the process of capitalist industrialization.

Once in power, the People's Reform/Republican Party put into effect now familiar policies that favored business interests generally and industrial capitalists in particular. Private capital accumulation was made easier by a sharp decrease in taxes and government spending on public projects. City expenditures dropped from $2.6 million in 1855 to only $353,000 in 1857. Some of this was due to city and county consolidation, but deep cuts in spending did take place. In addition, taxes declined a reported 40 percent, leaving more profits for investment in industry (Decker 1978, 139; Bancroft 1887, 649).

While some have argued that election fraud was stopped, it is doubtful that this was true, since the number of voters stayed about the same in the yearly elections of 1855 and 1856, something not likely if widespread ballot stuffing had occurred in 1855 and then stopped in 1856 (Bancroft 1887, 648–649; Senkewicz 1985, 119). Elections, which had been yearly events, were made less frequent by extending the term of office, reducing the people's influence on those holding elected office (Senkewicz 1985, 191). Overall, the city's reputation among Eastern businessmen undoubtedly went up, making it easier to borrow investment capital from that source (Issel and Cherny 1986, 21). The Vigilance Committee had in effect launched a successful capitalist revolution from above.

With political power secure in the largest and, by far, the most important city in the state, and with a new political party favorable to industrial capital established and driving toward state and national political power, the groundwork was in place for the establishment of a new economic order in California. Fully articulated industrial capitalism, characterized by the control of the means of production by a relatively few wealthy families and by alienated wage labor for the workers who made up the great majority, was now ready to make its decisive entrance on the stage of California history.

FOUNDRIES AND HARD ROCK MINES, THE ORIGINS OF CALIFORNIA'S CAPITALIST INDUSTRIALIZATION

As indicated above, San Francisco was at the forefront of the economic and social revolution represented by the process of capitalist industrialization. Manufacturers were concentrated in

San Francisco for a number of reasons, principally because both capital and markets were concentrated at this location (Trusk 1960, 36). It was the focus of a complex system of pre-capitalist, semi-capitalist, and capitalist social relations of production (that is relations between owners and producers) that were spread over California and the West and linked to each other by market relations of exchange. Prior to the 1857–1858 years, there was relatively little manufacturing in San Francisco or California. As one leading writer of the time expressed it, "The great danger from conflagrations, high prices of skilled labor, excessive rates of interest for money, and the then uncertain future of the country, all combined to prevent any extensive manufacturing … and it was not until about 1858 when large amounts of capital were invested (Langley 1869, 67).

Political control and security were therefore key background factors in investment decisions. Once the political/legal control of San Francisco was firmly in the hands of a pro-industrial capitalist government led by the People's Reform Party/Republican Party, merchants felt secure enough to make large investments in industrial development. The rapid and full development of capitalism required that merchant wealth move from mere circulation (buying and selling goods) into industrial production, putting machinery and workers in motion. As this investment accelerated, the market in human labor power also rapidly expanded. The worker was dispossessed, divorced from the ownership of the means of production; henceforth, the capitalists would own all significant productive property. Capitalism in its mature form, which used the commodified wage labor of propertyless workers to produce goods for sale on the market then came into being in California.

With important exceptions, pre-capitalist systems, such as debt peonage and small-scale commodity production, were gradually superseded statewide by capitalist wage labor, by which the lives of the workers *inside* the factory were strictly controlled by a boss who set the terms and conditions of work, while the workers were "free" *outside* the factory. In order to speed up efficiency and production, capitalists instituted the division of labor and a process of *deskilling* the worker. This process involved fragmenting the work process through the introduction of technologies and machines that could be operated by unskilled workers. This demeaned work, rendering it more mechanical and more alienated for the individual worker and those he worked with. Deskilled workers were also easier to replace, decreasing the chances for strong unions that could effectively make demands upon the owner.

Another central development of the 1850s, laying the groundwork for the entire process of industrialization, was the production and use of gas for lighting. Gaslight allowed work in interior spaces (such as factories) to take place both day and night. This also changed the concept of "day" into an abstract span of time, overruling organic life and opening the way for longer hours and the intensification of exploitation. Since large amounts of capital were required to establish such a facility, many investors were needed, creating corporations and uniting the wealthy in a common endeavor, raising the class-consciousness and unity of the rich. San Francisco's first gas plant, the west coast pioneer, was completed early in 1854; Sacramento's plant (the second) came in late 1855. Marysville's and Placerville's gasworks were completed in 1858; Nevada City's and Yreka's both in 1859, Stockton's in 1860, San Jose's in 1861, Grass Valley's in 1862, Oakland's in 1866, and Los Angeles's in 1867. All these plants used coal, pitch pine, or combinations of the two, heated in *retorts* to produce gas (*American Gas-Light Journal* June 1, 1863, 354–357; Coleman 1952, 11–13, 34–43).

While political control and gas production were key preliminaries, the core of the early (1850s and 1860s) industrial transformation of California was the development of metalworking, especially by the foundries of San Francisco. Several of these foundries were in existence as relatively small operations by the mid-1850s. At that point, their business was varied, consisting of repairing steamships, building and repairing steam engines, constructing and improving quartz-, saw-, and gristmills, producing boilers, making castings, and supplying equipment for gasworks. Then, in 1857, the stimulus from new quartz-embedded gold-mining development began to create a huge demand for practical and efficient mining machinery, and the booming foundries of San Francisco were ready for the challenge. The technological revolution they pioneered became the driving force in the capitalist industrialization of, first, San Francisco, then, step-by-step, the rest of California.

Quartz gold mining was industrial mining, and as such was entirely different from the simple placer mining of the Gold Rush era. Industrial mining required large capital outlays to purchase mining claims and supplies and to hire and pay a skilled labor force. Even more expensive and technically difficult to develop was the powerful machinery required to work underground, bring massive amounts of rock to the surface, crush it, and refine it to extract the precious metals. Mammoth steam engines, huge pumps, hoisting works, tram-cars, and large quantities of wire rope, blasting powder, leather, quicksilver, timber, lumber, food, and other supplies were all required to feed this giant industry.

California miners had initially expected to learn from Great Britain how to conduct deep mining and how to build stamp mills and other needed machinery, but the machinery imported from the East and abroad consistently failed. In 1853 and early 1854, complaints were common in California about this "miserably inefficient machinery" (*The Mining Magazine* November 1853, 507; January 1854, 63). Within a few years, inventors based in California's foundries changed this. Peter Donahue, one of the brothers who owned and operated the Union Iron Works, later said that 1855 was the year that the building of improved quartz mills was begun (Donahue n.d.). Langley and Mathews pointed out in 1857 that there were "recent improvements in the machinery employed …" in quartz mining (Langley and Mathews 1857, 214). Improvement continued, and by 1860, veteran miner Almarin B.

Paul could report that, "vast indeed is the advancement in mining knowledge; and I think I will be seconded by the experienced in saying that the past two years have outstripped, in progress, all the preceding eight" (*San Francisco Evening Bulletin* April 19, 1860, 1).

Thus, the key changes in the quality of machinery came in the 1855–1860 years, and California was the worldwide center of the new developments. California had a mixed population from many countries, was relatively isolated from the world, lacked restrictive traditions, and had a young and inventive population. These factors, combined with California's extensive deposits of complex and valuable mineral deposits, made it one of the first places in the world to extensively experiment and put mining on a fully industrial scientific foundation. The techniques and machinery it developed to solve key mining problems soon established the pattern and set the standard worldwide (Klein 1908, 61, 64; Bailey 1996, vii).

Quartz gold mining, where relatively small amounts of gold per ton of quartz rock are extracted and made to pay due to the large quantities of rock processed, had existed alongside placer mining since 1850, especially in Nevada, El Dorado, and Amador Counties, but early failures had set back the industry, and it was only in 1857–1858 that it really began to boom. As the Amador County Assessor's *Report* stated in 1858:

> *Quartz mining is now one of the most important branches of industry pursued in this county. The wild excitement of 1851–52, when little was known as to the practical working of gold-bearing quartz, brought ruin upon many of our citizens and deterred others for years from engaging in a branch of business which was deemed hazardous. A few enterprising men, however, persevered ... There are 32 quartz mills in operation, propelling 402 stamps, against 23 mills, with 268 stamps, last year. Total product of 32*

*mills per annum, $1,350,720. (Quoted in Langley
1862: 260–261.)*

The great expansion of Amador County's mills was typical;
the total number of quartz mills operating in California more than
doubled in the year and a half between April 1857 and November
1858, and the investment in them almost doubled during the same
time period. As the *Pacific Coast Business Directory* reported:

> *The number of quartz mills in operation in this State
> in April, 1857, was one hundred and thirty-eight,
> with an aggregate of fifteen hundred and twenty-one
> stamps; the cost of erection of which was one million
> seven hundred and sixty-three thousand dollars. The
> number in operation, November, 1858, was two
> hundred and seventy-nine, with an average of two
> thousand six hundred and ten stamps; the cost of
> erection of which was three million two hundred
> and seventy thousand dollars. (Langley 1867, 72)*

In mid-1857, during this boom, the quartz miners of California
met in convention in Sacramento. One of their leaders was a Grass
Valley (Nevada County) mine owner named James Walsh, later to
be a key early player in the development of the Comstock Lode.
One speaker at this convention stated that about $5 million was
currently invested in quartz mines (apparently including mines
and all their machinery) giving constant employment to at least ten
thousand people (*The Mining Magazine* November 1857, 472). The
great boom that this represented was the result of improvements in
machinery, more experienced operators, veteran prospectors who
found new mines, and the new political-economic climate in San
Francisco, where the mining equipment was being developed and
most investment capital resided. These developments provided the
essential industrial knowledge of tools and techniques as well as
a supply of liquid capital. They began to create the great demand
for the producer-goods that the foundries could fabricate.

In addition, other new industries were being established in San Francisco and California during the late 1850s: sugar refineries, sawmills, flourmills, woolen factories, and large-scale commercial farming also required foundry-produced machinery. Foundries and metalworking provided the initial base of the industrializing system, producing both the needed machinery as well as some of the economic demand-stimulus for the development of many other industries (Klein 1908, 67).

The Union Iron Works, Pacific Iron Works, and Vulcan Foundry, all established in the 1849–1851 years, led the foundry boom of the late 1850s and early 1860s. By 1858, there were five foundries listed in Langley's *San Francisco Directory*. The biggest were the three mentioned above, and each brought significant numbers of wage workers together under one roof. Their relative size can be gauged by the number of employees, which fluctuated due to layoffs and hires depending upon the level of demand (Langley 1858a, 43):

- Union: 50–170 men
- Vulcan: 45–90 men
- Pacific: 50–80 men

San Francisco was far in the lead among all the foundries of California. In his 1859 *California Register*, Henry G. Langley stated:

> *There is no department of mechanical industry in this state in which more enterprise and energy is exhibited than that of the manufacture of machinery. There are at the present time in operation, exclusive of the government works at Mare Island and those belonging to the Pacific Mail Company at Benicia, twenty iron foundries, of which five are located in San Francisco, three at Sacramento, two each at Calaveras, El Dorado and Nevada, and one each in Amador, Butte, Los Angeles, San Joaquin, Santa Clara and Yuba. The establishments at San*

*Francisco, particularly those of the Union Iron Works
and the Pacific and Vulcan Foundries, are of the
most extensive character, and being amply provided
with the necessary appliances for the construction
of the heaviest description of machinery. (Langley
1859a, 302)*

The largest foundry was the Union Iron Works, which had
"the best tools to be found in California" and had just received
a contract from the federal government to build the boilers and
steam engine for the new side-wheel steamer *Saginaw* (Langley
1859b, 37). One San Francisco newspaper commented on the
importance of this piece of machine work: "This, the first marine
engine constructed on the Pacific Coast, as a specimen ... is well
worthy of more than a passing notice, indicating the facilities
afforded by our machine shops and foundries as well as the ability
of our manufacturers to turn out work that will favorably compare
with that of older establishments in the Eastern states" (quoted in
Dillon 1984, 133).

QUICKSILVER, DEVELOPING THE NEW ALMADEN MINE, 1845–1860

Another important economic development of this era—and
one that soon fed into the ongoing process of the capitalist
industrialization of California—was the discovery and evolution
of a major quicksilver (mercury) mine near San Jose in Santa Clara
County. This mine became known as the New Almaden Mine,
after the famous Spanish quicksilver mine. The New Almaden was
the first major mine developed in California. It was discovered
by Native Americans in the distant past, and for hundreds of
years the Indians extensively used the mine's cinnabar ore for
body paint. A visiting Mexican cavalry officer claimed the mine
in 1845, soon turning it over to the British company of Barron
and Forbes, which had extensive operations and connections
in Mexico. In early 1848, as gold in large quantities was just

135

beginning to be found in the foothills of the Sierra Nevada mountain range, reports from San Jose estimated that the New Almaden was already yielding about $100,000 a year in profit to its British operators (Egenhoff 1953, 110–111).

During its early years, the New Almaden Mine was characterized by pre-industrial technology and methods of work, and this was only gradually changed during the mid- and late 1850s. The first miners at New Almaden were Mexicans and Yaqui Indians from the Gulf of California, imported by Barron and Forbes using their extensive Mexican connections. These imported workers were exploited under a type of peonage system, organized and supervised by bosses and mainly paid on a piece-work basis, depending upon the richness of the ore removed (Egenhoff 1953, 119–120; *The Mining and Statistic Magazine* August 1854, 232–233). The result was a mine in the early Mexican style, with a tortuous and irregular system of underground galleries cut into the interior of the mountain that were reached by wooden ladders consisting of notched logs. The miners, who were subject to silicosis, a disease caused by rock dust in the lungs, were required to carry the ore hundreds of feet out of the mine on their backs. As one eyewitness described the mine and its miners in 1854:

> *You descend a perpendicular ladder formed by notches cut into a solid log. You go down, perhaps twelve feet; you turn and pass a narrow corner, where a frightful gulf seems yawning to receive you. Carefully threading your way over the very narrowest of footholds, you turn into another passage black as night, to descend into a flight of steps formed in the side of the cave, tread over some loose stones, turn around, step over arches, down into another passage that leads into many dark and intricate windings and descendings or chambers supported, but by a column of earth ...*

These men work in companies, one set by night, another by day ... We inquired the average duration of life of the men who work underground, and found that it did not exceed that of forty-five years, and the diseases to which they are most subject are those of the chest ...

With a sigh and a shudder, we step aside to allow another set of laborers to pass. There they come; up, and up, from almost interminable depths; each one as he passes, panting, puffing and wheezing, like a high-pressure steamboat, as with straining nerve and quivering muscle, he staggers under the load, which nearly bends him double. These are the tenateros, carrying the ore from the mine to deposit it in the cars; and like the miner, he is burdened by no superfluous clothing. A shirt and trowsers [sic] ... a pair of leather sandals fastened at the ankle, with a felt cap ... completes his costume. The ore is placed in a flat leather bag ... with a band of two inches wide that passes around the forehead, the weight resting along the shoulders and spine. Two hundred pounds of rough ore are thus borne up, flight after flight ... Thirty trips will these men make in one day, from the lowest depths. (quoted in Egenhoff 1953, 116–119)

Once the cinnabar ore was in hand, it was smelted in a simple, wood-heated, brick, multi-chambered *reverberatory* furnace, which was very destructive to the lives of the workers who worked in and around these furnaces and breathed in deadly mercury fumes. Using such techniques, about a million dollars worth of mercury was mined, refined, and exported from the New Almaden in 1857 alone (*The Mining and Statistic Magazine* February 1858, 142; March 1858, 246).

By early 1860, some machinery had been added to increase the efficiency of the mine and relieve the Mexican miners from some of their hard toil. In March 1860, a visitor reported on the methods then in use, indicating how the process of industrialization had begun to transform this important mine:

> *The main entrance is a tunnel ten feet high, and about an equal width throughout, in which runs a tramway loading to the shaft. At the end of this tunnel a small steam-engine does the work of the poor "tanateros," or carriers, who until very recently, brought the ore and rubbish from the bottom of the mine on their backs … The next process is to be lowered down into the mine. Squeezing myself into a huge kind of bucket, and assuming as near as practicable the shape and position of a frog, my candle lighted … I find myself rapidly descending a damp dismal hole … The … Mexican miner deputed as guide leads the way along a narrow gully, and down an incline to the mouth of another hole, the descent to which has to be effected on a slanting pole, with notches cut in it … After this we scramble down a flight of steps cut in the rock, and reach the lowest excavation, about one thousand feet from the surface …*

> *All the work is done by contract, each gang taking a piece of ground on speculation, is paid according to the amount of ore produced … If a blast has been successful, often many tons of rock are loosened and torn out, to be broken into small pieces and conveyed to the bucket, and hauled the engine to the surface. The mining operations are continued night and day, seventy-four pounds of candles being consumed every twenty-four hours … The ore, on reaching the surface, is conveyed by the tram-cart to the sorting shed, where it is broken and carefully picked over … The picked ore is placed in large bags*

*made of sheepskin, weighed; and then hauled by the
mules to the lower works … quicksilver … here …
is found solely in form of cinnabar, and to reduce a
kind of reverberatory furnace is used, three feet by
five, placed at the end of a series of chambers …*

*Although … care has been taken to prevent mercurial
fumes from injuring the smelters, still a great deal
of it is necessarily inhaled, most injurious to health.
Clearing out the furnace is the most hurtful process,
the men employed working short spells, and resting
a day or two between. (quoted in Egenhoff 1953,
127-131)*

The importance of the New Almaden came from its ability to
supply the large amounts of quicksilver needed for gold and later
silver mining in California and Nevada. A pattern of gross abuse of
workers and the environment was set by the mine's owners, Barron
and Forbes. Illness and premature death among their workers was
common, and mercury pollution of the New Almaden area is
still a problem today. In the name of capital accumulation, this
pattern would be repeated again and again throughout California
and the West. Finally, this pioneer mine was a key part of the
transition from older labor and mine-development systems to
industrial mining and capitalist wage labor. The company also
employed and physically separated its Mexican and Cornish
workers in adjacent company towns in order to divide the labor
force and better control it. This also prevented a strong union from
organizing to protect worker interests and playing a role in the
mine's management and development. This divide-and-conquer
tactic by capitalist owners and the racialization and conflict that
resulted will be discussed in more depth below.

OTHER KEY CALIFORNIA INDUSTRIES IN 1859

Langley's *California Register* reported other key industrial developments in California as of 1859. San Francisco's industry again stands out. The *Register* identified fourteen metallurgical and gold-and-silver refining works in the state, of which eight were located in San Francisco, and two each in Sacramento and Placer counties. The eight San Francisco establishments included the California Metallurgical Works, founded in 1856. This was the largest in the state, built at a cost of $150,000 (Langley 1859a, 302–303). Two sugar refineries had also been recently developed in San Francisco, the only ones in the state. The largest refinery, owned by merchants becoming industrialists, was described:

> *The San Francisco Sugar Refinery is owned by a company of San Francisco and New York merchants ... The works of the company are ... of the most extensive character, and of a capacity sufficient to supply the entire consumption of sugar in this State. The main building is seventy-five feet in width by one hundred and twenty-two feet in length, and five stories high. Several small buildings are attached ... The raw material consumed at these works is obtained from Manila, Batavia [Dutch East Indies, today's Indonesia] and other Islands of the Pacific ... the number of hands employed is one hundred and fifty. Cost of buildings and grounds, one hundred thousand dollars. (Langley 1859a, 304)*

This sugar refinery was established in 1855 when George Gordon, the owner of the Vulcan Foundry, joined with eastern merchant capital to finance the construction of this facility (Trusk 1960, 128).

In 1859, another key industry—manufactured woolen goods—was being organized. Langley pointed out the essential background to this development, adding that an association of "capitalists" was behind it (1859a, 304–305):

> *The extensive growth of wool in this State, and the demand existing on this coast for goods manufactured therefrom, have engaged the attention of an association of capitalists, who have made the necessary arrangements for the early construction, in the vicinity of San Francisco, of a manufactory for the production of blankets and other woolen goods, to be of a capacity sufficient to supply the demand for home consumption and our export trade. This movement is but one of the many evidences, to be seen in almost every section of the State, of the rapid advancement of our manufacturing interests.*

Also ongoing during 1859 was the construction of steamboats at South Beach, San Francisco. Some of them were very large, as the *Bulletin* reported in January 1860:

> *The largest and most magnificent steamboat ever constructed on this coast, is rapidly approaching completion. The vessel is constructed of California timber, upon a beautiful model, and in the most substantial manner. Her length is 260 feet, and her entire breadth 70 feet. She draws 5 feet of water. Her engine is a low-pressure beam engine, with a cylinder of 60 inches diameter and 12 feet stroke. The wheels are 36 feet in diameter, with a face of 10 ½ feet. Besides a large ladies' cabin, there is a grand general saloon 170 feet long by an average breadth of 16 feet; and in addition to 66 staterooms, containing three berths each, there are 150 first-class open berths. It is supposed she will make the trip between San Francisco and Sacramento in six hours. No pains have been spared to make her in all respects*

> *equal to the best of the world-renowned floating*
> *palaces of the Atlantic States. She has been built for*
> *the California Steam Navigation Company, at a*
> *cost of $200,000.* (San Francisco Evening Bulletin
> *January 24, 1860, 3)*

In his 1859 *California Register,* Langley also describes the beginnings of the manufacture of chemicals, cordage and oakum, furniture, agricultural implements, paper, matches, perfumes, leather, brooms, macaroni, candles, soap, starch glue, beer and wine, camphene and oil, and stoneware. The *San Francisco Evening Bulletin* (January 24, 1860) reported that San Francisco also had rice-cleaning mills, glass-making factories, jewelry-making facilities, and cigar manufacturing. One of the leaders of the Vigilance Committee, Republican Party leader Edward P. Flint of Flint, Peabody and Company, was a key organizer of the cordage, oakum (cotton fiber used to seal joints on wooden ships) and rice-cleaning mills industries. In most cases, San Francisco was in the lead in establishing factories in all of these industries (Langley 1859a, 303–308).

The sources of capital needed to start a manufacturing concern in California primarily came from income gained in California, especially from merchant activity. Gold from the labor of miners passed through the hands of merchants who took a percentage as profit, often investing some of this profit in manufacturing (Trusk 1960, 173–174). The manufacturers themselves were mainly from manufacturing areas of the East Coast (49.3 percent) and Midwestern (9.9 percent) states, with a smaller number from Europe (29.6 percent) and Canada (7 percent) (Trusk 1960, 184). Strikingly absent from lists of early manufacturers in California were Latin Americans, Asian Americans, and Irish Americans. All made up a substantial part of the state's population, but they were workers, not the organizers of early capitalist industrialism. It was people from places that already had the factory system, gas lighting, steam power, scientific and mechanical education, and capitalist forms of work organization that became California manufacturers (Trusk 1960, 184).

Capitalism and industrialism were advancing rapidly at the end of the 1850s, but were still in their infancy. Capitalism still consisted of a few islands, San Francisco the largest by far, surrounded by a sea of pre- and proto-capitalist social relations of production. Then during 1859, 1860, and 1861, several developments rapidly accelerated the pace of capitalist industrialization in San Francisco and California. The first centered around the discovery of giant bodies of complex silver-gold ore in Nevada, initially the Comstock Lode, but followed by a number of smaller but still significant finds in both Nevada and California. The second was the growing sectional conflict threatening to tear the United States apart, leading to the Civil War of 1861–1865.

COMSTOCK

The extraordinary ore deposit called the Comstock Lode was discovered in 1859 only a short distance east of today's California–Nevada border. The yield of silver and gold from the mines that sprang up along this ore deposit established and maintained San Francisco's financial structure for over a decade and exerted an important influence on the monetary system of the entire world (Becker 1882, 1).

In the spring and early summer of 1859, a small group of self-employed gold miners, using the simple tools and organizational forms of the California Gold Rush, had followed the eroded trail of a gold deposit up a western Nevada hill to its source. The lode they found was strange, like nothing they had ever seen or heard of. At its core was a seam of black rock that increased in size as it went down. Since it was in their way, they saw the black vein as an obstacle to their gold-sluicing work and cursed it as they broke it up and threw it aside.

A local rancher visiting the miners was curious about the black seam, however, and took a sample, later giving a fragment to Judge

James Walsh, the Grass Valley mine owner who had been a leader of the 1857 California quartz miners' convention in Sacramento. Walsh entrusted the sample to Melville Atwood, a skilled assayer in nearby Nevada City (Lord 1883, 54–55; Carlson 1955, 36). It was at this point that California's earlier development in the fields of scientific/industrial mining began to pay off spectacularly, for Atwood could and did discover the secret of the seam of black rock—it was a well-defined vein of silver sulphurets, one of the largest and richest the world had ever seen. The gold that the first prospectors were focused on was a secondary deposit; the primary one by far, both by weight and value, was silver.

Veteran miner George Hearst was also mining in Nevada County and heard about the find. Walsh, Hearst, and other men resolved to travel immediately to "Washoe," as it was then called. When they arrived in July 1859, the surface of the lode had barely been scratched, but it was clear to them that an extraordinary mineral deposit had been uncovered. Even if much of the ore was much poorer in gold and silver than the ore already visible, the great length of the lode meant that it contained an incredible amount of wealth. The challenges facing the miners were, however, quite substantial. Mining historian Eliot Lord (1883, 56–57) later summed up the difficulties they faced in 1859:

> *The task presented to capital and labor was the development of a silver lode cropping out on the slope of a barren mountain more than a mile above the level of the sea. North, east, and south the mountain was surrounded by deserts. West lay the white capped range of the Sierras, a barrier penetrable only through a few steep passes blocked with snow during the winter months, which led over its summit and down the western slope to the young cities of California.*
>
> *The range, in the heart of which the lode was placed, was a lumpish ridge of discolored rocks and earth,*

partly covered but not concealed by underbrush and scrawny cedars. During the dry season no water flowed down into its ravines, and in the spring only meager brooks ran through the main canons ... If a city was to be built on the line of the lode, it must be a foreign creation. Water must be made to flow from the rocks or conducted from distant lakes; roads must be cut and blasted through the cañons and along the edge of mountain precipices; the frame-work of the houses and the timber used in the mines must be cut from the trees of the Sierras and dragged up to the mountain camp; food, clothing, tools, and supplies of all kinds must be transported by slow and costly methods from the Pacific sea-board ... Not only a gold mine was requisite to work a mine of silver such as this, but energy incessant and untiring faith which no discouragements could shake, and skill born of years of varied experience. California furnished the men, the methods, and the means. (Lord 1883, 56-57)

Large amounts of capital, industrial methods, and skilled labor were needed to develop the mines and mills that could successfully tap this lode. California supplied all three, along with capitalist production methods, namely the corporate form and wage labor. For those who could envision the future, the first step was to secure options on some of the mines and further prove the richness and extent of the discovery. With this in mind, large consignments of ore were sent to San Francisco and refined at the city's metallurgical works during the summer and fall of 1859 (Lord 1883, 59; *Daily Alta California* November 2, 1859, 3).

The results were spectacular, a reported gross yield of $112,000 from the ore, leaving a large profit even after the great expense of wagon transportation and ore reduction (Lord 1883, 62). A rush to purchase claims held by the original self-employed prospectors ensued, and by the spring of 1860 all the original claims but one had been bought out, most of them very cheaply. A large number of joint stock mining companies were then formed. The two leading ones were the Ophir Gold and Silver Mining Company in April 1860, and the Gould and Curry Silver Mining Company, formed in June of the same year. Among the founding officers and trustees of the Ophir were William C. Ralston, Joseph Woodworth, William F. Babcock, Benjamin Holladay, and William Blanding (*The Mining and Statistic Magazine* April to July, 1860, 410; Lord 1883, 89). The Gould and Curry's original leaders included George Hearst, Lloyd Tevis, John O. Earl, Alpheus Bull, Thomas Bell, B. F. Sherwood, along with Ralston and Blanding as well (Smith 1943, 84).

Meanwhile, a mad rush of erstwhile miners and prospectors traveled to Washoe that spring (*San Francisco Evening Bulletin* April 25, 1860, 2). The display of bars of silver bullion from the refineries of San Francisco conjured up the dazzling images of the galleons of old Spain, the riches of Potosi, and the wealth of Montezuma and Cortes. The rush collapsed with the realization that in most cases large sums of capital would be needed to fund the complex, developmental process required to tap the riches of the Comstock. In April 1860, the *Bulletin* ran an editorial stressing the need for capital to successfully work this lode, trying to discourage the mining rush that was underway:

> *Half a minute friend, if you are bound for Washoe …*
> *Valuable surface diggings have been found … but*
> *the country is absolutely without water for mining*
> *purposes … Capital must precede you, and make*
> *roads and ditches, many a weary mile in length,*
> *before you can hope to work the placers profitably.*
> *Your only other resource then is the silver mines.*
> *The mountains are already filled with prospecting*
> *parties, so that your chance of striking a rich "lead"*
> *and getting a claim on your own account is very*

*small. Have you then capital with which to buy
into a claim already discovered, and to contribute
your portion of the means necessary for its proper
development by an organized company? If so, go
ahead … But if you are without capital—if you
cannot become a stock-holder in mines already
discovered, there is nothing left for you at Washoe
except labor at days wages, for other parties. Labor
in the mines has been paying $5 per day, while the
cost of living is about $3; but the hundreds who have
poured into the Territory during the last few days,
depending upon their hands alone for subsistence,
must speedily reduce the price of labor one half.*

*Do not forget the vast difference between mining in
gold placers and working silver leads. In the former,
if you pan out even a dollar a day, you can take your
dust at night, go to the store and buy your flour and
bacon with it. Not so is it in silver mining, where
you must toil day after day, and week after week,
before getting any portion of the result in a shape that
will satisfy hunger and thirst. Laborers should cease
their exodus across the Sierras for the present. Even
good mechanics are in abundance now at Carson
and Virginia City, where they earn no more than do
the lowest grade of Mexican laborers, who "pack" on
their backs the ore from the Spanish claim.*

*To men of capital—even small capital—Washoe
offers a most inviting field. To those who have money
to spare, we say that we know of no better place to
invest it. (*San Francisco Evening Bulletin *April
23, 1860, 2)*

Of the millions of tons of ore that made up the Comstock Lode,
only a small percentage was rich enough to pay for transportation

to and smelting in San Francisco. No known process was capable of cheaply and efficiently reducing the complex ores characteristic of this lode. So, during the winter of 1859–1860 and the spring and summer of 1860, some of the best scientific and technological minds of the California mining community applied themselves to the problem.

Almarin B. Paul, who had worked with James King of William on the *San Francisco Evening Bulletin* and with the Vigilance Committee after King's assassination, found an initial solution. Paul had gone to Nevada City (California) to develop stamp mills there. Having kept up on the latest in quartz gold milling technology, Paul was familiar with a new circular iron pan invented in 1858 by I. W. and R. F. Knox, mechanics at a San Francisco foundry. This pan was found serviceable for the reduction of gold-bearing quartz and the new Miner's Foundry began to produce different kinds of such pans in San Francisco late in 1859 (Lord 1883, 82–83). Urged on by friends who had purchased claims, Paul decided to build a reduction mill in the vicinity of the Comstock Lode. He wanted the mill to process the tons of average-grade ore that were not rich enough to bear the cost of shipment to San Francisco.

He ordered his machinery from the Miner's Foundry, had it delivered across the Sierra, and was able to complete his mill by mid-August 1860. His trial run, using the most advanced steam-powered California stamp mill and the new pans, was a success. Although many improvements were still needed and would be made, the basic technology was in place to efficiently reduce the complex gold and silver ores characteristic of the Comstock (Lord 1883, 84–88). Over the next few decades, what became known as the "Washoe Pan" was the "chief agent" in the separation of a half a billion dollars worth of precious metals from its ore (Bailey 1996, 13).

California mining technology helped miners rescue the Comstock again in the fall of 1860 when mining efforts literally began to cave in. As the hired workers of the Ophir Company reached the depth of 175 feet, the great black vein of rich, silver sulphurets grew broader until it was sixty-five feet wide. The mass was so soft and crumbly that it was impossible to securely support, and the miners were in constant danger of being buried as they pursued their work. Historian Lord explained the problem and the solution:

> *The dilemma was a curious one. Surrounded by riches, they were yet unable to carry them off and their mass of black sulphurets bade fair to become a white elephant on their hands. The Ophir Company began to wish themselves less fortunate, as their miners narrowly escaped burial day after day in their attempts to stope out the ore.*
>
> *A young mining engineer, Philip Deidesheimer, was in charge of a quartz mine in Georgetown, El Dorado County, Cal., in the autumn of 1860, when this serious check to the development of the lode occurred. At the request of William F. Babcock, a trustee of the Ophir Company, Mr. Deidesheimer left his California mine and crossed the mountains with a letter from the directors of the Ophir Company, authorizing him to inspect the workings of their mines and make such changes in the method of timbering as should seem to him expedient. After examining the vein, he designed, in the course of a few weeks, a system of timbering which proved to be exactly adapted to the requirements of the work. Experiments which he had previously made in California gravel and quartz mines furnished the outline of his plan. This was to frame timbers together in rectangular sets, each set being composed of a square base, placed horizontally, formed of four timbers, sills, and cross-pieces from 4 to 6 feet long, surmounted at the corners by four posts from 6 to 7*

> *feet high, and capped by a frame-work similar to the*
> *base. The cap-pieces forming the top of any set were*
> *at the same time the sills or base of the next set above.*
> *(Lord 1883, 89–90)*

As the silver and gold ore was removed, these "square sets" were put in place as shoring. Square sets required huge amounts of timber. Logging and saw milling in the Sierra Nevada soon increased tremendously to satisfy the fantastic appetite of the Comstock for wood.

Men from California, especially San Francisco, who had capital, knew corporate organizational forms, and had experience with deep mining and the reduction and refining of ores had solved the basic problems presented by the discovery and early development of the Comstock Lode. This allowed the extraction and processing of huge amounts of rich ore, soon converted into vast wealth for California's new capitalists, wealth provided by nature's bounty, produced by the muscle, sweat, and very lives of workers.

THE COMING OF THE CIVIL WAR

Two 1859 events indicated that the national conflict between slavery and freer forms of labor was fast moving toward a climax. The first of these events took place in California and illustrated the growing split in the then dominant Democratic Party. California's two seats in the United States Senate were both held by Democrats—William Gwin, who was affiliated with what was called the Chivalry or pro-slavery faction of the party, and David Broderick, who was part of the "popular sovereignty" or anti-slavery expansion part of the party, and was allied with Senator Steven Douglas of Illinois. Votes on key issues were often close in the Senate, divided as it was between the pro- and anti-slavery forces in that body. With the election of the Chivalry Democrat Milton Latham as California governor, members of the Chivalry faction plotted to eliminate the anti-slavery Broderick and replace him with a pro-slavery senator.

The organizer of this plan was the Texas-born California Supreme Court justice David S. Terry, long a leader of the pro-slavery faction. Terry's plan was to challenge Broderick to a duel, kill him, and thus open the way for Governor Latham to appoint a pro-South US senator. Terry knew that Broderick was wary of duels and had to be seriously provoked, so he insulted Broderick by stating that Broderick was really a follower of Frederick Douglass, a former slave, who was strongly anti-slavery, rather than Steven Douglas, the senator. Broderick felt he could not back down from this perceived insult and challenge without a serious loss of face. Refusing the duel would also cost him political support among his Democratic Party followers, many of whom were racist and looked down upon Frederick Douglass and other African Americans. So Broderick accepted the fateful challenge.

Terry then resigned his seat on the California Supreme Court (he had only a few months left to serve) and on September 13, 1859, met Broderick near the Pacific Ocean south of San Francisco. Terry had learned from an accomplice that the pistols to be used in the duel had hair triggers that would cause either one to go off at the slightest touch. Not knowing this, Broderick touched the trigger of his pistol as he raised it and his gun went off too soon, the bullet harmlessly hitting the dirt in front of him. Terry was then able to aim and fire carefully at Broderick, hitting him in the chest with a mortal wound. Many believed that Broderick's dying words were, "They have killed me because I was opposed to a corrupt administration and the extension of slavery" (Bean 1973, 176).

Newly elected Governor Latham then appointed himself to the senate seat vacated by Broderick's death. Latham was a generally pro-slavery senator, and he favored secession in 1860–1861. The leaders of the Chivalry faction were successful, but at a serious cost. Broderick's murder widened the divisions in the California Democratic Party, with many members of the anti-slavery faction transferring allegiance to the Republicans. This in turn had an impact on the close 1860 election, and helped to swing California to Lincoln.

A second event was John Brown's Harpers Ferry raid. This took place in October 1859, just after Broderick's death, and the same month the Comstock Lode was in its earliest stage of development. Brown had long been a militant anti-slavery activist who believed that arming slaves to fight for their own liberation was the road to take to end the profound evil of slavery. With aid and encouragement from his northern supporters, Brown led a small interracial group of armed men, intent on seizing the federal armory in Harpers Ferry, Virginia, in order to try to spark a slave rebellion. The insurrection shocked the nation and put the slavery issue at the head of the national agenda. It was front-page news for days in California and stimulated wide discussion and debate in the state.

In 1859 California was, like the rest of the nation, in the midst of a political re-alignment stemming from the collapse of the Whig and Know Nothing parties and the rise of the Republican Party. This realignment was the political counterpoint of the ongoing capitalist industrial economic transformation of California and the nation, with the newly formed Republican Party leading both revolutions. Predictably, Democratic Party leaders blamed the Republicans for Brown and his insurrection. Democratic senator Steven Douglas said, for example, that the Harpers Ferry raid was the "natural, logical, inevitable result of the doctrines and teachings of the Republican Party, as explained and enforced in their platform, their partisan presses, their pamphlets and books, and especially in the speeches of their leaders" (quoted in Finkelman 1995, 131). Republicans said the Democrats were responsible, because it was their policies in Kansas and elsewhere that had driven men like Brown and those with him into open rebellion (*Daily Alta California* November 13, 1859, 2).

The tensions over how to deal with the slave-labor system were thus brought into the political system, and the 1860 election became, in part, a referendum on the future of slavery. The Republican Party platform of 1860 stressed the themes of no expansion of slavery, preservation of the Union, tariffs to help infant, domestic industries, a Pacific railroad, a homestead act for settlers, and freer immigration (*San Francisco Evening Bulletin* June 12, 1860, 1). This agenda aimed at helping the two main bases of Republican support: First, rising industrialists, who wanted a cheap, exploitable labor supply of immigrants and freed slaves, higher prices for foreign goods, and a railroad on that to ship goods. Second, small farmers, who wanted a homestead law, protectionism, and a railroad.

Lincoln's victory in California and the nation had huge implications for the future, and San Francisco's votes were central to Lincoln's victory in California. Lincoln won overwhelmingly in the rising capitalist city, but lost in most of the rest of California, winning by only a few hundred votes statewide. It was in this way that the Republicans, the party of capitalist industrialization, ascended to national power.

Once the Republicans were in power, the Southern slave-owning oligarchy felt that their best chance to preserve slavery and their way of life was to dissolve the Union, because Republicans would surely use federal power to wall off, undermine, and eventually crush the slave system. Republicans were rock solid on both forbidding any expansion of slavery, which required a vigorous assertion of federal power, and against secession. Their preferred labor system was exploitation of workers through wage-labor, and their economic system was industrial and agrarian (commercial farming) capitalism.

Both systems advanced tremendously in California during the Civil War of 1861–1865. To help this process along, Vigilance Committee member and long time Republican Party leader Leland Stanford was elected governor of California in 1861. The rise of the Republicans and the Civil War were thus tied to the rise of capitalist industrialization, a system focused both on the creation of surplus value and capital accumulation, as well as on the social, racial, or gender identities of the people it exploits. The Republicans developed ideological and practical pressures against extreme inequalities, preferring to employ all ethnic and racial groups equally, pitting them against each other to divide, conquer, and control the workforce. Capitalism thus represented a formal advance toward racial equality while at the same time informally creating racial and ethnic conflicts and intensifying class exploitation, an exploitation that increasingly shaped all social relations and identities.

THE 1860 CENSUS

In the summer of 1860, as the first Comstock mining corporations and the 1860 presidential campaign were both getting underway, the United States census was taken. The 1860 census presents a picture of California's people and development at this time. As such, it both measured the outcomes of the decade of the 1850s and was suggestive of things to come. In the area of population, the census found the aggregate population of California to be 379,994, with San Francisco County the most populated with 56,802 (14.9 percent), followed by Sacramento County at 24,142 (6.4 percent) and El Dorado with 20,562 (5.4 percent). Thus, a large majority of the population was still rural; while capitalism was advancing rapidly, pre-capitalist relations of production were still common in much of the state. This was reflected in the occupational structure for those 219,192 people listed as the economically active population of the state:

- Miners—82,573 (37.7%)
- Laborers—25,394 (11.6%)
- Farmers—20,836 (9.5%)
- Farm laborers—10,421 (4.8%)
- Servants—8,069 (3.7%)
- Merchants—5,082 (2.3%)
- Clerks—4,117 (1.9%)
- Carpenters—3,923 (1.8%)

- Mariners—3,078 (1.4%)
- All others—55,699 (25.4%)

Source: US Census Bureau 1864, 33–35

Trying to determine what percentage of the economically active population had been dispossessed, owned no means of production, and therefore had to work for others under the capitalist wage-labor system in order to compare it with the percentage that owned their own means of production is impossible to determine with any precision. The census takers did not gather data specifically on this topic. In addition, there were peons and workers held in various forms of caste control and economic bondage in both rural and urban areas of California in 1860 (mainly Native Americans and Chinese Americans).

The occupational statistics cited above, however, do give a general idea. The great majority of laborers, farm laborers, servants, clerks, carpenters, and mariners, amounting to 25.2 percent of those listed as having occupations, were undoubtedly wage laborers in 1860. Farmers and merchants (11.8 percent) were, on the other hand, large or small owners of productive property. Probably a majority of the miners of 1860 still owned their own claims, but industrial-capitalist mining was growing rapidly, constantly diminishing the independent miner category, and often employing those who lost or left their claims. Assuming the division to be 60:40 between independent miners who owned their own claims and waged miners, another 15.1 percent are added to the waged group, making about 40 percent for this category. Probably over half of the "all others" group can be assumed to be working for wages in 1860, making it likely that over half of the occupationally active population was working for wages at that time.

Thus, capitalist relations of production were likely already the most common kind of relations of production by 1860 and were expanding very rapidly. The two largest California cities, San Francisco and Sacramento, were already clearly capitalist dominated strongholds of the Republican Party.

California's population in 1860 was 61.4 percent US-born, a large majority of these natives having come from just seven states:

- California (33.3%)
- New York (12.3%)
- Missouri (6.0%)
- Ohio (5.4%)
- Massachusetts (5.2%)
- Pennsylvania (4.8%)
- Maine (4.2%).

The 38.6 percent foreign-born were mainly from four nations:

- China (23.8%)
- Ireland (22.6%)
- Germany (14.8%)
- England (8.3%)

Source: US Census Bureau 1864, 34

The fact that California's population overwhelmingly came from California, northern states, and foreign countries unsympathetic to slavery undoubtedly helped create a strong predisposition to the Northern side in the Civil War.

California's wealth was mainly concentrated in San Francisco, where ownership of natural resources and exploitation of workers was leading to the rapid accumulation of capital. A list of the richest San Franciscans, their occupations and incomes, compiled from the census of 1860, follows.

RICHEST SAN FRANCISCANS

1. E. P. Banker—banker—$515,000
2. Peter Donahue—foundry owner (Union Iron Works), $400,000. He was also a founder and one of the key owners of San Francisco Gas Company.
3. Daniel Gibb—merchant—$400,000. He was an owner of the New Idria Quicksilver Mine and, in 1858, the president of the San Francisco Chamber of

Commerce (*San Francisco Evening Bulletin* April 25, 1860, 1; Langley 1858b, 379).

4. Henry Gerke—farmer—$400,000
5. Augustus J. Bowie—physician—$310,000
6. Joseph Ginelli—merchant—$300,000
7. C. L. Wilson—contractor—$250,000
8. J. W. Tucker—jeweler—$240,000
9. Lafayette Maynard—real estate—$202,000
10. Samuel Inge—attorney—$200,000
11. R. B. Woodward—hotel owner—$180,000
12. Jas. R. Bolton—merchant—$170,000
13. Thomas Hayes—railroad stockholder—$160,000
14. Michael Hayes—railroad stockholder—$160,000
15. Andrew McCabe—real estate—$154,000
16. Oroville Pratt—attorney—$150,000
17. Cyrus A. Eastman—capitalist—$150,000 U.S. Census Bureau, 1860

This census also shows that six of the seventeen were foreign-born (two from Scotland, two from Ireland, one from Switzerland, one from Germany), and they collectively employed sixteen servants, (thirteen from Ireland, one from Canada, one from Germany, and one was a Native American from California). These seventeen men, mainly of white Anglo-Saxon background, made money from a mix of merchant (buying and selling), service, finance and law, and industrial activities. Much of the wealth had been accumulated during the 1850s, when industrialization was just getting underway, and so there are more merchants (three) than any other single group. But the dominant position of merchants and others was slowly declining, whereas that of industrialists was rising, as the 1870 census, covered in the following chapter, will illustrate.

In the area of manufacturing, San Francisco County with 16.2 percent of the firms and 26.3 percent of the capital invested was by far the leading manufacturing location in the state. Sacramento, with 8.7 percent of the firms and 8.2 percent of the capital invested, was in second place, and Santa Clara, with 3.2 percent of the firms and 6.6 percent of capital, was third (computed from Trusk 1960, 207–209). Politically these three counties were also the strongholds of Republican power and where Lincoln did best during the 1860 election. In terms of type of industry, and focusing on the larger firms with over $5,000 invested, food-related manufacturing was already in the lead with 40.2 percent of the capital investment, followed by lumber (24.4 percent) and metal working (17.9 percent). Leather, chemicals, textiles, stoneware, and others made up the remaining types of industry, with much smaller amounts of capital investment.

THE COMSTOCK ROARS: THE GOULD AND CURRY BONANZA, 1861–1865

The early Comstock had a number of rich mines, including the Ophir. Californians, especially San Francisco investors, owned most of them (Emmons and Becker 1885, 111–112). But none of these rich mines was more important for the early development of both the Comstock and the fortunes of the San Francisco rich than the Gould and Curry Mine, located on a 1,200-foot long claim south of the Ophir. The Gould and Curry began to develop its mine a few months later than the Ophir, but already by January of 1861, the *Bulletin* could report as follows on this mine:

> *The Gould & Curry claim is owned by an incorporated company with a capital stock of $2,400,000, in 4,800 shares at $500 ... This Company is running two tunnels into their ledge, the upper 150 feet long, to strike the ledge 70 feet below the surface, and the lower tunnel 700 feet long, to strike the ledge 200 feet below the surface. One thousand tons of ore are now out, which will yield from $150 to $200 per ton. All the ore under $300 in value will be worked on the spot ... The richer ores will be shipped as formerly ... Dividends will probably be declared*

*by this Company about the 1st of July, 1861. (*San Francisco Evening Bulletin *January 9, 1861, 2)*

At the same time that the Gould and Curry was getting underway, a number of new stamp mills were being built on a grand scale. Before the end of 1861, seventy-six mills, running 1,153 stamps, with an estimated crushing capacity of 1,200 tons daily, had been erected within a radius of sixteen miles from the mines, and twenty more were planned or under construction (Lord 1883, 114). The largest, called the Washoe Gold and Silver, was the one completed by Almarin B. Paul, discussed earlier, in early 1861. The *San Francisco Evening Bulletin* (January 9, 1861, 2) described the large size, scale, and extensive equipment used in this mill:

> *The ground occupied by it will be 500 feet long, by 300 feet wide, and the buildings will contain over 100,000 feet of lumber. The different operations will be conducted in separate departments, all of large size. When completed, it will contain 8 Howland's rotary batteries of 8 stamps each, and 48 Knox's patent amalgamating pans, driven by a steam engine of 60 horse power. The metal will be turned out in the shape of bars, ready for market. The weight of the machinery is about 120 tons, all of which was transported from San Francisco across the mountains, and over $25,000 will be paid by the company in freight alone. From 50 to 100 men were employed night and day in its erection. The entire cost will be about $200,000.*

At first, the Gould and Curry sent its lower value ore to custom mills like Paul's for processing, but in late 1861 and early 1862 discoveries were made at the mine that indicated even richer and more extensive deposits of ore existed than were initially anticipated. As the leading Comstock mine, the trustees of the

Gould and Curry decided to build their own mill on a grand scale. They chose a site at the junction of two canyons, about two miles northeast of Virginia City, Nevada. The site would become the largest and, at $1.25 million (including surroundings and accessories), the most expensive mill constructed on the early Comstock—and probably in the world up to this point (*Mining and Scientific Press* February 24, 1877, 120). When completed, the main mill building was reportedly the largest in Nevada Territory (Kelly [1862] 1962, 110). Lord (1883, 124) later described this gigantic mill:

> *The extraordinary mill of the Gould & Curry Company was ... the most conspicuous monument of inexperience and extravagance ever erected in a mining district. A rocky point ... at the junction of Six and Seven-Mile canons (sic), was transformed into an artificial plateau, on which was erected a building in the form of the Greek cross, 250 feet long, with arms 75 feet in length and 50 feet in width. The lower story and foundations were constructed of massive stone blocks supporting a heavy frame superstructure of finished wood, adorned with broad verandas, and painted inside and out. Smooth approaches were cut out and blasted over the hill-sides, arched sewers were built of hewn stone, and graded terraces, ascended by flights of broad stone steps, surrounded the mill. On the summit of the hill above the plateau a large reservoir was excavated in the solid rock and supplied with water from Virginia City ... A stranger, at sight of the stately edifice rising in the centre of a group of offices, shops, stables, and laborers' cottages, would naturally have supposed it the mansion of some wealthy land-owner rather than a mill built in a barren district to crush silver ore.*

The *Mining and Scientific Press,* (February 24, 1877, 120) later reported on the equipment and work practices at the mill, pointing out that it operated twenty-four hours a day in true industrial fashion:

> *The engine, of 150 horse power, a splendid piece of machinery, was built at the Pacific works, in San Francisco. There were eight batteries of five stamps each, capable of crushing 40 tons of ore per day. For generating steam to propel this engine, six furnaces, with three boilers, each 26 feet long and 42 inches in diameter, with 14-inch flues, were provided. In the various departments of this establishment, notwithstanding every labor-saving device then known in the business had been introduced, the services of 75 men were required, working in relays day and night, operations here never having been intermitted. With its terraced walls and numerous outbuildings, the place bore something of the appearance of a fortified city.*

Mining on the Comstock
This drawing illustrates the main mines, the square sets, tools, and techniques of these Nevada mines, which were especially active in the 1860s and 1870s. [Courtesy of the Bancroft Library, University of California, Berkeley.]

Another indication of the vast scale of this works was that labor costs alone for building this facility were $133,666.69, at a time when $1.25–$5 a day was the going rate of pay (Gould and Curry Silver Mining Company 1862, 9). The Gould and Curry Mine and mill and other mines and mills of the Comstock employed vast numbers of wage laborers. Soon, a large, propertyless mass of workers existed in and around Virginia City, which by 1863 had become not only the largest city in Nevada, but the second largest city in the West, almost twice the size of Sacramento, but still far behind San Francisco (*Mining and Scientific Press* August 17, 1863, 2). The city was basically a colony of San Francisco, however, as San Franciscans owned all of the main mines and mills. A working class was being created, a class that would eventually begin to organize and struggle to assert itself.

Unfortunately for Gould and Curry profits, their expensive mill was built to use an obsolete and inefficient technology; it had to be completely rebuilt the next year at a cost of almost $600,000 (Shinn 1896, 87). A key part of this new mill was a giant steam engine, the largest stationary engine ever built in San Francisco up to that point, and, as such, marked an important advance. This 300-horsepower engine, a product of the Vulcan Foundry, cost $30,000 and was described as follows:

> *The engine, at the time of our visit, had just been completed and set up, with every part in its place ... A massive bed-plate, 21 feet long and 6 feet wide forms the base of the structure. The cylinder is securely bolted to one end of this bed-plate, and is itself a fine piece of work, 30 inches in diameter and 6 feet stroke ... Some idea of the size and proportions of this engine may be formed from the fact that its main shaft weighs 7,000 pounds, the bed plate 14,000 pounds, its beam 7,500, its cylinder 4,200 and the entire engine exclusive of boilers, eighty tons. Every part of the engine has been cast, forged and finished at the Vulcan foundry, with the exception of the main shaft which has been made from a spare piston rod formerly belonging to the steamer Golden Gate. (*Mining and Scientific Press *February 27, 1864, 134)

The vast expenses of this mine and the enormous supplies and equipment it needed were paid for out of the even greater proceeds of its mine, which was, for a few years, one of the richest the world had ever seen. In 1863, the Gould and Curry even sent over twenty-four tons of its best ore—valued at $2,800 a ton—all the way to England for processing. The Gould and Curry mill processed the second-class ore, and third-class ore was sent to local custom mills (*Mining and Scientific Press* January 2, 1864, 21). Proceeds for the fiscal year ending November 30, 1863, were over $3.9 million and about $1.5 million was paid to its stockholders in dividends.

The fiscal year ending November 30, 1864, was also outstanding, with gross receipts of about $4.8 million and dividends of $1.4 million. Altogether, the Gould and Curry mined and milled 230,546 tons of ore between July 1, 1860 and November 30, 1866, producing $13.6 million in gold and silver and paying out at least $3.778 million in dividends, a vast sum for this time (Nevada 1866a, 94). This was many times the actual amount invested by the stockholders. While it was by far the richest of the early Comstock bonanzas, the Ophir, Savage, and Imperial were also substantial during this period, the three of them collectively producing almost as much as the Gould and Curry (Nevada 1866b, 23).

IMPACTS ON SAN FRANCISCO AND CALIFORNIA, 1860–1865

The new mining area opened by California's economic development and the Comstock discovery was vast in size and riches. It was an area of about 1.25 million square miles, an area with silver, gold, copper, quicksilver, and other minerals. San Francisco's *Mining and Scientific Press* (January 2, 1864, 2) expressed its excitement about the possibilities in early 1864: "The progressive development of this vast mineral region must soon build up an empire upon the Pacific, more vast, more wealthy and more powerful than any which the world has yet seen …"

The effective demand that these and the other new mines of Nevada and eastern California created was great, and generated an economic boom in San Francisco and the state. Vast quantities of lumber were cut for mine timbers and fuel. It has been said, for example, that by 1866, more board feet of timber had been used in the Gould and Curry Mine alone than was used in building the entire town of Virginia City (Nevada 1866b, 26). The Sierra Nevada mountain range served as the source of this wood; nature had stored an immense amount of energy in these trees, which were clear-cut for a distance of nearly a hundred miles around the Comstock mines, accurately nicknamed "the graveyard of the Sierra forests" (Brechin 1999, 46–47).

Food, machinery, quicksilver, draft animals, copper sulphate, salt, candles, and other supplies of all kinds, as well as human labor were other necessities that were supplied to the new mines. This demand had an immense impact on San Francisco and California. Serving the transportation needs of the Comstock alone required a tremendous, even an epic, feat of animal and human effort. By 1863, there were an estimated 3,000 teamsters using 15,000 draft animals carrying approximately 100 million pounds of freight a year to the Comstock over the Placerville Road alone. Other, less important routes also shipped great amounts of men and freight.

This river of commerce from California's cities and farms soon stimulated its own infrastructure of stations, hotels, saloons, stores, and stables along this and other routes through the central Sierras. Stage lines also ran along the Placerville road to Virginia City, carrying thousands of passengers back and forth between California and Nevada (Shinn 1896, 108–109).

The boom to the east immensely stimulated all of San Francisco's industries as well as its financial superstructure. San Francisco's foundries and machine shops played a central role as they greatly expanded under the impact of a continuous stream of large orders from the mines. By early 1864, San Francisco had twelve iron works employing twelve hundred wage laborers. They reportedly produced $3 million worth of machinery in 1863 and had a capital of $2 million (*Mining and Scientific Press* February 6, 1864, 88). By 1865, San Francisco foundries were already serving a territory bounded by Oregon and Idaho on the north, central Mexico on the south, the Sandwich Islands (Hawaii) on the west, and easterly to Colorado (*Mining and Scientific Press* May 18, 1863, 1; September 9, 1865, 150).

They had also begun to produce small locomotives by late 1859 and built increasingly larger ones year after year, until, in the summer of 1865, a heavy-class regular locomotive was completed by the Union Iron Works (*Mining and Scientific Press* May 23, 1862, 4; September 23, 1865, 182). This mechanical milestone was celebrated on August 30, 1865, when Governor Low, ex-governor Stanford, and other dignitaries enjoyed a ride, speeding at one point to sixty-six miles per hour, on the "California," the first heavy-class locomotive built in the western United States:

> *The trial trip of the splendid new locomotive, manufactured at the Union Foundry of Messrs. H. J. Booth & Co., ... on the route of the San Francisco and San Jose R.R., affords an opportunity, while noticing the excursion, to say a few words in relation to the establishment where it was fashioned. Of late years, such a degree of perfection has been arrived at on this coast, in the construction of all kinds of machinery, ponderous and otherwise, that we have not only ceased to look to the Eastern cities for our supplies, but to regard their manufactures of inferior quality, as compared with similar articles turned out from our own workshops. The extensive works of Messrs. Booth & Co. are located on First Street. The buildings cover a large space of ground, in which their own castings are made, and their own work performed in all the departments necessary to build a steam engine, a quartz mill, a water-wheel, an amalgamator, a force pump, or any and all other kinds of iron, brass or copper mechanism from the crude material, and with a compactness of form, extent of power, durability of parts, and elegance of finish, nowhere to be surpassed.*

The last, and perhaps the grandest, triumph of mechanical skill emanating from these works, is the immense locomotive, turned out a few weeks ago, and which to-day made its trial trip on the track of the San Jose Railroad. The Cylinders of this locomotive are 16 inches in diameter, with a 24 inch stroke; the driving wheels 5 feet in diameter, length of locomotive 26 1/2 feet over frame; diameter of boiler 44 inches, containing 141 two inch tubes, 11 feet in length; total weight of locomotive 30 tons. The manner of fastening the cylinders to the frames is entirely new; they being so placed that they can at any time be removed without interfering with other working parts of the machinery. The adoption of this plan is original with Messrs. Booth & Co ... The best of material has been used in its manufacture, and great care has been exercised, that its workmanship and finish should be perfect in every respect. It is no egoism for the builders to claim for it superiority over the Eastern build of locomotives; for our California mechanics rank among the best on the continent. (Mining and Scientific Press *September 2, 1865, 135)*

By 1865, Sacramento was also well on its way to becoming an industrial center. That summer and fall, the Sacramento Iron Works was building a giant steam engine for the pumping and hoisting works of the Savage Company on the Comstock. The engine itself weighed eighteen tons, and the total weight of the engine, iron bedplate, and other parts was over seventy tons. In 1865, this establishment was also doing a large amount of repair work for a mammoth new railroad then under construction, the Central Pacific (*Mining and Scientific Press* September 30, 1865, 198).

The more astute of early San Franciscans recognized the key role the foundries played in the development of California and the west. As a writer for the *Mining and Scientific Press* (May 21, 1864, 346) expressed it, "As a mining community, we are more indebted to and dependent upon the perfection of our foundries and iron-works for our material wealth, than any other branch of industrial art … we have nothing we can boast of with so much propriety and justice as the character, extent and perfection of our foundries and iron works …"

Another observer stated in 1865 that:

> *[T]the skill of our mechanics is perfecting appliances which enable us to increase our gold products from our quartz and gravel mines. The report of the Patent Office discloses this fact, the inventions, improvements in mining processes, machinery which have been made in California … are more numerous and perfect than all the previous inventions of similar character in the world; that during the last ten years, California has taken out more patents than any other State in the American Union, and especially in pumps, quartz machinery and chemical processes for extracting metals from ores, have our people been successful. (*Mining and Scientific Press August 12, 1865, 82*)

The great technological advances made by the foundries during the early and mid-1860s greatly solidified a trend already underway in 1859: the cumulative, self-sustaining, hand-in-hand advance of capital and technology. The repercussions of these advances were felt in all aspects of life and can be summed up by the word "industrialization." This radical and rapid change under capitalist conditions not only led to the conquering of time, space, and the environment, but also the commodification of everything, including human labor, and the creation of a full-scale market economy. This market economy existed side by side with key monopolies, controlled by those who owned capital for investment. The monopoly sector was always the locus of real capitalism; this is where the biggest profits and greatest exploitation have always taken place. Technological advances aided this sector, since they always created cost barriers to others on their way to closed and highly profitable areas of the economy. The monopolists were politically based; they needed the power of the state for protection, to constrain market forces and gain grants and subsidies.

These monopolists soon controlled the financial superstructure and made up the core of the new ruling class of California, organizing a regional economy centered in San Francisco. Increasingly, their favored form of organization was the corporation, divided into shares that could be bought and sold. This led to the formation, in September 1862, of the second stock exchange in the country and the first in California, the San Francisco Stock and Exchange Board.

Prior to 1862, individuals and some banks had been involved in buying and selling mining stocks, real estate, and other securities on a modest scale, but it was not well-organized (Carlson 1941, 3–5). With the discovery and early development of the Comstock, public interest in mining investments leaped, as did the possibilities for pure speculation, fraud, and deception. A formal, legal, stock exchange allowed for the purchase and sale of mining ground and stocks of all kinds on a much larger scale, increasing the speculative frenzy, while only marginally curbing fraud and deception. By early 1863, the following securities were already being sold and traded at the San Francisco Stock Exchange:

- United States Treasury Notes
- Legal Tender Notes
- Three kinds of San Francisco Bonds
- Twenty other California City and County Bonds
- San Francisco Insurance Company stock
- California Steam Navigation Company stock

- State Telegraph Company stock
- San Francisco Gas Company stock
- Sacramento Gas Company stock
- Bensley Water Company stock
- Spring Valley Water Company stock
- Some four different railroad companies' stocks
- Twenty-five mining companies' stocks from the Comstock Lode
- Fourteen other mining stocks, one of which was a copper mining company, and two of which were gold mines in Mexico

Source: *Daily Alta California* March 3, 1863, 4

Due to the need to raise capital, most of these companies had their headquarters in San Francisco and looked to the city for leadership. In the 1850s and 1860s, the state legislature passed specific incorporation laws that allowed corporations in many fields to be formed. The corporate structure then became the easiest way to collect the large sums of money needed to successfully start a business or open a mine. As the leading California mining journal of the time put it, "For the facilitating of business, the collection of assessments, and the general system of conducting the affairs of a Company—there is nothing like Incorporation" (*Mining and Scientific Press* November 29, 1862, 4).

Then in 1863–1864, came a frenzy of mining speculation. Thousands of mining companies were formed in 1863 alone, sometimes offering hundreds of thousands of dollars worth of new mining stock for sale in a single month. Thousands of San Franciscans from the rich to the poor engaged in the speculation, mainly in silver mines, many of them completely worthless. In August 1863, the *Daily Alta California* reported in detail about the city's stock exchange, silver mines, and the interconnections of capital accumulation, speculation, and mining development:

> *This city is unquestionably the greatest market in the world for the sale of shares in silver mines. The*

shares of one thousand mines are now in this market, and the sales have not been less than $50,000 in cash value on any one day during the last three months and have often risen to $300,000, averaging probably $100,000 ...

About two hundred and fifty companies are organizing monthly with a joint nominal capital of $100,000,000. The total number of silver mining companies incorporated in this city is about 1,600 with an aggregate nominal capital of about $600,000,000. Nine-tenths of these companies, probably a much larger proportion, have no claim that will pay, and their capital exists only on paper ...

Silver mining stock is now preferred as an investment for many over everything else. Those who have invested freely in it are the most prosperous men in California ... [W]ithin four years since the Comstock Lode was discovered the cash value of silver mining stock owned in California has risen from nothing to $50,000,000. This is a moderate estimate of the actual cash value of a permanent property which was obtained at an original cost of perhaps $3,000,000, leaving a profit of $47,000,000 to be divided among perhaps 5,000 persons who own shares in the rich mines ...

The mining regions of the coast are so numerous now that it is almost impossible to remember them ... all these regions consider San Francisco as the spot to which they are to look for help. Here alone stock can be sold, money obtained for starting business, and machinery purchased. (Daily Alta California August 3, 1863)

171

This speculative boom lasted less than a year more, fueled by the very real bonanza of several Comstock mines, led by the Gould and Curry, the stock of which rose to a value of over $5,000 a foot, or $6 million for this one mine alone (Carlson 1941, 18). Total stock value reached $81 million in May 1864. But then a break in the market occurred. The sudden heavy selling of Gould and Curry stock by some of its richest stockholders caused this decline. These insiders, who had connections to the company's trustees or officers, had been warned that the mine's rich ore had begun to play out. In the unregulated environment of the time, this confidential information could be used to speculate, enabling insiders to reap immense personal profits. This often had disastrous results for the larger system. Stock dumping caused a panic, bringing much of the market down with the Gould and Curry. In only ten days, there was a decline of $60 million in stock values, and hundreds of people who had considered themselves rich were suddenly bankrupt (J. Hittell 1878, 389). Most of the rich and well-connected emerged with their fortunes intact, having sold out in time.

Possession of privileged information was connected to the fact that small cliques often held enough shares to control a given company, and they increasingly came to wield immense economic and political power. There was no more important clique than those associated with William C. Ralston and the newly formed Bank of California. The formation of this bank in 1864 and the alliance it soon formed with the Central Pacific Railroad began a new era in California history, which would bring decades of domination by the "Pacific Coast Ring."

PART THREE

CAPITALIST CALIFORNIA, 1860–1901

The triumph of capitalism resulted in a new capitalist ruling class that consolidated itself as the "Pacific Coast Ring" during the 1860s and early 1870s. The Bank of California and the Central Pacific/Southern Pacific Railroad combine were the two dominant forces within this ruling class. Their control was periodically challenged by the propertyless wage workers that their system created. The two biggest upsurges of worker rebellion occurred in 1894 with a railroad strike and, in 1901, with a general strike on the San Francisco waterfront.

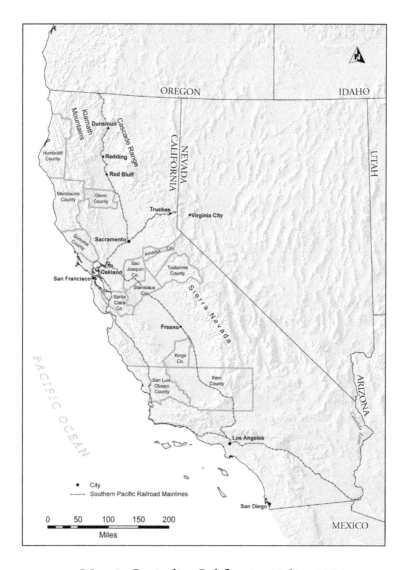

Map 3: Capitalist California, 1860s–1901

5

THE FORMATION OF A NEW RULING CLASS— THE "PACIFIC COAST RING," 1864–1870

In the late 1850s and early 1860s, the economic landscape of California was characterized by a number of corporations with relatively large amounts of capital (from $750,000 to $3 million), each of which largely monopolized their own economic sector. Examples included the California Steam Navigation Company, San Francisco Gas Company, Sacramento Valley Railroad Company, San Francisco City Water Works, New Almaden Mine, California State Telegraph Company, Pacific Insurance Company, and the San Francisco and San Jose Railroad. A large competitive sector of the economy was also growing, characterized by smaller firms, narrower focus, and discipline by the market, such as was typical of the foundry industry, which had fourteen establishments in San Francisco in 1860, none with a capitalization over a few hundred thousand dollars (US Census Bureau 1865, 29).

Into this environment came the two corporations that were to largely dominate the commanding heights of the political economy for the next several decades. These were the Bank of California and the Central/Southern Pacific Railroad.

RALSTON AND THE FORMATION
OF THE "BANK CROWD"

Banker William C. Ralston was an early director of many of the large monopoly corporations mentioned above. In 1860, he also emerged as the treasurer of both the Ophir and the Gould and Curry Mines. By 1864, he was treasurer of most of the important Comstock mines and also a leader of the San Francisco Chamber of Commerce.

Ralston's career had started in the shipping industry, managing steamship lines, and, through his close ties to C. K. Garrison, he had been associated with the interests of New York transportation tycoon and multimillionaire Cornelius Vanderbilt.

Garrison represented Vanderbilt on the West Coast and was also elected mayor of San Francisco in 1853 (Lavender 1975, 64). Ralston's Vanderbilt connection was apparently very strong; at one point he was reportedly in love with and planning to marry Vanderbilt's great-granddaughter, but she died before the relationship could fully develop (Tilton 1935, 183; Lavender 1975, 60–70).

Like Vanderbilt and other leading capitalist businessmen, Ralston could be calculating and duplicitous. In a letter to his colleague William Sharon, he suggested this approach to a potential business rival: "Remember he owns too much ... for us to make an enemy of him. Give him sugar and molasses at present, but when our time comes give him vinegar of the sharpest kind" (Ostrander 1966, 48).

On January 1, 1856, Ralston joined with Vanderbilt's representative Garrison and other former steamboat men in forming a banking partnership, Garrison, Morgan, Fretz and Ralston, a firm which very shortly became Fretz & Ralston (Kelly 1862, 12–15; Cross 1927, I:215). Then in mid-1861, Ralston joined with merchant Joseph Donohoe and others to form a new and bigger bank, Donohoe, Ralston and Company. This firm soon became the leading bank in the state, handling much of the immense output of the Comstock, and loaning money to the key mines. But the partners began to disagree about future plans, opening the way for Ralston to withdraw and form a new organization (Cross 1927, I:219).

The impact of the Comstock and the rapid industrial development of San Francisco was also opening up new possibilities. Earlier banks had been partnerships that mainly made small loans, sold exchanges, exported gold, and discounted notes. But by 1862, in the wake of Comstock developments, California's financial affairs had reached the point where larger blocks of capital were required. Therefore, in 1862 the state legislature revised California banking laws to allow for the incorporation of banks and joint stock companies (Kelly 1862, 18–19). During these years, Ralston began to accumulate both capital and connections with others who also had capital. In 1863, he helped form the Pacific Insurance Company. Through his varied connections, he built up a subscription list of those who would help him found a new bank, the Bank of California, and he launched it in June 1864. It was Ralston who was mainly responsible for the organization of this bank whose "original stockholders and directors embraced the most prominent and outstanding capitalists of the community" (Cross 1927, I:260).

DIRECTORS AND OWNERS OF THE BANK OF CALIFORNIA, 1864

The group of directors and owners who formed the new Bank of California in 1864 had long been leading capitalists and power brokers.

DARIUS OGDEN MILLS, PRESIDENT

—A well-known Sacramento banker and wealthy owner of a number of properties, Mills had been in California banking since 1849. He was ever the prudent, careful, conservative banker, balancing Ralston's frequent enthusiasms. In 1864, he was a director of the San Francisco and San Jose Railroad, later he was an owner and trustee of the Pacific Rolling Mill Company.

WILLIAM C. RALSTON, CASHIER

—With wide connections, both to the Comstock owners and key California corporations, he was the central organizer of the bank. He was a director of the Pacific Insurance Company, California Steam Navigation Company, California State Telegraph Company, and the Sacramento Valley Railroad, as well as the treasurer of key Comstock mines. He had been active in the Vigilance Committee in 1856 and in Union activities during the Civil War. One of his central goals was always to find places and situations where profitable new industries or businesses could be launched.

LOUIS MCLANE

—Manager of Wells Fargo and Company on the West Coast and head of the Pioneer Stage Company, he was also a trustee of the California Steam Navigation Company and a director of the Pacific Insurance Company. He was also an owner and incorporator of the California Telegraph Company and the San Francisco Gas Company. His brother Charles was president of the Pacific Mail Steamship Company.

J. B. THOMAS

—A commission merchant and a director of both the Pacific Insurance Company and the San Francisco City Water Works.

WILLIAM NORRIS, SECRETARY

—Later, he was a trustee of the California Steam Navigation Company.

JOHN O. EARL

—Wealthy merchant and mine operator, president of the Gould and Curry Silver Mining Company, and a director of the Pacific

Insurance Company. He was active in the Vigilance Committee of San Francisco in 1856.

THOMAS BELL

—A commission merchant and capitalist, he was one of the key owners of the Gould and Curry Mine and the New Almaden quicksilver mine in Santa Clara County. Later an owner of California mines in Bodie (Mono County, quartz gold) and North Bloomfield (Nevada County, hydraulic gold).

HERMAN MICHELS

—Capitalist and consul for the German state of Saxony, he was also a director of the Pacific Insurance Company.

A. J. POPE

—Partner in Pope & Talbot, lumber dealers.

O. F. GIFFIN

—Importer (Giffin & Brother) and president of the Empire Milling and Mining Company.

JAMES WHITNEY JR

—President of the California Steam Navigation Company and a director of the Pacific Insurance Company.

Sources: Hunter 1950, 27; Norris 1887; Lavender 1975, 179, 216, 226, 290; Langley 1863, xvii; Phelps 1881, 45

The stockholders of the Bank of California when it was established in mid-1864 included the above eleven men as well as the following businessmen:

MOSES ELLIS

—Importer, Moses Ellis & Company, San Francisco.

R. M. JESSUP

—A trustee of the California Steam Navigation Company, he was a leader of the San Francisco Chamber of Commerce and was an executive committee member of the Vigilance Committee of San Francisco in 1856.

WILLIAM E. BARRON

—A San Francisco commission merchant, the owner of Barron & Company. With his brother Edward, he was also an owner of various Comstock mines and the New Almaden quicksilver mine. When he died in 1871, his estate was valued at $5 million.

H. F. TESCHEMACHER

—A former mayor of San Francisco, he was a director of the Pacific Insurance Company as well as the California Mutual Marine Insurance Company.

WILLIAM ALVORD

—Owner of the mercantile firm Alvord & Company, San Francisco, he was also a director of the Pacific Insurance Company. He later became a trustee and president of the Pacific Rolling Mill and mayor of San Francisco. He became president of the Bank of California in 1878.

A. T. LAWTON

—Merchant.

A. B. MCCREERY

—Dry goods merchant.

R. S. FRETZ

—Former partner with Ralston in the firm Fretz & Ralston.

GEORGE H. HOWARD

—A large landowner, Howard was also president of the Central Wharf Company of San Francisco, a director of the Pacific Insurance Company and of the California Mutual Marine Insurance Company.

SAMUEL KNIGHT

—Superintendent, Wells Fargo & Company Express (banking and express).

J.C. WILMERDING

—Wells Fargo & Company
   Sources: Norris 1887; J. Hittell 1883, 45; Lavender 1975, 226, 290; Langley 1859B; 1863, xvii; J. Hittell 1882, 143
   Within a few years, these additional central figures joined in the affairs of the Bank of California:

ALVINZA HAYWARD

—A mine owner and trustee of the California Steam Navigation Company.

LLOYD TEVIS

—A lawyer, large stockholder of the California Steam Navigation Company, and a director of the Pacific Insurance Company, Tevis later headed the Wells Fargo Bank.

THOMAS SUNDERLAND

—Comstock mine owner.

SAMUEL BUTTERWORTH

—New Almaden quicksilver mine superintendent and owner, he was also a director of California Mutual Life Insurance Company.

HORACE W. CARPENTIER

—Carpentier largely controlled the Oakland waterfront and was president of the California State Telegraph Company.

Sources: Bancroft 1865, 88; Norris 1887; Lavender 1975, 179, 220–221, 226; Phelps 1881, 28–29; Langley 1863, xvii Lyman 1937:86

The formation of the Bank of California was a milestone in the financial history of capitalism in California and represented the initial consolidation of a new ruling class in the state. It could boast paid-up capital of two-million dollars, a vast sum for the time (only two of New York's fifty-five banks exceeded this figure), two of the state's best-known financiers at its head, and a list of trustees and stockholders which included many of the state's key business and industrial leaders (Wilson 1964, 21). Its trustees and major investors were from several of the largest corporations, especially the Pacific Insurance Company and California Steam Navigation Company, as well as the key Comstock mines. From its founding, it held the commanding position in not only financial affairs, but also social and political life. One writer went so far as to say that the bank was "supreme in the Pacific West in politics, in social matters and in business" (Lyman 1937, 70). The great mercantile and business establishments of the state soon saw it as the key power, the center of "Wall Street West." Its influence was indeed felt throughout the West. As a leading business journal commented:

> *The Bank of California … [o]rganized for general banking purposes from the outset, its capital contributed by men of wealth, its business relations enlarged and comprehensive, and its adaptability to commercial requirements are fully equal to that of first-class Banking institutions in any part of the world … [I]t introduces a new feature into our financial affairs. (*Mercantile Gazette and Prices Current *June 22, 1864)*

The bank soon focused on controlling Comstock mines during the 1864 to the early 1870s (Mills 1881, 85). To manage its Comstock affairs, Ralston organized the Union Mine and Milling Company and appointed William Sharon to be agent in charge of this firm and the bank's activities in Virginia City generally. A director of the Pacific Insurance Company, Sharon was a close friend of John D. Fry, Ralston's father-in-law, and Ralston viewed him as a reliable ally (Ralston n.d.). Under the direction of Ralston and Mills, Sharon soon became one of the leading Nevada financiers, often loaning money to the local mine and mill owners, who typically used their mines and mills as collateral.

The bank owners used dispossession to take over the property of other capitalists. This was achieved by controlling proxies, directly owning stock, and foreclosing on loans when the mine and mill owners failed to meet their obligations. In this way, Sharon, Ralston, and the Bank of California rapidly became the owners of nearly all the mines and mills on the Comstock, as well as the water system and railroad (T. Hittell 1898, 3: 552–553). This gave the bank, its directors, and its owners vast opportunities for both stock speculation and profit from these mines.

Ralston and his bank were also centrally involved in the key economic developments of San Francisco during the second half of the 1860s. One example was the Mission Woolen Mills, which was taken over by the Bank of California in 1865 after it had gained control of its rival, the Pacific Woolen Mills. Ralston's father in law, John D. Fry, was then installed as its president (Lavender 1975, 197).

Ralston and his "bank ring," as it was soon called, gained a reputation for both power and ruthlessness. As the banker John Parrott wrote in a letter to a fellow banker in mid-1867:

> *Ralston is a man of wonderful resources, people look upon him as a King. He has a ring formed of very strong people ... such as the Barrons, Bell, Butterworth, Hayward, Sunderland, Tevis, and their stripe, who are going in for a new gas company or depress the stock of the old one until they buy upon their own terms*

> *and get the control … They stop at nothing these days.*
> *(quoted in Lavender 1975, 206)*

For a time they were able to make the most of their opportunities. Meanwhile another capitalist group was forming, one which would eventually consolidate an even vaster power.

THE COMING OF THE RAILROAD

At the same time that Ralston was organizing the power of the developing capitalist class of San Francisco, a small group of middling Sacramento merchants with strong ties to the emerging Republican Party was considering grand plans for a transcontinental railroad. Despite the extensive and rapid economic development that had taken place in the state, California was still very remote from the rest of the United States. The sharp conflict over the expansion of slavery had blocked serious consideration of a national railroad connecting east and west. Leaders of the slave South were completely against and blocked for a time anything that would stimulate the settlement of the territories by the "free soil" men and women of the North. The Civil War and the withdrawal of Southern representatives from Congress immediately changed the dynamics of power nationally. The 1861 election of Leland Stanford as the first Republican governor of California did the same for the state.

Stanford had been an early supporter of Abraham Lincoln and had had extensive discussions for "many weeks" with the president-elect soon after his 1860 election, becoming a trusted adviser (Phelps 1881, 185–187). At the same time, Ralston was the head of a pro-Union committee that helped elect Stanford governor (Lavender 1975, 153–154). By the time of his discussions with Lincoln, Stanford was part of a group of four "associates," who were considering a plan for a transcontinental railroad put forth by an obscure engineer named Theodore Judah. Judah had done a significant amount of early development work for the railroad, including locating the best route through the biggest obstacle, the mountain range known as the Sierra Nevada. The "associates" group, consisting of Stanford, Collis

P. Huntington, Charles Crocker, and Mark Hopkins, had had their initial meeting with Judah in the fall of 1860.

Judah's original goal had been to get San Francisco capitalists to supply the money to build the line he envisioned, but they were deaf to his appeals. It was mid-1860 and they were instead busy investing in silver mines and other enterprises considered more secure than a railroad at the time being blocked by southern leaders and that also required crossing the mighty Sierra Nevada.

Additionally, San Francisco capitalists had investments in transportation enterprises, such as the California Steam Navigation Company, Pacific Mail Steamship Company, and Wells Fargo, all companies likely to be seriously harmed by the development of a transcontinental railroad (Bean 1973, 214). D. O. Mills later said, for example, that he doubted the railroad would be successful, and he felt that the associates' financial credit was "very poor" (Galloway 1950, 99). Lloyd Tevis stated he did not want to be involved at first, since he felt the project was tenuous and "liable to great embarrassment" (Galloway 1950, 98).

Leland Stanford (1824–1893)
Governor, president of both the Central Pacific and Southern Pacific railroads, and later a US Senator; he was a central figure of the California ruling class for several decades. [Courtesy of the Bancroft Library, University of California, Berkeley.]

Once the Civil War was underway, however, it appeared more likely that Congress would subsidize the project and, in late June of 1861, the Central Pacific Railroad was formally incorporated with soon-to-be Governor Stanford as president, Huntington as vice president, Hopkins as treasurer, and Crocker and Judah as additional directors. The railroad was built on credit and government subsidies, and the amount of money actually paid in to subscribe to company stock by these five and a few other individuals was pathetically small. The new company started out with only $15,800. The total combined personal assets of the four associates were only $108,987, a significant sum for the time, but very small compared to the wealth of many San Franciscans or the immense return the associates eventually received (Bean 1973, 212; Russell 1912, 118).

Once the incorporation was complete, Judah traveled to Washington, DC With the help of California's congressional delegation, at least two of whom, Aaron Sargent and early investor Cornelius Cole, were Republican friends and allies of the "associates," Judah successfully made the case to Congress for immense federal subsidies and loans for what was a private railroad project (Cole 1908, 148–149). The public would take much of the risk and pay immense sums up front, but the vast benefits would be privately appropriated, largely into the hands of only four men. At the same time, Stanford, operating as both governor of the state and president of the Central Pacific, used all his influence to get state and county subsidies for the railroad.

The 1862 and 1864 acts of Congress and state and local subsidies conferred huge benefits on the Central Pacific Railroad and its main owners. These included generous federal loans at a given rate per mile (average $35,000 per mile) depending on various factors, such as the difficulty of the terrain, which were secured initially by a first mortgage on railroad property, later changed to a second mortgage, allowing the railroad owners to get additional loans more easily. In addition, they received gifts of millions of acres of public land in alternating checkerboarded sections on either side of the right of way. The state of California gave a direct state gift of $500,000 for the completion of the first fifty miles of railroad, although this was later repealed and substituted with a measure to pay $2.1 million in interest on bonds. Three counties along the route also provided a $1.15 million in bond subsidies (J. Hittell 1882, 164; Bean 1973, 213).

The actual construction of the railroad began in January–February 1863 in Sacramento. At first, costs were heavy and cash short. The possibilities for alternative funding were limited for a time because opposition existed from the transportation corporations controlled by Ralston and other San Francisco capitalists, who correctly saw that the railroad could seriously damage their interests. But the associates, who increasingly saw themselves as the "Big Four," succeeded in fraudulently asserting that the Sierra Nevada began only seven miles east of Sacramento (twenty-five miles is closer to correct) in order to begin collecting larger federal government subsidies illegally.

People joked that the Central Pacific was the strongest corporation in the world, since it was able to move the Sierra Nevada Mountains nearly twenty miles closer to Sacramento (Russell 1912, 122). When the Big Four set up a dummy entity, Charles Crocker and Company, to handle all construction, Judah had had enough of the manipulations of his four associates, breaking with them completely. He accepted $100,000 for his interest in the Central Pacific and left for New York with options to buy out each of the four associates for the same amount if he could convince New York capitalists to invest in the enterprise. The associates were discouraged and willing to quit, but Judah caught yellow fever in Panama and died in New York on November 2, 1864.

The possibility of a new group of capitalists taking over from the four associates died with Judah. Instead, Stanford, Huntington, Crocker, and Hopkins continued in control, and things soon began to improve. With federal, state, and county subsidies rolling in, the cash shortage was soon overcome. Construction contracts granted to a monopoly dummy corporation without competitive bidding also meant large profits. With construction booming, a labor shortage became the major problem.

European American workers wanted fair wages and decent working conditions; but the Big Four knew they could make vast profits on this gigantic project with lower wages and worse conditions. So in 1865, and in line with their belief that all racial and ethnic groups were equally exploitable under capitalism, they tried Chinese laborers as an experiment.

The Chinese worked so hard and at such efficiency that the Big Four started recruiting them by the thousands, laying off their Irish and other ethnic laborers. At the peak of construction in 1866–1869, they employed over ten thousand Chinese workers, many brought all the way from China. They were paid low wages, only thirty dollars a month for an over-twelve-hour day, and many were killed during the epic work of blasting, digging, and laying a railroad through the vast Sierra Nevada range. The four Central Pacific owners pocketed an estimated $5.5 million in only three years by hiring the Chinese (Saxton 1971, 63).

Once through the mountains, and with another railroad, the Union Pacific, building westward, a frantic race between the two companies developed during 1869. Each one was trying to lay as much track and reap as many subsidies and as much profit as possible. They met at Promontory Point, Utah, in May 1869, and steel rails finally linked the nation.

At a crucial point in the early development of the railroad, William C. Ralston, seeing that the railroad project was viable and would be successful, overcame his earlier reluctance and decided to back the Big Four, arranging for a $100,000 loan from the Pacific Insurance Company for Stanford (Lyman 1937, 11). An alliance of sorts developed between the Bank of California and the railroad during the final few years of the Central Pacific's epic of construction. The Big Four depended heavily on Ralston and the Bank of California for loans and Ralston also brokered several of their purchases of other railroads. The Central Pacific's fluctuating account at the Bank of California at times reached over $1 million, and personal loans of over $100,000 each were made to both Stanford and Huntington (Lavender 1975, 278).

As the Big Four pushed construction eastward as rapidly as possible during 1869, loans from the bank to the railroad reached $3 million, a huge sum for the time (Cross 1927 Vol. I, 284). One author concluded, "Ralston was more efficient in his service to Stanford and the others than any other man outside the corporation" (Lyman 1937, 324n5).

A few years later, in return for his great services to their railroad enterprise, the Big Four offered to name a town site after Ralston on their new line through the San Joaquin Valley. When he refused, in an ironic twist, they named the town "Modesto," after Ralston's apparent modesty (Lavender 1975, 275–276). It is more likely that Ralston refused the honor because he wanted something more tangible from the associates than the mere naming of a town. He may have preferred, for example, that the Big Four purchase their railroad cars from the Kimball Car Factory that Ralston was helping to establish in San Francisco. The Big Four refused to do this, however, since they had built their own "car shops" factory in Sacramento (Lyman 1937, 84).

AN EMERGING TRANSPORTATION MONOPOLY

Once their railroad was well on its way to completion, the Big Four took steps to create a statewide transportation monopoly, using the great wealth garnered from subsidies, fraud, and the exploitation of their Chinese American workforce. First, in 1868, they seized strategic control of the best terminus on the east side of San Francisco Bay by creating and controlling the Oakland Waterfront Company with Horace W. Carpentier. Carpentier dominated early Oakland and was connected with Ralston both through the California State Telegraph Company and as an owner of the Bank of California. Through Stanford's political influence at the state level, they also were able to purchase, at nominal prices, sixty acres of waterfront land in San Francisco, although their attempt to gain an even larger part of the waterfront failed due to public outcry (Bean 1973, 221).

Next, the Central Pacific owners, together with lawyer Lloyd Tevis, formed the Pacific Express Company to threaten the east–west express business of Wells Fargo. The owners of Wells Fargo knew they stood little chance of competing head-to-head with the railroad, so they gave one-third of their stock to the Big Four and associates to absorb Pacific Express.

Wells Fargo's stock price then dropped, and Tevis and his partner James Ben Ali Haggin, together with D. O. Mills, H. D. Bacon, Stanford, Huntington, and Crocker, purchased additional shares, giving them a controlling interest in this important corporation. Then, in 1870, Tevis, Stanford, Huntington, and Mills became members of the Wells Fargo board of directors (Loomis 1968, 199, 204, 215; Russell 1912, 150–151; Hungerford 1949, 114–116). Tevis was thus closely connected to and an ally of both the Bank of California and the Big Four during this period. By 1869–1870, he was president of the Southern Pacific Railroad, one of the Big Four's new railroad enterprises, and in 1872, he began a long tenure as president of the newly railroad-allied Wells Fargo (Dumas 1936, 384–385; Phelps 1881, 28–29).

In 1869, the owners of the Central Pacific purchased one of its largest competitors, the California Steam Navigation Company. The latter company had long been a leading California corporation, but since its steamers were slower and more costly to operate than the railroad, its owners recognized that they were doomed in the head-to-head competition with the railroad, and so sold out.

The Big Four dealt with a final competitor, the Pacific Mail Steamship Company, which had a monopoly on ocean transportation to and from California, initially through a series of rate-fixing agreements to keep prices high, then in open competition, and finally through outright control of Pacific Mail (Bean 1973, 222; Decker 1978, 161).

With Ralston's help as a broker, the Big Four then purchased and extended the San Francisco and San Jose Railroad, renaming it the

Southern Pacific (Lavender 1975, 275). They also founded the San Joaquin Valley Railroad and the California and Oregon Railroad, building south and north, obtaining similar subsidies from federal, state, and local governments. By 1870, over two million dollars had already been invested in these two new railroad companies, both controlled by the Big Four. Their plan for encircling the state with steel rails and creating a vast transportation monopoly was well underway (Poor 1870, 402–403; J. Hittell 1882, 166–168). The pioneer Sacramento Valley Railroad and newer Western Pacific Railroad were also purchased, making the Big Four overwhelmingly dominant in California transportation (*Sacramento Daily Union* January 1, 1870, 3).

Not content with a horizontal monopoly in transportation, the Big Four began to develop a vertical one as well, building their car shops factory in Sacramento beginning in November 1863. This facility remained relatively small until 1868–1869 when it was greatly expanded by adding a roundhouse, car shop, wood finishing mill, and machine, paint, blacksmith, and boiler shops (ERM-West 1991, 2.2—2.3).

By 1869, the Sacramento Car Shops already had one of the largest industrial plants west of the Rocky Mountains. Already the political capital of California, this facility helped make Sacramento a main industrial center as well. Individual members of the Big Four also invested in and directed companies that produced the industrial goods that they required, such as the Pacific Rolling Mills for rails and other iron products.

By 1869–1870, less than a decade after the Big Four had been worth only an average of $25,000 each, they were all multimillionaires and the richest men in the West. Political influence, exploitation of workers, corruption, and public subsidies and loans were the real key to their wealth. Their railroad was, in the words of one historian, "a monstrous triumph of greed, fraud and corruption," (Russell 1912, 127). In 1870, they already owned nearly all the Central Pacific Railroad stock with a paid-in value of over $40 million; they held nine million acres of land with an estimated value of $50 million; they had received a loan of $24 million of national bonds and over $3 million in subsidies from state and local governments (J. Hittell 1882, 169; Poor 1870, 425; *Sacramento Daily Union* July 4, 1870, 1).

The Big Four also controlled several other already giant railroad corporations, as well as steamship lines. They were thus in a strategic position to totally dominate California's transportation system and, through their unregulated rate-setting power, the fate of nearly every farmer, merchant, manufacturer, and miner in the state. They used their monopoly to vastly enrich themselves and their friends and allies by setting freight rates according to the highest charge that the traffic would bear without bankrupting the shipper.

The public had largely paid for the railroad, but the Big Four owned it, soon establishing a vast network of corruption to prevent any serious rate (or other) regulation, let alone public ownership and control. Put simply, they set up a multi-state political machine to hand out large bribes to everyone necessary to assure control at all levels of society, from the newspapers to the judges to local, state, and national politicians (Russell 1912, 154–155; Ostrander 1966, 75–76, 82, 87–88). This allowed them, as will be discussed below, to become even wealthier and more politically powerful.

The completion of the transcontinental railroad had powerful effects in California. At the most general level, it spread and intensified capitalist development in the state. By connecting California with the East, it allowed the easy import of both workers and goods. This undermined a number of price-sensitive competitive California industries. Boot and shoe manufacturing was one example, an industry where labor costs were very important and for which California's relatively high wages were a major disadvantage. This was a key factor in some worker resistance and capital-labor conflict to be discussed in later chapters.

OTHER LARGE INDUSTRIES AND FIRMS, MID– AND LATE 1860S

In the wake of the capital conglomerations created by the events of the mid- and late 1860s and the demand created by the rise of the railroad and continued development of the Comstock, new and very large industrial enterprises were created or expanded during the last half of the 1860s. These corporations were mainly based in San Francisco but also in other California cities. In 1866, for example, Bank of California people, including D. O. Mills, William Alvord, and Alvinza Hayward, created the Pacific Rolling Mills (Pacific Rolling Mill Company 1866). Ralston was also an early director of this company. The value of its capital was initially listed at $1 million.

The goal of the new corporation was to manufacture railroad and merchant iron, taking advantage especially of the ongoing railroad boom (Langley 1867, xvi). Within a few years, Leland Stanford had joined Mills, Alvord, banker John Parrott, and others as the largest and dominant stockholders, making Pacific Rolling Mills, in effect, a joint venture of the bank and the CPRR (Judson Pacific-Murphy Corporation 1946).

Another large industrial corporation dominated by the Bank of California was the San Francisco and Pacific Sugar Company, capitalized at $800,000 and having as trustees Ralston and Nicholas Luning, who had joined the bank's board of directors in 1866 (Langley 1867, viii). This enterprise had been near bankruptcy when rescued and reorganized by Ralston. The Bank of California also controlled both of the main San Francisco woolen mills during the second half of the 1860s (Lavender 1975, 197).

In the spring of 1868, another heavy industrial enterprise was established in San Francisco. This was the Risdon Iron and Locomotive Works incorporated April 3, 1868, with $1 million worth of capital stock (Langley 1869, 50). Its first board of trustees included John Risdon, Lloyd Tevis, Charles McLane, and Samuel Butterworth, thus also bringing together men associated with both the bank and the railroad (California 1868).

Iron foundries were the key industry spreading capitalist industrialization. By 1867, San Francisco had no less than twenty-two foundries; twenty-seven additional such facilities are listed as existing in other California and Nevada cities, including two each in Sacramento,

Grass Valley, and Sutter Creek, California, and Gold Hill, Nevada (Langley 1867, 102, 460, 538). Their continuing central role in the development of capitalist industrialism was noted in 1868, "There is no other single branch of manufacturing in California in which even one-half as much labor and capital is employed as in the several departments of iron working …" (Conise 1868, 610). A leading industrial press of the time also pointed out that iron manufacturing and iron working were at the center of all industrial pursuits, "Without it, we could conduct neither mining, mercantile or manufacturing interests" *(Mining and Scientific Press* March 16, 1867, 168).

By 1866, sugar, iron castings, clothing, tobacco products, and furniture were the leading California-manufactured products; these five amounting to well over one-half of the total value of such products statewide (Hittell Scraps n.d., 1:439). While mining was still the most important economic interest of California, it was declining, while manufacturing and agriculture were both growing very rapidly (Appleton and Company 1870, 84). During the final years of the 1860s, both manufacturing and agriculture overtook mining as the chief economic activity of California. Even if Nevada's considerable output of silver, gold, and other metals is included (about $15 million a year), agriculture and manufacturing both well exceeded mining by 1869.

EARLY CALIFORNIA AGRICULTURE

During the 1860s, industrialized commercial agriculture, using machinery to plant and harvest on a large scale, also developed very rapidly. By the end of the decade, it had achieved second place in value of total production behind manufacturing, but ahead of mining. At the beginning of the decade, raising livestock was still by far the dominant agricultural activity, and California had over one million cattle and almost as many sheep. These animals ranged over a vast area in the central and southern parts of the state. Then came the great flood of the winter of 1861–1862, followed by a serious drought in 1862–1865. These two acts of nature substantially destroyed the open-range cattle industry and seriously affected the sheep industry, opening political and economic space for a new agriculture. In place of livestock, there grew a diversified agricultural economy with wheat farming in the lead. The world market for the dry and hard wheat produced under California conditions was substantial, and rich new lands were soon being opened up in the San Joaquin Valley. This agricultural revolution took place rapidly during the second half of the 1860s, and by 1868 wheat alone had already almost equaled gold in value of annual production. As the *Daily Alta California* (January 4, 1869, 2) reported:

> *The farmers of California have never had a more profitable year than 1868. The area sown and the average yield to the acre were larger than ever before; and the prices were very high … The total amount of the wheat crop of 1868 has been estimated at 20,000,000 bushels, worth, at the current rate, about $21,000,000—nearly as much as the gold produced in the State … The products of the agriculture of this State are worth at least 60 percent more than the yield of our mines.*

> *The most noticeable event in the farming of California in 1868 was the cultivation of a large area of land in the San Joaquin Valley previously regarded as valueless. It was offered for sale for years at $1.25 per acre in greenbacks, and now a large part of it is in demand at $20 in gold. In 1866 Stanislaus County was the seventeenth wheat county in the State, having produced only 150,000 bushels, and in 1868 it was first, producing 2,300,000 bushels … instead of being poor land, as was supposed, it is, all things considered, the best wheat land in the State.*

The main agricultural commodities were wheat and flour, of which exports alone jumped from $1.55 million in 1865 to an average of $11.6 million for the years 1867–1869 (*Daily Alta California* January 5, 1869; California Immigrant Union 1870, 21). Bancroft estimated California wheat production at 100,000 tons in 1861, increasing to 250,000 tons in 1867 (Bancroft 1890, 7:120). This vast increase in production and exports during the second half of the 1860s marked the rapid spread of industrial techniques to agriculture, helping to commercialize and capitalize the agriculture of the Central Valley and Coastal Plains. The arrival of the railroad promoted and intensified this trend. Thus, the new California agriculture was industrialized agriculture, characterized by the extensive use of labor-saving machinery and modern science. As the *Daily Alta California* (March 16, 1868, 2) explained,

> *The plains of San Joaquin County have ... borne more profitable wheat crops for the past two years than any other large district in the State ... The grain farms are large, and are prepared with gang-ploughs, six abreast, drawn by six horses—managed by one driver. A sower is attached to the ploughs, so that one man can, in good weather, plough and sow nine acres. The soil is sandy, so that it is easily broken up; and it can be worked in wet seasons, when farmers in clay districts have to lie idle. The grain is harvested with a header, which is driven by one man, and cuts a swath fifteen feet wide. The header throws the grain into attendant wagons, which carry it to the thresher, which is driven by steam.*

Agricultural industrialization was one of the keys to California's overall development, since an adequate local food supply allowed massive urbanization. A relatively small rural population could produce enough food for the entire California population and large exports as well, allowing California to become one of the ten most urbanized states in the United States by 1870. California, almost uniquely for the time, had great agricultural production without a large agricultural population.

During the 1860s and 1870s, Native Americans and Californios continued to be dispossessed of their land through squatterism, racialization, and mass murder of the Indians, and the exercise of the military and other powers of the federal government. It was redistributed to land speculators, railroad owners, the State of California, squatters and homesteaders, and those direct purchasers who had enough money to buy a farm. Relatively little was actually homesteaded; rather more typical was the monopolization of land. The giant Miller-Lux empire was a prime example. It began in the mid-1860s, eventually accumulating over one million acres of land through fraud, purchase, control of water (forcing others to sell), and bribes to county assessors to keep its taxes low (McWilliams 1949, 97–98). Miller and Lux also developed a close relationship with the railroad to get rebates on carload and trainload lots (Pomeroy 1965, 95).

The core agricultural tradition of California was thus rapidly established. It consisted of scientific, industrial agriculture on large farms, combined with oppressive rural social and agricultural labor systems, similar to Spanish haciendas and Southern plantations, with Indians, Chinese, and later Mexicans mainly playing the role of the sharecroppers and peons. This agricultural tradition soon became dominant in the coastal plains and great Central Valley, which were the key agricultural regions of California.

There was a second and less powerful agricultural tradition in California, one that was also developing during the decade of the 1860s. This was the small-scale family farm, more self-sufficient and oriented toward production for use as well as the market. Homesteading often established these farms, which tended to be located in the more isolated mountains and small valleys surrounding the great Central Valley. In these more marginal areas, worse climatic conditions, steeper terrain, poorer soils, and slower and less efficient transportation systems resulted in a greater variety of crops and much more production for local use. This resembled more closely the relative self-sufficiency of the northern and midwestern sections of the United States.

The exceptional variety of microenvironments in the state, combined with scientific farming and industrial techniques, also resulted in high productivity and a great diversity of agricultural products. As early as the first years of the 1870s, these results were already being remarked on in the eastern United States. Appleton and Company, in its *Annual Cyclopaedia* for 1870, summed up California agriculture, "In no State of the Union are the products of the earth so great where the population is so small, and outside of the cities, so sparse" (1873, 77).

In agriculture, mining, transportation, and manufacturing as well, the steam engine was crucial during this era. The *Mining and Scientific Press* argued that the steam engine was the …

> *indispensable assistant to the builder, contractor, manufacturer, merchant, ship-owner, farmer, miner …[O]n every hand, we see the steam engine being made subservient to the good of almost every conceivable avocation in which man can engage. What would become of the civilization and industrial interests of this nineteenth century were we to be deprived of the aid of steam without a compensating equivalent? It is the wonder of the age—the greatest instrument of social, intellectual and physical progress which the world has yet beheld. (December 15, 1866, 371)*

A MOMENT IN TIME, CALIFORNIA IN THE 1870 CENSUS

The 1870 census supplies us with the raw data to see how far the state as a whole had progressed along the road to a full-scale capitalist industrial society, with both urban and rural branches. In total population, the census found 560,247 Californians, an increase of almost 200,000 over 1860. Most of these people immigrated from outside California. Birth rates were relatively low, since women made up only 37 percent of the population in 1870, reflecting the long-standing shortage of women in the state (Wright 1941, 73). San Francisco continued to be the overwhelmingly dominant city, with 149,473 people, fully 26.7 percent of California's total. Sacramento remained second, with 16,283 people (2.9 percent), followed by Oakland and Stockton, each with about 10,000. Data from the 1870 census also illustrates the even more central role San Francisco played in the state's economic life, along with the supporting roles of Santa Clara and Sacramento Counties. These three held over half of the total wealth of the state, making up the main local pool of investment capital. The last column in table 5.1 below shows the cumulative percentage of California's total wealth held by the top counties together.

Occupational data show an increasing division of labor, one of the distinguishing characteristics of industrial capitalism. By 1870, capitalism, the labor market, and the exploitation of workers through wage labor were completely dominant. The major occupations and percentages of the total for California's 238,648 "economically active" people (as defined by the US Census, which left out women keeping home and other categories of people) are shown in table 5.2.

TABLE 5.1, **True Valuation of Real and Personal Estate in Leading California Counties, 1870**

County	True Valuation	Percent of State Total	Cumulative Percentage
San Francisco	$263,056,512	41.2%	41.2%
Santa Clara	39,877,413	6.2%	47.4%
Sacramento	38,870,795	6.1%	53.5%
Alameda	23,622,500	3.7%	57.2%
San Joaquin	23,472,805	3.7%	60.9%
San Mateo	23,286,825	3.6%	64.5%
Solano	19,357,710	3.0%	67.5%
Remaining 43 counties	207,222,508	32.5%	100%

Source: US Census Bureau 1872a, 3:18

TABLE 5.2, Major Occupations, 1870

Laborers	37,586	15.8%
Miners	36,339	15.2%
Farmers	24,061	10.1%
Agricultural laborers	16,231	6.8%
Domestic servants	15,472	6.5%
Carpenters and joiners	7,413	3.1%
Clerks, salesmen and accountants in stores	6,304	2.6%
Draymen, teamsters	4,582	1.9%
Hotel and restaurant keepers and employees	4149	1.7%
Launderers and laundresses	4043	1.7%
Sailors, steamboat men, water men	3485	1.5%

Source: US Census Bureau 1872b, 1:722

The workers in almost all these occupations typically survived by wage labor except farmers, a minority of miners who still owned their own claims, and some hotel keepers, restaurant operators, and similar, mainly small-scale, property owners. The large number of laborers and servants (together almost 30 percent of the total labor force) is striking and illustrative of both the rapid development of the class structure and fast accumulation of wealth at the upper end of that structure during the 1860s. The diversity of types of employment is also evident. The eleven categories of employment listed account for about two-thirds of those employed. Another one-third worked in a large number of other categories, each with a relatively small number of employees.

The ethnic background of California's labor force in 1870 was quite diverse. People born in the United States, China, Ireland, and Germany were most numerous. Children and married women "keeping home" were not counted in the census as "employed." Thus, the lower the percentage employed, the more wives and children there were in that group. Using this measure, people born in Canada and the United States had the most children and wives, the Chinese and Italian-born the least. Table 5.3 reviews the basic data on ethnicity and percentage employed.

TABLE **5.3, Ethnicity of California Labor Force in 1870**

Birthplace	Total	% of Labor Force	Number over 10 yrs old	% Employed
United States	110,124	46.1	224,351	49.1
China	33,768	14.1	46,070	73.3
Ireland	30,783	12.9	53,452	57.6
Germany	19,311	8.1	29,172	66.2
England/Wales	11,366	4.8	18,947	60.0
France	4,984	2.1	7,924	62.9
Canada	4,836	2.0	10,470	46.2
Italy	3,313	1.4	4,577	72.4
Other	20,163	8.4	35,471	56.8

Source: US Census Bureau 1872b, 1:722

In 1870, paid employment for women was scarce (women held only 5.8 percent of California jobs) and what employment existed was concentrated in a few occupations. A majority of all employed women worked as domestic servants. Almost all occupations open to women during this era were aspects of traditional women's work (table 5.4). Women dominated the occupations of dressmaking and teaching. The fact that there were very small numbers of women iron and steel workers, journalists, cabinetmakers, and government officials is an interesting footnote.

In terms of capital invested in various sectors of California's industrial economy (the census takers left the railroads out of this list), the state total was $39.7 million with gas manufacturing by far the largest, followed by lumber, quicksilver, iron and machinery, flour and grist mills, woolen goods, quartz mills, and sugar (see table 5.5).

Even more was invested in the mining economy, both in California and its neo-colony, Nevada (California controlled Nevada in numerous ways), a total of $52.3 million ($20.1 million in California and $32.2 million in Nevada). The bulk of this investment ($36.9 million or 70.6 percent) was in gold and silver quartz mining. California cinnabar mining was second with $11.9 million (22.8 percent of the total) invested (US Census Bureau 1872a, 3:760–761).

TABLE 5.4, Female Employment in the 1870 Census

Occupation	# of Women Employed	% of Employed Women	Women as a % of Total Employed in this Work
Domestic servants	7,735	56.1	50.0
Milliners/dressmakers	1,354	9.8	89.8
Teachers	1,150	8.3	58.9
Tailoresses/seamstresses	793	5.8	44.1
Laundresses	789	5.7	19.5
Boardinghouse keepers	362	2.6	47.4
Other	1,597	11.6	—

Source: US Census Bureau 1872b, 1:722

TABLE 5.5, Capital Invested in California Industry

Type of Business	Number of Establishments	Capital (in millions)
Gas	7	$6.49
Lumber, sawed	291	$3.9
Quicksilver	4	$3.5
Ironworks	81	$2.67
Flouring and grist mills	115	$2.6
Woolen goods	5	$1.8
Quartz mills	114	$1.7
Sugar, refined	3	$1.3
All others	—	$15.74

Source: US Census Bureau 1872a 3:497–498

The total cash value of all California farms in 1870 was $141.2 million, with another $5.3 million worth of farm implements and machinery (US Census Bureau 1872a 3: 81). Farms in the counties of Alameda, Santa Clara, Solano, Sonoma, Yolo, and San Joaquin had the highest value. Wheat was the key product, and, with only a few exceptions, the highest wheat producers also had the highest valuation (US Census Bureau 1872a, 3:104–105). These figures strikingly show the vast increase in California's agricultural economy during the 1860s. By 1869, it had risen to a point where the cash value of California farms and farm machinery was worth over one and a half times the combined value of both California industry and California and Nevada mines.

In 1869, California agriculture was already clearly divided into the two clear categories, discussed above, the larger and richer Central Valley and coastal plains farms and the smaller and poorer mountain farms. Table 5.5 offers 1870 census data on twelve counties, six from each category. The two groups are differentiated by much more than size, quality of land, climate, and topography. On the larger farms, an agricultural form of commercial, industrialized capitalism had rapidly developed. Wage labor had been brought in, often composed of single men and foreign-born or racialized people of color, such as the Chinese who were without social, legal, or political rights. Production was specialized and for sale (often abroad), rather than for local or regional use (wheat for example). Yearly profits were often large and farm cash-values high. Census data is by county and therefore large farms cannot be isolated for analysis; small and medium-sized farms are included as part of the average for the entire county. Even so, the Central Valley and coastal plains counties were characterized by huge farms—factories in the fields—with larger value, higher production, and more wages paid to greater numbers of workers.

The smaller scaled mountain county farms produced a greater variety of crops, often more for subsistence use at home and locally, instead of for sale on the market. They also had smaller production levels and used less wage labor. Yet since isolated mines were often close to these farmers, many also frequently

grew crops for sale to the mining population, increasing the size
of farms, production levels, and use of wage labor.

TABLE 5.6, Farm Counties Ranked by Size, 1869

County	Number of Farms	Average Size (in acres)	Cash Value per Farm	Production per Farm	Wages Per Farm	Production less Wages
1. Small-Farm Counties						
Inyo	73	176.5	$2,035	$2,154	$532	$1,622
Nevada	194	193.0	$2622	$1,916	$432	$1,484
Tuolumne	304	207.7	$975	$882	$114	$768
Shasta	181	213.7	$1,795	$1,655	$220	$1,435
Trinity	38	224.5	$2,067	$2,324	$665	$1,659
Sierra	96	240.0	$1,781	$1,971	$403	$1,568
2. Large-Farm Counties						
Kern	86	2,947.0	$3,949	$2,243	$526	$1,717
Colusa	428	1,122.3	$10,299	$4,701	$957	$3,744
Marin	433	726.9	$12,777	$3,753	$905	$2,848
Stanislaus	869	622.6	$4,952	$3,128	$929	$2,199
Solano	941	395.2	$10,809	$3,369	$587	$2,843
Santa Clara	936	339.9	$12,845	$2,949	$704	$2,245

Source: US Census Bureau 1872a, 3:104–105, 346

In terms of yearly production, statistics from the 1870 census
show how far both manufacturing and agriculture had come
during the boom decade of the 1860s. Table 5.7 offers basic
data on this topic. The divisions between the three categories
in census data are arbitrary, since, for example, "quartz milled"
is included in "manufacturing," as is "flouring and grist mill
products." Also worth noting is the sharp drop in wage scales
from the $3–$5-per-day characteristic of the late Gold Rush and
the fact that board was sometimes included in the agricultural
laborer's wage figure.

TABLE 5.7, California Manufacturing,
Agriculture and Mining Production in 1869

Type	Total Production	Wages Paid	Employees	Wages/ year	Wages/ day
Manufacturing	$66,594,556	$13,136,722	25,392	$517.36	$1.66
Agriculture	$49,856,024	$10,369,247	18,161	$570.96	$1.83
Mining	$26,452,652	$8,796,525	16,908	$520.26	$1.67

Source: US Census Bureau 1872b, 1:722; 1872a, 3:104, 496, 752

Table 5.8 summarizes much of the data on the California class structure in its various dimensions as of 1870. At the top stood a few thousand industrialists, lawyers, bankers, brokers, insurance executives, large mine owners, large farmers, large merchants, government officials, railroad owners, and their families.

The owning-class occupations are almost entirely male, overwhelmingly US-born and exclusive; Chinese Americans, for example, although 14.1 percent of California's labor force, are almost entirely missing from the owning-class group. The higher paid workers are also overwhelmingly male and mainly US-born. An exception was the high percentage of German-born workers among traders and dealers. Since higher paid workers were often skilled, they were also sometimes able to form and maintain craft unions, which usually focused on organizing only that narrow segment of the workforce working in one specialized skill. These unions, however, were usually divided by race and generally banned Chinese and African Americans from membership.

Women and people of color were allowed to have only lower-paid jobs where exploitation was greater. The Chinese, who had few legal rights, were employed in large numbers as miners, cigar-tobacco workers, launderers, and domestic servants. Unionization and participation by the US-born workers were correspondingly much lower in these occupations. Often lacking skills and legal rights, as well as solidarity from workers higher on the capitalist totem pole, these lower-paid workers were usually powerless

Laurence H. Shoup

against the employers, who exploited them unmercifully. If they tried to form industrial or craft unions to defend their interests and resist the capitalist drive to extract maximum surplus value and accumulate, such unions were crushed by the capitalist owners, as will be seen in chapters 7 and 10.

TABLE 5.8, The California Class Structure and Ethnicity in 1870

Occupation	Total #	percent Male	percent US-Born	percent China-born	percent Ireland-born	percent Germany-born	percent England-& Wales-born
I. Owning Class Sector							
Bankers/brokers	630	100%	69.7%	0.16%	4.4%	10.0%	4.9%
Lawyers	1,115	100	89.6	0	3.1	1.1	2.5
Insurance	377	100	77.2	0	6.1	6.6	4.8
Farmers and planters	24,061	99.6	69.5	1.4	8.1	6.3	3.9
Govt. Officials	1,731	99.8	74.7	0.17	11.1	5.1	3.5
II. Higher-Paid Workers							
Printers	1,045	99.4	74.6	0.38	7.1	3.9	5.3
Carpenters	7,413	100	63.7	2.0	9.4	6.6	6.5
Carmen, draymen & teamsters	4,582	99.8	64.6	0.39	15.5	6.1	3.6
Employees railroad co.	1,872	100	53.6	22.9	15.4	1.8	2.0
Iron workers, blacksmiths & machinists	4,165	99.9	54.5	0.89	14.6	8.9	7.7
Traders/dealers	10,734	99.4	41.0	7.6	8.6	23.7	3.8
Clerks, sales, accountants	6,304	99.5	59.1	3.2	6.2	15.9	4.7
Hotel & restaurant	4,149	96.0	41.4	2.4	14.6	19.7	5.1
III. Lower-Paid Workers							
Miners	36,339	100	34.4	25.0	7.9	4.0	8.6

206

Occupation	Total #	percent Male	percent US-Born	percent China-born	percent Ireland-born	percent Germany-born	percent England-& Wales-born
Laborers	37,586	99.6	38.1	20.6	20.4	5.0	2.8
Agricultural laborers	16,231	99.5	62.9	10.1	8.1	5.1	2.7
Domestic servants	15,472	50.0	25.0	28.1	28.7	6.8	2.8
Tobacco & cigars	1,920	99.8	2.7	89.6	0.36	3.2	0.21
Boots/shoes	2,501	97.8	27.5	15.7	21.7	18.4	4.4
Steamboat men/sailors	3,485	99.9	32.1	2.3	15.6	10.8	8.9
Lumbermen/ woodchoppers	2,517	100	52.5	19.5	4.7	3.2	2.1
Laundry	4,043	79.5	10.9	71.7	8.7	2.0	0.8

Source: US Census Bureau 1872b, 1:722

In sum, the US census shows that capitalism—and its unique constellation of class relations—was well established in California by 1870. The process of dispossession of most of the workers from ownership and control of any means of production was already well advanced by that point in time. Wage labor was overwhelmingly dominant, the capitalist class was increasing the rate of exploitation, and average wages were falling. The resulting rates of profit were very high and capital accumulation rapid for those at the high end of the capitalist economic (class) structure. The market was in control and everything was becoming commodified. Skin color, ethnicity, and gender were central factors in determining what occupations were open to a given person. Competition was sharp in many sectors of the economy, resulting in the beginnings of the characteristic capitalist drive to speed up production, cut wages, and increase the hours of work. Since the great majority of people had less to spend on necessities, the increase in exploitation helped create a crisis of effective demand in the California economy, resulting in the depression of the 1870s. This in turn sharpened the class struggle, a topic we will return to in detail in the chapters that follow.

THE CALIFORNIA RULING CLASS IN 1870, THE "PACIFIC COAST RING"

The data provided by the 1870 census also gives us a window on the status of the California ruling class at that moment in time. The decade of the 1860s had been an extraordinary, even revolutionary one. The capitalist industrialization that had triumphed during the decade had developed enormous means of production and also spawned the first California millionaires. By 1870, a number of them were also multimillionaires at a time when the daily rate of pay for most workers ranged from $1.50 to $4.00, and monthly rates from $20 to $80 (California Immigrant Union 1870, 19–20). A review of the US Census for San Francisco, Sacramento, and their suburbs produced a list of key millionaires, fifteen of the richest Californians as of 1870. These were the places where the rich were most likely to have lived in 1870. The census taker asked about wealth levels (real property and personal property) and wrote down the estimates given. In most cases, they are probably understatements. But the results largely conform to what we know about the 1860s and the richest Californians of this period. The list shows the emerging Central Pacific Railroad–Bank of California alliance in control of the biggest accumulations of capital, fully eleven of the fifteen being easily identified with this cooperating combination of financial-industrial capital.

The top two wealth holders were Leland Stanford and Mark Hopkins (railroads, $8.7 million each). Stanford's and Hopkins' listed wealth was mainly in "personal estate," overwhelmingly in Central Pacific Railroad stock. C. P. Huntington, one of the other two members of the Big Four, was on the East Coast in 1870, tending to the railroads' political and other business in Washington and New York. For reasons unknown, Charles Crocker listed a total estate of only $340,000 in 1870, although he later was known to have a similar wealth level to other members of the Big Four. Crocker also had seven servants (five California-born, two China-born) whereas Stanford had only four (three Irish and one from Nova Scotia); and the more thrifty Hopkins had only one Chinese servant. In 1870, Stanford, Hopkins, and Crocker all lived in Sacramento. Within a few years, they had all moved to San Francisco and built huge mansions in the exclusive Nob Hill district. In addition to being president of the Central Pacific Railroad and other railroads, Stanford also sat on the board of directors of Wells Fargo Express and owned at least one successful gold mine.

John Parrott (banking, insurance, industry, $4.6 million) was number three. Long a leading San Francisco banker, who owned his own company, Parrott was also a director of such firms as the Union Insurance Company (with Ralston and Mills) and Spring Valley Water Company (with Tevis). He was also a large investor (with Stanford, Mills, Ralston, and Hayward) in the Pacific Rolling Mills (Langley 1871, Lii). He lived in San Mateo County with ten servants (five Irish, three French, one Swiss, and one US born), along with nine Chinese day laborers.

Archbishop James P. Alemany was in fourth place with $3.84 million. This French-born Catholic church leader's holdings were almost entirely in real estate, undoubtedly church buildings and land he was holding in trust for the church.

Next was D. O. Mills with $3.0 million. As president of the Bank of California, Mills represented the bank's interest and his own on a number of leading corporate boards of directors, such as Wells Fargo Express and Pacific Rolling Mills.

Peter Donahue, Michael Reese, and Francois Pioche each held $2.5 million in wealth. Long a main owner of the Union Iron Works, Donahue was also a director (with Tevis, Huntington, Stanford, Hopkins, and others) of the Southern Pacific Railroad. He was also a key owner of the San Francisco Gas Company. Reese was a mine and real-estate owner, and Pioche, a banker. All three of these men were foreign-born, Donahue in Scotland, Reese in Prussia, and Pioche in France. Reese had gained a portion of his initial capital buying and selling slaves in the South before the Civil War. He became a real-estate speculator in San Francisco during the Gold Rush and after 1858 reportedly never suffered a reverse in his speculations (Cutter 1963, 132–134). His mine holdings included investments in Amador County quartz gold mines. When Reese died in 1878, he reportedly was worth $6.4 million (Cutter 1963, 140). Pioche was an owner and partner in the San Francisco banking firm of Pioche, Bayerque and Company. He and his firm prospered with investments in real estate, mines, utilities, and railroads. Following economic losses during the depression of the 1870s, he committed suicide.

Alfred Borel was worth $1.9 million. The Swiss-born Borel owned a large part of the firm of A. Borel that had been the main financier behind the Sacramento Valley Railroad and was also involved with the Spring Valley Water Company. He had two Swiss-born servants in 1870.

Samuel C. Hastings, a New York–born lawyer, had assets worth $1.85 million in 1870.

George H. Howard, with $1.8 million, was the next wealthiest. This Massachusetts-born landowner was also a director of the Pacific Insurance Company and the California Mutual Marine Insurance Company. He was also president of the Central Wharf Company of San Francisco.

William C. Ralston had assets worth $1.75 million. As we have seen, this Bank of California leader was also the director or treasurer of a number of key mines and industrial establishments.

Partners Lloyd Tevis and James B.A. Haggin had $1.5 million each. These two lawyers both listed their occupation as "capitalist" and were also directors of leading corporations. They were business partners, were both from Kentucky, married to sisters, and even lived next door to each other. Each had four servants. Tevis was president of Wells Fargo Bank for many years and was associated with the Big Four in their railroad enterprises. They jointly owned large agricultural estates and important mines located in different western states.

Finally, Alvinza Hayward was worth $1.44 million. By 1870, Hayward was a director of both the Bank of California and the Union Insurance Company. He was also an owner of gold and silver mines in California and Nevada, including Amador County quartz gold mines (US Census Bureau 1870; *The San Francisco Call* August 6, 1871, 3, August 8, 1871, 3).

Eleven of these fifteen wealthy Californians can be placed into two primary interest groups, with four apparently outside:

- Central/Southern Pacific/Wells Fargo—Stanford, Hopkins, Reese, Donahue, Tevis, and Haggin
- Bank of California—Mills, Ralston, Parrott, Hayward, and Howard
- Mainly independent—Alemany, Pioche, Borel, and Hastings

It should be understood that in 1870 there were numerous links and minimal conflict between the two most powerful interest groups, although divisions were soon to develop. The interconnections between them helped foster cooperation in running the California and western United States economy. Tevis was, for example, also connected with the Bank of California group through the Pacific Insurance Company (Ralston, Hayward, and Tevis were all directors of this company). Mills was also on the board of directors of Wells Fargo with Stanford and Tevis. Stanford was a large stockholder in the Pacific Rolling Mills, which had Mills, Ralston, Parrott, and Hayward among its leading investors, officers, and directors. In 1869, the Union Insurance Company had Ralston, Hayward, and Parrott as directors (*San Francisco Alta* May 19 1869, 1). Parrott was also an investor and trustee (with Ralston and Louis McLane) in the San Francisco Assaying and Refining Works (Mills 1881, 160). Although apparently independent, in 1870, Reese traveled to Europe to sell bonds for the Big Four, and a few years later acted directly for Stanford when he brought suit against Milton

Latham, a former Democratic governor and senator (Cutter 1963, 135, 143–144n29).

The consolidation of a new ruling class whose dual base was the Central Pacific Railroad and the Bank of California was thus largely complete by 1870. By this time, it was also dominant in the economic and political life of the state. One journalist of the period argued that the railroad and the bank were "one and the same thing," best labeled the "Pacific Coast Ring," a "circle so powerful and complete that it laughed at opposition" (Bancroft Scraps 1877, Set W 24:56–57). Besides having great influence upon the Democratic and especially the Republican Party and local and state politics during the 1860s and early 1870s, it even exercised a strong influence on national legislation affecting the Pacific Coast, for example in the issue area of mineral lands controlled by the Department of Interior. Raw economic power, the ability to bribe, as well as financially reward and punish were the main sources of their political power. Another writer of the time viewed the Bank of California in 1869 as the center of economic power in the West, the "financial king of the Pacific States" and influencing or controlling the following companies or areas of enterprise, The Central Pacific Railroad and its affiliated enterprises, Wells Fargo Express and Stage Company, California Steam Navigation Company, Oregon Steam Navigation Company, the great woolen mills of San Francisco, the great machine shops of San Francisco, the Comstock mining companies, the large farms in the interior valleys, and the wheat trading "rings" of San Francisco (Bowles 1869, 341).

The establishment of unregulated industrial capitalism in a state and region with great and untapped mineral and agricultural resources resulted in rapid accumulation of capital and great wealth at the top. Another result was a racial and gender hierarchy typical of a new capitalist society.

The other side of this accumulation and ruling-class control was the creation of a stratified working class of often poorly paid people who owned no productive property and were exploited by their employers. The social imbalance this created was not only unjust and alienating for the majority, it was also dysfunctional for the economy. Overproduction in an unplanned economy and the lack of effective purchasing power for the majority laid the basis for the long depression that afflicted California throughout the 1870s. This depression also tested the unity of the newly consolidated ruling class and spawned sharp conflicts over accumulation and the developmental process.

6

CONFLICT AND UNITY—
THE EVOLUTION OF THE CALIFORNIA RULING
CLASS,
1870–1877

Although the largest and most successful capitalists of late-nineteenth-century California monopolized huge sectors of the economy—railroads, banking, Comstock mining, water and gas utilities, steamship lines—the overall system was still unregulated laissez-faire capitalism, and it was strongly competitive. Sharp competition, capital vs. capital was central to economic life. This reality, in the context of a decade of depression necessarily led to double-crosses, business failures, and even, on rare occasions, intraclass violence involving some of the less socialized members of the capitalist ruling class. During this period, the chief monopoly of the time, the Central Pacific/Southern Pacific Railroad combine—leader of the Pacific Coast Ring—successfully built rail lines north and south from the San Francisco–Sacramento axis, economically unifying and integrating the state as a single market and fostering capitalist relations among farmers, miners, and merchants statewide.

At the same time, the growth of the working class and its resistance to being victimized by the exploitation and political schemes of capitalist corporations impelled the upper class to become more class conscious and gradually unify. The result was a multitude of "cautious dances of scorpions at the alert" (Ross and Trachte 1990, 27), in a variety of settings during the 1870s, maneuvers that resulted in a growing ruling-class unity under the leadership of the most successful capitalists. Leisured upper-class women had a key role in this development of unity, for it was they who ran "society." The social ties of the higher circles gradually became central to political and economic life.

The Republican Party, mainly the party of industrial, retail, and banking capital, was dominant. The Democratic Party, which had been the party of agrarian capital and racism, with occasional, mainly rhetorical flourishes about workers' rights, was essentially in a junior partnership with the Republicans. Both parties were part of a political boss system run by the railroad and its corporate and upper-class allies.

During this period, the Comstock Lode, a key prop of the San Francisco and California financial superstructure, experienced ups and downs as new bonanzas of silver and gold were discovered, quickly exploited, and exhausted. Towards the end of the 1870s, as the last and greatest of these bonanzas played out, the already depressed California economy hit bottom, with unemployment and mass suffering at a high level. The crisis of the system then became part of the continuing transition of California from a mining to an agricultural and manufacturing state. Within this context of economic depression and transition, economic conflicts within the state's new ruling class became intense, amounting to a war over who would be successful in the ongoing struggle for accumulation. This conflict eventually left William C. Ralston as its chief victim. Conflicts continued following Ralston's fall, being eventually resolved by a general recognition of the Big Four and the Central Pacific/Southern Pacific empire, the core of the Pacific Coast Ring, as the key leaders of the ruling class of California.

THE CONFLICT OVER THE SAN FRANCISCO GAS MONOPOLY

One of the largest and most lucrative monopolies in California during this era was the gas monopoly of San Francisco, which provided gas lighting to the Queen City of the West. It was owned and operated by the San Francisco Gas Company, a corporation that was not controlled by the Bank of California ... at first. The San Francisco Gas Company, whose president was Peter Donahue, had a capital of six million dollars, and in 1869, its annual rate of return on this capital was fully 54.4 percent, as reported in the 1870 census. A good part of the reason for this princely rate of return was the fact that gas-rate ceilings were set by the San Francisco Board of Supervisors. Using a common term of the time, "engaging in the monied fight," a majority of these supervisors could be directly or indirectly bribed to ensure both a high price and an excellent rate of return on capital, all at the expense of rank-and-file consumers.

By the end of the 1860s, the Bank of California crowd decided to establish a rival firm to undercut and try to gain outright control over this gas monopoly. So in April of 1870, they incorporated the City Gas Company with a capital of $1.5 million dollars. They then built a large, state-of-the-art gas manufacturing facility in the Potrero, part of the rapidly industrializing section of the city south of Market Street. City Gas Company's initial small board of directors included Bank of California directors Alvinza Hayward and Nicholas Luning, as well as the bank- and Southern Pacific–connected Lloyd Tevis. Once the Potrero plant was functional, a few years of sharp rate competition followed. Then came a compromise; in 1873, the two rivals merged, forming the San Francisco Gas Light Company (Coleman 1952, 28–30). The Bank of California sector of the Pacific Ring had successfully seized a piece of the ownership and profits of the most lucrative gas monopoly in the West.

GOAT/YERBA BUENA ISLAND AND
THE "COMMITTEE OF 100"

Another source of conflict within the California ruling class during the early 1870s was the 1871–1872 attempt by the Central Pacific's Big Four to obtain a grant of Goat—also called Yerba Buena—Island from the federal government. This island lay in San Francisco Bay across the sea lines of communication for the Port of San Francisco. The Big Four's potential ownership, control, and development of the island as their transcontinental railroad terminus angered and alarmed many San Franciscans.

There were a number of reasons for this feeling. First of all, the city had already given the Central Pacific sixty acres of land along the Mission Bay waterfront in the southern part of the city for this purpose, and in exchange, the Big Four had agreed to establish their western terminus in San Francisco. Quite naturally, many San Franciscans wanted the Big Four to live up to their agreement and not continue to develop their western terminus on the Oakland waterfront. Second, the specter of a large railroad facility, headed by a small group of very ambitious monopolists answerable only to themselves, lying on Yerba Buena (Goat) Island across the main avenues of commerce in San Francisco harbor made many of the city's leading businessmen very nervous. Many wanted to organize and fight against such a federal grant. Therefore, a "Committee of 100" was organized in April of 1872 to oppose the takeover. They stated their aims and purposes as follows:

> *Whereas, the Central, Western and Southern Pacific Railroad Companies have received enormous grants of lands, subsidies in lands and money from the Federal Government, from the State of California, from various counties in the State, and from San Francisco, which grants and subsidies were more than sufficient for the construction and equipment of said roads; and whereas, this State and city have*

given said railroads large subsidies and valuable grants of land within this city, with the intention and understanding that said roads should make their western terminus within the city of San Francisco and upon the tract of land granted for that purpose in Mission Bay; and whereas, said companies have obtained large grants of land on the opposite side of the bay in front of Oakland, and have directed the entire railroad system and all railroads of the coast towards the last mentioned point in disregard of the conditions of said compact; and whereas said companies have been, and are now, making strenuous efforts to obtain from the Federal Government a grant or lease of Goat Island, lying in the Bay of San Francisco, midway between this city and the Oakland shore, for the purpose of a terminus of all the lines aforesaid, in spite of and against the expressed wishes of this city, and in defiance of damage or danger to the harbor and commercial interests of this port …

Resolved, that the city of San Francisco has expected and does expect from the railroad companies a strict compliance with the terms and conditions of the compact made by said companies to and with the actual and immediate location of the terminus of said railroads, now merged into one ownership, and upon the sixty acres of land in Mission Bay, in this city …

Resolved, That the citizens of San Francisco believe that said company should withdraw from Congress every claim … of using or connecting said roads with Goat Island, and at once cease all further construction of wharves, piers or slips in the waters of this bay at the terminus of their present Oakland wharf …

> *Resolved, That in case said company shall decide to*
> *refuse ... to comply with this reasonable request, it is the*
> *right, duty and purpose of the citizens of San Francisco to*
> *take all lawful measures for maintaining their rights ...*
> *and to prevent said unlawful acts of said company.*
> (Sacramento Daily Union, *April 18, 1872, 3)*

The Committee of 100 was a powerful group of ruling-class leaders, and they threw down the challenge to the Big Four. Former San Francisco mayor William Alvord, who was also a director of the Bank of California and president of the Pacific Rolling Mill, headed up the committee. No less than four other current Bank of California directors were also members of the "100" (Alvinza Hayward, John O. Earl, Nicholas Luning, and Drury J. Tallant). Four of those listed in the previous chapter as being among the fifteen richest Californians in 1870 were also among them (foundryman Peter Donahue, lawyer S. C. Hastings, mine owner Hayward, and large landowner George H. Howard). Other wealthy men who signed up to confront the railroad included sugar baron Claus Spreckels, foundryman J. M. Scott, large landowner and cattleman Charles Lux, and banker Robert Tobin. In addition, former Vigilance Committee president William T. Coleman was an executive officer for the Committee of 100, and treasurer James Dows was a member of the new committee. Other former Vigilance Committee leaders on the Committee of 100 included Earl, Howard, and industrialists A.L. Tubbs and Ira P. Rankin (*Sacramento Daily Union* April 18, 1872, 3).

It is notable that neither Ralston nor D. O. Mills formally joined the committee; apparently, they were too close to the Big Four and their interests. But it was nonetheless a very formidable group. Faced with the actual threat of litigation and political action and the implied threat of another military uprising similar to the 1856 Vigilance Committee, the Big Four wisely backed down from their attempt to seize Goat/Yerba Buena Island. They saw the wisdom of not pushing San Francisco and the Committee of 100 too far. They decided to be conciliatory and conduct a flanking operation. Soon, three of the Big Four moved to San Francisco, built fantastic mansions on Nob Hill, and began to play a leading role in the social and economic affairs of the city. This eventually put them in a position to control—and not be controlled by—the ruling class of the Queen City of the West.

J. NEWTON BOOTH AND THE ANTI-MONOPOLY MOVEMENT, 1871–1874

The conflict over Goat Island partly merged into the anti-monopoly and anti-corruption struggle led by J. Newton Booth. Booth was a Sacramento merchant, a partner in the mercantile firm of Dodge, Booth and Company, importers and wholesalers who dealt in produce, liquors, and tobacco products. Dodge handled the San Francisco branch of the firm and Booth the Sacramento branch. The firm was medium-sized, with combined assets in the hundreds of thousands in the mid-1870s, an agent in New York with correspondents in St. Louis, Chicago, Boston, and Yokohama, Japan (*Sacramento Record Union* January 1, 1883, 1; *The San Francisco Examiner* July 15, 1892, 5). Therefore, Booth was representative of both the merchants and the smaller capitalists of Sacramento and San Francisco.

During the last years of the 1860s, Booth and many other California merchants, newspaper owners, and some Republican Party leaders foresaw that the growing political ascendancy of the railroad and other corporate monopolies was a menace to their own interests and the future of political democracy in the state. As it was, political democracy was already quite limited. A majority of adults, consisting of women and immigrants who were not citizens, could not even participate or vote. Political resources, (such as funds for staff and election campaigns and access to the press) were available only to the few who were relatively wealthy.

Furthermore, corruption and bribery were rampant, giving an additional advantage to the rich and well-connected. Booth and others were concerned that the already evident development of the Central Pacific/Southern Pacific Railroad's political machine, in frequent close and growing alliance with other large corporate interests like the Bank of California, would create an even narrower, more oligarchic plutocracy than already existed, both leaving them largely powerless and also possibly eventually leading to a radical revolution to overthrow such an oligarchy.

A gifted orator, Booth was able to win a following and was elected to the state senate as an independent Republican in 1869. His articulate attacks on Democratic Governor Haight's opposition to the Fifteenth Amendment to the Constitution, expanding voting rights, made him a leader of the Republican Party and a possible candidate for governor in 1871. Booth's speeches made it clear that he was against corporate monopoly and the ongoing corruption of the political system, so the railroad's political machine did all it could to prevent his nomination, even putting forward Thomas H. Selby, San Francisco's popular mayor, as an alternative (*The San Francisco Examiner* July 15, 1892, 5). W. W. Stow, the railroad's San Francisco boss, played a large role in Republican politics in the city and was able to bring a united San Francisco delegation to the Republican state convention for the purpose of defeating Booth (*The San Francisco Examiner* July 15, 1892, 5; *San Francisco Chronicle* August 20, 1871, 1; September 10, 1871, 1). The balance of forces was nevertheless against the Central Pacific/Southern Pacific machine in this case, and Booth won the Republican nomination.

In his 1871 acceptance speech, Booth summed up his anti-monopoly and anti-corruption stance, asking rhetorically, "Shall this government be and remain a mighty agency of civilization, the protector of all, or shall it be run as a close corporation to enrich the few?" (Crane 1894, 143).

During the 1871 campaign, Booth elaborated on this theme, outlining what he considered to be the "ideal republic," one that would foster both equality and justice and check revolutionary outbursts:

> *The Ideal Republic would be a community where wealth would be so equally distributed, that the possessions of each would represent actual services rendered. There would be no Vanderbilts, Stewarts and Astors, and no men would toil through a lifetime to reach a pauper's grave … legislation should prevent as far as possible those immense combinations of capital, which draw to themselves more than imperial power. The law should do this in the interests of the rights of property itself; for if the tendency to centralization continues to increase, the time may come when social order and the tenure of all property will be shaken by the volcanic outburst of revolutionary forces.* (Daily Alta California *July 22, 1871, 1*)

In this campaign speech, Booth also outlined his strategy and tactics to move towards his ideal republic, focusing first and foremost on the need to control the vast and growing power of the railroads, the giant corporations of the time:

> *The introduction and vast extension of the railroad system in the United States, placing our interior trade and communications largely under the control of great corporations, present some difficulties to practical statesmanship. The world has seldom witnessed so great and rapid a material change as that wrought by railroads … More than any other branch of business … they represent capital massed. In our own day there is a strong and increasing tendency toward the centralization of wealth. The great business absorbs the small, the powerful company the weak … It is a struggle between giants—a struggle in which popular rights … the rights of the weak, are*

> *liable to be disregarded … [C]oncentrated capital is*
> *becoming so vast a power, it is necessary to detach it*
> *from all control of the government … to … shut out*
> *from legislation all schemes, of whatever nature, of*
> *money-making and corruption … speculation which*
> *is absorbing our public lands, and converting what*
> *should be held as homes for the toiling millions, into*
> *imperial donations … the overshadowing danger of*
> *the hour [is] that this Government may be run in the*
> *interest of money and not of manhood—that Gold*
> *may become king and Labor its vassal.* (Daily Alta
> California *July 22, 1871, 1)*

Newton Booth won big in the Republican strongholds, the more urbanized parts of California—San Francisco, Sacramento, and Alameda Counties—and defeated Haight, the Democratic governor (*San Francisco Chronicle* October 5, 1871, 3). The railroad and other large corporations still controlled much of the government, however, and the railroad in particular had a well-funded and well-organized political machine, which operated on a local, state, and national basis. Without a large, activist, grassroots movement of the people with a political party of their own, Booth could not achieve his ideals. He evidently did not want to help create such a movement and party, or even promote the full political participation, unity, and real political empowerment of the only force that could achieve his goals: the great majority of the people, including all workers, women, and youth.

The serious divisions among the mass of the people led to a politics that stressed outstanding personalities such as Booth, not the empowerment of citizens aware of their common interests and pursuing them collectively. Booth either did not understand how or was unwilling to try to transcend the individualism of existing politics within California and instead decided to withdraw from the governorship and seek the position of United States senator. This office was the most powerful and prestigious elected office available in the state of California; therefore, there was frequently a struggle over who would receive this plum and the political and economic benefits that went with it.

Such conflicts are instructive about which interest groups are important players statewide and their relative strength, revealing the structure of political and economic power in graphic terms. Throughout this era, the state legislature decided who would represent California in the Senate, making the development of a statewide political machine imperative to assure that the votes would be there when a term expired or vacancy occurred. The Big Four of the Central Pacific/Southern Pacific Railroad first successfully took over one of the US Senate positions in the 1860s when Republican Cornelius Cole was elected senator by the legislature. When Cole's term was up, Republican Aaron Sargent, another close friend and ally of the railroad, was chosen by the legislature to take his place. Sargent's term had almost expired when the other senator, Eugene Casserly, resigned in late November of 1873. The state legislature suddenly had to decide on two senators, one for a short term (two years) and one for a full six-year term.

The California legislature decided on the two senators in December 1873. Just before the legislative vote, with the railroad ring's lobbyists, led by president Leland Stanford of the Central Pacific/Southern Pacific, working overtime to gain both offices, *The San Francisco Call* printed the following editorial:

> *Stanford & Co. have not yet oppressed the people to the full measure of endurance. They want two United States Senators at Washington to help them in carrying out various projects to further oppress the people … Stanford & Co. desire more money, and that is why they contest every movement made by the people. The struggle will not be given up until the community, in its might, arises and sweeps away the horde of retainers who throng about the Legislature*

> *whenever it assembles at Sacramento. (*The San
> Francisco Call *December 20, 1873, 2)*

Governor Booth's personal popularity and vast public support overcame the machine, and he was elected to the US Senate on December 20, 1873, for the full term. Stanford, who tried to influence the Republicans, and Billy Carr, one of his political bosses (who tried to influence the Democrats), had failed to achieve their objectives. This failure was despite the likely expenditure of large sums to bribe the legislature. Such bribery was a common practice of the time—expenditures by the Central Pacific/Southern Pacific for legislative favors in Washington, DC up to 1887 were reported to be about $5.5 million, a huge sum for the period. The famous secret letters between railroad leaders David D. Colton and C. P. Huntington, released as part of a court case, amply illustrate the immense corruption that the railroad used to secure the votes and cooperation of public officials at the state and national levels (Bean 1973, 299–300; Russell 1912, 171–181).

The defeat of the railroad led to what turned out to be premature rejoicing by the anti-monopolist newspapers, led by *The San Francisco Call* and *San Francisco Chronicle*. The *Call's* special correspondent in Sacramento wrote about the victory:

> *[F]or once the voice of the people has been respected. It is a new revelation in California politics, and one which promises well for the future … In past days the richest candidate, with the best wire-pullers to manage the fight, had by far the best chance. It was money to buy up County Committees, money to carry the primaries, money to secure the nomination of legislative candidates, money to elect them, and then money to keep them from bolting … Money represented principle, party, constituency and everything else, and no secret was made of the fact that Senators were elected by the money power.*

This contest has been different. Of the three candidates, one was the declared choice of the people, the others were the nominees of party caucuses. Farley, the Democratic candidate, stood no chance to win by the party vote, and the result was an unholy coalition with the railroad. Farley, anxious for the place, was willing to accept the aid of the railroad manipulators, although he represented anti-monopoly principles. Carr and Stanford were also willing to use Farley as a means of defeating Booth, whom they cherish as their dearest enemy. So completely has the railroad gang controlled the Republican party of this State in the past, by having possession of the inside machinery, that it presumed that it could dictate to Republican legislators, and even compel them to support a straight out Democrat if need be …

Both the local railroad organs, the Record *and the* Bee, *received their instructions, and the novel sight was presented of two newspapers, ostensibly devoted to the interests of the Republican party, urging the claims of a Democrat and never mentioning the name of their party candidate. (*The San Francisco Call *December 21, 1873, 3)*

The *Chronicle* called it a "remarkable event" in California political history:

… marking the beginning of a new era in which the people will themselves control the selection of their highest legislative representatives, independent of any … party, clique or corporation … The reform movement … has had the power of a revolutionary mass, and with such leaders as Booth it will not be difficult to transform this mass into an army. Other States have failed to produce any individual of his

227

> *prominence in connection with this anti-monopoly
> and anti-corruption revolution, and in no one State
> has there been ... the elevation of a champion of the
> people to the dignity bestowed upon Governor Booth.*
> (San Francisco Chronicle *December 21, 1873, 4).*

The *Sacramento Daily Union* (December 22, 1873, 2) editorialized:

> *The election of Governor Booth to the United States
> Senate ... deals the first telling blow to corruption,
> intrigue, bargain and sale in the senatorial elections.
> It vindicates the right of the people ... to control
> these elections ... to ... beat the insolent, autocratic
> and corrupt corporation, in league with an army
> of corrupt and selfish politicians. It was something
> new in the history of the state ... that the voice of
> the people, and not the conclaves and caucuses of the
> demagogues, should elect the Senator.*

The *Call* also seized on the occasion to repeat a warning about the dangers of a "subsidized" press, owned and operated by and for the railroad and other monopoly corporations:

> *Had it not been for an unpurchasable press, Stanford
> and Carr would, in all probability, now control
> the Legislature, and be able to dictate the passage
> of such laws as would please them. If the people are
> wise, they will now put their feet upon those viper
> newspapers which have betrayed them at every step
> of the Railroad controversy.* (The San Francisco
> Call *December 21, 1873, 2)*

Several newspapers of the time, among them the *Sacramento Record,* the *Sacramento Bee,* and apparently the *San Francisco Bulletin,* were secretly subsidized or even owned by the railroad. On the other hand, the owners of the *Sacramento Union* refused railroad bribes and stood up to railroad threats until the mid-1870s. By that time, it was losing money due to successful ostracism by the railroad and its allies and had to sell the newspaper to the railroad, creating the railroad-controlled *Sacramento Record Union* (Crane 1894, 130; Clark 1931, 286–288). Over time, the influence of the railroad and other corporations over the press grew even more, and a press independent of the overpowering influence of the largest corporations almost disappeared.

The legislative election of a second United States senator still had not taken place however, and following their defeat, the monopolist forces, led by Stanford and Carr, launched an even stronger and ultimately successful effort to install their choice for the second senator. Their choice was John S. Hager, a politician and judge who had fought for turning Goat Island over to the railroad and for other corrupt railroad schemes (*San Francisco Chronicle* December 22, 1873, 2; December 23, 1873, 5). The *Chronicle* reported:

> *John S. Hager was yesterday elected United States Senator … Hager was the railroad candidate … he was nominated by the same Carr Democratic Caucus that placed James T. Farley in the field to defeat Newton Booth … John S. Hager goes to the United States Senate by the votes of Railroad Democrats, assisted and finally decided by Railroad Republican votes. (December 24, 1873, 2)*

The railroad crowd in San Francisco was reported to have joyously received the news of the victory:

> *The news of the election of Judge Hager seemed to afford unbounded satisfaction to the railroad officials of this city. Congratulatory telegrams were exchanged with Sargent and the other railroad Congressmen in Washington, and last night a general jubilation took place at Billy Carr's headquarters on Montgomery*

229

> *street ... at which were present many of the Federal*
> *officials and prominent railroad politicians. (*San
> Francisco Chronicle *December 24, 1873, 3)*

During his final months as governor, Booth advocated a government takeover of the railroads, arguing that the government gave the railroads construction subsidies, land grants, and credits, giving the government the right to take possession (Crane 1894, 173). He added that, "There is no danger that we will lose the form of a republic. There is a danger that we may ultimately retain *only* the form" (Crane 1894, 123–125).

Booth suggested further that the people had a right to revolution, "That tyranny which is so potent ... must be destroyed by a general uprising of all individuals and interests, heralded by a new declaration of independence" (Crane 1894, 174).

Once in the United States Senate however, Booth acted more the statesman than the revolutionary or man of the people. He remained a member of the Republican Party and retired quietly from politics at the end of his first and only term in 1881. The failure of Booth to transcend the Republican Party and lead a mass people's anti-monopoly fight sidelined a leader who might have been able to make a fundamental difference for democracy in California in the long run.

NO HONOR AMONG THIEVES: HAYWARD'S DOUBLE CROSS

Alvinza Hayward had been a leading member of the "Bank Crowd" from at least 1865 when he became both a major stockholder and a member of the Bank of California's board of directors (Wilson 1964, 23). In the late 1860s, John P. Jones, Hayward's brother-in-law, and a sometime politician (he had been a state senator), needed a job. Hayward was able to successfully recommend Jones to William C. Ralston to be the superintendent of first one and then another bank-controlled Comstock mine. It was as superintendent of the second of these mines, the Crown

Point, that in 1870–1871 Jones, with Hayward's cooperation, made the fortune that enabled him to later purchase one of the two Nevada seats in the United States Senate for a reported half a million dollars (Lyman 1937, 172–178, 344n2; Lavender 1975, 321–330, 371).

When Jones took over as superintendent, the Crown Point was in barren rock, and its stockholders had already been hit with a number of assessments to search for a bonanza deeper underground. These assessments had driven the stock of this mine down to only two dollars a share. Ralston believed there was rich ore at a deeper level (something he had to believe and act upon in order to keep intact the speculative financial structure he was developing), and so he assessed the stockholders another $250,000 to prospect further.

Working at the 1,100-foot level, Jones's miners broke through a clay seam and came into white quartz, which held pockets of rich ore worth millions. But Jones kept the find a secret, telling no one but Alvinza Hayward. Soon the brothers-in-law had decided to try to steal the mine from Ralston and the Bank Crowd. They secretly invested their savings in Crown Point stock, trying to get majority control. Close to success, but with the stock's price rising due to their purchases, Hayward and Jones decided to try to achieve victory by tricking other stockholders and market speculators into a lower price. Jones went onto the San Francisco Stock Exchange floor, telling people he would have to sell out because his son had been "taken ill in the East." Speculators interpreted this to mean that Jones had failed to find ore and the mine was now barren and worthless. The stratagem worked, enough stockholders sold out to allow Hayward and Jones to accumulate their majority. They even purchased the decisive shares from William Sharon, the bank's main financial and political representative in Virginia City (Ostrander 1966, 50–52; Stone 1956, 306–307).

Sharon was from Illinois, a college graduate, and had studied law with Edward Stanton, later secretary of war under Lincoln. Engaging in various speculations in Gold Rush California,

Sharon had both successes and failures, making and losing a small fortune. He was also elected to minor public office. Sharon was an old and dear friend of John D. Fry, Ralston's father-in-law. So when Sharon lost his original small fortune, Ralston gave him a key job as manager of the Bank of California's activities in Nevada (Muscatine 1975, 297–298). Over time, Ralston and Sharon developed a close partnership.

Once in total control of the mine, Jones and Hayward ordered their miners into the bonanza ore and took out about $30 million in gold and silver. They even organized their own milling company to process the ore, so they did not have to depend upon the bank-controlled Union Mill and Mining Company (Stone 1956, 307). The successful double-cross made Jones rich and expanded Hayward's already considerable fortune. It also deprived Ralston and the bank of this bonanza, hurting them economically. But the Bank of California's loss of Crown Point bonanza was small-scale compared to what was to follow.

THE RISE OF THE IRISH SILVER KINGS

During the early 1870s, four Irishmen, three of them born in or near Dublin and the fourth in New York to impoverished immigrant parents, stole an even bigger bonanza from the Bank Crowd. Between 1849 and 1851, John W. MacKay, James G. Fair, William S. O'Brien, and James C. Flood had all come to Gold Rush California to find a fortune. Following a few years mining, Flood and O'Brien became small businessmen and MacKay and Fair continued with mining careers, gradually becoming hard-rock mining experts. By the end of the 1860s, MacKay and Fair were partners, working in the Comstock mines. As deep lode experts, they believed that there were still very valuable ore bodies at deeper levels, the trick was to acquire and own the right mines, nearly all controlled by the Bank Crowd. The first focus of attention was the bank-controlled Hale and Norcross Mine. To acquire control, they needed help.

That help came in the form of Flood and O'Brien, who meanwhile had become partners and established the "Auction Lunch," a saloon and restaurant in downtown San Francisco, cultivating the stockbrokers and Comstock insiders who came in to eat, drink, and conduct business. Acting on the tips and inside information they received at their saloon, they bought and sold stocks, and by 1868 had put away enough money to sell the Auction Lunch and open a stock-brokerage office. Soon their partnership merged with the partnership of MacKay and Fair, and together they laid plans to gain control of the Hale and Norcross Mine (Phelps 1882, 169, 196; Stone 1956, 307–309).

Using Flood's skill and adroitness in secretly purchasing stock, in 1869 the partners were able to buy up a controlling interest in the Hale and Norcross before Sharon, Ralston, and Bank Crowd suspected anything. When the board of directors of the mine met, the four Irishmen had a majority and kicked the bank's directors off the board. Striking in new directions in what was now *their* mine, they brought in a small bonanza and were able to purchase Virginia City's water company as well as two mills to crush their ore (Phelps 1882, 16 9, 196; Stone 1956, 309; Lavender 1975, 267).

This was mere prelude however. The four then decided to try to gain control over an area which they firmly believed held rich ore buried at deep levels—the 1,300-foot long part of the Comstock Lode lying between the two most productive original mines, the Gould and Curry and the Ophir. The Consolidated Virginia Mine occupied this area, where the Bank Crowd had already expended no less than $1 million in fruitless underground exploration. Sharon believed the mine was worthless, but since this time he was able to detect the stock purchases of Flood and O'Brien, he was able to force them to pay an extra $100,000 (over and above the hundreds of thousands they had already invested) to gain control of the Consolidated Virginia (Ostrander 1966, 55). Sharon happily reported to Ralston that the Irish Americans had been royally taken; they had bought a nearly bankrupt property for far more than its market value. But Sharon again failed to have the last word.

MacKay, Fair, Flood, and O'Brien gained control of the Consolidated Virginia in February of 1872. Not having adequate funds to probe the deeper levels of their newly purchased mine without a shortcut, the four men requested and were granted permission from Sharon and the bank to use the deep workings of the bank-owned Gould and Curry Mine to drift into their own ground, paying the bank a fee to bring their waste rock up through the Gould and Curry shaft.

Sharon again thought he got the better deal, since he believed that the four would waste all their money on a futile endeavor with the bank gaining profit through payments for the use of the Gould and Curry. Soon Sharon was again proved wrong. Mining experts MacKay and Fair discovered a thin vein and began to follow it into the richest of all the Comstock bonanzas, one of the biggest precious metal strikes in world history, worth about 150 million in 1870 dollars, many billions in today's values. Once poor, the four Irish Americans then became multimillionaires, the "Silver Kings" of San Francisco (Loomis 1968, 205–207, 214).

Dumbfounded at the turn of events, Ralston and Sharon decided to explore more deeply in one of their Comstock mines, which was located nearby the Consolidated Virginia, coming up with a $35 million strike in the Belcher Mine. This made William Sharon one of the richest men in the Far West. Sharon then decided that he would like to become a United States senator. Since most of the Nevada state legislators, who choose the state's two senators, were selected, financed, and elected by the Bank of California, Sharon thought he could easily be elected.

His candidacy caused an outcry in Nevada, however, where he was deeply disliked by many. A Virginia City newspaper editor called him a "hyena" in an editorial, saying that Sharon's career had been one of "merciless rapacity" making him "feared, hated and despised" in the community. John P. Jones then stepped forward to become a candidate, and Sharon tried to destroy Jones's reputation and finances, provoking more anger at Sharon. At this point Ralston intervened, demanding that Sharon resign from the senatorial race before more damage was done to the bank's interests. Sharon did withdraw, but thereafter held a serious grudge against Ralston, a feeling he would soon be able to act upon (Stone 1956, 312–313). It was during this period that Sharon purchased the *Daily Territorial Enterprise* newspaper of Virginia City in order to further his political career.

THE FALL OF RALSTON

As we have seen in a prior chapter, William C. Ralston was one of the most ambitious among powerful San Franciscans during the 1860s and 1870s. By the mid-1870s, he had had many successes and only a few embarrassments. He was one of the richest men in the West and sat on many corporate boards of directors. Through the usual means of big money in politics, he had political power at the local and state level, giving him the best political allies and confederates money could buy. His elite social ties gave him access to the highest social circles of the city and state. Ralston had a grand vision for San Francisco as a world-class city, a vision that often went together with the development of his own and his bank's moneymaking plans and schemes.

These plans and schemes ranged from establishing normal businesses like the Kimball Carriage Manufactory, the Cornell Watch Factory, and the Pacific Woolen Mills to speculative mining activities on the Comstock to involvement in fraudulent ventures like the attempted diamond swindle of 1872. This latter incident involved salting worthless desert land with diamonds in order to sell it for high prices to unsuspecting investors (*San Francisco Evening Bulletin* August 30, 1875, 1; Stone 1956, 316–317). As time went on, and especially after the big Comstock bonanza that Ralston had planned, worked, and hoped for went to the rival Silver Kings, he became even more of a gambler.

Around this time, Bank of California president D. O. Mills, who had often put a brake on Ralston's more risky ventures, decided to retire, leaving the bank presidency in Ralston's hands.

The bank's board also often failed to pay enough attention to bank business, so there was no real check on Ralston's vast ambitions and increasingly wild speculations. By 1874–1875, he was taking the bank's funds for his own personal ventures, leaving only IOUs. These funds increasingly went into dubious investments. One such investment involved a complex real-estate development scheme in San Francisco, which required approval by the state government (reportedly secured by the payment of $35,000, intensive lobbying of legislators, as well as daily restaurant bills of $400) and the construction of two massive new and expensive hotels (the Grand and the Palace) (Issel and Cherny 1986, 124).

Another speculation involved the massive purchase of Ophir Mine stock from, among others, E. J. "Lucky" Baldwin. This Comstock mine had been an early leader on the lode, but the great bonanza at deep levels did not extend to it, and its stock price later collapsed, causing Ralston another huge loss (Bean 1973, 231).

By this time, Ralston was overextended by millions of dollars. Growing desperate, he conceived a plan that would rescue his fortune and position at the expense of the City of San Francisco's taxpayers and water ratepayers. As part of this plan, Ralston would acquire a controlling interest in the Spring Valley Water Company, which supplied the city's water needs, and then use his substantial political power to secure the city's purchase of this company for an inflated price. This would result in a profit of millions for himself and his friends, who also invested in the scheme (Lavender 1975, 371).

By using the technique of the "monied fight" (a polite way to describe bribery), Ralston was able to influence the San Francisco Board of Supervisors over a time. One newspaper argued that Ralston controlled a majority of the board of supervisors from 1863 until 1875, adding that he was "overbearing," "domineering," and a "political dictator" (*San Francisco Evening Bulletin* August 30, 1875, 1). Ralston's proposal was exposed as a fraud on the city's taxpayers by several newspapers however, and a strong wave of opposition resulted. Fearing for their own political futures, the supervisors decided to stand up to Ralston, and refused to authorize the purchase (Issel and Cherny

1986, 125; *San Francisco Evening Bulletin* August 30, 1875, 1). Ralston hoped to win new supporters in the coming election for the board of supervisors, but the Bank of California's resources were by this time (mid-1875) stretched very thin by Ralston's many speculative activities during depressed times. At this decisive moment, the Irish Silver Kings decided to establish their Nevada Bank with a capital of five million dollars. Their conflict with Ralston and Sharon was a factor in their establishment of their own bank to compete with the Bank of California. Oscar Lewis later wrote that:

> *It was understood that the partners' entry into the banking business was an outgrowth of their feud with William Sharon and that their real purpose was to challenge the long-established supremacy of the Bank of California. (Lewis 1947, 257)*

The Palace Hotel San Francisco, 1875
This was one of William Ralston's major investments; one which helped bankrupt him. [Courtesy of the Bancroft Library, University of California, Berkeley.]

Flood, O'Brien, MacKay, and Fair had meanwhile become allied with the Big Four barons of the Central Pacific/Southern Pacific. The Big Four had also abandoned Ralston and his bank. The new president of the Nevada Bank was Louis McLane, president of the Pacific Mail Steamship Company and one of the main owners and former president of the Wells Fargo Bank, both corporations with increasingly close ties to the Central Pacific/Southern Pacific combine. McLane had also been on the board of the Bank of California until 1873, but left when Ralston took over as its president.

In an exchange between the leaders of the now rival banks, Ralston said he "would send Flood back to selling rum at the Auction Lunch Saloon." Flood answered that if he "should ever sell drinks again, it would be over the counter of the Bank of California" (Loomis 1968, 208).

It was Ralston who turned out to be wrong, as the new Nevada Bank drained needed cash both out of the Bank of California and out of the general economy at a crucial moment. Confidence in the future of the Bank of California collapsed and there was a rush by many to withdraw their funds. The money was not there to pay the creditors, since Ralston had depleted it in his overextended speculative ventures. The leading financial institution in the West then failed and was forced to suspend operations and close its doors on August 26, 1875. Many believed that the Silver Kings had brought Ralston and the Bank of California down (Lewis 1947, 258).

The bank directors met that afternoon. Ralston gave them a complete report, admitting that he had used the bank as his personal fiefdom, and now owed it $9.5 million. He could muster personal assets of about $4.5 million, leaving a huge deficit. He proposed a reorganization scheme to reopen the bank and repay the depositors. Upset, the other bank directors asked him to leave the room so they could discuss the situation and his proposal. William Sharon immediately moved that Ralston be forced to resign. The motion carried.

Suddenly out of power and in disgrace, that afternoon Ralston went on his usual swim towards Alcatraz Island in the cold waters of San Francisco Bay and died—drowned either by suicide or accident. Thus ended what was one of the most extraordinary business careers of nineteenth-century California, called by one historian, "a combination of blindness, negligence, splendor and magnificence" (T. Hittell 1898, 4:552). Over fifty thousand people reportedly attended his funeral; the procession was said to be six miles long.

The Bank of California was then rescued by a group of prominent and wealthy men, among them Sharon, D. O. Mills, and stock speculator E. J. "Lucky" Baldwin, each of whom pledged one million dollars to the fund to satisfy the bank's debts. The San Francisco Stock and Exchange Board pledged $250,000; Nevada senator John P. Jones pledged $200,000; and foundryman Peter Donahue and mine owner Thomas Bell pledged $150,000 each.

When the bank reopened in October 1875, among those present were most of the above named along with ex-mayor William Alvord, ex-governor Leland Stanford, Charles Crocker, Lloyd Tevis, J. B. Haggin, grain king Isaac Friedlander, millionaire Michael Reese, industrialist J. D. Fry, and banker John Parrott (*Daily Alta California* October 3, 1875, 1). It is interesting to note that although key railroad men like Stanford, Crocker, Tevis, and Haggin attended the reopening ceremonies, they were not listed among those who pledged money to reopen the bank.

Sharon was able to take over all of Ralston's extensive personal property, and tried to settle with the estate's creditors for sixty cents on the dollar. Following a court case, Sharon was forced to pay them all in full. Sharon also quickly moved into Ralston's Belmont house, sending the grieving widow Ralston and her family into the servant's quarters. Mrs. Ralston finally had to sue Sharon to get a settlement of $250,000 out of the many millions that her husband had once controlled. Sharon then boasted that he was the second richest man in California, behind only D. O. Mills, an overstatement since both the Big Four and the Silver

Kings were probably wealthier, but Sharon was now indeed a very wealthy man (Ostrander 1966, 58).

At a deeper level, the fall of Ralston and his bank was symbolic of the passing of an age, an age of excessive, even wild, speculation—in mining, in the San Francisco stock market, and in real estate. In this respect, it is interesting to note that none of Ralston's wealthy ruling-class friends were willing to come to the aid of the Bank of California while he ran it. This indicates that the ruling circles of California had largely repudiated the man even before his bank had failed, and that the bank's failure was needed to rid the economic and political body politic of a man increasingly seen as out of step with a more regularized and less speculative business and capital accumulation system.

THE CORPORATE SYSTEM AFTER THE FALL OF RALSTON, 1875–1880

On July 24, 1877, a California newspaper published an article on the rich men of California (Bancroft Scraps 1877, Set W, 30:14). With one major exception, the list appears accurate. The exception is its estimate of the collective wealth of the Big Four and their Central Pacific/Southern Pacific railroad empire at only fifty million dollars. Other sources during the same general period give a far higher figure. The New York–based business newspaper, *The Commercial and Financial Chronicle* (September 11, 1875, 251) stated that the directors of the Central Pacific Railroad "estimate the company's assets, including lands, at $183,971,054," for example. The *San Francisco Directory* estimated the Central Pacific alone as worth $187 million in 1878–79 (Langley 1879, 20). *Poor's Manual of the Railroads of the United States* for 1880 lists Central Pacific assets at $161.35 million and Southern Pacific assets at $68.24 million, giving a total of almost $230 million for both together (Poor 1880, 976, 991). Since the Big Four owned almost all of these two railroads, even after subtracting liabilities, they were probably collectively worth well over one hundred million in 1880, just counting their two main railroads and not their land and numerous other properties.

A close contemporary observer wrote in early 1883 that Huntington, Crocker, and Stanford together held a total of $155 million worth of stocks and bonds in the various railroad lines (*The Commercial and Financial Chronicle* January 20, 1883, 71). Turning to earnings, the Central Pacific alone had net earnings (after expenses), of about seventy million dollars in 1871–1879, and stock dividends were high. Retained land grants for the Central Pacific alone were estimated at twelve million acres (about 12 percent of the entire land area of California), alone worth fully thirty million dollars at the government minimum price (Poor 1880, 976, 980, 991). Clearly, the estimate of fifty million dollars total worth was far too low.

An analysis of the above-mentioned newspaper list discovers that there were three main groupings of California capitalists who were far richer than the others in 1877. These main groupings, the silver kings, the railroad barons, and the leading bankers—along with their wealth levels (understated in the case of the railroad barons)—were stated as follows:

- Flood, O'Brien, MacKay, and Fair (Silver Kings)—$100 million
- Stanford, Huntington, Crocker, and Hopkins (the Big Four)—$50 million
- Tevis and Haggin, allies of the Big Four—$10 million
- Bank of California Group—$46 million divided as follows:
  o D. O. Mills—$10 million
  o Michael Reese—$10 million
  o William Sharon—$8 million
  o Murphy Grant and Company—$5 million
  o E.J. Baldwin—$5 million
  o H.M. Newhall—$4 million
  o Nicholas Luning—$4 million

Other corporations and wealthy individuals, while important, followed:

- Donohoe-Kelly Banking (part of the Eugene Kelly banking firm of New York City)—$10 million
- Levi Strauss and Company (wholesale clothing and dry goods, real estate)—$10 million
- Pope and Talbot (lumber, timberlands, sawmills, urban real estate, ships)—$8 million
- John Parrott (banking)—$7 million
- S. and I. Glazier—$6 million
- James Phelan (banking)—$5 million
- Lazard Freres (French firm, banking, dry goods)—$5 million

Source: Bancroft Scraps 1877, Set W, 30:14.

Therefore, the ownership and control of most of the leading California corporations of the late 1870's, and, therefore, key sectors of the state's economy were held by only three interconnected groupings of capitalists.

The corporations of the Silver Kings included:

- Consolidated Virginia and California Mines (Comstock)
- Nevada Bank (Flood, MacKay, Fair, and Louis McLane directors)
- Selby Smelting and Lead Company (Flood and O'Brien, directors) The Silver Kings bought most of the stock of this firm from Thomas Selby in 1877.
- San Francisco Assaying and Refining Works

The corporations of the Big Four/Tevis and Haggin included:

- Central Pacific/Southern Pacific Railroad (Stanford, president of C. P., Huntington, Crocker, Hopkins, and Tevis, directors)
- Wells Fargo Bank (Tevis president, Stanford, Charles Crocker, and Charles F. Crocker, directors)

- Occidental and Oriental Steamship Company (jointly owned with the Union Pacific Railroad)
- Capitol Gas Company, Sacramento
- Huntington and Hopkins, wholesale hardware (Sacramento and San Francisco)
- *Sacramento Record Union* newspaper
- Tevis and Haggin partnership, allied with large mine owner George Hearst and reportedly included large ownership stakes in:
  - Wells Fargo bank
  - California Dry Dock Company
  - San Francisco Gaslight Company
  - Risdon Iron Works
  - California Street Railroad
  - Pacific Ice Company
  - Homestake Mining Company
  - Utah Mining Company
  - Spring Valley Water Company
  - Pacific Mail Steamship Company.

This partnership also included hundreds of thousands of acres of land in California's Central Valley, with a concentration in Kern County.

The Bank of California Group included:
- Bank of California (directors during 1875–1880 period):
  - D. O. Mills
  - William Alvord
  - William Sharon
  - Nicholas Luning
  - Drury J. Tallant
  - E. J. Baldwin
  - Charles Mayne
  - Michael Reese
  - Adam Grant
  - C. Adolph Low

- o Jerome Lincoln
- o H. M. Newhall
- o H. W. Carpentier
- Union Mine and Mill Company and Comstock mines
- Mission and Pacific Woolen Mills (J.D. Fry, president; he was a close and old friend of William Sharon and Ralston's father in law.)
- Virginia and Truckee Railroad (Mills and Sharon, directors)
- H. M. Newhall and Company (real estate, auctioneers, J. O. Eldridge a partner)
- Murphy, Grant and Company (wholesale dry goods)
- C. Adolph Low and Company (a Far Eastern trading company, connected to W. W. Montague)
- *Daily Territorial Enterprise* newspaper, Virginia City, Nevada (Sharon, owner, mainly used it to further his political career.)
- Security Savings Bank (Lincoln, vice president and a director; Alvord and Grant other directors)
- Kimball Car and Carriage Manufacturing Company
- Palace Hotel (owned by Sharon)
- Connections with Baring Brothers international bankers in London through C. Adolph Low, Baring's agent in San Francisco

There were direct economic ties between the silver kings, the railroad barons, and the bankers, as well as close social links, as we shall see. For example, two of the Bank of California's directors—H. M. Newhall and Charles Mayne—were also directors of the Southern Pacific Railroad in 1880, sitting on the Southern Pacific board with Charles Crocker and his son Charles F. Crocker; Stanford's representative and former business partner, N. T. Smith; and Collis P. Huntington's nephew and representative, W. V. Huntington (Poor 1880, 992). Wells Fargo

Bank, while mainly controlled by the Central Pacific/Southern Pacific group, also had D. O. Mills of the Bank of California as a director. The Pacific Rolling Mill was another key point of economic connection—in 1875, the main stockholders of this large firm included Mills and William Alvord of the Bank of California; Alvord was also president of Pacific Rolling Mill. Other large stockholders included Leland Stanford of the Central Pacific Railroad, Louis McLane of the Nevada Bank, and Oliver Eldridge of the Pacific Mail Steamship Company. When Pacific Rolling ran into financial problems in 1876, James Flood and Louis McLane of the Nevada Bank, D. O. Mills and Jerome Lincoln of the Bank of California, and banker John Parrott took over the firm.

Another key point of economic connection between the three groups was the California Dry Dock Company, whose main stockholders in the mid-1870s were Lloyd Tevis, J. B. Haggin, D. O. Mills, Louis McLane, Isaac Friedlander (a grain trader and speculator, a.k.a. the "Wheat King") and Oliver Eldridge. Finally, by 1886 the Anglo-Nevada Assurance Corporation of San Francisco had James L. Flood, John W. MacKay, and J. B. Haggin as directors, further linking the Nevada Bank and the Tevis-Haggin-Central Pacific/Southern Pacific combine together. At the same time, the higher circles of San Francisco were beginning to coalesce into a coherent whole.

SAN FRANCISCO HIGH SOCIETY MAKES NEWS IN NEW YORK, LATE 1876

In late 1876, San Francisco "high society" was still dominated by members of the transplanted, southern Chivalry, the former slave-owning nobility of the old South. One chronicler of San Francisco society explained as follows the key role of the old South's transplanted ruling class in imposing aristocratic standards on the rest of the San Francisco community:

> *Although the Southern influence represented by the tone of Chevy Chase[2] often merged with social traditions brought from Philadelphia, New York, New England, and Europe, it was the most important formative influence by far on emerging San Francisco society. The more prosperous the community became, the more it abandoned the easy, egalitarian standards of its early days in favor of stereotyped criteria of wealth and class distinction, as most readily defined by the Southern contingent. (Muscatine 1975, 356)*

The Chivalry was, however, generally much less wealthy than the "shovelry," the new industrialists like Stanford, Crocker, and Hopkins and the new mining millionaires like Flood, Fair, MacKay, and O'Brien. The difference between the class exclusiveness and "taste" of the established old rich and the desire of the new rich to be accepted was a main tension in the ruling class of the time. Such tensions were being overcome, slowly at first, then more rapidly due to the emerging class struggle with the working class (discussed in a later chapter). The first stage was reported on in the pages of *The New York Times*, which stressed the role of upper-class women. These ruling-class women, who had servants to do their housework and were banned by the men from direct involvement in politics and the economy, found their outlet in society and artistic endeavors; they held the power in the realm of "high society."

The fall of 1876 was a benchmark for San Francisco high society for it was then that *The New York Times* first noticed its existence in a serious way, printing three long articles on San Francisco society. The first of these articles pointed out that unlike New York society, which was based on church cliques, San Francisco society was secular and based on the leading wealthy families. *The Times* summed this up as follows:

---

2 Chevy Chase was an affluent suburb of Washington D.C.

*The social world of San Francisco may fairly be
represented by a pyramid, of which the first four steps
alone concern the reader, since these are the only ones
which are likely to have any effect upon the fortunes
of the city. Proudly mounted on the apex are three
"first families," all of whom are either Southerners, or
of Southern affiliations. These three are the McLanes,
formerly of Baltimore; the Hagginses and the Tevises.
Among the members of this triumvirate there is a
perfect equality, and the strangers whom any one of
the three take up are at once adopted without dispute
by the others. Social matters being here absolutely
and entirely in the hands of the fair sex, the female
heads of the triumvirate are despots as to who shall
be received and who shall be banned. Fortunately for
the world of the Pacific slope, they are ladies of high
refinement, much culture, and thorough believers in
the old-fashioned Southern style of social intercourse.
(November 26, 1876, 10)*

The article then elaborates on activities and the nature of the
highest circles of society, led by the "three great sisters," Mrs.
McLane, Mrs. Haggin, and Mrs. Tevis:

*One sees in all the entertainments of San Francisco
the secret pleadings of refined taste overcoming the
influence of commercial men, and the barbarism of
mining men. Dinner parties here are more prevalent
than they are in the East, and the style in which the
tables are set is captivating in the extreme to those
who are aesthetically inclined. The floral decorations
on such occasions are exceedingly tasteful ... Instead
of the very stiff and formal manner in which
tables, even in New York, are adorned, here the
beautiful blossoms are scattered profusely over the
whole damask ... On reception days the floral*

decorations partake of the same wild grace and unstudied elegance, but they are on a larger scale. All the ladies of any standing have receptions once a week, and by some tacit understanding these are arranged according to localities. Thus the ladies of Taylor Street receive on a Tuesday, the ladies on Bush Street on a Wednesday and the ladies of Nob Hill—as a part of California Street is profanely called—on a Thursday and so on …

There is a curious feature about visiting in San Francisco, which I must not fail to note. Having been regularly introduced to several very pleasant families, and having attended various receptions, I thought I would pay a little evening visit at a very charming house. I rang the bell accordingly, and when it was answered by the Chinese servant, handed my card. "Missus not leceiving," said the yellow minion. "Missus night Toosday; you come Toosday." I answered indignantly, "Take in my card at once." But he reiterated stoically, "Not leception night; wait Toosday, you come," and shut the door in my face …

I thought to myself this thing had gone far enough, and so I sought comfort and instruction from the lady who had presented me, and had been my social sponsor. "Bless you," she said, with a laugh, "you might ring the bell in vain at every house in San Francisco, even if you were as rich as Croesus instead of being a poor newspaper scribbler. These ladies only see visitors when they receive, and you cannot get a glimpse of them any other night." "Isn't that strange?" I said. "What does it mean?" "Well," she replied, "I don't know exactly. Slanderers and gossips say that half the ladies are in the suds, if you will

*understand that expression, but then, the other half
are certainly presentable on all occasions and at any
time. I have thought," she continued, "that people
have adopted this rule so as to prevent themselves
from being overrun by disagreeable visits."*

*The barbarism of "long lunches," which are gorges
for the exclusive delectation of the fair sex, forms
an integral portion of this letter, because it receives
the sanction of the "three great sisters," and must
therefore be noticed before I pass to a consideration of
the second step in the social pyramid of San Francisco.
The long lunch is a stand-up feast, accompanied
with an immense flow of champagne and with a
sufficiency of cordials … to which gentlemen are not
only not invited, but absolutely forbidden to come.
It is a sort of revenge which the fair sex has taken
as a compensation and set-off for the stag parties
in which the men of '49 delight.* (The New York
Times *November 26, 1876, 10)*

In the second article, *The New York Times* correspondent
focuses on the second, third, and fourth levels or "grades" of San
Francisco "society":

*The second grade in the social pyramid of San
Francisco, however, is a very peculiar one. It
consists … of the railroad aristocracy. The three
ruling families recognize them and are intimate
with them to a certain point, but are not intimate
with the people who comprise the third grade of the
social pyramid, with whom the railroad aristocracy
are intimate, also, up to a certain point. So, also, the
third grade, composed of the banking and brokering
element, the professional and commercial classes,
who are intimate up to a certain point with the*

mining millionaires, who form the fourth grade of society here. I must confess that this second grade, with one luminous exception, is for me the most disagreeable of all. The ruling families have some wealth, have culture and refinement, and hide their consciousness of their social supremacy with considerable tact and affability. The third grade contains social fractures of a very varied character, embracing all that is most pleasing in Eastern society, Western society, Southern society, and even French, English, and Spanish society. And it has more heartiness, more real culture than any other. The fourth grade is ostentatious in the display of a vulgar magnificence, but there is no assumption of superiority, and there is a genuine joviality and good humor and frankness that are very alluring. But the second grade, the railroad aristocracy, is bumptious and most disagreeably impressed with a sense of its wealth and its importance. And with the exception of one family—the Coltons—the railroad people are almost universally detested.

Perhaps this is because they are not Friscans. Truth to tell, they all, with the exception of the Coltons, hail from Sacramento, where they were petty shopkeepers. Of the manner in which they acquired their wealth, I have nothing to say … from the moment that this clique of Sacramentonians became wealthy, they launched out into absurd and laughable social displays … they deserted Sacramento and came to San Francisco, where they pitched upon the top of Clay Street hill and purchased entire blocks of land upon … California Street. They engaged Bugbee, the leading house architect of San Francisco, to erect structures for them … and then they announced

*their intention of being very exclusive. Whereupon
the Friscans laughed heartily at them, and christened
the locality they had chosen "Nob Hill."* (The New
York Times *December 3, 1876, 10)*

The correspondent also discussed the Charles Crockers'
massive mansion and the famous "spite fence" which Crocker
built around the house of a family which refused to sell their
property to him so he could own the entire block:

*In rear of this wonderful edifice … there is an
extraordinary wooden structure which, at first sight,
I took to be a California conservatory. It looked like
a gigantic fence some thirty feet high. But when,
like the moon, I had walked all around the house,
I found that it was no conservatory but an actual
fence. On the street in rear of Nob Hill there was
a meek little house of brick covered with adobe,
with its little garden in front. The great being who
owned the big mansion wanted the little house, and
the owner absolutely refused to sell it to him. Then
the great man in his wrath enclosed the little house
in a big fence, so that nothing can be seen of it from
three sides, save an inch and a quarter of chimney.
The house is suppressed, but the fence is a thousand
times more obnoxious than the house could have ever
been. It would have been so easy to mask the walls
with shrubs and evergreens and creepers, which are
here perennially in bloom, but then the great man
wanted the whole block to himself, and could not
bear the thought of having one corner lot in the
possession of a mudsill, who positively was not worth
more than twenty-five thousand dollars. He could
not exactly take Naboth's blood, so he penned him
in, and kept the sunshine and air from him. How
differently Gen. Colton has managed under precisely*

251

the same circumstances. He had only the front of the block, and at the rear, where his neighbors' houses touch his grounds and enclose him with their walls, he has raised a bank of green turf and has planted rows of beautiful evergreens ...

And so, when the Friscans inveigh against the railroad monopolists and gibe scornfully at the inhabitants of Nob Hill, Gen. Colton and his family are carefully separated from the others and are mentioned with praise and friendly feelings. (The New York Times *December 3, 1876; 10)*

Finally, *The New York Times* printed an article on the "Mining Aristocracy," the lowest "grade," and not really a part of San Francisco "society":

It often happens that objects which are most conspicuous at a distance are unimportant features of a landscape ... And so it is with the mining aristocracy of San Francisco. Here, with few exceptions, they are nothing, and in some instances, less than nothing; but viewed from a distance of three thousand miles the names of Flood and O'Brien, Fair and Mackey, Morrow and Lucky Baldwin loom up like mountain peaks and seem to be all California in themselves. Here in San Francisco not one of these potentates, viewed socially, has any standing whatever, save among the camp followers that follow his fortunes and pick up the speculative crumbs that fall from his table of mining accounts. (The New York Times *December 15, 1876, 7)*

The Irish Silver Kings were only recently poor men, and were therefore seen as of much lower rank. Furthermore, they had also tried to ruin the Bank of California and all the industrial establishments that depended upon this institution, making them (at least temporarily), beyond the pale:

> *Ralston and Sharon had for a time indeed contested the supremacy with the bonanza kings, but finding them too powerful, had yielded the palm and had retired from the mining arena. Messrs. Flood and O'Brien in pursuing them further and attempting to ruin the Bank of California and the companies that depended upon its … care, committed a crime against the well-being of the community, and therefore, when they attempted to profit by their success, society rose against them. All-powerful in everything relating to the mines, they found themselves completely ignored socially.* (The New York Times *December 15, 1876, 7)*

In one of its articles, *The Times* wondered about how the San Francisco-based California ruling class could be unified, asking, "How shall the best elements be cemented into one harmonious whole?" *The Times* answer was only through "strong leadership and rigid censors" (*The New York Times* December 11, 1876, 3). Leadership and unity were, in fact, soon to see rapid development, due to ruling-class fear of the dissatisfaction and rebellion of the San Francisco rank-and-file.

7

Resistance and Racialization—Capitalism and the California Working Class, 1850–1885

For the majority of the population, the three-decade-long period from the decline of the gold placers to the mid-1880s was marked by two main themes, the beginnings of working-class self-organization in a racially-charged capitalist setting, and the impact upon workers of a serious depression in the 1870s.

The decline of the gold placers, the landed monopoly, and the rise of capitalism in California during the 1850s and 1860s created a class of working people who owned no means of production (land, factories, or other large productive property), and had to survive by selling their labor power on the market. These workers had little individual social or economic power. As a result, they often recognized that they had to organize collectively and strike to gain their goals, which included a measure of control over their working lives and the surplus they created. This was manifested especially in the nineteenth century struggle for the eight-hour day and a living wage, a struggle that continues into our own time. The resulting organizing, strikes, and other on-the-job conflicts with the property owners are thus social markers, representing periodic revolts for worker self-realization against the autocracy of capital. They are the class response of workers who feel exploited and alienated by existing conditions. As the great socialist and labor leader Eugene V. Debs put it, "The strike is the weapon of the oppressed, of men capable of appreciating justice and having the courage to resist wrong and contend for principle. The nation had for its cornerstone a strike" (quoted in Boyer and Morais 1955, 119).

A strike often appears to be a struggle only over the terms and conditions of work (that is, only as an economic struggle) not over accumulation of wealth and power (a political struggle). But in fact, nearly all strikes represent conflicts that are both economic and political, whose outcomes shape future relations between the owning/ruling class and the working class, the plutocrats and proletarians, the rulers and rebels. Therefore, we can accurately speak of the historic responses of California's workers as resistance to the capitalist system, a political rebellion that began early in the history of capitalism in California.

If strikes were a central part of working-class attempts at self-actualization during this era, a second key aspect of the period was both the development of a culture of racism and white supremacy in America and the establishment and evolution of capitalist labor dynamics. In its struggle to survive and accumulate capital in what was a ruthlessly competitive system, the ruling class was relentless in its drive to extract more value from workers by speeding up the pace of work and cutting wages and conditions. To foster their accumulation, the capitalists continually searched for sources of cheaper, more exploitable labor.

One obvious source of such cheap labor was the use of non-white peoples who could be enslaved or made into debt peons either to avoid paying wages altogether or to at least keep wages very low. This strategy had the added advantage of fostering competition and division among the workers themselves. This also allowed the capitalists to play off different elements of the working class against each other, usually by race, but sometimes also by ethnicity and gender.

Workers tried to address this competition among workers both by creating unions and by using white supremacy to restrict the occupational access of those racial groups who were identified with more exploitative labor systems. White supremacist mob violence was also used to physically try to drive some racial groups out of certain jobs or out of the state. The exact role played by different elements among European-American workers— organized workers, unorganized workers, the unemployed, youth, various ethnic groups, and criminals—in such outbursts or "riots" as they were labeled by the newspapers of the time, is difficult to precisely determine. But the phenomenon of mob action was important and specific examples will be discussed below.

The 1870s represented an era of serious economic depression and conflict as California's infant political economy came into competition with eastern capital. The completion of the transcontinental railroad in 1869 was a mixed blessing for the state of California. On the one hand, railroad connection with the rest of the country made travel and the shipment of goods much easier. On the other hand, this very ease of commerce greatly increased the competition faced by California's young manufacturing industries and commercial establishments, causing layoffs, wage cuts, and bankruptcies in San Francisco, Sacramento, and other cities. *The New York Times* (July 13, 1870, 4), expressed the situation as follows:

> *All accounts, both from private and public, indicate a state of extreme depression in business matters in the Pacific States … The great cause of this unfortunate dullness of trade is, as is well known, the Pacific Railroad, which was dreamed of and hoped for as the great blessing of the State. There has been no great panic or financial disaster, or important failure of crops, or dearth of precious metals in the mines.*

> *The great basis of prosperity and financial wealth—
> the agricultural interest—remains substantially
> untouched. The simple fact is that California is now
> brought near the Eastern States, and all who carry
> on the exchanges of the country must compete with
> the retailers or wholesale dealers of other sections.
> Hitherto they have enjoyed a "protective tariff" laid
> by nature in separations by mountains and deserts
> of three thousand miles.*

> *Now, free communication is opened, and the
> commission-merchant of Chicago, or the dry-goods
> dealer of St. Louis, or even the jeweler of New York,
> sends his wares right to Virginia City, or Stockton, or
> San Francisco, and beats his California competitor
> out of the field.*

As the lawyer, banker, and society leader Lloyd Tevis later
observed:

> *[T]he completion of the railroad brought San
> Francisco merchants, in markets in which they
> before had undisputed control, face to face with the
> competition of the larger capital, the lower interest,
> the more active solicitation and rivalry of the great
> Eastern cities ... [T]he completion of the railroad,
> instead of bringing at once the rapid growth that was
> expected, brought rather a time of transition ... the
> accommodation of business to new relations and new
> channels. (Tevis 1881, 11)*

Perhaps as a compensating factor, in 1868 the federal
government signed the Burlingame Treaty with China, allowing the
importation of bonded Chinese laborers to increase substantially.
This gave California's employers access to an inexpensive pool of
unfree labor to cut wages, and meet the new competition.

The result was a transition that involved serious impacts to the jobs and wages of the rank-and-file worker. As the US Census Report on the *Statistics of Wages* expressed it, "From the completion of the Pacific railroad can be dated the beginning of the reduction of wages of all kinds" (US Census Office 1886, 56).

Unemployment and underemployment also became very high. While accurate figures are unavailable, some estimates suggest that as much as 20 percent of the state's labor force was unemployed by 1870. Whatever the real figure, it is clear that many people were desperate for work. When a job requiring 115 men was advertised in March of 1870, two thousand men showed up and a riot almost resulted (Shumsky 1972, 115). The crisis was thus a classic capitalist one: sharp competition between capitalists; a decline in the sale of California products; a falling rate of profit and a descending spiral; fewer sales; less production; and a push to lower wage costs, including layoffs.

CAPITAL, RACIALIZATION, AND THE ROLE OF NON-CAPITALIST LABOR SYSTEMS

It is not uncommon for a social formation to have a variety of different labor systems; what makes it a specific social formation is the *dominant* labor system. Capitalism, with its characteristic wage-labor system, rapidly came to preeminence in California during the years between the late 1850s and late 1860s. The organization of capitalist production, with its emphasis on efficiency and division of labor, tended to divide workers, making them easier to control.

The fact that the California working class was, from the beginning of the Gold Rush, multinational and multiethnic made it even more difficult for workers to develop the class consciousness and unity required to develop fully as a class and assert their interests. An aspect of this situation was the continued existence of other, non-capitalist labor systems in California during this period, and the use and abuse of people of color in these other, more oppressive labor systems. Two non-capitalist labor systems—peonage and slavery—continued to exist even after the advent of capitalist wage labor. The eventual identification of oppressed nationalities of color with these more backward and oppressive labor systems played an important role in creating a racist, white supremacist capitalism in California.

Slavery and peonage were exclusively reserved for colonized people of color—African Americans, Native Americans, and Chinese Americans. Both of these oppressive labor systems existed for decades in San Francisco, the heart of early capitalist California, as well as other cities and rural areas of the state. The basic function of maintaining and at times even expanding the number of racialized and colonized people who were deprived of basic civil and democratic rights, such as citizenship, the right to vote, and the right to testify in court, as well as economic opportunities, such as the right to own productive property, was to institute a cheap, reserve army of oppressed and desperate labor that would be available to use as strikebreakers and wage-cutters on a continuing basis, whenever the capitalist class wanted. Workplace demands over wages and working conditions could be more readily deflated with the existence of this reserve army of people who where culturally and ethnically different, denigrated, discriminated against, and forced to accept more oppressive conditions.

Thus, the capitalists understood, at a very early date, that if it could divide labor into more-favored (white) workers and disadvantaged (non-white) workers, they could cut both groups off at the legs and dominate them. A competitive antagonism between white and non-white workers already existed due to the long history of racialization and white supremacy in the United States; that cultural legacy was used and reinforced by the developing system of capitalist labor relations in California. This carefully fostered white supremacist system of racial oppression was characterized by internal colonialism and occupational apartheid. This was to be the basic strategy of the capitalists and sectors of the white working class throughout this and later periods.

Important examples of slavery and peonage in California during this period illustrate the exclusive application of these labor systems to people of color, the forces that benefited from this oppression and exploitation, and the development of resistance to such systems.

AN AFRICAN AMERICAN EXAMPLE

African Americans, who made up a very small percentage of California's population during this period, were sometimes kept as slaves in the 1850s by Southerners in violation of the California constitution. Federal and Southern-states fugitive slave laws complicated the situation, making it more difficult for these slaves to gain their freedom by living in a free state.

In 1858, the northern part of California was stirred into excitement over the fate of Archy Lee, a young African American slave whose owner, one C. V. Stovall, wanted to return him to Mississippi. Stovall had used Archy as wagon driver and cook on his trip across the plains to California in 1857. Upon arrival in Sacramento, Stovall had opened a school and hired out Lee to make additional money. Then Stovall decided to return to the South, taking Archy with him.

Upon learning of Stovall's plan, Lee escaped, having found out (probably from free African Americans in Sacramento), that California law might protect him. He was recaptured, however, and taken to county court, the owner arguing that Archy Lee was a fugitive slave who should be returned to slavery. The local judge decided that Lee was not a fugitive slave within the definitions of state or federal law, because Stovall had lived and engaged in business in the free state of California.

The owner then appealed to the California Supreme Court, which was dominated by pro-slavery Southern Democrats. They ruled that, although they recognized that the California constitution and law was clearly on the side of Archy Lee, Stovall could still take the young African American back to Mississippi, due to the fact that Stovall, although young, was not in good health and so needed the services of "his" slave!

Many Californians refused to take the biased and unfair decision of the California Supreme Court as the last word. The newspapers of the state were immediately filled with strong protests, and some rebels, led by local African Americans, determined to resist the Supreme Court and free Archy by mass, direct action. When Stovall tried to bring a heavily manacled and guarded Lee to San Francisco to leave by ship for Panama, he found a waterfront patrolled day and night by fifty to a hundred African Americans, one of whom had secured a writ of habeas corpus from a local court for Archy and also sworn out a warrant charging Stovall with kidnapping. Although Stovall tried to avoid capture by boarding a ship after it had already gotten underway, he was nevertheless captured and arrested.

Archy Lee was subsequently set free after a court hearing in San Francisco (Eaves 1910, 99–103). Although African Americans were disenfranchised and not allowed to testify against European Americans in the courts, they had successfully organized a mass action to counter those in the state who were supporting slavery and other oppressive labor systems.

THE OPPRESSION OF NATIVE AMERICANS

California Indians were a second, and much larger, group of people who were often enslaved or kept in peonage well into the capitalist era. California laws made the enslavement of Indians (technically, indentured servitude) legal during the 1850–1863 years, and the practice even continued after 1863 (Heizer and Almquist 1971, 39–58; Almaguer 1994, 131–136). Anthropologist and historian Sherburne Cook estimated that between three and four thousand Indian children were kidnapped and sold as "servants" during the 1852–1867 years alone, along with an unknown number of Indian women taken and sold for concubinage and labor purposes (Cook 1976, 315; see also Almaguer 1994, 120). Contemporary observers often conveniently claimed that this was not slavery but merely a kind of servitude, even though these Indian children were sometimes sold and were often only captured after their parents' murders. Thus, government surveyor William H. Brewer could write in 1863:

> *It has for years been a regular business to steal Indian children and bring them down to the civilized parts of the state, even to San Francisco, and sell them— not as slaves, but as servants to be kept as long as possible. Mendocino County has been the scene of many of these stealings (sic), and it is said that some of the kidnappers would often get the consent of the parents by shooting them to prevent opposition. (Brewer [1863] 1966, 493)*

Although understating its extent, in 1861, the federal government's Indian agent W. P. Dole was more blunt in his description of the practice of enslavement of Indians:

> *In the frontier portions of Humboldt and Mendocino Counties a band of desperate men have carried on a system of kidnapping for two years past. Indian children were seized and carried into the lower counties and sold into virtual slavery. These crimes against humanity so excited the Indians that they began to retaliate by killing the cattle of the whites. At once an order was issued to chastise the guilty ... a company of United States troops, attended by a considerable volunteer force, has been pursuing the poor creatures from one retreat to another. The kidnappers follow at the heels of the soldiers to seize the children, when their parents are murdered, and sell them to the best advantage. (Cook 1976, 312–313)*

Many of these reports make it appear that these crimes were isolated in time and space, and only a relative few were guilty. In fact, this "enterprise" was widespread, and the massacre and enslavement of Indians was standard practice. In Sacramento during the early 1860s, for example, Indian slave children were reported seen in "every fourth white man's house." When a relatively few of these crimes reached the courts, the European American perpetrators were invariably set free to prey on the innocent again (Cook 1976, 313–314). The resistance of native people to this exploitation was as unsuccessful as it had been during earlier phases of California history, resulting in a sharp and continuing decline in Indian population and self-control over land and other resources.

CHINESE PEONAGE AND SLAVERY IN CALIFORNIA

A third, and by far most important, example of the use of pre-capitalist labor systems during this era was the extensive practice of holding Chinese men in a system of debt peonage and Chinese women in a system of debt slavery. The Chinese in California had begun to arrive in significant numbers during the Gold Rush, and the majority of those who came remained in the mining industry until the mid-1860s. The Chinese mining population reached a peak in 1863, and then sharply declined over the next several years, as the last worthwhile placer gold deposits were exhausted (Chiu 1967, 28–29).

Most of the thousands of Chinese leaving the placer mines, along with new arrivals, became waged laborers, some with the Central Pacific Railroad and others in varied urban and rural occupations (especially agriculture, construction, woolen mills, boot and shoe making, fishing and fish packing, canneries, tobacco, and clothing). Chinese workers were usually not independent agents individually applying for a job, however; most were part of an organized system of power and control extending all the way back to China. An understanding of this larger power structure of peonage and slavery, its connections with the US white system of power and exploitation, and the resulting subordination and control—as well as the resistance to it—is fundamental to a comprehension of the history of both Chinese workers and of the wider California working class during this era.

Even today, over one hundred and fifty years since the beginnings of Chinese California, there is still controversy and distinct perspectives about the essence of its power structure. Observers generally agree that associations based on place of origin, ancestry, occupation, or creed made up the complex network of social power that controlled Chinese California. But there is no general agreement on the real nature of these various groups. Some experts have stressed the benevolent and charitable functions of these associations, while others have focused on the oppressions and abuses imposed by the exact same bodies. In reality, both aspects are in varying degrees true, and only a careful consideration of the whole Chinese experience can approach an accurate historical evaluation.

The overwhelming majority of California Chinese came from the Pearl River region of South China. Most were poor males who had close ties to family, clan relations, and homeland. Wanting to help their extended families survive in the difficult economic and political environment of the mid-nineteenth century, these "Sojourners," as they came to be called, were willing to travel far from home and, temporarily, work in difficult conditions in a foreign land in order to send money back to their relatives. Trusting the agents of "companies" (associations) who were willing to advance them money for the passage to California, they left expecting to make a decent living, pay off their debt, then return to China (Loomis 1868, 224–225). But when the Sojourners arrived in California, they found themselves to be largely powerless indentured emigrants, in debt-bondage to merciless merchant-creditors who hired them out to others, often for a pittance.

In 1870, the *Daily Alta California,* quoting *The New York Times,* called this bondage system "modified slavery," adding that, "Ship loads of Chinese have been brought over under contract for years—their labor mortgaged for a lengthened period, at wages on which a white man could not live, in consideration of their passage ... in effect they are but a few degrees removed from slavery (*Daily Alta California* July 17, 1870, 1).

Low wages, combined with the legendary Chinese ability to be extremely frugal, did allow a certain percentage of these debtors to accumulate enough to pay their debts and return home. After becoming independent agents, some stayed in California. But in the late 1860s and throughout the 1870s, more new debtors were coming into California than were leaving, assuring that the debt peonage system was maintained and expanded, and that the Chinese American population increased.

This population, able-bodied adult men, went from 34,933 in 1860 to 49,310 in 1870 to 75,218 in 1880, making the Chinese American labor force over 20 percent of California's total during this era (Loomis 1868, 224–225; US Census Bureau 1883, 382, 811). This development was fostered by the policies of a Republican-controlled federal government, which, in 1868, signed the Burlingame Treaty with China, guaranteeing free migration and facilitating the importation of bonded labor forced to work for low wages under harsh conditions.

The keystone of the debt-peonage system was the power over the Chinese population of a few large district-based associations, called the "Six Companies." This control was usually reinforced by what were called "tongs," which consisted of a varied group of smaller family associations, guilds, and secret societies. Tongs could be family-, occupation-, or district-based, and often operated independently, although under the overall influence of the larger Chinese power structure. As a result, the tongs sometimes violently conflicted with each other and other elements of the Chinese power structure.

These groups were necessary because the debt-peonage (for men) and outright slavery (for most women) that resulted from the indentured emigrant system lacked the support of American law and custom. Extralegal, often violent, controls therefore had to be exerted by the Chinese power structure. The Chinatowns of California were thus merely the visible parts of a hidden world, where the social and economic ties created by these organizations guaranteed the continuing functioning of the indentured emigrant-debt-peonage system.

Such a system, operating as it did within a very different set of laws and customs, could not work perfectly, since the supreme arbiter (the district associations or Six Companies) did not have legal police and military power to completely enforce its will with the legitimate use of force. Therefore, conflicts were constant, involving everything from tong wars and wildcat strikes to individual escapes from bondage. The social and economic pressures exerted by both the companies and the tongs substituted for police, to some extent, and were enough to keep the system in place for many decades, but not without frequent disruption. The goals and actions of the emigrants who rebelled also sometimes had an effect, as we will see below.

The associations that brought together and enforced this system also had their "benevolent" aspects, such as organizing limited medical services for some of the sick and indigent, legally defending Chinese in American courts, hiring private police to guard Chinese stores, shipping the remains of the deceased back to China, and keeping track of all Chinese by registrations and bookkeeping (Hoy 1942, 20–21). But, as Gunther Barth put it:

> *[T]he dividing line between outright oppression and hidden exploitation under the guise of self-help or benevolence, always remained thin … Behind a facade of benevolent precepts, the companies and tongs of Chinese California … supervised or oppressed their countrymen. With the aid of district companies and clan associations, the merchant creditors controlled the mass of indentured emigrants. (Barth 1964, 79–80)*

The district associations/Six Companies (the actual number over the years varied between five and eight), led by "merchants" (Chinese commercial capitalists), were initially at the apex of the system controlling Chinese debtor emigrants. Chinese culture stressed that the gentry and scholar-officials should rule, but few from these higher levels of Chinese society came to California, so "merchants" rose to fill leadership roles (Muscatine 1975, 392–393). The term "merchant" included, for the Chinese, the following monied occupations: traders, manufacturers, agents, contractors, managers, bankers, and proprietors. These merchants combined "the prestige of mandarins, the wealth of gentry, the authority of family heads, the status of scholars, and the power of creditors" (Barth 1964, 81).

The firms they controlled were the usual connection point between the Chinese and American worlds. Centered in San Francisco's Chinatown, merchants were the leaders of the associations or companies of people from certain Pearl River districts, and virtually all the Chinese Sojourners belonged to one of these organizations. The Six Companies enforced the rules of debt bondage, keeping track of all the emigrants from their district by requiring all new Sojourners to register with their district association, pay a fee, and keep up interest on their debt.

The Six Companies also kept account books on each person so they could be prevented from leaving the United States if they still had outstanding debts. The Six Companies had close ties to the corporate shipping firms (such as the Pacific Mail Steamship Company) and entered into agreements with them to require a certificate from the association prior to the purchase of a ticket back to China. This certificate showed that they were debt free and could be allowed to leave (Dillon 1962, 78; Barth 1964, 91). The Six Companies spoke for the Chinese, acted as their highest court, and even, for a time, their diplomatic representative from the Chinese government. It was in effect, the governing body for all Chinese Californians (Muscatine 1975, 394).

Each of the Six Companies also had smaller companies associated with it, and it was these small companies that did the actual labor contracting, supplying California's industrialists, mine owners, large farmers, and railroad companies with inexpensive Chinese workers, men who were their debt peons and therefore forced to work cheaply and often in dangerous conditions. San Francisco newspaper articles based on legislative investigations during the mid-1870s illustrate the workings of the Chinese labor system at the most basic level. For example, a lawyer for Einstein and Brothers, a boot and shoe company employing two hundred to three hundred Chinese workers, stated that his company paid "E. Chy Lung and Company" to organize and send these workers to them, and directly collected the wages of these workers. "E. Chy Lung and Company" was further identified in the newspaper as one of the companies forming the Hop Wo Company, one of the Six Companies of Chinatown (*Daily Alta California* April 15, 1876, 1). A similar system operated in agriculture.

A reporter on late nineteenth-century California described his discussion with a large-scale farmer about the advantages of the system as follows:

> *[T]he admirable organization of the Chinese labor is an irresistible convenience to the farmer. "How do you arrange to get your Chinese?" I asked a man in the country who was employing more than a hundred in several gangs. He replied, "I have only to send to a Chinese employment office in San Francisco, and say I need so many men for such work and such pay. Directly up come the men, with a foreman of their own, with whom alone I have to deal. I tell him only what I want done; I settle with him alone; I complain to him, and hold him alone responsible. He understands English; and this system simplifies things amazingly. If I employed white men I should have to instruct, reprove, watch, and pay each one separately; and of a hundred, a quarter, at least, would be dropping out day after day for one cause or another. Moreover, with my Chinese comes a cook for every twenty men, whom I pay, and provisions of their own which they buy. Thus I have nobody*

> *to feed and care for. They do it themselves." (Derks*
> *2000, 36)*

Since it was these smaller associated companies who did the actual labor contracting, the Six Companies could argue that they were not directly involved in the exploitation of labor. This was mere subterfuge, however, for the Six Companies kept the books, enforced the rule that no one could return to China without permission and also coordinated the overall system. Their leaders also greatly benefited economically from the system and lived in wealth and luxury (Barth 1964, 93). As Bancroft's *History of California* summarized their power:

> *The Chinese Six Companies were really contractors and importers, although they attempted to pass themselves off as benevolent organizations. They governed and controlled with an iron hand, all the Chinese in the country, and sustained a secret organization of highbinders, who were not only detective police, but secret avengers of any infraction of the companies' rules. So swift and mysterious were their blows that the San Francisco police seldom succeeded in capturing a highbinder who had extracted "blood atonement" in the Chinese quarter. (Bancroft 1890, 7:344)*

Even the Six Companies themselves, in their own publications, admit to being the controlling force in Chinese California, "When, therefore, the seven district groups—which sociologically speaking, constitute the basic social control groups among the California Chinese—unite together to form a coordinating organization such as the Chinese Six Companies, the social power that such an agency would wield is practically without limit" (Hoy 1942, 18).

To sum up, in the case of the Chinese, the system for the exploitation of Chinese labor was based on an informal alliance between the merchant-capitalist-controlled Six Companies and leading California capitalists and landowners. One visitor to California remarked in 1869 that the managers of the Six Companies and the leading Chinese merchants "all hold friendly relations with the leading citizens and public men of California" (Bowles 1869, 407). One result was cheap Chinese labor, undercutting the wages, hours, and working conditions of the "free" workers, along with super-profits for capital. Another was the near total control over the tens of thousands of Chinese workers in California and the West. As one knowledgeable observer wrote in the mid-1870s, "These Companies are said to hold almost despotic sway over the Chinese laborer … It is believed, by those who are best informed, that there is not a Chinaman working in the mines, on the ranches, in the depth of the forest, at points the most remote from civilization, whose movements, plans, prospects, are not regularly reported to his company in San Francisco" (Minturn 1877, 320).

The Six Companies held the Chinese workers through tight organization, debt-peonage, and violence. The worker was in debt and had to repay it through work and future earnings. The Six Companies, which also served as a kind of supreme court for the Chinese in California, was the main organizing and coordinating force for the overall system (Chinn et al. 1969, 15–17, 64–66). Discipline was enforced, Mafia-like, both by secret tribunals and the violence of gangs of toughs called "highbinders" (Minturn 1877, 320). The overall result was that these workers were more like slaves and peons than wage workers.

In 1869, when the use of Chinese labor was under attack by the rising working-class movement in California, San Francisco merchants and others who benefited from the exploitation of these Chinese workers formed a "San Francisco Chinese Protection Society" to defend their exploitation and extol the benefits of this system. In an 1869 newspaper article, their secretary, H. C. Bennett, stated:

> *There is no people in the world who conduct their business more systematically than the Chinese. Those here, from the richest merchant to the … rag picker, are all directly or indirectly under the supervision of what are known as the "six companies," organizations similar in their operations to our express companies. These companies are managed by Boards of Trustees residing here, but having their chief officers in China … The managers of the branches here keep a record of every man, woman and child who arrives in this State, also a list of all who return, die or leave the State … The six companies collect and remit to China the savings of the Chinese, aggregating from $20,000 to $100,000 by each steamer. (*Sacramento Daily Union *November 27, 1869, 8)*

Secretary Bennett had access to records of the Six Companies and therefore could offer specifics on the numbers, occupations, and locations of employment for about 89,500 Chinese in California, other Western states, and even the Southern states of the United States. California had by far the largest population of Chinese, and, in 1869, Bennett listed their main occupations, approximate numbers, and places of employment (San Francisco and interior counties of California) as follows (*Sacramento Daily Union* November 27, 1869, 8):

- Construction of Central Pacific Railroad—8,500 (in interior)
- Females—7,350 (4,800 in San Francisco, 2,550 in interior)
- Miners—6,500 (in interior)
- Male Domestic Servants/Cooks—6,000 (4,500 in San Francisco, 1,500 in interior)
- Laborers—5,500 (1,000 in San Francisco, 4,500 in interior)

- Factory/Mill Workers—3,000 (1,500 in San Francisco, 1,500 in interior)
- Cigar Makers—2,750 (in San Francisco)
- Shopkeepers/Traders—2,700 (1,200 in San Francisco, 1,500 in interior)
- Farmhands/Woodchoppers—2,500 (in interior)
- Shoemakers—830 (in San Francisco)
- Laundrymen—764 (in San Francisco)

Interestingly, Secretary Bennett failed to mention the occupations of the 7,350 females he lists in his article, but this is not a surprise given that his main purpose is to justify a slave/peonage system that mainly benefited the wealthy, both Chinese American and European American. In fact, the great majority of these poor Chinese women were slaves, forced to be domestic servants and prostitutes in the homes of the rich and the brothels of San Francisco's Chinatown and smaller Chinatowns all over California and the West.

It is unclear exactly when the practice of enslaving and buying and selling Chinese women began, but a court case during April 1861 indicates that it was already established by that time. The case, an early one of many thousands to come, told the sad story of a poor Chinese mother, Chang Mong, who was forced to sell her daughter Sing Ye into servitude for a term of four years or until Chang Mong's loan was repaid. The terms included the usual usurious 5 percent per month interest. The essence of the agreement, which was reprinted in the newspapers, was as follows, "Whereas, one Chong Tong has advanced passage money for Sing Ye in order that she should cross the waters for California, therefore the sum of $370 is hereby borrowed by her mother ... Chang Mong, stipulating that the said Sing Ye pledges her body and services to Chong Tong for the term of four years, or until full payment of same, when this agreement shall be canceled" (*Sacramento Daily Union* April 12, 1861, 3).

In fact, of course, there was no escape for Sing Ye and thousands of other working-class Chinese women. They were forced into a

permanent state of slavery, were bought and sold, and forced to
work as servants and prostitutes by the Six Companies, tongs,
and powerful European American capitalists, who benefited from
this infamous system (Wegars 1993, 231–234). Among the latter
were the Pacific Mail Steamship Company, one of the largest
corporations in California and the holder of profitable contracts
to transport US Mail. As Secretary Bennett pointed out in his
defense of the system, "all the females come here on board the
Pacific Mail Steamship Company's vessels" (*Sacramento Daily
Union* November 27, 1869, 8).

Once in the United States, Chinese women were under the
control of a combination of tongs and the Six Companies. During
the long history of the Chinese in California, one or another of
the tongs were powerful actors within the Six Companies, and
sometimes they conflicted with the Six Companies. Some tongs
successfully achieved control over certain economic fields, mainly
those that were illegal or occupying the borderlines of the law,
such as opium smuggling, gambling, and prostitution. The tongs
made their own connections with California's dominant society
by bribing police and politicians, and hiring prominent lawyers
to defend them when they were caught violating the law (Barth
1964, 100–107; Bancroft Scraps 1877, Set W, 6:224).

One of the laws that were regularly violated was the
constitutional prohibition on slavery. Chinese females were
regularly sold as slaves in San Francisco throughout the late
nineteenth century, a practice that continued as late as 1909 (*The
California Weekly* January 26, 1909, 213). One such brutal slave
market was known as the "Queen's Room." This location was
apparently St. Louis Place off Jackson Street in San Francisco's
Chinatown (Lawson and Rufus 2000, 210). In his book *Pigtails
and Gold Dust,* Alexander McLeod (1948, 178) described what
went on at a San Francisco slave market:

> *Here Chinese slave girls were brought from ships and
> exposed for examination to the prospective buyers,*

*who rated them according to their various standards
of physical beauty. Sometimes the girls were treated
in a horrible manner which was supposed to render
them more valuable for the purpose for which they
were purchased ... they were placed on sale in the
Queen's Room at from 100 to 300 per cent profit on
their cost in China, and were critically examined by
purchasers from town and country.*

Some of these women became the wives of the more prosperous
Chinese, but most were forced into prostitution. San Francisco
alone had a thousand or more Chinese prostitutes at any given
time in the 1870s, 1880s, and 1890s. Prices for these slaves were
as high as one thousand dollars on the San Francisco market,
although in earlier days they sold for half that price (Bancroft
Scraps 1877, Set W, 6:224). Many women were locked up and left
alone to die or were murdered once they became too unattractive
or diseased to be of use to those who owned them. In late 1869,
the *San Francisco Chronicle* described the horror of what took
place in such a "hospital," as it was called:

*When any of the unfortunate harlots is no longer
useful and a Chinese physician passes his opinion that
the disease is incurable, she is notified that she must
die ... Led by night to this hole of a "hospital" ... she
is forced within the door and made to lie down ...
A cup of water, another of boiled rice, and a little
metal oil lamp are placed by her side ... those who
have immediate charge of the establishment know
how long the oil should last, and when the limit is
reached they return to the "hospital," unbar the door
and enter ... Generally the woman is dead, either
by starvation or from her own hand; but sometimes
life is not extinct ... but this makes little difference
to them. They came for a corpse, and never go away
without it ... A woman—helpless, useless, without*

> *value to those who claim to own her—is murdered.*
> (San Francisco Chronicle *December 5, 1869, 3)*

A final group of important organizations in Chinese California were the Chinese trade unions that tongs organized around occupation and skill. They were organized like other trade unions to set up apprenticeship training, prevent destructive competition, take care of sick members, negotiate with employers, and if necessary, strike for better wages and conditions (Dillon 1962, 85). As was the case with California's European American unions of the period, these were mainly craft unions, excluding the unskilled in order to increase bargaining power. These unions were apparently a late development, but by the mid-1880s, San Francisco had Chinese craft unions that included carpenters, bricklayers, gold and silver workers, jewelers, bakers, shoemakers, clothing workers, and cigar makers (California Bureau of Labor Statistics 1888, 184–185).

THE BEGINNINGS OF WORKING CLASS ORGANIZATION AND RESISTANCE

Unlike the California upper class, the working class of the state was far short of being an organized, unified, and conscious class-for-itself during this era. Most union leaders and rank-and-file members responded to capitalist exploitation and the use of un-free labor by taking an "exclusionist" or craft-union approach to the problem, trying to narrow the labor market by excluding those who were not part of the favored race or gender or did not have the required skills. By narrowing the labor market, they hoped to increase the price of labor and improve hours and conditions. Making exclusionary deals with the employers on the basis of class collaboration and white supremacy/white solidarity against workers of color and the unskilled was also part of this approach. A more inclusive or industrial union approach was generally not common during this era. This latter approach could have strengthened the working class *as a class* by organizing everyone, irrespective of skill level, race, ethnicity, or gender, working towards the free association and free development of all. This could have led to a more confrontational approach in relations with the bosses, could have used the collective power of all working people to fight not only for better hours, wages, and conditions but also to advance a vision of a different future, one of self-realization, solidarity, real democracy, and social justice.

Although the California working class was weakened by the dominant craft unions' exclusionism, elements of the class frequently organized unions and conducted strikes and political struggles. Out of such organized struggle and collective action, developed tendencies toward self-management, solidarity, and unity—all characteristics required to move existing society toward more equality and justice. An important example of this early organizing that was instrumental in the development of a conscious working class was the 1864 strike against the foundries.

With the rise of large-scale capitalist relations of production in the late 1850s and early 1860s, a number of wage workers' protective organizations began to be formed, especially in San Francisco, where industrial capitalism first had a serious impact. By 1863, there were a number of these unions, and the tailors union took the lead in organizing a central labor council (Cross 1935, 31–33). Called the San Francisco Trades Union, by early 1864 the council included fifteen unions with a total membership of about three thousand (Knight 1968, 8). In April of that year, the first of the struggles of rebellion and resistance by working people against capitalist exploitation began. The "Journeymen Iron Moulders' Protective Union" went on strike against Peter Donahue's Union Iron Works and other San Francisco foundries due to, as the strikers expressed it, "the refusal of employers to pay a reasonable rate of wages to those in their employ ... We ask only a living price for our labor, and we are determined to stand by it" (*Daily Alta California* April 3, 1864, 1).

This language was in a notice sent out to other iron moulders in California that San Francisco Iron Moulders were on strike and that no one should believe they could work in this occupation in San Francisco without first joining the Journeymen Iron Moulders Protective Union, the members of this organization "being prepared for any and all emergencies which may arise during the 'strike'" (*Daily Alta California* April 3, 1864, 1).

In this strike, the iron moulders established some important trade-union principles—in addition to the need for a living wage—such as the power to set wage rates, solidarity among journeymen workers, and the concept of the union shop; in short, a defining of the union as a place for working people to participate in decision making in the economic realm. On the negative side, it institutionalized exclusionism as a union principle. Apprentices, men and boys who lacked the training and experience to be journeymen, were excluded from the union and the strike, and so continued to work during the struggle. This lack of solidarity, growing out of the narrowness of craft union organization and often connected to white supremacy, was to prove, over and over again, to be a major problem for the full self-actualization of California's working class.

Within a week, the strike expanded, when about half of San Francisco's boilermakers joined the struggle for higher wages. Whereas the moulders had demanded four dollars for the prevailing ten-hour day as their living wage, the boilermakers wanted $4.50 to $5.00 for a ten-hour day (*Daily Alta California* April 8, 1864, 1).

The owners of San Francisco's foundries responded to this early strike in a way that would become typical. First, they tried to divide the striking workers by offering higher wages to some, but not all. The union men refused this "compromise" which would have destroyed their unity and solidarity. Second, the bosses attempted to find other workers—strikebreakers, derogatively known as scabs or blacklegs—who would work on the strike and do the job of the striking men. Both apprentices and what were called "irregular" workers were used, but this proved inadequate to maintain production. The moulders and boilermakers were skilled workers and difficult to replace. As a final tactic, the employers decided to use new channels of transportation and communication to rapidly bring scab workers from the eastern states to break both the strike and the union. As the *Daily Alta California* reported on April 8, 1864 (1):

> *The proprietors of leading machine shops have telegraphed to New York, Boston, Providence, and Portland, Maine, where they have engaged all the men they require—though, practical workmen—at rates they feel able to pay; and by advancing their fare to this city, will be able, in some twenty days from this time, to resume work with full force.*

This attempt to import strikebreakers failed, however, when union representatives met the potential scabs as they were crossing Panama en route to California, successfully persuading them to join the strike upon arrival. The employers then had to capitulate and agree to the union's demands. In this initial struggle, the workers had won, encouraging them to begin an even more important and difficult struggle: the demand for the eight-hour day (Cross 1935, 35–36; Knight 1960, 8).

THE INITIAL STRUGGLE FOR THE EIGHT-HOUR DAY, 1865–1870

Beginning in 1865, San Francisco unions launched a major effort to achieve the eight-hour day. A legislative strategy was adopted initially, but a coordinated effort to get the state legislature to pass an eight-hour law was narrowly defeated in 1866 (Knight 1960, 9). This led some workers to begin to enforce the eight-hour day through job actions—working for eight hours and no more. That summer, employers countered the workers efforts by organizing a Ten-Hour Association, agreeing not to employ wage workers except on a ten-hour a day basis. Large, waterfront employers like the Pacific Mail Steamship Company then fired all employees who would work only eight-hours (Cross 1935, 48).

The unions redoubled their efforts on the political front, forming a statewide "Mechanics State Council," and supported the long out-of-power Democrats in the 1867 election (Cross 1935, 50–51). Hungry for success and power after the bitter experience of the Civil War, the Democrats decided to sign on to an eight-hour law. With labor support, the Democratic Party then won this contest, electing a governor for the first time since 1860. The result was the passage of an eight-hour-a-day law, signed by Governor Haight on February 21, 1868 (Eaves 1910, 206). The following night there was a torchlight parade of about three thousand San Francisco workers to celebrate a great victory for working people. About twenty different unions participated in the march, carrying thousands of torches and signs. Called *transparencies*, these signs expressed basic sentiments bonding the working class: "Sweethearts and clean hands at 5 P.M."; "Man is not a machine, he needs a rest"; "We will help the Ladies' Cooperative Union" (*The San Francisco Call* February 23, 1868, 3; *San Francisco Evening Bulletin* February 24, 1868, 3).

The celebration was premature, however, since the capitalists were intent on maintaining the ten-hour day, and the new law was weak and had no real enforcement provisions. Unions and workers then attempted, throughout 1868 and 1869, to enforce the law through strikes and other job actions. San Francisco street graders undertook one of the first such strikes in May 1868. The *Daily Alta California* (May 8, 1868, 1) reported:

> *The laborers engaged in street grading … in San Francisco … are now on a strike. They demand an increase of 25 per cent on their present wages, or what is equivalent to it, a reduction of 20 per cent on the hours of labor, with no diminution in the rates of wages. There are plenty of men who would gladly accept the wages hitherto paid, and take the place of the strikers … [who] went around yesterday, and by a liberal display of clubs and threats of violence*

> *compelled all who were willing to work ten hours to*
> *desist at once … No arrests have been made as yet.*

In an attempt to solve this impasse, about a hundred contractors met and decided to allow the men to work by the hour instead of by the day, so that some could work eight hours if they so chose. The contractors offered twenty cents an hour pay—or $1.60 for eight hours, and $2.00 for ten. The laborers refused to accept this compromise, however, and the strike went on (Eaves 1910, 208; *Daily Alta California* May 9, 1868, 1). The contractors then decided to try to break the strike, importing scabs from the eastern states for that purpose. The *Alta* (May 13, 1868, 1) reported, "Several thousand able-bodied men from Pennsylvania and New York, accustomed to labor upon public works, have arrived here within a few days by steamer, and went to work with alacrity at the wages offered … Many arrived on Sunday and went to work on Monday. The contractors say that they are generally unusually good workmen …" (*Daily Alta California* May 13, 1868, 1). The strike was over, broken by imported scabs, and the ten-hour day remained in force (*Daily Alta California* May 15, 1868, 1).

There were other similar efforts to enforce the new law by strikes and the creation of cooperative industries operating on the eight-hour-a-day principle, and some short-term successes were achieved. But the arrival of the transcontinental railroad in 1869 made it easier than ever to import strikebreaking scabs, and the 1870s saw such depressed economic conditions that workers' power was sharply undercut by competition from other workers. The attitude of the ruling class was also very aggressive, undercutting labor's power by organizing the California Labor and Employment Exchange, which advertised widely to attract eastern and foreign workers to California (Cross 1935, 54). As discussed above, the importation and wide use of ill-paid Chinese workers was another aspect of the employer plan to greatly overstock the labor market, increase hours, and drive down wages and conditions.

Waged workers, the overwhelming majority of whom owned no productive property and had to work to eat and support their families, had great difficulty maintaining the solidarity and unity fundamental to achieve victory in the long struggle that the employers made them fight. Workers also lost on the legal front. In the fall of 1869, the California Supreme Court, in a decision written by Justice Alonzo Sawyer (a close personal friend of Leland Stanford and other wealthy California industrialists, and part of the social set of the San Francisco upper class), ruled 3–2 that the eight-hour day statute also allowed contracts for a longer working day and provided no penalty for violations (Eaves 1910, 210–211). After a number of bitter strikes and job actions, California's workers had to give up the dream of an eight-hour day. This milestone on the road to workers' rights and greater self-realization as human beings would be postponed for an entire generation.

JOB COMPETITION AND ATTACKS ON CHINESE WORKERS

One of the reasons for the long postponement of shorter hours was the intensifying conflict within worker ranks, something employers had tried very hard to create with their divide-and-conquer tactics. On February 12, 1867, the *San Francisco Evening Bulletin* reported on a violent "riot" in San Francisco, pointing out that the cause was the employment of Chinese labor for less pay than white, in this case Irish, labor:

> *It seems that Weed & Anderson, contractors, recently took a contract for grading some lots on Townsend street … and engaged as laborers in the work of excavating about thirty Chinamen. When it became known to the Irishmen and other parties who had been engaged in this kind of employment that Chinese labor was to be employed, they threatened to prevent them from working …*

About eight o'clock this morning a party of fifteen Chinamen were set at work by the foreman … They had no sooner commenced work than a party of white men appeared on the hill above and commenced throwing stones … In a few minutes … a large party came round by way of Third Street and another by Second Street, the two crowds meeting in front of the Chinese workmen, when … they commenced throwing stones and bricks assaulting and beating the Chinamen in the most cruel and outrageous manner. The poor creatures attempted to escape … but … they were surrounded by the crowd and beaten …

The foreman, Marshall, endeavored to resist … when he was felled by a heavy rock, which struck him on the head … One Chinaman was so severely injured that he was subsequently taken away in a wagon, being unable to walk. His skull was supposed to be fractured. Others sustained serious although not fatal injuries about their face and limbs. One of them had his face almost beaten to a jelly …

After the Chinamen's house had been demolished, and no more victims were immediately at hand, one of the crowd proposed to "clean out" the Chinamen at the ropewalks at Hunter's Point. The proposition was taken up with yells of delight, and shouting and yelling the crowd started off on a run … A party of Chinamen engaged in grading on the Potrero fled at their approach, but one of the number fell into the hands of the rioters and was severely beaten. The crowd then continued on in their mad career until they reached the rope factory, but … the Chinese laborers in the factory had fled to the surrounding hills. Being disappointed in not finding the Chinamen there, they set fire to and burned two shanties which

> had been occupied by the Chinamen, destroying the buildings and contents. (San Francisco Evening Bulletin *February 12, 1867, 6*)

At least one of the Chinese workers later died as a result of this violent attack (*Sacramento Daily Union* February 22, 1867, 3). Such mob attacks on Chinese workers were fairly common during this era, part of a nationwide pattern of violent job competition among workers created by a capitalist system in search of cheaper labor, lower costs, and greater profits (Ignaliev 1995, 100–112).

Another and even more murderous example of the violently racist aspects of job competition took place in Los Angeles and became known as the "Chinese Massacre of 1871." Background to this event was the familar fact that Chinese immigrants were willing to work long hours for low pay, which was very threatening to white workers. One mainstream historian noted white workers' response to the Chinese: "Labor ... had a constant tendency to regard them as unwelcome competitors, and whenever the demand for labor fell off, this intolerance was apt to manifest itself vociferously or even violently" (Caughey 1940, 451).

As was the case for the rest of California, the 1870s was a period of depression in Los Angeles, and job competition created the conditions for conflict. When a white person got shot while caught in the crossfire between two rival Los Angeles Chinese tongs in October of 1871, hundreds of whites went on a violent rampage against the Chinese community. A newspaper report said the rioters were "mainly ... native Californians, the dregs of society," and thus, those in direct competition with the Chinese for low-paying jobs (*Sacramento Daily Union* October 26, 1871, 2). The Chinese ghetto was invaded, and every Chinese American encountered was attacked; between eighteen and twenty-two were killed, most of them hanged on makeshift gallows. No one was ever convicted for this outrage, which for years was the shame of Los Angeles.

The competition among workers that characterizes capitalism had become especially severe in the late 1860s and early 1870s as

California capitalists imported workers from many places. With an ample labor supply, the capitalists fired one group of workers (often the Irish) and hired cheaper Chinese workers. The capitalists were very successful in driving down wages in this way during the 1867–1870 years, despite a number of strikes of resistance to try to prevent such cuts. The newly arrived Chinese, under the lash of debt peonage, were especially useful to the capitalists in their resistance to the eight-hour day and desire to cut wages and smash unions. One newspaper report in July 1870 stated that the employment of Chinese had resulted in a reduction of 50 percent in the wages of a number of trades, including boot and shoe making, and had driven many into the ranks of the unemployed, threatening their families with starvation (*Sacramento Daily Union* July 11, 1870, 1).

This process created a culture of poverty. Low-waged, unskilled poor people, without access to any means of production, were forced to compete with each other in a system plagued by unemployment and underemployment, causing alienation, hostility, hatred, and violence. Largely powerless people occupying marginal class positions, in an individualistic, class-stratified system, began to feel desperate and react violently against their competitors, resulting in riots like the Chinese Massacre of 1871 discussed above.

Thus, part of the reason violent attacks on the Chinese occurred and reoccurred was the labor competition continually fostered by the system of competitive capitalism, as well as a blame-the-victim mentality on the part of workers who were themselves victims and near the bottom of the class structure. In its origin then, the violent racial conflict between the Chinese and European Americans was, in fundamental respects, an artifact of the alienation between people growing out of capitalist labor dynamics. But more was involved. There was an entire system of white supremacy that was embedded in the culture and encouraged by both the Republican and Democratic parties.

WHITE SUPREMACY

Labor competition is only one reason for the massive and sustained attack on Chinese Americans in California during the 1860s and 1870s. Another root cause lay in the entire historical cultural development of the United States as a slave-owning, racist nation. By the 1860s, the nation had long been a white supremacist society, and most of the Irish and other European immigrant groups clearly wanted to identify themselves as white in order to gain a competitive edge in ongoing economic and political struggles (Ignaliev 1995, 1–2).

THE ROLE OF THE REPUBLICAN AND DEMOCRATIC PARTIES

White supremacy was reproduced and perpetuated by both of the main political parties, the Republicans and the Democrats. The Republicans, the party of industrializing capital during this era, tended to be harder on class questions and softer on race issues (Saxton 1990, 343). They wanted to unify the white ruling class and white professional/manager class with appeals to class interest while exploiting the poorer people of all races on an equal basis. High profits and rapid capital accumulation was their central goal, so employing members of all races and ethnic groups, subtly or overtly playing them off against each other in a divide-and-conquer strategy to lower wages and conditions was a natural part of their business and political practice.

The Big Four's extensive use of Chinese labor in building their railroad, their threat to import thousands of freed African Americans as strikebreakers to replace Chinese strikers (reported later in this chapter), and their practice of using a number of different segregated nationalities in their operations was the typical Republican approach and illustrates a conscious divide-and-conquer strategy against wage workers. Other ruling-class Republicans, such as William Ralston, also employed many Chinese alongside whites to encourage divisions among workers and reduce wages in their San Francisco factories such as the Mission Woolen Mills.

The Democrats, on the other hand, practiced a policy that tended to be hard on race and soft on class. Tapping into and building on the long tradition of white supremacy in United States history, which the slaveholder-run Democratic party had had a key role in creating during the period prior to the Civil War, Democrats focused on softening class conflict and encouraging class collaboration by solidifying "white" European Americans across class and ethnic lines. Their hard-on-race stance involved blunt racial appeals, blaming problems on supposedly "inferior" races and appealing for "white" unity. This helped bring together a white population divided into many occupational, class, ethnic, and national groupings, creating a race-class coalition that was able to achieve substantial Democratic party political power. It was the Democrats, who by rhetorically crusading against ruling-class domination and upholding egalitarianism within the white community as well as white superiority, helped steer the workers' cause into the dead end of white supremacy and division.

Over time, the development of the white workers' movement continued to be infused with socially constructed concepts of race, precluding the development of full class consciousness, since class was subordinated to race. This naturally led many craft unions to use racial discrimination to reinforce their exclusive positions, remaining all white and, in effect, joining with the white supremacist ruling class in a colonialist, collaborationist stance. European Americans unified against workers defined as "non-white."

Capital's dominant role was then left largely uncontested by these workers and their unions, since white solidarity often precluded challenges to capitalists who were almost all white. The exclusive membership strategies of skilled craft unionism dovetailed well with racial exclusion and class collaboration. Capitalists were more likely to accept unions and their demands if there was a craft union approach by skilled white workers infused with class collaboration. Employers would still sometimes attack, giving the craft unions no choice but to resist, but the heaviest guns of the ruling class were usually aimed at industrial unions, which had to be inclusive of all workers (the unskilled and workers of color included), because only inclusiveness would give workers and their unions maximum bargaining power against the class warfare of the rulers.

In early 1867, the Democratic Party, which had been the "out" party in the state since 1861, decided to do what was natural for them—use the Chinese labor issue to both attack the Republicans (whose leading members often used this type of labor) and unify their base among the racially conscious European American population, especially white workers who were either directly harmed or felt threatened by lower-paid Chinese workers. In this the Democrats linked the Chinese to the general hatred and contempt for people of color created in the white population by hundreds of years of white supremacist culture, including enslavement of African Americans, the wars against Native Americans, and even the recent war against Mexico (Saxton 1990, 295).

In the 1867 campaign, Democratic Party leaders blatantly played the "race card" against the Chinese, more firmly establishing hostility against them as part of the prevailing white supremacist perspective. Joined by unions fighting to preserve wage levels and for the eight-hour day, the Democrats won by posing as defenders of egalitarian goals. The victory speech of Henry Haight, the new Democratic governor, linked the Chinese to African Americans and the Reconstruction of the South, expressing well the Democratic Party's white supremacist outlook during this period, "I will simply say that in this result we protest … against populating this fair state with a race of Asiatics—against sharing with inferior races the Government of our country … and this protest of ours will be re-echoed in thunder tones … until the Southern States are emancipated from negro domination" (Saxton 1990, 296).

THE ROLE OF CRAFT UNIONS

The developing attack on the Chinese at the highest political levels of the state helped influence the developing union movement in an anti-Chinese direction, giving union leaders and the rank-and-file the hope that the Chinese could be banned from the state; labor kept scarce; and wages, hours, and working conditions thereby improved. So in February and March of 1867, the *Sacramento Daily Union* reported that pro-slavery Democrats were lining up to oppose the Chinese, and workingmen were meeting and passing resolutions condemning Chinese immigration as well as the Big Four for using Chinese labor (*Sacramento Daily Union* February 22, 1867, 3; March 7, 1867, 3). Conflicts over use of Chinese labor gradually escalated, with craft unions often leading the charge, pursuing the mistaken path of exclusionism as a way to gain traction in the ongoing class struggle. In so doing, they helped prevent both their fellow Chinese workers and themselves from ever achieving the unity needed to put a different and more just social and economic system on the agenda.

In March 1868, the Mechanics' State Council of California, this state's first statewide federated labor organization, affiliated with the National Labor Union, pointed out that the importation of the Chinese was an "injustice" to white workers, adding, "That whatever present benefit may be derived from the employment of Chinese, as a cheap system of labor, is chiefly confined to a few capitalists—any real advantage in the State being neutralized by the system of peonage under which they are introduced" (Mechanics' State Council 1868, 4).

The exclusionist approach failed initially, however, since the Republican Party dominated the national political scene, and it was intent on opening the doors even further to Chinese immigration. With an increase in Chinese immigration and the completion of the transcontinental railroad in 1869, the time came for both Republican and Democratic employers to go on the offensive, to break unions and drive wages and conditions downward. Labor-contracting businesses were established in San Francisco to supply employers with as many workers as they needed, and the ruling class founded new organizations to widely advertise the wonders of California, attracting even more immigrants (California Bureau of Labor Statistics 1887, 45).

Workers' strikes to try to preserve existing conditions failed as a wave of new and often desperate workers arrived to serve as strikebreakers. For example, hundreds of San Francisco boot-and-shoe workers struck in early 1867 and again in early 1869 to try to prevent wage reductions. In the 1867 strike, violence was followed by police intervention and replacement of the shoemakers by Chinese scabs. In the summer and fall of 1869, strikes by the iron moulders against wage reductions began. Scabs were brought in and replaced the striking workers. The moulders held out for about a year before their union disintegrated in utter defeat (Cross 1935, 56, 63, 308; Knight 1960, 13; *Sacramento Daily Union* April 3, 1869, 5).

The resulting anger led to violence against the Chinese, with the more extreme of the "anti-coolie" groups ("coolie" being a racial slur for Asian workers), even establishing armed military companies to violently drive the Chinese from the state. The Irish, another oppressed group of workers, were usually the leaders of this approach. In 1870, one such Irish-led military group was called "St. Crispin's Guard" (*Sacramento Daily Union* July 13, 1870, 1).

The "Knights of St. Crispin," an early, mostly Irish American San Francisco shoemakers craft union, had gone on strike in the spring of 1869. As part of this class struggle, an association of shoe manufacturers was also formed that hired Chinese workers to break the strike (*Sacramento Daily Union* April 3, 1869, 1). The resulting bitterness led to the founding of St. Crispin's Guard to threaten and engage in attacks on the Chinese (*San Francisco Chronicle* July 12, 1870, 3). A union-led anti-Chinese convention was held in San Francisco in August 1870 to respond to the crisis. This convention was noteworthy because it agreed to affiliate with the National Labor Union, a nationwide labor organization founded in 1866, which invited African Americans to join its effort. The adopted platform included the following planks:

> *—man, his labor and the fruits thereof, life, liberty and prosperity are the primary objects of government ...*

—the eight-hour system of labor is a natural division of time for labor, recreation and rest … It meets with our warmest approval. This due degree of labor develops the body, expands the mind, dignifies labor and elevates man.

—the system of importing Chinese or Asiatic coolies into the Pacific States … is in every respect injurious and degrading to American labor, forcing it as it does into unjust and ruinous competition, placing the white workingman entirely at the mercy of the coolie employers, and building up a system of slavery in what should be a free land.

—the treaty known as the Burlingame Treaty should be abrogated and annulled.

—the interests of the colored working classes are identical to our own, and we hope and trust that representatives from that class of citizens will be welcomed into all labor conventions.

—we announce the foregoing as the principles and political doctrines of the workingmen of California concerning the Chinese question and we call upon the laboring classes … to endorse, support and carry out by cooperative measures these doctrines …

(Daily Alta California *August 19, 1870, 1*)

ONGOING RACIALIZATION IN CALIFORNIA

The result of these structural and ideological factors—US white supremacist culture, material interests, capitalist divide-and-conquer tactics, job competition, racial ideologies, the association of people of color with oppressive labor systems, political opportunism, and narrow exclusive craft unionism—worked together to intensify and expand the racialization of California society, a system that had already been developed in the case of the California Indians. As capitalism transformed the state during the 1860s and 1870s, these factors institutionalized a white supremacist system.

Each of the colonized non-European ethnic groups was racialized in specific ways, restricting the life chances of members of each group in relation to the dominant white majority. At the bottom of this hierarchical system of discrimination were the Native Americans and Chinese, with African Americans and Mexican Californios occupying slightly higher positions (Almaguer 1994, 8–9). There were few African Americans in nineteenth-century California, and the Mexican Californios were both culturally much closer to European Americans and still had some political and economic power in the state. Therefore, the weight of the racist oppression fell most heavily on rural Native Americans and urban Chinese Americans.

California's European American workers themselves obviously had a central role in this process, since they could and did gain narrow short-term advantage by excluding people of color. As the California working class was gradually formed, a sense of whiteness and non-whiteness also developed. White workers received the "hidden wage" of a feeling of racial superiority and greater political rights and material benefits. White supremacy undermined in turn the political and economic vision of most white workers and made it impossible to unify more than a fraction of the working class at a time.

The capitalists had an even bigger role, however, because they used un-free labor systems (especially debt peonage), both to gain super profits and divide-and-conquer the workforce. The state, largely beholden to the ruling capitalist class, passed discriminatory laws, making people of color second-class citizens and, at the same time, opening the door for more immigration. White workers often supported the former, but not the latter. Both capitalists and white workers were therefore responsible for the development of the institutional pattern of dual labor markets, segregated unions, and exclusionary legislation that created and perpetuated color lines within the working class and greater society.

Race consistently became the primary stratifying variable in the minds of most Californians. Class relationships were often secondary and usually only became primary as a defensive response to ruling-class offensives. Most white workers wanted capitalism, but without the un-free labor systems and the minority racial groups they associated with these systems. They did not get their wish, since the capitalists were by far the stronger party and they created a system to suit themselves, a complex labor and social system that included slaves and peons as well as waged workers. This often doomed workers to weakness in a race- and class-divided society. But it did not have to be that way. Chinese workers were willing to engage in the class struggle against exploitation and could have provided strong allies in the fight for justice and a new society.

RESISTANCE

The late 1860s and early 1870s saw a number of examples of resistance by rank-and-file workers in the form of important strikes. Two examples of such strikes were the first Chinese workers' strike and the Amador Country miners' strike, in 1867 and 1871 respectively.

THE FIRST CHINESE WORKERS' STRIKE 1867

The cheap and efficient labor of Chinese Americans immensely helped capital in building the Central Pacific and other railroads, as well as working in the mines, the factories, the farms, and the homes of the rich. By using their organized power, however, the Chinese also sometimes resisted capital. It is a surprising fact that the biggest strike (in terms of numbers of workers involved) in this era of California history was organized and conducted by Chinese immigrant workers. These workers were often operating under extremely difficult conditions, yet were still able to achieve the unity and solidarity necessary for several thousand workers to simultaneously down their tools and go on strike to assert themselves and try to improve their conditions. The Chinese workers' ability to organize was apparently based on their strong collective and community traditions. About them, one European American woolen mill worker said, with apparent respect, "They will combine … The lot will stand up for each other, and as a general thing, go together" (Chinn et al. 1969, 51).

Chinese Workers Filling in the Secret Town Trestle
The Chinese workers who were instrumental in building the Central Pacific Railroad through the Sierra Nevada conducted the first mass strike in California history in July 1867. [Courtesy of the Bancroft Library, University of California, Berkeley.]

The first large-scale example of the Chinese workers' willingness to organize and resist capital on a mass scale was the strike against the Central Pacific Railroad in June–July 1867. The Central Pacific Railroad employed thousands of Chinese workers in building the transcontinental railroad over the Sierra Nevada Mountains. The company paid these workers thirty dollars a month for twelve-hour days (although for tunnel work the hours were shorter), and used violence against them. Responding to handbills in Chinese that asserted the right of workers to higher wages, shorter hours, and no physical restraint or punishments by company supervisors, thousands of Chinese went out on strike. The *Sacramento Daily Union* reported it on page two, July 3, 1867:

> *This placard is said to have set forth the right of the workmen to higher wages and a more moderate day's work, and to deny the right of the overseers of the company to either whip them or to restrain them from leaving the road when they desire to seek other employment. About two thousand Chinamen responded to the appeal, and work was entirely suspended in the tunnels along the line of the road near the Summit. The Railroad Company refused to pay the wages earned since last pay day, and the Chinese refused to leave the line until paid.*

The *Daily Alta California* (July 1, 1867, 1) reported on its front page that between three and five thousand Chinese were on strike by July 1. The specific pay and hour demands of the Chinese workers included an increase in pay to forty dollars a month, ten-hour days on open ground, and eight-hour days in tunnels. The leaders of the Central Pacific, Stanford, Crocker, and Hopkins, responded by cutting off the workers' food supply and telegraphing east to Huntington to hire and send west several thousand African American "freemen" to California to take the place of the Chinese and break the strike. Interestingly enough, the Chinese reportedly had been used to break an earlier strike against the Central Pacific by Irish and other European American workers (Chiu 1967, 44).

Before African Americans could be sent, however, the Chinese, who were in remote mountain locations, and under pressure from the food stoppage, gave up the strike and returned to work on the old terms. Charles Crocker later admitted that he had used "coercive measures" in order to force the Chinese to return to work (Chiu 1967, 47). There was no reported solidarity by other workers with these Chinese who were fighting what was rapidly becoming the dominant monopoly corporation in the state.

THE 1871 AMADOR COUNTY MINERS' STRIKE

While the system of white supremacy was developing, and the working class on the railroad and in San Francisco was resisting the accumulation schemes of its capitalists, miners in the industrial mines of the Comstock Lode and Grass Valley, California, went on strike during the mid- and late 1860s (Lord 1883, 181–190; Mann 1982, 183-194). These led to the biggest and most important mining strike of the era on California's mother lode during the summer of 1871. By that year, San Francisco and Sacramento capitalists, as well as some of the local gentry, owned many of the leading California gold mines. Such was the case with the Amador County quartz gold mines, owned largely by several men from the Central Pacific Railroad and Bank of California. This county was one of the top two gold-mining counties of California, the other being Nevada County. Several of these mines were extremely valuable; the Amador Mine was reportedly sold for $800,000 in 1867, for example, and it distributed $379,400 worth of dividends to its owners in 1869 alone (*Daily Alta California* June 26, 1871, 2; July 7, 1871, 1). Jackson and Sutter Creek were the main cities of Amador County, located in the foothills of the Sierra Nevada Mountains about 150 miles east of San Francisco.

The absentee owners of the Amador County mines included both Democratic and Republican political leaders and other capitalists:

- Milton S. Latham, a San Francisco banker and former Democratic US senator

- David D. Colton, a major stockholder of the Central Pacific Railroad
- Michael Reese, a San Francisco millionaire
- John D. Fry, San Francisco Woolen Mill president and father-in-law of William Ralston
- Leland Stanford, Central Pacific Railroad president and former Republican governor
- George Hearst, Comstock millionaire and future Democratic US senator
- William M. Stewart of Nevada, Republican US senator
- Thomas C. Bell, a leader of the Bank of California

(*Daily Alta California* July 7, 1871, 1; *Mining and Scientific Press* April 8, 1871, 211)

Tired of being exploited by rich capitalists who were reaping large benefits while they struggled to survive, the Miners' League of Sutter Creek met on the night of May 31, 1871, and decided to strike for a wage of at least $2.50/day. The *Daily Alta California,* (June 25, 1871, 1), an anti-worker newspaper, soon engaged in red-baiting and immigrant bashing, charging that this union was made up of "communists, Irish, Italians, and Austrians." Early in the morning of June 1, the miners met at their hall and, accompanied by two locally elected officials, marched behind an American flag to seven of the local mines and one mill, closing each one in turn, ending up at an eighth mine, which was the Amador. The superintendent of the mine, who was also the president of the company, "General" David D. Colton of the Central Pacific Railroad confronted them there. The two company officials, typifying the "no-compromise" attitude of the capitalists of the time, informed the men that the company " was paying to-day the wages they did twelve years ago; that the company would make no concessions; that while they owned the mine they would run it to suit themselves" (*Daily Alta California* June 2, 1871, 1).

The strike went on for two months. During its course, the miners revised their goals, demanding three dollars per day for workers blasting underground and $2.50/day for other employees and the union shop, in which all workers at a given mine had to be union members. The owners of the mining companies refused to meet these demands, and the miners were faced with the need to develop ways and means to completely shut down production.

The *Alta* reported that the "market price" for commodified labor was then less than two dollars per day, but the miners were using violence to shut down the mines and to prevent scabs from breaking the strike. The striking miners notified all potential scabs that those who disregarded the strike would "suffer the consequences." As the *Alta* explained, "These consequences are not stated by the league, but they are well understood. They include such coercion as shall be sufficient to punish disobedience ... and secure obedience for the future. The coercion is applied by members of the league in their individual capacity. Usually the offender is attacked and brutally beaten by a dozen men" (*Daily Alta California* June 22, 1871). Siding with the owners, the *Alta* recommended that the "guilty authors of these outrages," including union leaders, be sent to prison and laws passed to prevent a union from controlling the actions of non-members.

Meanwhile, the mine pumps were not operating and many of the mines were filling with water, causing the owners to seek state intervention to break the strike and reinstitute their control. By late June, the miners had an additional demand. Perhaps aiming to unify strikers during a tough struggle and also fearing the introduction of Chinese American or African American workers to break the strike, the Miners' League stated that they wanted to protect " white labor ... and to discourage the competition of inferior races" (*Daily Alta California* June 23, 1871, 1).

In 1867, Henry Haight had been elected and was later re-elected governor on the Democratic ticket with strong labor support. Faced with the continuing success of the strike and strong pressure from the ruling class to do something about it, he decided to call out the California National Guard against the miners. His argument was that the mines would fill with water if they were untended for too long, but it is more likely that Haight agreed with the owners that seizure of the means of production by workers had to be answered with decisive force. The *Alta,* a mouthpiece for capitalist interests, argued that the rule of law and property rights were involved and so the strike and strikers had to be smashed: "they deliberately made war upon the laws of the State, and … the entire resources of the State, and of the Republic, if necessary, would be used to crush them" (*Daily Alta California* June 23, 1871, 1).

To lessen the chances for insubordination or rebellion by the National Guard, Governor Haight called out units from San Francisco rather than from a city or county closer to Amador County. Breach-loading Henry rifles, revolvers, and a six-pound field piece, together with munitions, stores, ammunition, and camp equipment, were transported with the soldiers via steamer and railroad to Latrobe in the Central Valley. One of the officers of this small army knew that they were taking sides in the class struggle and openly stated that they were "going to fight for the Bank of California" (*Daily Alta California* June 27, 1871, 1). From Latrobe, wagons and horses aided their march eastward to Sutter Creek, reestablishing the cut telegraph lines as they proceeded (*Daily Alta California* June 23, 1871, 1).

The arrival of the soldiers in Sutter Creek was unopposed, and no casualties were reported, allowing the owners to regain control of the mines. At this point in the strike, the owners resolved to employ only non-league miners, firing all members of the League and hiring only scabs (*Mining and Scientific Press* June 17, 1871, 372; July 1, 1871, 404; *Daily Alta California* June 27, 1871, 1; July 1, 1871, 1).

James Byrne, the president of the Miners' League, vowed to continue the strike, arguing that the use of troops to attempt to break it was "an outrage on the laboring classes" (*Daily Alta California* June 30, 1871, 2). Negotiations were initiated, and a tentative agreement between the league and the owners was reached in mid-July. Most of the troops were then withdrawn, but the strike was renewed when the owners failed to fulfill their promise to discharge the scabs who had been hired as part of the strike breaking effort (*Mining and Scientific Press* July 15, 1871, 20; July 22, 1871, 40; July 29, 1871, 52, 55; *Sacramento Union* July 22, 1871, 4; *Daily Alta California* July 16, 1871, 1; July 30, 1871, 1).

This increased the bitterness on both sides. The leading officers of the mines and the leaders of the league were becoming more aggressive, and fistfights and assaults were increasing, leading to a fatal gun battle in the streets of Sutter Creek on July 24, 1871. J. W. Bennett the superintendent of the Amador Mill was heavily armed, with two revolvers and a shotgun. Hughey McMenomy, a member of the league's executive committee, only had a revolver. The shooting started following "hard words" between the two men, whereupon Bennett lost his temper and gave McMenomy what he later called a "heavy push in the face" (*Daily Alta California* July 28, 1871, 1). Bennett, not only more heavily armed, was also apparently the more accurate shooter. He was only slightly hurt, but McMenomy was fatally wounded. At the same time, E. W. Hatch, the bookkeeper of the Amador Mine and a bystander to the gunfight, also drew his pistol and began firing, presumably at McMenomy. He was then also fatally shot, apparently by another member of the Miners' League (*Daily Alta California* July 26, 1871, 1; July 27, 1871, 1; July 28, 1871, 1; July 30, 1871, 1; *Mining and Scientific Press* July 29, 1871, 52, 55).

The violent deaths of these two men soon led to a compromise and the end of the strike, reportedly on terms more favorable to the owners than to the workers (*Daily Alta California* August 1, 1871, 1). There was also political fallout from the strike, which caused a serious split in the local Democratic Party. Leaders of the miners were bitter towards the Democrats and Governor Haight, who had sent troops against the miners. Local Democratic leader John Eagan, secretary of the Miners' League and an Amador

County supervisor, asserted that league members were merely "men who had asserted their rights" and that "it was time they asserted their rights and protected themselves from the capitalists" (*Daily Alta California* August 1, 1871, 1). He added that the Democratic Party Convention then underway was a party of men sent to "array capital against labor" (*Daily Alta California* August 1, 1871, 1; August 2, 1871, 1). With Democrats split, Republican Newton Booth was elected governor in his race against Haight a little over a month later.

THE 1870S, ORGANIZED LABOR AT A LOW POINT

The period from 1871 to 1877 saw unions and the organizing of working people in their own interests at a low ebb. The overall conditions for the working class, already difficult for many in 1870, declined further during the next decade. Data for this assertion is scanty, but comparing wage rates as reported in the 1870 census with those reported in the 1880 census, we find that the already low rates for many occupations *dropped* during the decade of the 1870s. For example, whereas the average daily wage for boots-and-shoe work in San Francisco was only $1.70/day in 1870, it had sunk to $1.40/day by 1880. For San Francisco tobacco workers, the daily wage had dropped from only 92¢/day in 1870 to an even more dismal 86¢/day in 1880. These were both occupations where use of Chinese labor was common, and the low wage rates indicate a very high rate of exploitation.

Statewide, the daily average manufacturing wage dropped from $1.66 in 1870 to $1.55 in 1880 (US Census Bureau 1883b, 2:92, 435–436; 1872a, 3:497, 640). In the woolen industry, wage rates published by the 1880 census show that an unnamed "establishment in California" had twenty "classes" of workers, and eight of these classes consisted entirely of Chinese. Seven of the eight Chinese classes saw a decline in wages between 1870 and 1880, from between $1 and $1.20/day for eleven hours of work, and the other one stayed the same. Only two of the remaining twelve classes of workers saw a small raise in pay between 1870 and 1880, most stayed the same, and several saw a pay reduction by about a third during the period, while still working eleven hours a day.

The 1880 Census report mentioned that the employment of Chinese American and European American labor side-by-side was a common employer tactic to divide the workforce and keep wages down, with the overt or implied threat to employ all Chinese if the other workers made any demands (US Census Bureau 1886, 15, 41, 56–57, 242, 310, 379, 435). Bancroft reported that in shoe making, the influx of Chinese shoemakers resulted in a drop of wages from twenty-five dollars per week in 1870 to only nine dollars per week in 1878 (Bancroft 1890, 7:353). In addition, in some occupations, such as laborers, the two largest groups were two of the poorest, the Chinese and the Irish. This fact led to alienation and continuing conflicts between these two groups of workers.

By 1876, widespread unemployment and destitution was reported in San Francisco. The San Francisco Benevolent Association estimated that there were fifteen thousand unemployed and seven thousand on relief (Bancroft 1890, 7:352–353). Many of the unemployed blamed the Chinese for their plight, and even Bancroft, who was generally pro-employer, later wrote, "There was truth in what was alleged, that the presence of the Chinese in California reduced the chances and earnings of citizen laborers, while it strengthened the power by adding to the wealth of capitalists" (Bancroft 1890, 7:351).

Very few labor organizations survived the consequences of the depression during the decade of the 1870s. There were only twenty-eight unions (mostly for skilled workers) listed in existence in the entire state of California in 1880. As of 1880, there were no unions for teamsters, boot and shoe workers, laborers, or textile workers in the state. Only three small, recently formed, building-trade unions existed, only nine transportation-related unions, and only four in the entire iron-and-steel industry (Weeks 1884,

2, 14–18). With very few unions, and large numbers of Chinese usually available as a low-paid reserve army of workers, it was nearly impossible for workers to adequately take care of themselves and their families, let alone improve their conditions.

The *San Francisco Chronicle* reported on the city's day laborers in a December 1873 article, interviewing one family man for the article:

> *Notwithstanding the boasted perfections of this Pacific Coast, it is a fact that even in the commercial Capital of the far West hundreds are dependent upon the charity of strangers, and the incomes of hundreds more are so scanty that it is a wonder how they manage to support themselves and families … There are thousands in this city who manage to eke out a bare subsistence on wages which, to a great many people, would prove insufficient to furnish cigars and other useless luxuries … Reporter—How can a man support a family on the pittance you have mentioned? The Laborer—They are obliged to resort to many shifts; but there are no luxuries for a laborer in San Francisco, unless he is a single man … When I am in constant work all goes well. But when I am not—well, we are obliged to run up bills that we find … very difficult afterwards to pay. (December 21, 1873, 3)*

The less-skilled and lower-paid segments of the workforce were the most affected by the importation of Chinese workers. Capital had created a disposable, commodified mass of workers at the bottom end of the class structure, grading into the chronically unemployed and "tramps"—marginalized people, with no regular employment and barely surviving as day laborers, petty thieves, or scavengers in the city dumps. In the summer of 1878, an enterprising reporter from the San Francisco's *Daily Evening Post* disguised himself as a tramp or "bummer" to penetrate and report on this world of the marginalized. He slept with the homeless in rundown vacant houses, hay bunks, and lumberyards along the waterfront, and at the city dump. His descent into the world of the poor was graphically described as he traveled with a "bummer guide" from the richer part of San Francisco to the waterfront area:

> *Down Pacific street, from Dupont to Kearny, the reporter and his bummer guide made their way. Saloons, restaurants, Chinese washouts, dives, fourth-class hotels, "Bottle Koenig's" wherein the giant organ gives out its uproarious notes, were all mixed in promiscuously—evidentially a forced kind of happy family. Small wonder that in such a locality street fights and midnight broils should be the constant harvest. Across Kearny street and thence down to Davis street, the diversity of character and pursuits of the denizens were equally as noticeable. There were cheap lodging houses, second-hand clothing stores, wherein the ragged could dress themselves in cast off clothing for a very small sum of money. There were slop-shops that retailed paper-soled shoes, glued rubber goods, shirts that would go to pieces at the first washing; hose that would walk off in one day's wear; shoddy blankets that divide themselves on a person's bed.* (Daily Evening Post *August 6, 1878, 1*)

After several days, the reporter finally ended up at the city dumps, where "could be found penniless humanity engaged in its daily struggle with want and privation."

> *In the southern part of the city, on Berry street, between Sixth and Seventh, I came to where is daily deposited the refuse of the city. Here were congregated many people of all nationalities, their wan and pinched countenances plainly showing the inroads*

that want had made there. Their clothes, ragged and soiled, and their faces and hair, unwashed and unkempt, were in keeping with their general air of dejected doggedness. Many were busily engaged with pitchfork, shovel or stick, poking, sifting each load as it was dumped from the reeking, overflowing carts. Nothing was too small for their quick, sharp eyes to discover, or too little valuable for their wits to utilize. Rags of any kind and every description, old bottles, cans, scraps of iron, glass, oil sacks, corks, pieces of wood, brick, oystershells—all was preserved with an eye to the future dimes their accumulated store would yield. Half-decayed fruit or vegetables, old bones that had passed from royal roast to humble soup, were prizes not to be overlooked.

*Close by were the habitations or quarters ... a description of one of these abodes of squalid misery will comprehend them all. They were uniform in their squatter style of architecture, in size about ten feet square and six in height, and the material used in their construction was of every variety and substance known to the building world. The frame had been constructed out of fence posts, pieces of scantling, old gaspipe, etc. foraged from some neighboring lumberyard, the whole covered with old matting, pieces of carpet, blankets, tin roofing, etc. Some of the most aristocratic of the habitations could boast of an old stove, which usually emitted more smoke from its numerous rents than went up the ragged, dissipated looking pipe. (*Daily Evening Post *August 10, 1878, 4)*

WOMEN IN THE WORLD OF WORK

White women increased their position in the workforce in this period, in large part because they represented a cheap and efficient labor force similar to the Chinese, only white. Government employers wanted to save the taxpayers money and capitalist employers were always on the lookout for a way to increase profits and best the competition with lower wages. Women and girls sometimes represented just the ticket for both needs. *The San Francisco Call* (September 29, 1878, 7) reported as follows on the "Feminine Toilers" of San Francisco:

> *Year after year woman is steadily pushing her way into newer fields of industry. Long ago she asserted her claims to recognition in the realms of literature and art; but all feminies cannot be Rosa Bonheurs, George Eliots or Ristoris, nor can they all be journalists, lawyers and physicians; but they may be practical and useful members of the community … The number of working women in every large American city will far exceed the estimate of anyone who has given the subject little attention. In San Francisco it may be truthfully said that girls and women are particularly industrious, and manifest an unusual disposition to take care of themselves by honorable toil. The number of our female workers is very large and can scarcely fall below eight or ten thousand. There are few commercial or manufacturing branches of business in the city in which women are not more or less employed, and such excellent satisfaction do they give, as a rule, that the constant tendency with employers is to enlarge the domain in which their labor may be utilized.*

The same article in the *Call* reported that female labor was greatest in the following occupations: at the US Mint, in city departments, retail stores, hotels, photographic galleries, as school teachers, journalists, dressmakers, milliners, bookbinders, cigar-box makers, cigar makers, paper-box makers, in candy manufacturing, shoe fitting, manufacturing of general clothing, and as house servants and housekeepers. The pay of these women and girls ranged from four or even less than four dollars a week for paper-box makers and house servants up to two hundred dollars a month for a few high-level educators. Hours of work ranged from eight up to twelve or more a day (*The San Francisco Call* September 29, 1878, 7).

Women also organized as women to assert themselves. At a meeting at which men were completely banned, women gathered in mid-March of 1880 under the leadership of local feminist Mrs. Anna F. Smith, to form a "Women's Protective Union." At this meeting, wage rates, the need for women to have the right to vote, and the Chinese as the cause of the unemployment and destitution among women were all discussed (*The San Francisco Call* March 14, 1880, 4). While this union did not survive, a start had been made towards raising consciousness and asserting women's rights in the industrial realm.

With such oppressive conditions, many working and poor San Franciscans were ready to rebel against those whom they saw as their oppressors. Even one San Francisco newspaper could say, "The truth is that the condition of the laboring classes in the United States has been growing harder year by year and there is now … an increasing class of men who are rendered desperate" (*The San Francisco Examiner* July 25, 1877, 2).

Years of low wages, recurrent unemployment, lavish displays of wealth by the rich, and growing numbers of Chinese competing for their jobs had created mass resentment among rank-and-file workers. This anger came to a head in late July 1877.

SAN FRANCISCO'S JULY 1877 RIOTS

Street riots can be a prelude to revolution; it was the "Paris mob" which had stormed the Bastille on a July day eighty-eight years before. The Russian Revolution of 1917 would also involve such actions. Spontaneous mob action throughout history has been a way for people to protest against existing conditions; this frequently results in injustices but no solutions for society.

On the evening of July 23, 1877, a mass meeting was held on the "sand lots" in front of San Francisco's city hall. The meeting was called and advertised through handbills and newspaper announcements by a new left-wing political group called the Workingmen's Party of the United States. The purpose of the meeting was to express solidarity with the large number of railroad and other workers then on strike in what became known as the Great Railroad Strike of 1877. The striking workers came under attack by police, state militia, and federal troops in St. Louis, Baltimore, Chicago, Pittsburgh, and other eastern cities. A few days before, state militia had opened fire on striking workers in Pittsburgh, killing and wounding almost fifty people. Similar, although less violent, incidents had taken place in other cities as well.

About ten thousand people attended the San Francisco meeting, which was entirely orderly until, near the end of the meeting, an "anti-coolie" group with band and banner reading, "Anti-Coolie Club-Self-preservation is the First Law of Nature," marched up Market Street and, upon arrival, demanded a resolution against the Chinese. Those in charge of the meeting were against this, as they believed in the solidarity and universal brotherhood of working people.

Once the demand was refused, a huge mob of thousands of people, reportedly consisting in large part of young men and boys led by a smaller number of adults, organized at the fringe of the crowd and began to roam the city attacking Chinese citizens and destroying and burning Chinese property, especially Chinese laundries, which were obvious targets. A number of laundries were sacked and torched and at least one Chinese man was burned to death (*The San Francisco Examiner* July 24, 1877, 3; July 25, 1877, 2–3; *San Francisco Chronicle* July 24, 1877, 2; July 25, 1877, 3; *The San Francisco Call* July 25. 1877, 1; Knight 1960, 15–16).

The next morning, a group of ruling-class leaders of the city, led by William T. Coleman and others from the 1856 Vigilance Committee, as well as D. O. Mills and other leading businessmen, met and decided to form a new committee, patterned in many ways after the 1856 one, but called the "Committee of Safety." The mayor, police, national guard, and federal officials were all working in cooperation with the committee to nip what one of the leaders labeled "the germ of communism" in the bud (*The San Francisco Call* July 25, 1877, 1). Thousands of recruits soon signed up to join the committee in suppressing what were insurrectionary mob actions. Before the committee could get fully organized and National Guard or federal troops brought in, however, another night of rioting occurred.

The second night of rioting was marked by an attempt by the organizers of the mob to target and destroy capitalist enterprises such as the Mission Woolen Mills, which employed large numbers of Chinese, as well as several shoe and match factories, in fact any and all corporations which were closely associated with the importation or employment of peon and slave labor from China. Foremost among these was the Pacific Mail Steamship Company, which brought the Chinese to California.

This giant corporation, allied with the Central Pacific/Southern Pacific Railroad combine, was one of the most important monopolies of the time. Since their property was heavily guarded, members of the mob set on fire an adjacent property, which had warehouses containing whale oil and other combustible material, as well as lumber piles at the wharf at the foot of Beale Street. Some also tried to prevent firemen from arriving and putting out the fire, hoping delay would increase the fire and lead to the destruction of Pacific Mail's wharf, docks, and other waterfront property. This led to large-scale fighting that night between the mob on one side and the police and Committee of Safety men armed with pick handles on the other. As the *Chronicle* reported:

> *Beale street wharf lies at the foot of a precipitous bluff … This bluff was covered by a dense mass of humanity, composed principally of hoodlums, who amused themselves by throwing stones down upon all passers-by …*

> *Officer Wilson and one or two others went up to quell the disturbance, when the officer was hit upon the side of the head with a stone and entirely disabled, and it is stated, suffered paralysis on one side in consequence …*

> *Meantime a detachment of the Vigilance Committee, 400 strong, under General H. A. Cobb, reached the scene … armed with pick handles sawed in half. On the march to the fire they were hooted at and insulted by the hoodlums, and on Fremont street one of the Committee was shot and severely wounded … at the fire the Committee formed a cordon partly around it and prevented all unauthorized outsiders from breaking through. This was done at all points save the bluff on First street, which was occupied by the mob … Some of the hoodlums even … set fire to the lumber-yard fence, but did not succeed in getting their fire to burn. Several charges were made by the officers on the lower point, and that was finally cleared, though many of the officers came back with severe contusions on their heads and bodies, caused by the volleys of stones …*

> *An engine and hose-cart drove furiously around the corner, and were greeted with a volley of missiles during*

the passage. The hose-cart ran over a man named Joseph Wentworth, a sailmaker ... who was fatally injured. Finally Sergeant Harmen, with officers ... ascended Rincon Hill at its eastern extremity, and crawling along the edge of the bluff attacked the mob, which numbered about 2,000 on First street. The thud of the clubs could be distinctly heard on the plain below as they came down on the heads of the hoodlums. The crowd melted away almost instantaneously before the vigorous attack of the officers, but about half-way down the hill ... the hoodlums made a stand, and a stubborn fight ... ensued.

From one of the houses volleys from revolvers and showers of stones issued, and in very self-preservation the officers were compelled to draw and fire in return. About this time about 75 of the Committee charged up the hill in the face of a shower of stones. As they went up the hill several dropped out of the ranks through the persuasive influence of some of the stones, but ... finally resulted in a total rout of the hoodlums ...

The officers fired with the intention of hitting their men, and the result was a hoodlum named Bailey was shot behind one ear, and another named Thompson in the shoulder ... the officers ... reported that two or three other wounded ones were carried away by their companions. For the remainder of the night the crowd made itself scarce in the vicinity of the fire, though it divided up into various small detachments which made themselves felt in various portions of the city. (San Francisco Chronicle *July 26, 1877, 3*)

Following these events and the destruction of more Chinese property, especially laundries, the authorities and the committee

311

were better prepared and more ready to use deadly force the next night. Ten thousand arms, including rifles, carbines, and navy revolvers with ample ammunition, had arrived from federal government stores at the Benicia Arsenal. Many of these arms went into the hands of the thousands of Committee of Safety volunteers, and the mayor and William T. Coleman warned people not to gather on the streets after nightfall. The police were also instructed to shoot into any crowd that attacked them with stones or weapons of any kind.

The Pacific Mail Dock and other facilities, which had escaped the fire of the previous night, were guarded by two hundred Marines from Mare Island Naval base who had howitzers loaded with grapeshot and Gatling guns, along with a navy warship, and hundreds of volunteers from the committee. More Committee of Safety men were stationed in the main working-class sections of the city, including 200 at nearby Tar Flat (First and Howard), two hundred more at Hayes Valley (Western Addition), 150 more at various south-of-Market locations, as well as one hundred more near Chinatown (*San Francisco Chronicle* July 27, 1877, 3; *The San Francisco Call* July 27, 1877, 3).

In addition, extra force was stationed to guard the water mains leading to Chinatown. As the *Chronicle* (July 27, 1877, 3) explained, "Among the special forces now on duty is a strong guard watching the Spring Valley mains from Russian Hill reservoir. The authorities received direct information of a plot to blow up the main to cut off the supply of water from the Chinese quarter, with the design of burning that section of the city."

The strong show of force by the authorities prevented any further serious mob action. What did happen during the following day's business hours was the appearance of squads of men systematically visiting San Francisco employers asking if they employed Chinese, and then leaving once they got an answer. At least a few of these employers, in the cigar and boot and shoe industries, took the hint, firing their Chinese workers and hiring white workers, at least some of them boys and girls (*The San*

Francisco Call July 27, 1877, 3). Under pressure from the depressed economic times, some employers were obviously set on paying low wages, even if they had to employ children.

What happened during the week of July 23 to July 26, 1877, can best be summed up as an incipient rebellion by large numbers of angry rank-and-file people with specific grievances growing out of capitalist labor practices. This proto-political rebellion was limited to securing modifications of private capitalist and government policy in regard to the importation and employment of low-waged Chinese labor. It revealed the existence of a dissident political culture that was largely hidden. The semi-insurrectionary actions were carried out by a highly excited crowd, best labeled a mob, which had a common belief system, was unified and intense in its purpose, and engaged in at least partly planned collective behavior.

The mob action directly and destructively attacked another sector of working people, diverting a critique of the capitalist system and actions of the capitalist class mainly into cultural/racial attacks directed against other workers. White supremacy and attacking the Chinese had proved much more popular to most workers than confronting capital directly. Anger built, but the class struggle against capitalist exploitation was converted into the much cheaper currency of anti-Chinese behavior. This discredited those involved, allowing the establishment to mobilize strong repressive forces to suppress the semi-insurrectionary mob with reactionary counter violence. The rebellion, growing as it did out of the long struggle against low wages, long hours, and insecurity of work, represented a symptom of social and economic distress, and a warning to capital that the limits to working people's toleration of harsh conditions was being reached.

This class-conscious warning from working people was reflected in a statement passed during the crisis by a group of workers meeting in Oakland, located across the Bay from San Francisco:

> *Whereas, the usurpation on the part of the self-styled ruling class has become unbearable by a freedom-loving people, inasmuch as they have disregarded our rights, degraded our manhood and brought the whole nation to starvation, while, under the pretense of law, they hold unbounded wealth and are wasting the same in luxury, debauchery and crime, and are now the aggressors, having called upon the Government for soldiers, for ordering the reduction of wages, knowing that if these men were not abject slaves they must strike, and proclaiming that the first movement toward a strike should be put down, although they might have to sacrifice life, thus avowing their right to sacrifice the life of the people whenever they stand in the way of the growing profits of property. (*Daily Alta California *July 25, 1877, 1)

THE WORKINGMEN'S PARTY OF CALIFORNIA

Immediately following the July events, a Workingmen's Party of California (WPC) began to be organized. As the WPC was forming, echoes of the July rioting in San Francisco were felt in other parts of California. For example, in mid-September of 1877, three people were murdered on a ranch near the town of Rocklin, located about twenty miles northeast of Sacramento. Chinese were accused of the crime and the entire Chinese community of Rocklin was blamed. A meeting of the white citizens of Rocklin was held and the Chinese were given until 6:00 the same evening to leave town with whatever possessions they could carry. After the Chinese had departed, "the citizens marched to the Chinese quarter and every house in that section, numbering twenty-five in all, was torn down and demolished" (*The Placerville Mountain Democrat* September 22, 1877, 2). Following this episode of ethnic cleansing, four Chinese men, accused of being accessories

314

to the crime, were almost lynched by a mob as they were being transferred by train to the county seat. Armed officers of the law foiled the attempted lynching (*The Nevada City Daily Transcript* September 18, 1877, 2).

In early October of 1877, the WPC was formally established, with the Irish-born Dennis Kearney as president. This party was different and separate from the Marxian Workingmen's Party of the United States, which later became known as the Socialist Labor Party. Kearney himself was an opportunist and in July had even joined and served with the Committee of Safety as a member of what was already called the "pick-handle brigade." When Kearney applied for membership in the Workingmen's Party of the United States in July 1877, he was rejected (Shaffer 1952, 13). But his language against both capitalists and the Chinese captured a wide following in San Francisco and other parts of California, and so he was able to become the head of WPC. At its founding, the WPC outlined its principles and political perspective, designed to appeal to those who felt that both the capitalist class and governmental forces were allied against them:

> *The object of this association is to unite all the poor and working men and their friends into one political party for the purpose of defending themselves against the dangerous encroachments of capital on the happiness of our people, and the liberties of our country.*
>
> *We propose to wrest the government from the hands of the rich and place it in those people where it properly belongs.*
>
> *We propose to rid the country of cheap Chinese labor as soon as possible, and by all means in our power, because it tends still more to degrade labor and aggrandize capital.*

315

We propose to destroy land monopoly in our state by such laws as will make it impossible.

We propose to destroy the great money power of the rich by a system of taxation that will make great wealth impossible in the future.

We propose to provide decently for the poor and unfortunate, the weak, the helpless, and especially the young, because the country is rich enough to do so, and religion, humanity, and patriotism demand we should do so.

We propose to elect none but competent workingmen and their friends to any office whatever. The rich have ruled us till they have ruined us. We will now take our own affairs into our own hands. The republic must and shall be preserved, and only workingmen will do it. Our shoddy aristocrats want an emperor, and a standing army to shoot down the people. (Bancroft 1890, 7:356n20)

Kearney devoted himself to agitation, and amid continuing depression and unemployment, he began holding open-air meetings in San Francisco, both denouncing capitalists and threatening the Chinese. This kept San Francisco on edge, and property owners and the police and militia were alert to further outbreaks of mob action. During the winter months, state legislation and San Francisco city ordinances were passed to limit free speech and assembly, and the public advocacy of destruction of property was made a felony. Class lines were hardening in San Francisco and California (Knight 1960, 16–17).

By 1878, the WPC was a political force in some parts of California, throwing fear into the Democratic and Republican Parties alike. In fact, the two major parties took the extraordinary step of fusing their electoral tickets in many places during that summer's election for a constitutional convention to revise the state's constitution. Despite their show of force, the WPC elected about one-third of the delegates to the constitutional convention, as well as the mayor of Oakland and a number of other candidates for state and local office. While wielding some influence at the convention, the WPC was yet unable to control it, and the result was disappointment for many people (Bean 1973, 241–242). Nevertheless, an alarmed *The New York Times* (June 22, 1878, 4) made these comments on the victory of the WPC:

> *The party represented by Kearney is the result of a revolt against the monopolies which have long ruled the State. Like most new communities, California has been afflicted with "rings" and oppressive corporate monopolies. From the earliest times to the present, the State has been largely managed by successive rings. Beginning with stage and express companies, there have flourished steam-ship companies, banking corporations, and railroad companies, each one of which, or a combination of which, has dictated political candidates of all parties, controlled Legislatures and Municipal Governments, crushed out or fostered private enterprises as they chose, and organized lesser rings in nearly every department of business activity. The concentration of great wealth in the hands of a few has not only made this possible, but it was the inevitable result of such a condition of affairs … No wonder the people grew restive. Whichever way they turned, they touched the iron ring of a corporation.*
>
> *But the revolution which brings to the surface such a man as KEARNEY is like a fever dream. This pestilent fellow is simply an anarchist. There is no "Communist" in New York so dogmatic, frantic, and threatening as he … This insolent ruffian has*

> *been permitted to advocate murder, and the objects of his wrath have been specially mentioned by name. The destruction or deportation of the Chinese, the Eight-hour law, maintenance of the poor by State appropriations, prohibition of convict labor, repeal of charters of corporations, unlimited issue of government currency, and other things contained in the Kearneyite platform are comparatively harmless heresies. But the men of KEARNEY'S kidney do not hesitate to declare that confiscation, incendiarism, and murder will figure in their programme if they ever get the upper hand in society. Of course, much of this talk is mere bluster. But ... the men who have blustered and threatened have very nearly come into power in a Constitutional Convention.*

In the 1879 election came the zenith of the WPC's power. It elected the chief justice of the supreme court, five out of six associate justices, the mayor of San Francisco, other city officials, eleven state senators, and sixteen assemblymen (Bean 1973, 242).

A newspaper report on a Workingmen's leadership meeting in February 1880 helps to capture the spirit of the times when fears of assassination and threats of violence were common:

> *A meeting of the Workingmen's Ward Presidents and several municipal officers was held at the headquarters yesterday afternoon. Dennis Kearney presided. Among those present were Mayor Kalloch, Auditor Dunn, City Attorney and Counsellor Murphy, and Railroad Commissioner Beerstecher, a full body of Presidents, and about one hundred idlers. Kearney called the meeting to order, and stated that it was for the purpose of enquiring into a reported plot to assassinate the leaders of the Workingmen by hirelings of capitalistic thieves and villains.*

A star-chamber session of capitalists and friends of the Chinese had been held at the Palace Hotel, Tuesday night and they had planned a Vigilance Committee to overthrow the Workingmen. A price had been offered for his life, and he supposed that of other leaders. He asked for suggestions as to action from any one present.

*L. J. Gannon said that there was so much talk of a Vigilance Committee and hanging that he thought it would be well to hang the leaders of the Vigilance Committee to the street-lamp posts. He believed that every man should arm himself and be ready for a fight ... the clubs should organize for the coming struggle ... O'Shaughnessy applauded the idea of hanging their opponents to lamp-posts; he believed executive sessions of the clubs should be held to properly organize for the hanging picnics. (*Daily Alta California *February 26, 1880, 1)*

Despite the brief success of the WPC, its direct involvement in party political struggles led to its demise in 1880 when a serious split occurred in the party. One group wanted to bargain with the Democratic Party and, depending upon the outcome of negotiations, return to that party. Kearney himself led a second faction, which wanted to ally itself with the Greenback-Labor Party, a national third party. This latter party was allied with the Grange and the Knights of Labor and favored inflationary currency as well as the eight-hour day, breakup of monopolies, graduated income tax, and an end to Chinese immigration. This party had elected fourteen members to Congress in 1878 and appeared to be gaining strength (Olson and Wladover 1992, 264–265).

The split in the WPC was deep, and one faction soon broke away and joined the Democrats. Although elements of the party continued on for a short time, the WPC was fatally wounded by the split and was effectively dead by mid-1880 (*The New York Times* May 19, 1880, 2; May 20, 1880, 2; May 21, 1880, 1; May 22, 1880, 1; April 24, 1881, 2; *Mariposa Gazette* November 5, 1881, 3; Issel and Cherny 1986, 126–129). At their last full convention, in May of 1880, the WPC platform included some planks that were reactionary (the anti-Chinese stance for example), but many of them, such as government control of corporations, direct election of the US president, and the right to vote for women, were very advanced for the time:

> *In the afternoon the Committee on Platform, Resolutions, and Constitution reported. The platform is anti-Chinese, anti-subsidy, anti-national banks, anti-monopoly, and favoring greenbacks, Governmental control of corporations, female enfranchisement, compulsory education, the creating by tax of a fund to be used in assisting heads of families in settling on public lands, and the election of President and Vice President of the United States and Postmasters by a direct vote of the people. (The New York Times May 19, 1880, 2)*

RURAL REBELS, SQUATTER TRADITIONS, THE RAILROAD, AND THE 1880 MUSSEL SLOUGH SHOOTOUT

In frontier regions of the West, there was a long tradition of settlers occupying and developing unoccupied, (or occupied "only" by Indians), public lands and lands with unclear or not-finalized titles. The usual outcome of such actions was the subsequent purchase of the land at the low, government price, under the 1841 Preemption Act, the 1862 Homestead Act, or other laws designed to encourage the settlement and agricultural development of "vacant" land—defined as territory not occupied by European Americans. Sometimes, however, serious conflicts developed when settlers were judged to be illegal squatters subject to forcible eviction from their homes. The settlers in such cases often organized, armed themselves, and resisted.

The conflict between the Central Pacific/Southern Pacific Railroad empire and the settlers of the Mussel Slough area of today's Kings County (then part of Tulare County) developed out of the same traditions of settler direct action. What was new was the rise of corporate power in the form of the railroad, making it much harder to achieve victory over this power than the government of the earlier years. Some settlers had arrived and occupied land in the area as early as 1870, years before the railroad company built through the region and acquired formal title to its land grants from the federal government.

Meanwhile, the Southern Pacific published pamphlets inviting the settlers to occupy the lands of this part of the San Joaquin Valley, promising that as soon as the railroad acquired full legal ownership that the settlers would be given the right to buy the land they had occupied and developed. While the actual prices to be charged for the land were kept vague in these pamphlets ("from $2.50 upward"), it was clearly stated that the price of the land would not include the settlers' own houses, barns, and other improvements. By 1875, these improvements included a cooperative irrigation system as well as the many houses and developed farms.

Then, in 1878, once the railroad had built its line and acquired title, it sent out letters to each settler stating that the land now could be purchased by anyone at prices ranging from seventeen dollars to forty dollars an acre. The settlers immediately charged that these prices included their own improvements and that the Big Four, all vastly wealthy multimillionaires, were grossly cheating them out of values built by years of their hard labor. The railroad answered that they were violating no specific legal contract and that, furthermore, it was the railroad's existence, not the settlers' improvements, which made the land worth the price the railroad set (Bean 1973, 226–227; Conlogue 1999, 43–44).

321

The action of the Big Four set the stage for organized resistance by the settlers. About six hundred formed a Settlers' Grand League to fight the railroad and organized armed paramilitary operations of secret, hooded, night-riding cavalry who terrorized, burned out, or tried to evict those who agreed to purchase the land at the unfair terms the railroad demanded.

Many of the settlers in this section of California had originally come from the South and the area had a pronounced Democratic Party voting pattern, both factors tending to make the settlers hostile toward the Central Pacific/Southern Pacific, which was Yankee and closely connected to the Republican Party. The Workingmen's Party also became involved, passing a resolution that supported the settlers and condemned the "grasping greed of the railroad monopoly." One of the settlers' leaders, John J. Doyle, was also affiliated with the Workingmen.

The conflict soon was in the courts, where the friends of the railroad far outnumbered the friends of the settlers, especially at the higher levels. In 1879, the legal dispute went to the federal circuit court, where Judge Lorenzo Sawyer, long an ally and social friend of Stanford, Crocker, and other wealthy Republicans, ruled in the railroad's favor (Brown 1994, 399; Conlogue 1999, 44–45). This led to the May 11, 1880, attempt by a federal marshal, Alonzo W. Poole, and two heavily armed land purchasers, Walter J. Crow and Mills D. Hart, to evict settlers at Mussel Slough, so that land could be taken over by Crow and Hart. A group of about forty armed settlers stood in their way, trying to disarm the trio. Crow and Hart then opened fire on the settlers, killing five before the remaining settlers shot and killed them both (Conlogue 1999, 43).

This battle represented the only important armed clash between the railroads and nineteenth-century US farmers and inspired several anti-railroad novels and plays, the most famous being *The Octopus,* a book by Frank Norris. The seven deaths in this shootout far exceeded the three killed in the legendary 1881 shootout at the O.K. Corral in Tombstone, Arizona. Later, seven league members were tried and five were convicted of resisting a federal marshal. They served eight months in jail. Public opinion was generally on their side, however, and they were seen more as heroes and martyrs than criminals. The losing settlers had to pay the railroad for their own improvements or leave their farms. Most refused to pay, left the area, and deeply resented the railroad as an oppressive ruling-class enemy.

THE 1883 CHINESE RAILROAD WORKERS' STRIKE

At least partly as a result of the years of direct action and political struggle by many of California's workers, by the early 1880s both major parties favored the restriction of Chinese immigrants. As a result, in 1882 the Chinese Exclusion Act was passed, limiting Chinese immigration for a ten-year period. Knowing that the supply of Chinese railroad workers was now more limited and hoping that this fact would result in an advantage for them, Chinese workers organized and conducted a large-scale strike against the Central Pacific/Southern Pacific monopoly, near Redding, California, in the summer of 1883.

Chinese railroad-construction workers were receiving one dollar a day for ten-hour days. In late June, they all set down their tools, with a daily wage of $1.25 as their central demand. The workers apparently had no formal union, yet 3,022 Chinese workers struck, maintaining solidarity for over three weeks (California Bureau of Labor Statistics 1888, 171–177). But there was no class solidarity across ethnic boundaries. As one newspaper put it, "all the white men continue to labor" (*Sacramento Record Union* June 29, 1883, 1). A few days after the strike began, the same newspaper reported that the Chinese laborers were standing firm, and optimistic about winning the strike or finding alternative employment, "The outside Chinese insist that the railroad company will eventually make the concessions demanded by the strikers. The strikers seem very independent, as they say they can go to work in the mines if the company doesn't want them" (*Sacramento Record Union* July 2, 1883, 2).

By mid-July, as the strike continued, it became evident that a key factor was the strikers' stockpiled supply of food, which was beginning to run low. The *Record Union* reporter predicted that this would be the decisive factor, "The strikers still hold out, and probably will, as long as their stock of provisions last, which will not be a great while now, and then they will probably go to work on the old terms" (*Sacramento Record Union* July 13, 1883, 1).

A few days later, the strike was nearly over, with many of the strikers returning under the old wage rates. Of the original strikers, a reported one thousand did not return with the others, but many of these were expected to return within a week (*Sacramento Record Union* July 17, 1883, 3; July 24, 1883, 1).

THE VICTORIOUS 1885 IRON WORKERS' STRIKE

Another illustration of the revival of union struggles during the mid-1880s example was the successful 1885 San Francisco ironworkers' strike. Due to a 15 percent cut in wages, on February 9, 1885, about two thousand men from several craft unions struck. They were led by the iron moulders', blacksmiths', and boilermakers' unions, and had the support of the machinists and patternmakers, who were both in the process of organizing unions of their own. At the mass meetings of the men involved, militant views were often expressed, opposing any compromise on their wages (*The San Francisco Call* February 10, 1885, 7). One unionist stated, for example, that, "Workmen must not allow themselves to be ground down to the level of European pauper labor. Sooner than that this should come to pass, they should throw up barricades and shoot their oppressors down" (*The San Francisco Call* February 10, 1885, 7).

Another unionist had a more moderate, but still firm view:

> *What we wish for is our right, and no more. We don't want to crowd the bosses, of course, but at present we*

*are only getting living wages. Suppose the times are dull just now, why should they wish us, who are poor workingmen, only living by what we earn day to day, to tide them, who have capital, over ... We cannot afford to do it. It means starvation for ourselves and our families if we do. (*The San Francisco Call *February 10, 1885, 7)*

UNION IRON WORKS
SAN FRANCISCO

The Union Iron Works

Located in the Potrero District of San Francisco by the mid-1880s, this firm was a leader of the early industrial development of San Francisco, and a stronghold of craft unionism. [Courtesy of the Bancroft Library, University of California, Berkeley.]

Discussions between the employers and workers took place, but these initial attempts to affect a compromise of a 7.5 percent reduction in pay were hooted down by the workers, and both sides became more stubborn (*The San Francisco Call* February 13, 1885, 3).

Solidarity among the strikers was high; the joint strike committee "emphatically informed" one of the employers that, "no man would be allowed to return to work unless every man who struck in the same shop went back with him ..." (*San Francisco Call* February 18, 1885, 4). There were reportedly only nine scabs or "rats" still working during the strike and they were either expelled from their union, declared renegades or visited by a committee of strikers. The workers also began to discuss establishing a cooperative factory on the model of several boot-and-shoe establishments "which have proved very successful" (*The San Francisco Call* February 18, 1885, 4).

After only ten days on strike, the solidarity of the strikers paid off, and the employers surrendered, restoring the old wage rates. The nine scabs that had broken solidarity and continued working during the strike were all discharged from their jobs, this being one of the conditions set by the strikers for returning to work (*The San Francisco Call* February 20, 1885, 3).

In contrast to many other strikes, this strike was relatively mild, with skilled workers, organized in craft unions, using their solidarity as leverage to force the bosses to capitulate. Craft unions were often in a kind of junior partnership with their employers, but they could only be pushed so far before they would strongly fight back.

THE 1885 CHINESE CIGAR MAKERS' STRIKE

Another example of a Chinese strike during this era came in October of 1885 when about seventy Chinese American cigar makers walked out of the factory of Koenigsberger, Falk and Mayer on San Francisco's Pine Street. This strike intensified the long-existing conflict between European American and Chinese American workers. The unmet demand that caused this strike related to the factory owners' policy of gradual replacement of all Chinese American cigar makers with European Americans. This process was underway when the Chinese complained that the new, white cigar makers were insulting and abusive towards them, even threatening violence, a fact denied by the factory owners. When the Chinese workmen demanded the removal of the offending white cigar makers, Mr. Falk, the owner of that department, refused, and the Chinese struck (*The San Francisco Call* October 24, 1885, 3; October 30, 1885, 3).

San Francisco's cigar makers were now between eight and nine thousand strong, with about eight thousand Chinese Americans and four hundred to eight hundred European Americans engaged in the trade. About seven thousand of the Chinese cigar makers were unionized and considering a general strike to achieve their goals. The white workers were represented by two separate unions; one willing to work with Chinese in the same establishment, and one absolutely refusing to do so (*The San Francisco Call* October 24, 1885, 3; October 25, 1885, 5; October 29, 1885, 1).

As the strike continued, threatening to grow much larger, other craft unions in San Francisco began to take notice and develop support for the two white unions against the Chinese. As the *Call* reported in a typically racist fashion, "The aggressive action of the Chinese in refusing to work with the whites is yet the all absorbing topic among the laboring classes, and great indignation is expressed that the heathens should be bold enough to make such a movement" (*The San Francisco Call* October 27, 1885, 1).

Soon the Knights of Labor became involved and led an organizing effort to bring all European American unions together with a march and mass meeting to, as the *Call* put it, "carry war to the Coolie camp" (*The San Francisco Call* October 29, 1885, 1). Over the next few days, various San Francisco unions joined the conflict, all supporting the white cigar makers and declaring they would march and rally against the Chinese cigar makers. The day of the march and rally the *Call* had an article on the topic:

The Workmen's War

All the necessary arrangements for the white cigar makers' mass meeting to be held to-night, at Union Hall, under the auspices of the Knights of

> *Labor, were completed last evening ... the joint committee of the Knights of Labor and the Cigar makers Union received delegates from the various trade unions ... There were fifteen trades union represented by delegates. These latter reported that their respective unions were in sympathy and accord with the white cigar makers, and would stand by them in their fight against the coolies ... The following labor organizations will participate in the parade, The Sailors' Union, the Boiler-makers, the Pattern makers, the Iron moulders, the Blacksmiths, the Machinists, the Cigar makers Union, the Cigar makers Association of the Pacific Coast, the Carpenters, the Bricklayers and the Painters ... The line of march will ... be taken down Market Street.* (The San Francisco Call *October 31, 1885, 3*)

That evening, the Knights of Labor were in charge of what the *Call* labeled a "huge" march and rally. A list of examples of the signs carried by the marchers and printed in the *Call* included both racist and anti-Chinese slogans, as well as more generic pro-working-class ones:

> *"Cheap Labor Destroyed Rome"; "Buy Only White made Cigars"; "Is America to be a Patron of China"? "Our Own Race for Us"; "One Blow, Strike Together, Now or Never"; "We Are Opposed to All Degraded Labor"; "An Injury to One is an Injury to All"; "Must the White Man Go?" "Loyalty to Ourselves and Race"; "Wage-workers, Strike for Your Rights."* (The San Francisco Call *November 1, 1885, 5*)

The march's Grand Marshall Frank Roney, who had once been a revolutionary in Ireland and was currently a leader of the Iron Moulders' Union, gave one of the last speeches:

"An injury to one in this cause," he said, "is the concern of all." He referred to the great and increasing numbers of men who have been thrown out of employment by reason of the Chinese, and who are vainly walking the streets looking for work. He remarked that those followers of O'Donnell who talk of shouldering muskets and driving the Chinese out would not, in his opinion, have the courage to do the fighting. The greatest courage is moral courage, he said, and this kind should be practiced. For the present, he thought the driving of the Chinese out of the cigar making business should be particularly attended to, and then they can be forced out of other trades. (The San Francisco Call *November 1, 1885, 5)*

This is what the world of San Francisco white workers had come to by the end of 1885. An important union leader (and a former Irish revolutionary, no less), was openly advocating driving out a militant sector of the working class on the basis of race. The narrow craft-union point of view was dominant; class consciousness had come to a low point and racialization to a high level.

Industrial unions, bringing together both the skilled and the unskilled while organizing entire industries, were usually up against total hostility from the corporate bosses, and so faced much more serious struggles. One such union was the Sailors' Union of the Pacific, which was founded that same year of 1885 in a torchlit meeting on San Francisco's Folsom Street Pier. The next year, a national confederation of craft unions was formed, the American Federation of Labor, with the eight-hour day one of its main demands. At the same time, the old Knights of Labor was slowing dying.

The long struggle of the California working class for basic rights like the eight-hour day, unionization, an end to corporate exploitation, a living wage, and women's equality and voting rights had not been achieved by the mid-1880s. It would take several more decades and a new century of rebellion and struggle to achieve even some of these rights.

8

UNITY—
THE SOUTHERN PACIFIC RAILROAD AND THE DEVELOPMENT OF THE CALIFORNIA RULING CLASS, 1877–1890

The period from the last years of the 1870s until the beginning of the 1890s was marked by increasing unity among ruling-class forces, largely led by the owners of the Central Pacific/Southern Pacific Railroad. The insurrection of 1877 provided the shock that led the San Francisco-based California ruling class to recognize the common threat to its long-term existence and begin to organize and unify itself into a coherent class for itself. They gave two grand social parties for ex-President Ulysses S. Grant in 1879 that were concrete expressions of this new unity. The glaring exception to the new ruling class togetherness was the continued exclusion of the Jewish upper class, which remained outside this circle. Its time of integration would come some years later, as part of the rise of an even broader ruling-class consensus.

The California ruling class also had a rural wing, consisting of land barons who owned millions of acres of the best lands in the state, employing and exploiting tens of thousands of dispossessed, landless workers. Brief case studies of two of the biggest of these barons are presented here.

By 1886, when the Southern Pacific Railroad achieved victory in the United States Supreme Court and C. P. Huntington succeeded the newly elected Senator Stanford as president of the Southern Pacific Railroad Company—the Christian sector of the California ruling class, in the words of one upper-class publication, had been brought together as an entirely consistent mass. Southern Pacific domination was nearly complete by 1890, but the ever-present forces of capitalist innovation and accumulation were gradually maturing, forces which would eventually challenge and overthrow their control.

THE DEVELOPMENT OF RULING CLASS UNITY: THE COMMITTEE OF SAFETY, 1877

During the summer of 1877, the developing unity and power of the higher circles had been tested by the crisis provoked by the mass dissatisfaction of thousands of workers due to economic depression and high unemployment, at the same time that vast wealth was being accumulated by the rich. As touched on earlier, when white workers rioted against the Chinese and those corporations employing Chinese at low wages, a new Vigilance Committee calling itself the Committee of Safety, was established, again under the leadership of leading merchant William T. Coleman. It is important to note the nature of the upper-class response to working-class rebellion and how it helped develop ruling-class unity.

Like the Vigilance Committee of 1856, the Committee of Safety was a violent group, composed of the leading businessmen of the time, usurping governmental authority to carry out their aims of protecting property during a period of crisis. The *Daily Alta California* (July 25, 1877, 1) described the initial meeting of this group:

> *[A] meeting of principal business men and representative men of solid property and social interests of San Francisco was held in the Chamber of Commerce yesterday afternoon, to take into consideration the grave conjuncture arising from the turbulence of Monday night ... over two hundred men were present ... The 1877 Committee of Safety was different from the 1856 Vigilance Committee in that it had the direct support of city, state and federal governments. San Francisco Mayor Bryant attended and spoke at the first meeting of the Committee, the San Francisco Board of Supervisors held a joint meeting with the Committee at the Chamber of Commerce headquarters, California's Governor came to the city and supported Coleman's activities and the federal government supplied 2,500 rifles to the Committee of Safety. (Bancroft n.d., 352–364; Daily Alta California July 25, 1877, 1)*

Besides Coleman, who was chairman, the Committee of Safety included leading ruling-class figures, many of whom exploited low-waged Chinese workers in the mines, factories, and farms they owned. They represented many key corporations and economic interest groups, especially the Bank of California, and included the following people:

Banker D. O. Mills, who at the initial meeting moved to entrust the entire organization to Coleman; Isaac Bluxome, a leader of the 1856 committee; industrialists Hiram Tubbs and J. C. Tubbs; Silver King and banker James C. Flood; clothing manufacturer Levi Strauss; Wm. Alvord of the Bank of California; large landowner George H. Howard; industrialist Ira P. Rankin; "wheat king" Isaac Freidlander; woolen mills president Col. John D. Fry; mine owner John O. Earl; former head of the Pacific Mail Steamship Company W. F. Babcock; merchant Horace Davis; merchants and bankers F. F. Low and C. Adolph Low; Prentiss Selby of Selby Smelters; banker R. C. Woolworth; and sugar baron Claus Spreckels (*Daily Alta California* July 25, 1877, 1; *Daily Evening Call* July 25, 1877, 1).

In only two days, these men and others subscribed the sum of forty-eight thousand dollars for the work of the committee, and a few days later San Francisco bankers offered up to one hundred thousand dollars to hire more police for the city (Bancroft 1891, 360, 364). These amounts of money were very large for the time; today's equivalent would be about fifty times as much. Within forty-eight hours, about five thousand men were mustered in companies of a hundred, commanded by "prominent citizens" under the overall direction of Coleman. Coleman argued that the actions of the Committee of Safety were necessary because there ...

> *was an agitation among the workingmen, and of a socialistic nature, aggravated by disagreements between the railroads and their employees ... aggravated further by financial disturbances and hard times, culminating in various serious outbreaks in New York ... the labor organizations, and particularly those of a communistic character, were actively in motion. (Bancroft 1891, 372)*

As described in the previous chapter, the Committee of Safety's attack on the rioters helped end the disturbances in forty-eight hours. But the fear of "socialistic" agitation was impressed upon the corporate rich. One result was the recognition of the need for more unity among the ruling class and a concomitantly more rigid division between the wealthy and the rest of the population.

THE DEVELOPMENT OF RULING-CLASS UNITY: THE 1879 PARTIES FOR U. S. GRANT

By 1879, social dividing lines that had been historically more flexible in California than in the East were becoming more rigid in relation to the working-class and rural-agricultural majority, even while the ruling class was becoming more inclusive and unified. In 1879, the first edition of *The Elite Directory for San Francisco and Oakland* appeared with the following commentary on the state of high society and what it termed the "lower classes":

> *Society in San Francisco has in it the possibilities of the greatest refinement and best culture. It is at present liable to the reproach of the nouveaux riches, as are most communities that have had similar experiences. The lines that divide its different classes are not yet distinctly drawn. The different sections overlap at the edges. If we speak of it as composed of superimposed strata, we may say that the composition of the lower classes changes insensibly into the next higher, and so on to the aristocratic capstone. It is not always easy to see where the adventurer merges into the gambler, the gambler into the stock-sharp, the stock-sharp into the regular broker, the broker into the man who follows occupations of greater certainty, until we reach the summit of wealthy leisure and unexceptional gentility. In reply to this it may be urged that it is changing rapidly. The lines are year by year more tightly drawn. (The Argonaut Publishing Company 1879, 21)*

In 1879, only a few years after *The New York Times* correspondent pointed out that the mining aristocracy was on the outs socially, members of this self-same group were invited to attend the two most important social events ever held in California up to that point. Two grand parties given for former President and Civil War hero Ulysses S. Grant, who visited San Francisco in the fall of 1879, illustrate the growing unity of the California aristocracy. The divisions between the San Francisco branch of the old Southern ruling class (the Chivalry), and the newly rich still had an edge, but there was clearly an ongoing process of unification. For one thing, these two great soirees were hosted by a leader of the Bank of California and a leader of the

Central Pacific/Southern Pacific Railroad, yet were attended by the key families and many of the members of the Chivalry.

By the time Grant arrived, the Southern influence on society was losing its dominance as other wealthy elements were being assimilated into the higher circles. One historian of San Francisco society later noted, "Many years passed before the Southern influence on society lost its dominance. By the time that former President Grant arrived in San Francisco, the entire city, Southerners, Northerners, laborers, and millionaires alike, could turn out to honor him with warmth and spontaneity" (Muscatine 1975, 360).

William Sharon of the Bank of California gave one party for Grant on the night of October 8, 1879, and Charles Crocker of the Central Pacific/Southern Pacific Railroad the other on the night of October 21, 1879. These two men represented the two dominant and overlapping economic and political interest groups of California during this period. Grant recognized the importance of these two key groups and their leaders, and so naturally was open to attending the gatherings. For their part, Sharon, who had successfully achieved his dream of becoming a United States senator from Nevada—where it was easier to purchase political power, even though Sharon lived in San Francisco—and Crocker were interested in impressing the former president with the wealth, elegance, and prestige of the arrangements and the people attending. In many respects, these events represented the coming of age of the California ruling class on the national scene.

Sharon's party was held at Ralston's former estate in Belmont, south of San Francisco, which Sharon now owned. It was the larger of the two parties, with sixteen hundred guests. The correspondent on the scene for the *Daily Alta California* enthused at length about the setting, decorations, arrangements, and elite guests for this grand party: "[The estate] is preeminently a magnificent house for princely entertainment. As this mansion is approached from the railroad station, the view in daylight reminds the traveler of an English park. The house is on the slope of the hill to the right of the road, resembling, with its many roofs, higher and higher up the hillside, a great Swiss chalet ... something sublime" (*Daily Alta California* October 9, 1879, 1).

He described the gathering as "one of the grandest yet assembled in this State. Few persons of distinction in political and social life of this city were absent. The representatives of wealth, beauty, intelligence and power were all there, and the scene, as the assembled hundreds passed through the capacious mansion, baffles description" (*Daily Alta California* October 9, 1879, 1). He added the following details:

> *Toward nine o'clock ... the first special train of nine cars arrived at the depot at Belmont, and ... the guests were soon furnished with carriages to convey them to the Sharon Mansion ... all along the route the variegated lanterns hanging from the branches of trees and projecting from the walls and buttresses ... had a very enchanting appearance ... At the mansion, the guests were received by Miss Sharon, Mrs. U. S. Grant, and Mrs. J. D. Fry in the principal drawing room ... Stepping forward to the vestibule, the guests at once saw that nothing which art and wealth could contribute to please the eye and gratify the taste for the beautiful had been withheld ... the scene of grace and beauty was perfectly bewitching. Over the entrance to the drawing room where General Grant received the visitors, there was hanging one of the prettiest works of floral art, in the word "welcome," that we ever looked upon.* (Daily Alta California *October 9, 1879, 1)*

Sharon's guest list for the party was broad and inclusive, and the *Alta* listed the names of nearly a thousand out of the sixteen hundred guests present. Both Sharon, a Republican senator, and Grant, a Republican Party leader, had an interest in upper-class inclusiveness, as did the upper class itself. The leaders of the Bank of California were, of course, present in force as were other bankers like Louis McLane, president of Nevada Bank; Lloyd Tevis, president of Wells Fargo Bank; H. L. Dodge of Union Trust; Edward Martin of Hibernia Bank; as well as John Parrott and Henry Barrollet of California Trust Company.

Numerous leaders of the California and Nevada mining world were also present. These included Silver Kings James C. Flood, John W. McKay and J. G. Fair (who were all also owners of the Nevada Bank); Thomas Bell and J. Barron of the New Almaden Mine; future Democratic United States senator George H. Hearst, who owned mines all over the West; L. L. Robinson, a hydraulic gold miner and president of the California Miners' Association; and A. J. Ralston, William C. Ralston's brother and an owner of Selby Smelting and Lead Company.

The owners and executives of California's key transportation companies were also prominently in attendance, including Charles Crocker, Leland Stanford, E. W. Hopkins, and A. N. Towne of the Central Pacific/Southern Pacific Railroad; Oliver Eldridge of the Pacific Mail Steamship Company, and William Norris, a former leader of the California Steam Navigation Company. Industrialists Peter Donahue and Irving Scott of the Union Iron Works, A. L. Tubbs (rope), and J. D. Fry (woolen mills) were also present.

From the realms of politics and the law, both Republicans and Democrats were well represented; men like Governor-elect George C. Perkins (R); former governors Stanford (R), Romualdo Pacheco (R), John B. Weller (D), and William Irwin (D); former and current US senators and representatives William Gwin (D), Cornelius Cole (R), William Stewart (R), John S. Hager (D), Aaron A. Sargent (R), Horace Davis (R), and John P. Jones (R); Judges Belcher, Hydenfeldt, Lorenzo Sawyer, Ogden Hoffman, A. C. Niles, Davis Louderback, E. McKinstry, and Selden S. Wright; and prominent attorney Hall McAllister. Military men like Generals McDowell, Leynard, Burns, and A. C. Kelton, and Admiral McDougold were also in evidence.

The representatives of the old-line Southern upper class, the Chivalry, who made up a prominent part of San Francisco high society, were a different category of guests. It is worth noting the irony of inviting large numbers of these Southern Democrats to a party honoring the man who did so much to win the Civil War for the North, then served as the Republican President during much of the Reconstruction of the South. Many of the Chivalry had favored both slavery and succession, yet the Sharon guest list had the following number of members of these Southern or Southern-connected families:

Parrotts (6)	Bowies (3)
Crittendens (6)	Poetts (3)
Gwins (5)	Tevises (3)
Haggins (5)	Breckenridges (2)
McAllisters (4)	Reddingtons (2)
Kings (4)	McKinstrys (2)
McLanes (4)	Blandings (2)

(Atherton 1914, 203–204; Muscatine 1975, 357)

Members of the eastern aristocracy (such as Mr. and Mrs. John Q. Adams), were also at the party, and even a member of the Southern California Carrillo family, Romualdo Pacheco, whose mother was a Carrillo and whose daughter later married Lloyd and Susan Tevis's son. The presence of old-monied Southern aristocratic families in large numbers is strong evidence for the growing unity of the higher circles of San Francisco and California. It also shows a high level of class consciousness as well as a clear willingness to let bygones be bygones in the interest of broader upper-class goals and unity.

A final notable fact was that brothers-in-law Alvinza Hayward and John P. Jones (now a US senator from Nevada), who had successfully double-crossed both Sharon and Ralston and stolen the Crown Point bonanza, were both invited and came to Sharon's party for Grant. By 1879, ruling-class unity clearly came first, before old conflicts.

The party for Grant held at Charles Crocker's mansion on Nob Hill took place on October 21, 1879, a few weeks after the Sharon fête. A reporter from *The San Francisco Call* opened his story on the event as follows:

The second momentous society event of the season took place last evening. The occasion was another tribute offered by the beauty and wealth of San Francisco to the distinguished citizen and soldier General Ulysses S. Grant. It is not frequently that any of the palaces on California Street Hill are thrown open to society, and more rarely that such a grand reception is planned and carried out, as that tendered last evening by Mr. and Mrs. Charles Crocker to the city's guest. The list of invitations issued was smaller than that sent out by Senator Sharon on the occasion of his recent reception in honor of the General, but the event equaled, if not eclipsed in grandeur and magnificence, the gathering at Belmont ...

Soon after nine o'clock, when carriages began to arrive with the hurrying guests, the streets and carriageway were crowded with horses and vehicles. The inner portion of the mansion never looked to better advantage. The floral decorations, although not profuse or gorgeous, were rich and expensive, and arranged in superb taste. The splendid adornments of the mansion, the rich frescoes, mahogany panels, marble and bronze statuary, prismatic chandeliers and all the articles which combine to make the residence a modern palace, were shown to unusual effect ...

The costumes of the ladies, some three hundred of the wives and daughters of our most distinguished citizens being present, were most elegant and expensive, and some were marvels of the modiste's art. The reception was in every sense a credit to the city, its society and the prominent millionaire who gave it ... [I]t was an assemblage of representative aristocracy, and therefore a most notable event ... it will long be remembered as

one of the most brilliant society events of the decade.
(The San Francisco Call *October 22, 1879, 3)*

It is notable that the *Call* reporter stated at the outset that "society" did not often have an opportunity to see the interiors of the giant Nob Hill mansions of the newly super rich. The opening of the Crocker mansion to a high society that was strongly Southern and Democrat in its origins was another important step toward ruling-class unity.

The *Call* reporter described Crocker's "magnificent palace" as 250 feet square (62,500 square feet per story) and three stories high" (not including the basement and tower), and built in the French Renaissance style. Sanborn maps and other sources indicate that the building was somewhat smaller, but still huge, one of the largest buildings in the western United States (Sanborn Map Company 1886; Shumsky 1972, 221). The other grand mansions, those of Stanford, Hopkins, Colton, and Flood—all located nearby on Nob Hill—were slightly smaller.

The Crocker mansion's ground floor was divided into a drawing room, a library, main hall, billiard parlor, dining room, Mrs. Crocker's boudoir, and art gallery. Bedrooms occupied at least part of the upper floors. The *Call* reporter's brief description of the art gallery gives an idea of the character of the whole:

> *The handsomest room in the Crocker mansion, and one which reflects credit upon the esthetic tastes of the proprietor, is the Art Gallery ... It is an apartment at once simple, unique, elegant, of graceful shape, and as pure and beautiful to the eye as a poet's dream ... {A] polished inlaid floor of oak, ash, manzanita ... of light and dark colors, in square and diamond-shaped figures, is perhaps the humblest of the features of the graceful and refined picture. The gallery is well lighted by three skylights ... From each of these skylights descends a large and costly cut glass chandelier ... Around the dark and purple walls of the room are hung the works of some of*

*the most noted native and foreign masters. (*The San Francisco Call *October 22, 1879, 3)*

The guest list for Crocker's party included about eight hundred persons (about five hundred men and three hundred women), only half the size of the crowd invited to Sharon's. How this more select group was chosen is evident: the members of the Southern "old rich" society people and those associated with mining were much reduced. There were also fewer Democrats. Charles Crocker and the Big Four railroad barons and their close business associates; generally admired European royalty and Northern, not Southern, American aristocracy. Politically, they had strong Republican Party ties and believed that, economically, California should focus on developing its long-term agricultural and industrial potential, not the relatively short-term and more speculative mining interests. Crocker's guest list therefore reflected this perspective.

Charles Crocker's Mansion
This Nob Hill palace was the location of the October 21, 1879 party for ex-President U. S. Grant. [Courtesy of the Bancroft Library, University of California, Berkeley.]

Only the upper echelon of the old-rich Southern–born or connected society, such as former Senator William Gwin and Hall McAllister, whose highly accomplished wife was a Southerner, were invited to the Crockers' party. Kentucky-born Lloyd Tevis, whose wife was a daughter of the former attorney general of that state, and whose own daughter married a Breckenridge (John C. Breckenridge had been the slaveowners' candidate for president on the Democratic ticket against Lincoln in 1860), was also in attendance, but he had close business connections with Crocker and the Big Four in Wells Fargo Bank and Express and the Southern Pacific Railroad. With only a few such exceptions, virtually all the other upper-class members of the Chivalry, so prominent and numerous at Sharon's event, were not invited to Crocker's party. This was also true of the miners.

One of the few miners invited was Silver King James C. Flood, but he was, by 1879 also a leading banker and stockbroker, and not just a miner. Only a few prominent Democrats were in evidence, including former Senators Gwin and John S. Hager. Republican Party leaders were numerous, including Stanford, Sharon, Cole, Congressman Horace Davis, and Governor-elect and future US Senator George C. Perkins. Railroad leaders were, of course, well represented, as were leading bankers, merchants, and industrialists, including five directors of the Bank of California (Sharon, William Alvord, Adam Grant, D. O. Mills, and C. A. Low), along with many of the same business leaders who attended the Sharon party, such as Homer King, William Babcock, J. B. A. Haggin (who was also a Southern aristocrat), Edward Martin, H. L. Dodge, W. T. Coleman, A. L. Tubbs, Peter Donahue, Irving Scott, Oliver Eldridge, and William Norris.

Four judges were at both events: Lorenzo Sawyer, Ogden Hoffman, E. McKinstry, and Selden S. Wright; and the only military leaders at both parties were General Irwin McDowell, General Kelton, and Lt. H. G. Otis.

Curious absences were those of Henry Miller and Charles Lux, California's "cattle kings." By 1879, they owned hundreds of thousands of acres of land and tens of thousands of sheep, cattle, horses, and pigs. Their large landholdings and other property holdings heavily influenced rural social and economic development, making them an important element of the local ruling class in a number of areas in rural California. Both Miller and Lux had developed close ties to both the Bank of California and the Central Pacific/Southern Pacific Railroad. But Miller was often on the road visiting his vast holdings, and did not generally like high society. Lux may have attended, but not listed by the newspapers, or he could have been out of town.

Also missing was Sugar King Claus Spreckels, whose wealth and economic power were already substantial by this time. Spreckels often acted the part of the outsider rather than the team player, and so may have been unwelcome.

One group that was later to become prominent in higher social circles was still excluded in 1879. This was the Jewish upper class, which was becoming increasingly successful in mercantile, banking, and industrial pursuits in San Francisco and Los Angeles. It had its own clubs, the leading one being the Concordia of San Francisco, established in 1865. An examination of the Concordia's 193 members in 1879 with the known guest list for Crocker's party found that not one member of this leading Jewish upper-class club attended (The Argonaut Publishing Company 1879; *The San Francisco Call* October 22, 1879, 3). This exclusion gradually changed over the next several decades, but in 1879, upper class Jews were still mainly outside of Christian high society.

A final and interesting category in attendance at the Crocker party was the "Misses," young, unmarried women who were the daughters of the rich and powerful. Their families were socially or economically well connected enough to command their attendance at such prestigious events, however only the top families had enough "pull" to get their daughter or daughters invited to *both* the Sharon and Crocker events. Only five young ladies were apparently in that category, reflecting the wealth and social power of their parents and their desirability as mates for men of the *right* social and economic status.

These included the daughter of former Democratic senator William Gwin, whose social standing was higher than her family's wealth; the daughter of Charles Crocker, whose wealth and social standing were both very high; the daughter of industrialist Peter Donahue, who was the heir to her father's great wealth and her mother's high social standing; the daughter of Republican senator William Sharon, who had both great wealth and rapidly rising social standing; and the daughter of Silver King James C. Flood, whose family was very wealthy, but as newly rich, was less well accepted in "high society."

These two important 1879 social events show that, following the conflicts of a decade of depression, the core of the California ruling class remained the wealthy men whose interests were focused around the Bank of California and the Central Pacific/Southern Pacific Railroads (including the Wells Fargo Bank, which was controlled by the owners of the railroad). Others, such as a few key San Francisco industrialists like Peter Donahue, the three remaining Silver Kings (William O'Brien had died in 1878), and a few members of the old Chivalry aristocracy like William Gwin and Hall McAllister, also had economic and social power, but the first two groups were dominant, and as we have seen, interlocked socially as well as economically.

INCLUSION AND EXCLUSION: KEY SOCIAL EVENTS, 1882–1885

Four major social events in 1882—hosted by Mrs. Mark Hopkins, Mr. and Mrs. Charles Crocker, Mr. and Mrs. Lloyd Tevis, and Mr. and Mrs. D. O. Mills—illustrate the increasing social unity of the top aristocratic and corporate sectors of the California ruling class. Representatives of all of the "grades" of San Francisco high society mentioned by *The New York Times* in its 1876 series were present at each party, showing a definite mutual recognition and integration.

On January 5, 1882, the widow Mrs. Hopkins held a party for Lord Beaumont, the holder of the English Barony of Beaumont, which dates to the fourteenth century. The guest list was a mix of Southern aristocrats, (for example, members of the Gwin, Tevis, McAllister, Ashe, Poett, Reddington, and Blanding families); railroad and industrial magnates (members of the Crocker, Towne, Scott, Donahue, and Tubbs families); and merchants, miners, and bankers (members of the Coleman, Newhall, and Flood families) (*The San Francisco Call* January 10, 1882, 5).

Later that month, Lloyd and Susan Tevis held a reception for 250 guests at their mansion at Taylor and Jackson in San Francisco in honor of their son Hugh's twenty-first birthday. The *Call* reported on the occasion:

> *It was an occasion of unusual brilliancy. The ordinary and permanent embellishments of the interior of the house required no elaboration for the special occasion … Art has in this private residence one of her temples: here beauty nestles in ample folds of the richest tapestries; here is the unrestrained exemplification of home and social aesthetics, profusion presided over by good taste, beauty written everywhere, with a royal hand; grandeur looking down from the walls where hang paintings from the master's easel … Flowers, rich, rare and fragrant, lent their charms to the picture, while rich carpets of the mansion were spread over … The great mirrors reflected and re-reflected this charming combination of beauty…*
>
> *The apartments on the main floor are large and numerous … The parlors, the billiard-room and the supper-room, supplemented by the verandas and balconies, afforded an area for promenading,*

*dancing or resting that precluded the discomfort of
a jam.*

*At eight o'clock the stream of carriages began to
arrive. Mrs. Tevis was assisted in receiving by
her daughters—Mrs. Gordon Blanding ... Mrs.
Breckinridge, and Mrs. Rathbone. Dancing was
promptly inaugurated, and continued almost
without cessation until three o'clock in the morning
(*The San Francisco Call *January 24, 1882, 5)

The *Call*'s reporter also described the elaborate attire of many
of the ladies, showing the time, expense, and effort they put into
their gowns:

*Mrs. Tevis was costumed in a robe of royal blue
velvet and delicate pink satin-finished silk. The waist
and long sweeping ... train were composed of the
velvet, showing at the sides a facing of pink silk ...
Pink feathers were arranged in her hair. Diamond
ornaments.*

*Mrs. J. B. Haggin was attired in a costume of cafe au
lait and a darker shade of silk ... The waist, sleeves
and sides of skirt were elaborately trimmed with
wide passementerie ... The back of the skirt was en
train, with bouffant drapery, and finished off with
a large butterfly bow. Diamond ornaments.*

*Mrs. Gordon Blanding wore a robe of pale blue
satin, profusely trimmed with wide bands of silk
embroidery, worked in variegated colors of silk floss.
Bouffant drapery.*

*Mrs. Breckinridge was attired in a costume made
a la Marie Antoinette, and profusely trimmed with
creamy Spanish lace ... In the back the tails of the*

> *coat were lined with pink satin and fell into a long*
> *train. Her hair was ornamented with a diamond*
> *star. She also wore a diamond cross at her neck.*
> *Corsage bouquet of fine roses. (*The San Francisco
> Call *January 24, 1882, 5)*

The Tevis reception was the most inclusive of these four major social events of early 1882. Most of the old South's aristocratic families attended, including the McLanes, Haggins, Gwins, McAllisters, Ashes, and Parrotts. Also present were railroad barons like the Crockers and Hopkins; bankers, large landowners, and merchants, including members of the Sharon, Friedlander, Babcock, Davis, and Coleman families. Public officials like California Supreme Court Judge Lorenzo Sawyer and General McDowell of the army, as well as Bishop Kip of the local Episcopalian church were also in attendance *(The San Francisco Call* January 24, 1882, 5).

A third key social event was a ball held by Mr. and Mrs. Charles Crocker at their residence on February 2, 1882. The *Call* reporter wrote about the Crocker mansion that evening: "Perhaps there is no residence in this city more attractive in its furnishings and finish than that of Mr. Crocker. The building, a perfect palace in itself, was brilliantly illuminated throughout, and with floral decorations everywhere in the greatest profusion, the effect was one of rare beauty and grandeur" *(The San Francisco Call* February 7, 1882, 5).

The Crocker guest list was similar to that of Mrs. Hopkins, except there were fewer members of the Chivalry and more railroad and industrial capitalists. Notably, there were no members of the McAllister, Ashe, and Gwin families reported to be present, but members of the Tevis, Blanding, King, Carolan, and Kittle families were in attendance, representing the western branch of the old South's aristocracy. Lord Beaumont and most of the same representatives of railroad, industrial, banking, and merchant families who had attended the Hopkins' event were present, with the notable additions of bankers Grant, King, Fair, and Dodge and industrialist Eldridge. Crocker also included three generals (McDowell, Houghton, and Kautz), Judge Sawyer and even Commodore Lebrano of the visiting Italian Navy (*The San Francisco Call* February 7, 1882, 5).

The final key social event of 1882 was held at Mr. and Mrs. D. O. Mills' residence at Millbrae. The *Call's* reporter described the arrangements as …

> *complete, the minutest detail that could insure the enjoyment of the guests not being neglected. A special train had been chartered, which left the depot at Fourth and Townsend streets at nine o'clock, having on board a goodly assemblage of the fashionables of San Francisco. Needless to say that quick time was made, and almost before the ladies had settled themselves for a little quiet chat Millbrae was reached … Vehicles awaited the guests, to transport them to the scene of the festivities.*

> *The well-kept grounds through which the route lay were brilliant with the light of many hundred Japanese lanterns, which shed a soft and pleasing glow athwart the darkness of the night. The lake gave back an added radiance to the strings of lanterns the rays of which were reflected upon its lucid bosom. The effect of the exterior decorations was noticeably pretty, and evoked from the guests many exclamations of admiration … The guests then repaired to the reception rooms, where they were received and welcomed by Mr. and Mrs. D. O. Mills and Mrs. Whitelaw Reid, the latter lady's husband being unavoidably called to New York on important business. Every minute brought new accessions, till at last the beautifully decorated parlors were thronged.* (The San Francisco Call *September 12, 1882, 5)*

As was the case for other "high society" events of the period, the *Call*'s reporter offered endless details on the attire of the upper-class women, including the fact that diamonds were by far the most common ornaments, although gold and pearls were also often mentioned, "The toilets of the ladies were miracles of the dressmaker's art, and made the scene a brilliant one. Even in the ... days of the Second Empire we doubt if Paris itself could have gathered into one salon so many elegantly attired ladies" *(The San Francisco Call* September 12, 1882, 5).

The guest list for the Mills' reception reaffirms the overall conclusion deduced from the prior three social events. By 1882, the Southern aristocracy had largely united with and were part of the same social set as the leading railroad, banking, industrial, and merchant families. At the Mills' event the Tevises, Crockers, Colemans, Donahues, Floods, Parrotts, Gwins, McAllisters, Ashes, Hopkins, Tubbs, Kittles, and others were again together socially. Key judges like California Supreme Court justice Lorenzo Sawyer and United States Supreme Court justice Stephen Hill were also present along with General McDowell *(The San Francisco Call* September 12, 1882, 5). By this point, this group was not only socializing, but also intermarrying. The Parrott family for example intermarried with the Donohoes, and the Sharons with the Tevis family *(The San Francisco Call* April 20, 1882, 1). The young women were also marrying upper-class New Yorkers—a Crocker with an Alexander, a Fair with a Vanderbilt, a Mills with a Reid. They were also (for a large dowry price) marrying titled European royalty. For example, historian Francis Moffat described the making of the match between Flora Sharon and a British baronet:

> *In 1880 Sir Thomas George Fermor-Hesketh sailed into San Francisco aboard his steam yacht Lancashire Witch ... As he rode the new hydraulic elevator of the Palace Hotel, his eyes caught those of a pretty young lady ... Her eyes probably would not have*

stayed on his for long had she not known that he was the seventh baronet of Lancaster ... The young lady, Flora Sharon, was the daughter of William Sharon, the owner of the Palace Hotel.

When he left the elevator, Sir Thomas made inquiries ... Her father (noting who Sir Thomas was) arranged for an introduction ... After the payment of a dowry of almost five million dollars, Flora Sharon became Lady Hesketh. (Moffat 1977, 93–94)

Thus by the mid-1880s, the dominant element of the California ruling class was fused and had become a conscious class for itself. Ruling-class publications recognized this class unity. For example, *A Social Manual for San Francisco and Oakland*, published in San Francisco in 1884 stated,

During the last few years ... the social elements new and old have been fused into a consistent mass ... Stylish and expensive weddings have been numerous. Every season has had its large parties to which invitations have been general. Smaller parties have gathered members of the various cliques ... Society ... cannot be said to have new constituents, but a process of assimilation has gone on rapidly with those already in existence. (Anon 1884, 23–24)

At the same time, the Jewish upper class, a much smaller and less powerful group, had social lives largely separate from the gentile aristocrats and capitalists mentioned above. A major Jewish wedding, joining two prominent German Jewish families, Ehrman and Heller, took place in early 1885. The extensive guest list included members of the Heller, Ehrman, Sachs, Adler, Stern, Hecht, Levy, Michaels, and many other leading Jewish families, but not one of them had been invited to any of the four important society events of 1882 or to similar events that took place in 1885 *(The San Francisco Call* February 10, 1885, 3; February 17, 1885, 3). There remained a definite disconnect between the gentile and Jewish upper classes, a split which would only be rectified in the next few decades.

INDUSTRIALIZED AND COMMERCIALIZED AGRICULTURE: TWO GIANT OPERATORS

The rulers of the 1870s and 1880s also included landowners based in rural California, families that owned vast estates amounting to latifundia (large farms). They employed thousands of farm laborers, an occupation which was one of the most numerous of the period. Small- and medium-sized farms were also important, but their farmers were often marginalized by large corporate groups, especially the Bank of California and the Central Pacific/ Southern Pacific Railroad.

This increasingly powerful railroad corporation worked with the biggest agricultural interests and wheat-trading rings of San Francisco to dominate the field and reap the bulk of the profits. Government land grants had given the Central Pacific/ Southern Pacific a vast amount of land, and the giant, Spanish- and Mexican-era land grants were frequently transferred as a block to new owners, resulting in a feudal-like concentration of land-ownership patterns in many regions of the state. This resulted in the rapid industrialization and commercialization of California agriculture as distinct from partly self-sufficient family farms. Two of the largest owners during this era were examples of this monopolization, industrialization, and commercialization. These were the partnership of Miller & Lux, whose livestock and commercial meat business operated mainly in Central California, and Dr. Hugh Glenn, who was one of the state's largest wheat growers and a Democratic Party candidate for governor. Glenn County was later named after this big landowner. Both of these large operations created conflictive class situations, ones that reflected the exploitation of the farm laborers, and resulted in both alienation and violence.

THE EMPIRE OF MILLER AND LUX

Two German immigrant butchers, Henry Miller and Charles Lux, founded the Miller & Lux firm in 1858. It focused on supplying meat to urban markets, especially San Francisco. In an industrial fashion, Miller and Lux engineered the California landscape, transforming nature by applying labor, capital, and science to the constant problems of irregular rainfall and drought. Everything about their firm was on a grand scale. First, their business strategy involved control of the supply end of the market for meat. Their power and profit therefore depended upon vast land purchases, land that was needed to produce the large amounts of meat needed to dominate the market. To acquire this land, Miller and Lux forged links to the corporations and individuals who could help them gobble up both former Mexican land grants and land in the public domain. These links included John Parrott and Company, the trial lawyer Hall McAllister, bankers D. O. Mills and William Ralston of the Bank of California, and land lawyer Henry Haight, who was also a former governor of California.

Miller & Lux also had strong connections to the Bank of California, which provided loans to the company and kept its accounts (Treadwell 1931, 180–181). This cooperation led to closer ties. J. Leroy Nickel, Miller's son-in-law, was for many years both a vice president of Miller & Lux and a director of the Bank of California (Walker 1910:372). Miller and Lux were also members of the San Francisco-based California upper class, and Lux especially had close social relationships with many in positions of influence who could help the firm achieve their land acquisition goals. The two partners also married upper-class sisters, members of the Sheldon family, which traced its ancestors to the early founders of Rhode Island. Henry Miller maintained his connection to this family after his first wife died, by marrying his former wife's niece (Igler 2001, 16–17, 40).

John Parrott was a banker at the center of a group of land brokers operating out of his Parrott Iron Building in San Francisco. This building also housed the United States Land Office, which disposed of the public lands. Insider deals, as well as personal influence facilitated many of these transactions. Corruption and fraud were often key elements in acquisitions, with the use of lobbyists, bribery, and political influence used to pass laws allowing Miller and Lux—and a small number of other owners— to claim vast tracts of prime land. As a result, Miller and Lux, at the height of their power, held 1.25 million acres in three states. Without defining exactly what he meant, Henry Miller stated that Miller & Lux controlled ten times this amount of land, probably referring to deals with other landowners relating to irrigation and boarding cattle and sheep.

The Miller & Lux agricultural empire was centered in the San Joaquin Valley, where it owned about 421,000 acres by 1874. These vast holdings were part of a larger picture of concentrated landholdings in California. Already by 1872, only a hundred individuals owned over 5.46 million acres of California land (Igler 2001, 60–62). By 1900, the Miller & Lux operation was reportedly the largest agricultural corporation in the United States; quite a feat in a state that still had only a modest population (see Igler 2001).

As was the case with most of the other giant California corporations of this time, Miller & Lux had offices in San Francisco. Within a five-block radius of the Miller & Lux central office on Kearny Street resided the headquarters of most of the West's leading firms, including the Pacific Mail Steamship Company, Bank of California, Union Iron Works, Comstock mining syndicates, New Almaden Mining Company, and California Redwood Company (Igler 2001, 58).

Once Miller & Lux had its land, it had to have a hedge against nature's uncertainties, such as drought. For this, it needed to buy or develop irrigation systems and water rights. By 1878, it had purchased enough shares to control the San Joaquin and

Kings River Canal and Irrigation Company, the largest irrigation company in the American West (Igler 2001, 84–85). Second, Miller & Lux hired thousands of mainly immigrant workers to expand its irrigation system, which became the region's largest in this era.

The Miller & Lux workforce was not only mainly immigrant, it was also segregated along racial and ethnic lines and worked for low wages in a union-free environment. Native-born Mexican Americans and immigrant Mexican, Italian, Portuguese, Germans, and Chinese were all employed in their own distinct spheres of unskilled labor. This was a form of racialization, assigning specific characteristics to different groups and enforcing it on groups of workers through work assignments.

Most of the Miller & Lux workforce was what we would call "casual" today. Workers were hired for a specific job, such as digging an irrigation ditch and, when that job was over, they were laid off and told to move on. Such rootless, causal workers were used as strikebreakers or to replace workers who walked off the job. But such men could also be dangerous, so Miller and Lux decided that they would always provide free meals to anyone who passed through their lands looking for work. Feeding such "tramps" also assured that an abundant supply of cheap labor was available for the company's operations.

Feeding this army of tramps created more work for Miller & Lux's Chinese cooks, however, as they would have to wash the extra dishes that the tramps ate on. The Chinese cooks rebelled, refusing to wash the extra dishes. The outcome was the famous "dirty plate route." The mobile laborers could have free meals at the Miller & Lux mess hall, but they would have to eat off of the dirty plates left after the regular employees had finished eating. This procedure also humbled the tramps, helping to keep them insecure and tractable.

This and other aspects of the Miller & Lux labor system were very oppressive. The company immediately fired any suspected union members or sympathizers, so that no union could become established. At least one attempt was made to organize a union in the Miller & Lux butchering operations in San Francisco's Butchertown, but this never succeeded because the organizers were fired (Igler 2001, 143–144). One former Miller & Lux superintendent later stated that the company's labor system "was vicious and bred industrial oppression on a large scale, with the accompanying resentment and hatred" (Igler 2001, 142).

The oppression and exploitation of labor characteristic of the Miller & Lux operation did occasionally lead to violence. One incident in April of 1890 resulted in two deaths. August Keonig was a low-waged German immigrant worker who had worked for some years for Miller & Lux and felt he should have been promoted and paid more than the one dollar per day that he always received. His frustration boiled over one Sunday after a heavy bout of drinking, and he decided that he wanted to kill Henry Miller or the ranch superintendent, E. L. Davis. Grabbing his pistol, he looked for Miller and Davis in vain. Not being able to find either, he decided to shoot and kill the ranch foreman, Henry Berger. With Berger dead, Koenig tried to escape, but he was tracked down, shot, and killed by a posse (Igler 2001, 138–139). Koenig's act of murder and his own demise was a predictable outcome of the injustice of corporate rule over waged laborers who were not allowed to organize unions to humanize their working and living conditions and overcome the alienation they felt due to their powerlessness.

Miller was able to escape the sometimes violent effects of his rule over others and die a natural death as a very wealthy multimillionaire at over ninety years old (*The San Francisco Call* June 5, 1909, 7). Dr. Hugh Glenn, another of California's large landowners, was not as fortunate.

THE RISE AND FALL OF HUGH GLENN, THE "WHEAT KING OF THE WORLD"

Dr. Hugh Glenn, a medical doctor originally from Virginia, began accumulating wheat land on the Sacramento River north of Colusa in the mid-1860s. By 1870, he already owned about 35,000 acres and had one of the biggest agricultural operations in the state (*Sacramento Daily Union* November 4, 1870, 3).

During much of the 1870s, he kept purchasing land, leasing it to tenants who cultivated wheat on a commercial basis on large tracts. By June of 1873, Glenn reportedly had 45,000 acres with a frontage of eighteen miles on the Sacramento River, extending back from the river about five miles, and 140 miles of fencing on his property. In 1873, his tenants used new industrial methods with threshing machines powered by steam engines, along with hundreds of horses and men to plant, thresh, sack, and transport hundreds of thousands of bushels of wheat and barley. Industrial commercial farming thus reached a peak on Glenn's ranch, and he was reputed to be the largest wheat grower in California (*Sacramento Daily Union* June 21, 1873, 4; June 23, 1877, 1; US Census Bureau 1883d, 77).

By 1879, Glenn owned 132,000 acres—66,000 in California and almost as many acres in Oregon and other states. He was not only a wealthy landowner and farmer, but was also active in Democratic Party politics. He became the Democratic gubernatorial candidate in 1879, but lost the election. It was during his campaign that unsavory details about Glenn's farming and business practices began to be unearthed and published in the *Sacramento Union* newspaper. He was a major exploiter of Chinese "coolie" labor, and systematically cheated his tenants and hundreds of employees at his farm headquarters "Jacinto" (*Sacramento Daily Union* August 2, 1879, 3–4). At harvest time, Glenn had around eight hundred workers, making him one of the largest employers of farm labor in California. As was the case for other farm workers, his employees typically worked twelve to fourteen hours a day (Street 2004, 193, 197). As the *Sacramento Daily Union* reported in August of 1879, "There can be no more aggravated illustration of the evils of land monopoly than Glenn's ranch and system affords." The newspaper pointed out the nature of the problem:

Glenn is too cunning and selfish to do his own farming. He rents three-fourths of his land, and makes such arrangements with his tenants that they have all the risk and he secures all the profits. It is said that he has ruined every man who has ever held land under him, and when his terms are considered this is not surprising. He takes half the crop, and he insists on making himself a preferred creditor. All the expense of production is borne by the tenants, but when they are hard up Glenn is willing to assist them; that is to say, he lends them money at 18 per cent, which he himself borrowed at 9 per cent ...

The treatment which his white laborers receive is also deserving of examination. They are used like tramps and beasts, and like nothing else. No attempt is made to secure any comfort for them ... They are worked as cattle could not be worked. Roused up at half-past three in the morning, they are kept going until nine at night, and when, utterly fagged out, the poor fellows sink into their filthy bunks at last, they have the consolation of reflecting that they have received about nine cents an hour during the sixteen hours of their "days work." Nine cents an hour, and such board as they share with the mules, is the form which the Colusa monopolist's extreme love for the working-men takes.

But we are in fact assuming too much in saying that the laborer on Glenn's ranch obtains nine cents an hour. He would receive so much if he were paid promptly and fully. But he is not so paid. He may be kept waiting for his money for months, and then be paid in a check which he can only cash by bringing it to Sacramento, and which he must submit to discount if he wishes to realize upon it *at Jacinto … So it appears that Dr. Glenn first pays his men the lowest conceivable wages, and then juggles them out of a part of even that miserable pittance … All things considered it would be scarcely possible to find a mode of managing such an estate more utterly antagonistic to the public welfare than that which this man practices. (*Sacramento Daily Union *August 2, 1879, 4)*

A later 1879 report stated that Glenn was the "Boss wheat grower of the world" (*Sacramento Daily Union* November 17, 1879, 2).

True or not, Glenn was certainly one of the largest, with 45,000 acres in wheat and an 800,000-bushel harvest. In 1880, he reportedly shipped 27,000 tons of wheat to England alone and was paid eight million dollars (*Sacramento Daily Union* November 17, 1879, 2; Baker and Ewing 1968, 56). Glenn's headquarters in Colusa County, where there were a number of large farms, was the most elaborate of the "wheat camps." It was a small town with many conveniences, including a general store, hotel, post office, telegraph office, saloon, two-story brick mansion, butcher shops, slaughterhouses, smokehouses, machine shops, blacksmith shops, a large number of barns and houses, sheds, stables, dining halls, wash houses, grain warehouses, and other buildings (Street 2004, 192, 201, 219).

In July 1879, Glenn's men, animals, and machines set a one-day record for cutting, threshing, and stacking wheat—2,748 sacks. When Glenn's crew tried to break this record in October of 1880, the boiler on the steam engine that ran the threshing operation was pushed too hard and exploded, killing four men and seriously wounding a number of others. One man was blasted apart, his remains landed 180 feet away (Street 2004, 208).

Glenn continued to grow wheat and exploit and dispossess his workers for the next several years, making many of his employees angry and resentful. Some began to say that the MD after Glenn's name stood for mule driver not medical doctor. His employees even went on strike for higher wages, winning a raise to $1.80/day. Then, in February 1883, Glenn was shot and killed by Huram Miller, a discharged employee.

The circumstances surrounding the murder came out in Miller's trial, further illustrating the exploitative labor practices that Glenn used. The accused murderer's attorney brought out the fact that Miller, who was an old friend of Glenn, was employed as a bookkeeper at Glenn's farm headquarters. Part of his job was to help another friend, the widow Mrs. "Rosebud" Posten, who worked closely with Glenn in the exploitative company store. Glenn paid his workers by check, which, unless they wanted to go all the way to Sacramento, they could only cash at a reduction at Glenn's store. The rate of discount was "such as the temper of the men would stand," according to the *Sacramento Record Union* (June 26, 1883, 1). Mrs. Posten was a key part of and profited from this arrangement. While she was making money, Miller had the difficult job of executing the exploitation of Glenn's employees through the paycheck discount.

Miller's defense attorney related his situation:

> *He soon found that his position was a most unpleasant one. Dr. Glenn was much under the influence of the woman, Mrs. Posten. She was in the store and everywhere. The prisoner [Miller] could not talk of business with Dr. Glenn, but Mrs. Posten would take part in it. In short, Mrs. Posten ran the ranch. The woman became much dissatisfied with the manner in which Miller ran the discount business, and what with her complaints and having a quarrel with each man with whom he settled, owing to the Posten discount, his position became very unpleasant.*
> (Sacramento Record Union *June 26, 1883, 1*)

By February, 1883 Miller and Posten became increasingly at odds, with Rosebud influencing Glenn against his old friend. As

Miller's attorney later explained, "At this time, Mrs. Posten had complete control of Dr. Glenn. She sat at his right hand at the table. His sons and other members of his family would sit at the same table" (*Sacramento Record Union* June 26, 1883, 1).

Soon Miller and Posten were having words with each other, and Posten told Miller of scandals in the Glenn family which involved Mrs. Glenn—evidentially offered to Miller as an excuse for the affair she was apparently having with the doctor. Then one night Mrs. Posten used her influence on Glenn to bring matters to a head, and Glenn called Miller to a conference in Posten's bedroom. As Miller's attorney later stated:

> *The "Rosebud" was also there, and the doctor accused Miller of having insulted the woman. Miller said that he had merely sought to protect the honor of Glenn's family, whereupon the doctor struck him between the eyes, breaking the bridge of his nose. The doctor's rage increased and the "Rosebud" pointed a pistol at Miller, daring him to deny that he had insulted her. Whereupon the doctor again struck him, blacking his eye and knocking him down...*
>
> *Miller being drenched in his own blood...the frenzied man would have undoubtedly killed Miller, had not the "Rosebud" said, "you have done enough, boy;" she always called him boy. "Don't strike him any more." Glenn then discharged Miller from his employ.* (Sacramento Record Union *June 26, 1883, 1*)

Miller shot and killed Glenn soon thereafter. The Miller trial ended in a hung jury, one that agreed that Miller was guilty, but strongly disagreed as to whether he should be convicted of first- or second-degree murder, largely because Miller had been able to portray Glenn as a violent, ruthless employer and a womanizer (*Sacramento Record Union* June 27, 1883, 4; June 28, 1883, 2;

July 2, 1883, 2). A second trial found Miller guilty, and he was sentenced to life in Folsom Prison. He served only about seven years; his case for parole strengthened by a petition signed by 135 local citizens (Street 2004, 223).

During Miller's years in prison, Glenn's friends were able to get a corrupt state legislature "to memorialize him and wipe from the records any mention of him as an oppressive and hated employer" (Street 2004, 223). Their efforts were successful in 1891, when the northern section of Colusa County was split off and renamed Glenn County.

THE SOUTHERN PACIFIC AT THE APEX OF POWER

The period of the mid-1880s into the early 1890s marked a high point in the power of the Southern Pacific/Central Pacific railroad combine. In early 1883, the *Commercial and Financial Chronicle* estimated that the three remaining partners—Stanford, Huntington, and Crocker—had joint personal assets worth almost two hundred million dollars—the equivalent of about ten billion dollars in 2010 values (*Commercial and Financial Chronicle* January 20, 1883, 70–71).

At the same time, the Southern Pacific/Central Pacific combine continued to grow in wealth and power. In 1884, the Southern Pacific Company was incorporated in Kentucky as a holding company for all of the railroad lines controlled by the three men and their families. The Central Pacific was then leased to the Southern Pacific for a yearly rental fee. After 1884, the combined line was simply referred to as the SP. The earnings and assets of the combine continued to grow rapidly, reaching $14.4 million in earnings over expenses in 1888, with total assets of $393.8 million that year (*Commercial and Financial Chronicle* May 10, 1890, 661–665). By 1890, assets had reached $430.7 million and net earnings $17.2 million (*Commercial and Financial Chronicle* May 19, 1891, 716, 722). These figures put the Southern Pacific (the SP) in a class by itself. "The Octopus," as the railroad combine was being called, after the Norris novel, dwarfed all other corporations, the biggest cities, entire industries, and even the State of California itself.

Several legal and political events collectively illustrate the growing dominance of the Southern Pacific during the decade.

GOLD VS. GRAIN

In early 1884, the same year that the Southern Pacific was becoming a holding company, federal judge Lorenzo Sawyer made a ruling that helped assure the dominance of agricultural over mining interests in California. Woodruff vs. North Bloomfield Gravel Mining Company had been brought by Sacramento Valley farmers angry about the debris pouring out of the mountains onto their lands, houses, and cities as a result of hydraulic mining for gold.

In 1868, William Ralston and other San Francisco capitalists had established the North Bloomfield Gravel Mining Company to mine gold using a part of the great water resources of the Sierra Nevada. Their favored hydraulic mining technique employed large fire-hose-like devices, called "monitors" or "giants," to play strong streams of water on the ancient gravel banks left by Tertiary-era gold-bearing rivers. The technique yielded great quantities of gold, but produced as waste vast amounts of muck, sand, and rocks that poured through the sluice boxes into the rivers and downstream, sometimes burying a distant farmer's property.

Judge Sawyer was part of the ruling-class social set that included Stanford, Huntington, and Crocker, and he also owned shares in the Southern Pacific. His ruling, granting a "perpetual injunction" against hydraulic mining, represented one of California's first pro-environmental decisions. The ruling also helped the Southern Pacific, because a good part of its business consisted of carrying the farmers' products to market, and the more money they made, the more the SP could charge them (see Kelley 1959).

SANTA CLARA COUNTY VS. SPRR

In 1886, a United States Supreme Court ruling found in favor of the railroad in Santa Clara County vs. Southern Pacific Railroad. This famous case was successfully used to assert the doctrine of corporate personhood; that is, that corporations have the same rights as natural persons and therefore cannot be strictly controlled and regulated, as they usually had been earlier in US history. Besides contributing to the SP's dominance, the ruling had a very negative influence on the democratic development of the United States, empowering corporations over individuals and other groups.

This case was brought by Santa Clara County because the Southern Pacific had refused to pay its assessed taxes to the county. These taxes were based upon the full monetary value of the railroad track existing in the county. Southern Pacific lawyers used several arguments, one being that the entire assessment was null and void because there was no discount for the mortgages that covered the tracks. In the case of natural persons, such a discount was allowed, and since the Fourteenth Amendment of the Constitution stated that United States citizens were entitled to "equal protection of the laws" and their "privileges and immunities" could not be abridged, corporations—specifically the Southern Pacific—should have the same rights.

The Southern Pacific had made a similar argument in winning cases in the years immediately prior to 1886, but the court had not made a specific ruling on the argument. This time, the Supreme Court also ruled in favor of the railroad and also declined to rule on the question as to whether the Fourteenth Amendment applied to corporations.

However, Chief Justice Morrison R. Waite made the following statement in regard to the decision, "The Court does not wish to hear argument on the question whether the provision in the Fourteenth Amendment to the Constitution, which forbids a State to deny a person within its jurisdiction the equal protection of the laws, applies to these corporations. We are of the opinion that it does." The court reporter included Waite's statement in the background history of the opinion, but it was not part of the Court's official opinion. Therefore, it had no value as a precedent. Yet it influenced future decisions, becoming a key part of American law without ever being enacted by statute or formal judicial decision.

The revolutionary result of that one ruling has been a vast extension of constitutional rights to corporations. A judicial interpretation of a constitutional amendment intended to protect freed slaves against attacks on their rights had been used to extend personhood to corporations. Legally such human rights were not meant to apply to corporations, and prior to 1886, were not. Before that point, corporations were much more constrained and subject to the conditions placed in their legal charters by state legislatures. Corporations, which had been mainly subordinate to government, now could more easily control government, an outcome that gave validity to Jefferson's fear that the "aristocracy of our monied corporations," if not crushed, would "challenge our government in a trial of strength, and bid defiance to the laws of our country" (Ford 1904, Vol. 12, 43).

STANFORD, BRIBERY, AND THE US SENATE

A disturbing example of the corrupting power of the railroads during this era is the way that Southern Pacific president and Republican leader Leland Stanford used bribery to gain and keep his seat in the United States Senate. Stanford, Crocker, and Huntington all had such high levels of personal assets that they were among the wealthiest men in the entire world, and together had monopoly control of California transportation. There were, therefore, few things unavailable to them, including personal political power and the prestige and publicity that go with it. Stanford could not resist the temptation to bribe his way to a seat in the United States Senate.

The Democrats were also guilty of bribery and could win the senate seat when they had a wealthy candidate willing to spend enough money. The corruption was pervasive. There was illegal voting, with voters being paid to vote a certain way, fraudulent vote counting, and the purchase of nominations for office.

State legislators elected senators prior to 1913 when a constitutional amendment provided for direct election by the voters. Legislators therefore could be bribed to vote for a specific US Senate candidate. *The New York Times* covered California politics extensively during this era, and pulled no punches in its comments about the sea of corruption characteristic of the state during the era of Southern Pacific rule. In a November 1886 article on the recent election in the state, *The Times* (November 23, 1886, 2) summed up its politics:

> *California has as stringent laws against bribery in election as any State in the Union, but these statutes might just as well not have been put upon the books, for no attention whatever is paid to them. Indeed, when unusually flagrant cases arise, and the purchasers of votes make no secret of their work, many of the newspapers make jocular mentioning of it as if it were a good joke rather than a penitentiary offence.*

As background to Senator Stanford's well-documented bribery to win the election of 1890, it should be mentioned that mining tycoon and Democrat George Hearst (father of William Randolph Hearst) won his senate seat through spending an estimated five hundred thousand dollars in bribes (*The New York Times* January 19, 1887, 1). The fact that it took a fortune to be elected to the senate discouraged some ruling-class figures who either had enough principles or not enough money to bribe their way into high office. M. H. de Young, the wealthy owner of the *San Francisco Chronicle* who also wanted to be a senator, stated in a September 1890 interview, "the cost of getting elected to the Senate from California is about $300,000. I will not buy an office for that or any other figure. Of course, I would not refuse the office. Who would?" (*The New York Times* September 26, 1890, 1).

Leland Stanford had vastly greater wealth than de Young or even Hearst; he was the functional equivalent of today's billionaires in terms of his economic power. He did not hesitate to use it to assure Republican Party power and his senate seat. In prior years, Stanford could rely on the Central and Southern Pacific corporations to supply much of the cash, but by 1890, Charles Crocker had died, and a rift had developed between Stanford and C. P. Huntington, the other surviving member of the Big Four. Huntington, who, in the past, had conducted extensive bribery campaigns himself to control congressional votes, even went so far as to accuse Stanford of causing the "rottenness of the politics" of California (Tutorow 1971, 276).

Huntington's attitude meant that Stanford was often largely on his own in corrupting the political system from the Republican side during the 1890 election. He was apparently up to the task, willing to "open the sack," which was the era's slang term for bribery. Just prior to the November 1890 election when seats in the state legislature were at stake, *The Times* reported from San Francisco under the heading "Senator Stanford Relying on Vote Buying":

> *Senator Stanford is here overseeing the legislative fight in person, and the details of its management are in the hands of an able general, experienced in the financial persuasion of voters. The sack has already been opened to a considerable extent, and the Democrats are expecting the strings to be cut on election day. This is a serious matter, for the floating vote in California is very large.*
>
> *Of course Mr. Stanford is primarily interested only in his own fight, but when he buys a vote for his*

> *candidate for the Legislature it goes into the box for
> the straight Republican ticket, from Governor down.
> The Stanford sack might easily make a difference of
> 10,000 votes in this State. For months the Senator's
> agents have been at work colonizing the doubtful
> legislative districts with tramps and bummers of every
> species. The cheap lodging houses have been filled with
> cots, and in many cases two voters have registered
> from every cot, one occupying it, or assuming to do
> so, by day and the other by night. The Registrar of
> San Francisco, himself a Republican, has expressed
> the opinion that there are 10,000 "stuffers" on the
> register, and nobody doubts which side is employing
> them. The local Democratic managers are none too
> good to resort to fraud, but they have no money this
> year. There is no Democratic millionaire in the field
> for the Senatorship against Stanford. (*The New
> York Times* November 4, 1890, 9)*

The *Times* pre-election article proved accurate; Stanford and
the California Republicans won the state, even as the rest of the
country was going Democratic. As the *Times* reported under the
heading, "Stanford's Money Won; How California was Brought
by the Republicans," the key factors included Stanford's money
and the sellout by Christopher Buckley, the "blind boss" of the
San Francisco Democrats:

> *If there had been a general Democratic defeat
> throughout the country there would be no particular
> interest in knowing why the Democrats failed to win
> in California. But it happens that California is the
> only State in the Union, without a single exception,
> in which last week's elections showed Republican
> gains over those of the Presidential year. Under such
> circumstances there may be a natural desire to know
> what the phenomenon means.*

> *The causes of the Democratic defeat in this state were foreshadowed in* The Times *during and before the campaign. They were lack of organization, mistaken tactics, Stanford's money, and Buckley … Mr. Stanford fairly submerged the State with money. The amount has been estimated as high as $700,000. No such open, wholesale bribery has ever been known on the Pacific coast outside of Nevada. At the last moment the Democrats secured a small corruption fund too, but they were sold out by their own brokers. Buckley's men took Democratic money and used it to buy votes for Republican legislative candidates. (*The New York Times *November 17, 1890, 2)

One upshot of the corrupt election was a court order for Senator Stanford to appear before a San Francisco court Commissioner to answer charges of bribery. A defeated Democratic state senate candidate brought the charge, which Stanford ignored, leaving town and arguing that he had been called to Washington DC to attend to official duties (*The New York Times* November 25, 1890, 1; November 27, 1890, 1). Stanford not only believed he was above the law, he actually was.

Another consequence was that the California State Legislature of 1891–1892, elected by the "Stanford sack," was one of the most corrupt in state history. As the *Times* expressed it, "The late Republican 'Legislature of a thousand scandals' is admitted by Republicans themselves to have been the most shamelessly disreputable horde of political tramps that ever camped in the State Capitol, and that structure has sheltered some pretty scaly legislative bodies (*The New York Times* September 4, 1892, 16).

9

CALIFORNIA'S POLITICAL ECONOMY AT THE END OF THE NINETEENTH CENTURY

This chapter will review key census data from 1880, 1890, and 1900 to produce a general portrait of California's political economy and society at the end of the nineteenth century. Knowledge of central aspects of the California social formation during this era will yield a deeper understanding of the community rebellions that took place at the end of that century and the beginning of the twentieth.

CALIFORNIA'S POPULATION AND ECONOMY IN 1880

By 1880, California had developed a complex, multifaceted capitalist economy and society. California's population was 864,694 in 1880. A total of 571,820 (66.1 percent) were native born, and fully 88.7 percent (767,181) were classified as "white." The next largest group was the Chinese, at 75,132 (8.7 percent). Indians, making up 1.9 percent (16,277) and "colored," making up only .7 percent (6,018), were the other census categories used in 1880 (US Census Bureau 1883a, 3).

In terms of occupational structure, the state had 376,505 people employed, 348,303 male (92.5 percent), and 28,202 female (7.5 percent), a ratio of over 12:1. United States-born workers numbered 175,406 or 46.6 percent of the total labor force. There were 101,452 (26.9 percent) people from "other countries." The Chinese made up the biggest part of this "other" category. They were followed by the Irish with 9.5 percent followed then by those from Great Britain/British America (8.4 percent) and the German-born (7.3 percent) (US Census Bureau 1883a, 811).

The female sector of the labor force was concentrated in a few occupations, with domestic servants, dressmakers/seamstresses/tailors, teachers, laundresses, musicians, hotel and restaurant keepers and employees, boarding and lodging housekeepers and nurses/midwives making up well over 80 percent of total female employment. There were also smaller numbers of female farmers, agricultural laborers, authors, store and government clerks and officials, doctors and dentists, journalists, lawyers, bankers and brokers, saloon keepers and bartenders, woolen mill operatives, box factory workers, boot and shoe makers, bakers, glove makers, photographers, cigar makers, cabinet makers, and fishermen/oystermen. Women were making some progress on the long road toward a measure of occupational equality (US Census Bureau 1883a, 793–798).

The male labor force had a much more complex division of labor, but men also tended to be concentrated in certain occupations, with 50 percent working in only five fields—general laborers, farmers/planters, miners, agricultural laborers, and traders/dealers. Table 9.1 offers details on the occupational division of the male workforce in 1880, most of which was engaged in waged labor.

TABLE 9.1: California Male Occupations in 1880

Occupation	Capital or Waged Labor	Number	% of Total	Cumulative%
General Laborers	waged	57,158	16.41	16.41
Farmers/Planters	capital	43,091	12.37	28.78
Miners	mixed	37,141	10.66	39.44
Agricultural Laborers	waged	23,722	6.81	46.25
Traders /Dealers	capital	14,656	4.21	50.46
Domestic Servants	waged	12,160	3.49	53.95
Clerks/Salesmen	waged	11,553	3.32	57.27
Carpenters/Joiners	waged	9,056	2.60	59.87
Drayman/Teamsters	waged	6,007	1.72	61.59
Launderers	mixed	5,996	1.72	63.31
Sawmill/Lumbermen	mixed	5,714	1.64	64.95
Hotel/Restaurant	mixed	5,672	1.63	66.58
Sailors/Steamboat Men	waged	5,523	1.58	68.16

Source: US Census Bureau 1883a, 760–766

The system of class and racial hierarchy favored the native-born white males. Table 9.2 illustrates that the poorest paid and physically most difficult jobs were disproportionately filled by the "other" group, mainly Chinese. Conversely, US-born white males had the best paying and least dangerous work. Women dominated the dressmaking/tailor and teaching fields and were nearly half of the domestic servant labor force. Omitted from the table are workers from Sweden, Norway, and British America/Canada, which together amounted to only a few more than fifteen thousand people. The traders/dealers category evidentially included small-scale Chinese peddlers, as well as merchants and dealers in stocks and bonds.

TABLE 9.2: The California Class Structure and Ethnicity
as Reported in the 1880 Census

Occupation	Total #	Male%	US-Born%	Other %	Irish %	British %	German %
I. Owning Class Sector							
Farmers/Planters	43,489	99.1	67.0	10.2	7.5	5.3	6.0
Traders/Dealers	14,920	98.2	39.4	23.2	8.5	5.5	20.7
Govt. Officials	3,789	95.6	74.2	4.0	10.3	4.6	4.2
Lawyers	1,899	99.9	86.0	2.4	3.6	4.1	1.9
Physicians	1,851	96.5	64.2	17.3	3.3	5.3	6.1
Bankers/Brokers	1,431	99.4	66.8	6.8	6.1	7.3	10.8
Manufacturers	1,203	99.1	54.7	15.5	4.6	6.7	15.4
II. Higher-Paid Workers							
Clerks/Salesmen	11,553	97.6	66.8	9.6	5.2	5.4	10.1
Carpenters/Joiners	9,056	100	60.6	6.9	8.0	8.4	7.1
Draymen/Teamsters	6,007	100	61.8	6.8	14.9	4.8	6.4
Sailors/Steamboat	5,523	100	28.1	20.1	11.9	10.9	12.8
Teachers	4,788	35.3	82.9	5.1	3.3	3.2	2.6
Saloon Keepers	4,015	98.8	37.5	12.9	14.2	5.6	25.2
Railroad employees	3,961	99.9	51.1	20.8	17.6	4.6	2.1
III. Lower-Paid Workers							
Miners	37,147	99.98	24.8	51.4	6.8	10.1	3.9
Gen. Laborers	23,856	99.4	41.3	33.8	13.9	3.1	4.2
Agricultural Laborers	23,856	99.4	61.2	23.7	5.1	2.7	3.7
Domestic Servants	22,858	53.2	25.8	48.1	15.9	2.8	4.9
Dressmakers/Tailors	9,516	26.7	53.5	19.8	9.3	4.2	9.4
Laundry	7,013	85.5	9.8	81.8	5.4	1.0	1.5
Blacksmiths	4,689	100	56.1	5.8	12.6	8.7	7.4
Boots/Shoes	4,577	96.4	19.5	47.9	12.8	4.3	11.8
Wood/Lumber	4,433	100	40.5	31.7	4.8	3.9	2.4
Cigars/Tobacco	3,217	98.3	7.9	85.7	0.3	0.8	4.9
Cotton/Wool Mills	776	80.2	44.2	30.3	12.4	8.6	2.4

Source: US Census Bureau 1883a, 811

Data on assessed valuation of property (table 9.3) illustrates the continuing dominance of the City of San Francisco, which with only 27.1 percent of the state's population, had over 40 percent of the total property of all kinds, and combined with adjacent Alameda County, made up almost one half of the property value of the entire state in 1880.

TABLE 9.3: Assessed Valuation of California Real and Personal Property, 1880

Total for State of California: $584,578,036

County	Assessed Valuation	% of State Total
San Francisco	$244,626,760	41.8%
Alameda	$42,822,877	7.3%
Santa Clara	$27,603,240	4.7%
Sacramento	$18,416,338	3.2%
San Joaquin	$17,377,129	3.0%
Los Angeles	$16,368,649	2.8%
Sonoma	$15,569,362	2.7%
Colusa	$12,420,308	2.1%
Forty-five remaining counties		32.4%

Source: Porter 1884, 206–208

An 1880 Census Bureau report has an instructive comparison to these valuation figures (US Census Bureau 1883c, 124–131). It lists the total assets of the Central Pacific/Southern Pacific Railroad, showing that only four people owned the bulk of the shares (Huntington, Crocker, Stanford, and Hopkins' widow). This meant that each one individually was worth at least thirty million dollars, the functional equivalent to the mega-billionaires of the early twenty-first century. These two companies under the same centralized ownership had almost as many assets ($231.5 million) as the entire assessed valuation of all the real and personal property of San Francisco ($244.6 million), which the largest city in the entire West. The Central Pacific Railroad, with 209 stockholders, was worth $165.1 million; the Southern Pacific had 35 stockholders and was valued at $66.4 million. This illustrates the truth that workers under capitalism create vast wealth, but that this wealth is monopolized by those at the top of the class structure.

In 1880, capital invested in 5,885 California manufacturing establishments was reported to be $61,243,784. Over half (57.7 percent) was invested in San Francisco. For some unexplained reason, gas manufacturing, which had been the single biggest category in 1870 at over six million dollars, was not listed in 1880. The largest manufacturing investment categories listed in the 1880 census are shown in table 9.4 below.

TABLE 9.4: **Largest Manufacturing Categories by Amount of Capital, 1880**

Lumber, sawed	$6.5 million (mainly northern rural counties)
Flouring and grist mill products	$4.4 million (widely dispersed around state)
Foundry and machine shop	$3.0 million(concentrated in San Francisco)
Liquors, malt	$2.8 million (concentrated in San Francisco)
Gunpowder and high explosives	$2.4 million (Contra Costa and Santa Cruz)
Slaughtering and meat packing	$2.1 million (San Francisco)
Tobacco	$1.8 million (San Francisco)
Printing and publishing	$1.8 million (San Francisco)
Shipbuilding	$1.8 million (San Francisco)
Woolen goods	$1.7 million (San Francisco)
Leather, tanned	$1.7 million (San Francisco)
Sugar and molasses	$1.6 million (San Francisco)
Boots and shoes	$1.3 million (San Francisco)
Furniture	$1.3 million (San Francisco)
Clothing, men's	$1.2 million (San Francisco)
Liquors, distilled	$1.2 million (widely dispersed)
Fruits and vegetables, canned	$1.2 million (San Francisco)

Source: US Census Bureau, 1883b, 92–94; 195–199; 435–437

The investment of these sums, the equivalent of amounts fifty or more times as much in today's money, had some impressive results in development of the means of production. In shipbuilding, for example, the 1880 census reported:

A great variety of steam craft—tugs, ferry-boats, transfer steamers, propellers, and launches—have been made from Pacific Coast fir within the last five or six years, one of the largest being the Transit car-ferry, built at the Central Pacific ship-yard in Oakland. This large vessel is 338 feet long over all, 316 1/3 feet between perpendiculars ... and is supplied with vertical condensing engines with 60-inch cylinders and 11 feet stroke. The wheels are 29 feet in diameter, carrying 20 paddles 12 feet long and 20 inches wide. A still larger one is the Solano, of 3,549 tons, a sidewheel transfer boat employed to ferry the overland railroad trains across the river. She is the largest transfer boat in the United States. Her dimensions are: length, 407 feet; beam of hull, 65 1/2 feet; hold 17 1/2 feet. Four tracks are laid upon her decks, capable of receiving 48 cars and engines. (Hall 1884, 162)

The 1880 census also covered the California mining industry in its report on precious metals. California gold and silver mines produced $18.3 million in 1879, in contrast to the $38.6 million produced by the Comstock mines at their peak in 1876. We can understand the importance of the Gold vs. Grain case when we see that only $16.3 million worth of capital was invested in nine leading hydraulic gold mines, led by North Bloomfield/Milton with an investment of $4.1 million (Emmons and Becker 1885, 185, 307). This report also points out a key fact of the time: Californians owned 93.1 percent of the deep mines in their state (ninety-four out of one hundred one) and also owned 70.1 percent of the deep mines of Nevada (sixty-eight out of ninety-97). Smaller numbers of Californians owned deep mines in Arizona (sixteen), Dakota (nine), Idaho (eight), Utah (three), and Oregon (one). New York-based investors were especially important in Colorado and outnumbered Californians in the ownership of Arizona's deep mines.

These facts illustrate that Californians were largely masters of their own fate in the mining field in their state and Nevada, but that New York capital was more powerful in the rest of the West (Emmons and Becker 1885, 111).

The 1880 data on capital invested, wages paid, materials purchased, and value added allow a calculation of profit and annual rate of return on capital in the manufacturing sector. This is done by adding wages and the cost of materials and subtracting the resulting sum from the value of production amount. Table 9.5 gives the details for the state and main fields of manufacturing.

TABLE 9.5: Yearly Rates of Return on Invested Capital, 1880 Census

Industry and Location	Capital Invested ($ millions)	Number of workers	Amt. of Profit ($ millions)	Yearly Rate of Return on Capital
Calif. manufacturing	61.2	43,693	22.5	36.8%
S. F. manufacturing	35.4	28,442	14.9	42.2%
Lumber sawed	6.5	3,434	1.1	16.9%
Flouring and grist mill	4.4	888	1.1	25.6%
Foundry/machine shop	3.0	2,384	.9	28.5%
Liquors, malt	2.8	1,201	1.1	41.0%
Explosives/gunpowder	2.4	260	1.1	45.8%
Slaughtering/meat	2.1	487	1.8	84.7%
Printing/publishing	1.8	1,629	.8	44.7%
Tobacco	1.8	3,551	.9	50.8%
Shipbuilding	1.8	534	.2	13.8%
Leather, tanned	1.7	627	.7	41.7%
Woolen goods	1.7	907	.3	18.1%
Sugar and molasses	1.6	280	.2	14.1%
Boots and shoes	1.3	2,994	.9	71.4%
Furniture	1.3	999	.3	27.5%
Clothing, men's	1.2	1,799	.7	60.6%
Liquors, distilled	1.2	112	.2	13.2%
Canned fruits, vegetables	1.2	1,173	.3	23.0%

Source: US Census Bureau, 1883b, 92–94, 195–199, 435–437

Average daily wages for these industries were generally low. This exploitation of surplus value from the worker allowed a high rate of return for most industries and firms. Of those listed above, the highest daily wages were in shipbuilding, at $3.54/ day average wage (a little over one thousand dollars per year). Lower average wages, but still relatively high for the time, existed for workers in printing/publishing, slaughtering/meatpacking, sugar and molasses, and foundry/machine shop work. The poorest paid workers labored in fruit and vegetable canning, tobacco, sawed lumber, woolen goods, and boots and shoes. They received between $248/year and $435/year (less than a dollar a day to less than a dollar and a half a day). The state average was $482/year, a little more than a dollar and a half a day (US Census Bureau, 1883b, 92–94, 195–199, 435–437).

The Agricultural Census of 1880 also illustrates some key facts about California at that time. There were 35,934 California farms, covering 16,593,742 acres, and having a collective value (land, fences, buildings, farm implements and machinery, livestock, etc.) of almost $306 million. In addition, there was a reported $59.7 million of agricultural production reported for 1879 (US Census Bureau 1883d, 3, 4). Thus by 1880, agriculture clearly outranked both mining and industry in economic importance. The wealth and power of the Central Pacific/Southern Pacific derived in part from its monopoly in transportation of agricultural products and supplies.

California agriculture in 1880 was characterized by two extreme patterns, each with its own economic, social, and political characteristics, with a number of mixed cases lying in-between. These were the latifundia, or large-farm counties, and the small-farm counties. Table 9.6 gives the basic statistics for these two extremes, showing that many of the large farms were operated by tenants who paid rent or were sharecroppers (see the last column of table 9.6):

TABLE 9.6: Statistical Characteristics of Latifundia and Small-Farm Counties, 1880

County	# farms	Average farm size (acres)	% cultivated by owners	% 500+ acres cultivated by renter/ sharecroppers
State of California	35,934	462	80.2	25.2
Latifundia Counties				
Merced	388	2,362	60.8	48.2
Kern	282	1,844	78.4	35.2
San Luis Obispo	832	929	68.4	34.3
Colusa	1,073	834	82.9	20.2
Stanislaus	692	826	75.1	30.1
Tehema	636	820	83.8	30.3
San Diego	696	804	93.5	25.0
Santa Barbara	713	786	71.4	38.4
Fresno	926	748	85.6	21.7
Small Farm Counties				
Tuolumne	721	186	95.4	15.7
Santa Cruz	584	189	86.1	41.9
Inyo	242	209	90.5	10.0
Santa Clara	1,492	213	76.7	16.3
Nevada	356	214	94.4	14.3
San Bernardino	709	238	86.2	17.4
Amador	531	243	92.7	8.0
El Dorado	542	244	96.5	7.7
Sierra	156	250	93.6	17.0
Shasta	544	273	92.5	10.8
Calaveras	467	274	97.9	0.0
Alpine	33	282	100	0.0
Modoc	472	299	94.5	4.5

Source: Computed from US Census Bureau 1883d, 34

Closely examining the two extreme cases of latifundia and small-farm counties illustrates the different economic, social, and political patterns and implications of each. In the case of Merced County, the average farm size was over twelve times as large as the average farm size for Tuolumne County. Fully 42.3 percent of Merced's farms were over five hundred acres, whereas only 12.3 percent of Tuolumne's were. The percentage of renters and sharecroppers working large (over five hundred acres in size) tracts was three times greater in Merced than in Tuolumne, which had a much greater percentage of small owner-operators.

The large-farm counties were generally counties where there was a lot of money to be made in producing and exporting wheat to world markets and meat to San Francisco. In these places, the pattern of large commercial/capitalist farms with a powerless, dependent, and often racialized labor force (first Indians, later Chinese) had been established either during the Spanish/Mexican period or soon thereafter. These latifundia counties tended to be dominated politically and economically by the owners of giant parcels of land who were connected with the Central Pacific and Southern Pacific railroads. Prime examples were Lloyd Tevis, James B. A. Haggin, and W. B. Carr in Kern County (who formed the Kern County Land Company in 1890); Henry Miller and Charles Lux in Merced, Madera, and Fresno Counties; the Irvine Ranch in Orange County; the Hearst holdings in Monterey and San Luis Obispo Counties; and Hugh Glenn in Colusa (later Glenn) County.

The small-farm counties, on the other hand, were generally those on poorer land and in more remote areas, producing more diverse crops for local and regional consumption. A more egalitarian and progressive political and social order developed in these places.

CALIFORNIA'S POPULATION AND ECONOMY IN 1890: EVIDENCE FROM THE CENSUS

In 1890, there was another national census, and it confirmed California's continued development as a complex, multifaceted, capitalist economy and society. California's population was 1.21 million in 1890. There were only four general ethnic categories covered by the 1890 census. These were native whites born of native parents, 497,729 (41.2 percent); native whites with foreign-born parents, 320,390 (26.5 percent); foreign-born whites, 293,553 (24.3 percent) and non-white or "colored" 96,458 (8 percent). Of the last named category, the great majority were Chinese Americans (US Census Bureau 1895a, 396).

In terms of occupational structure, the state had 544,165 people employed, 483,622 male (88.9 percent) and 60,543 female (11.1 percent), a ratio of almost exactly 8:1. This showed a substantial gain for women workers, who made up only 7.5 percent of all workers in 1880. "Native white" workers dominated, with 281,598 people (51.7 percent) of the total labor force. "Foreign white" was the next largest category in the records at 185,536 (34.1 percent). Native Americans, Chinese Americans, African Americans, and Japanese Americans, 77,031 strong (14.2 percent) made up the colored workers category (US Census Bureau 1895b, 536).

The female sector of the labor force was concentrated in a few occupations, with domestic servants, dressmakers/seamstresses/tailors, teachers, laundresses, musicians, hotel and restaurant keepers and employees, boarding and lodging housekeepers, and nurses/midwives making up over 77 percent of total female employment. There were also smaller numbers of female farmers, agricultural laborers, general laborers, artists, physicians, hotelkeepers, bookkeepers, clerks, merchants, saleswomen, stenographers, typewriters, telegraph and telephone operators, boot and shoe makers, cotton and textile operatives, printers, engravers, and bookbinders (US Census Bureau 1895b, 536).

The male labor force had a much more complex division of labor, but men also tended to be concentrated in certain occupations, with 52.95 percent working in only seven fields: farmers/planters, general laborers, agricultural laborers, merchants/dealers, miners, bookkeepers/clerks, and servants. Table 9.7 offers details on the occupational division of the male workforce in 1890 engaged mainly in waged labor. Over two-thirds of those listed in table 9.7 were waged workers, while only 17.2 percent were unambiguously owners. The balance consisted of groups of capitalists and workers, such as miners and steam railroad workers who the census lumped into the same category.

TABLE 9.7: California Male Occupations in 1890

Occupation	Capital or Waged Labor	Number	% of Total	Cumulative
Farmers/Planters	Capital	59,356	12.27	12.27
General Laborers	Waged	58,022	12.0	24.27
Agricultural Laborers	Waged	51,532	10.66	34.93
Merchants/Dealers	Capital	23,712	4.9	39.83
Miners	Mixed	21,965	4.5	44.37
Bookkeepers/Clerks	Waged	21,642	4.47	48.84
Domestic Servants	Waged	19,880	4.11	52.95
Carpenters/Joiners	Waged	17,105	3.54	56.49
Drayman/Teamsters	Waged	11,571	2.39	58.88
Steam RR Employees	Mixed	9,067	1.87	60.75

Source: US Census Bureau 1895b, 536

Census data make it clear that there was a system of class and racial hierarchy that favored white people, especially white males. Table 9.8 illustrates that the "colored" group, mainly Chinese, disproportionately filled the jobs that were the poorest paid and physically most difficult. Note that while the non-white population was 15.4 percent of the male working population, it made up 61.1 percent of the servants and 72.5 percent of the tobacco workers, but only 1.5 percent of the farmers and only 0.2 percent of the lawyers. There were a fair number of Chinese merchants, and the railroad hired Chinese for construction, accounting for the relatively higher levels in the merchant and steam railroad categories.

TABLE 9.8: The Male California Class Structure and Ethnicity
as Reported in the 1890 Census

Occupation	Total Number	% White	% Colored
California	**483,622**	**84.6**	**15.4**
I. Owning Class Sector			
Farmers/Planters	59,356	98.5	1.5
Merchants/Deal.	23,712	84.1	15.9
Agents/Collectors	7,241	99.1	0.9
Bankers/Brokers	3,994	98.5	1.5
Manufacturers	3,940	97.4	2.6
Lawyers	3,217	99.8	0.2
Physicians	2,844	91.0	9.0
Govt. Officials	2,654	98.4	1.6
II. Less Exploited, Higher Status Workers			
Bookkeepers/Clerks	21,642	95.0	5.0
Carpenters/Joiners	17,105	99.2	0.8
Draymen/Teamst.	11,571	98.0	2.0
Steam RR Employ.	9,067	77.5	22.5
Blacksmiths	6,934	99.1	0.9
Painters/Glaziers	6,206	99.0	1.0
Restaurant/Saloon	5,718	96.1	3.9
Machinists	3,953	99.0	1.0
Iron and Steel Men	2,295	99.0	1.0
III. More Exploited, Lower Status Workers			
General Laborers	58,022	72.5	27.5
Agric. Laborers	51,532	80.2	19.8
Miners	21,965	78.8	22.2
Domestic Servants	19,880	39.9	61.1
Tobacco Factory	3,281	27.5	72.5

Source: US Census Bureau 1890b, 2:536

Manufacturing statistics further illustrate the class and sexual division of labor, with the bigger rewards going to the males with higher levels of authority. At the bottom, were the women and children working as pieceworkers in such jobs as fruit and vegetable canning, tobacco, clothing, and woolen goods.

Table 9.9: Statistics on Manufacturing Wages and Salaries California, 1890

I. Officers, Firm Members, and Clerks

9,972	Adult Males	$980.24/year
974	Adult Females	$606.69/year

II. Operatives

50,569	Adult Males	$650.87/year
6,968	Adult Females	$305.71/year
1,513	Children	$172.82/year

III. Pieceworkers

8,496	Adult Males	$550.24/year
4,086	Adult Females	$241.13/year
344	Children	$97.75/year

Source: US Census Bureau 1895c, 347)

The largest sectors for capital investment in manufacturing as of 1890, are shown in the following table:

TABLE 9.10: Largest Manufacturing Categories by Amount of Capital, 1890

Manufacturing Category	Capital
Lumber, mill prod. (total)	$18.9 million
Gas	$13.1 million
Liquors (total)	$9.3 million
Shipbuilding	$6.9 million
Flouring and grist mill products	$6.1 million
Printing and publishing (total)	$5.6 million
Sugar	$5.5 million
Iron and steel (total)	$3.9 million
Cars/Shop RR (total)	$3.2 million
Leather, tanned	$3.1 million
Woolen goods	$2.6 million

Source: US Census Bureau, 1890c, 346–352

The Agricultural Census of 1890 illustrates the continuing rapid expansion of the agricultural sector of the California economy. In 1880, there were 35,934 California farms, covering 16,593,742 acres, and having a collective value (land, fences, buildings, farm implements and machinery, livestock) of almost $306 million. In 1890, these figures had grown to 52,894 farms, covering 21,427,293 acres, and worth over $772 million. Yearly agricultural production had increased to an estimated $87 million in 1889 (US Census Bureau 1895d, 200).

California agriculture in 1890 continued to be characterized by two extreme patterns, each with its own economic, social, and political characteristics, with a number of mixed cases in-between. The two extremes remained the latifundia (large-farm) counties and the small-farm counties. In comparison with the small-farm counties, a significantly greater number of the very large farms were cultivated by renters and sharecroppers, while a smaller percentage of such farms were cultivated by owners.

The number of latifunda counties and the size of farms had dropped between 1880 and 1890. As the number of farms grew, a somewhat more egalitarian ownership pattern emerged in rural California. Many giant farms run by firms like Miller and Lux still existed, but there was less concentration overall. Table 9.11 gives the basic statistics for these two main types of counties as of 1890. It should also be noted that the 1900 census illustrates that concentration of land ownership increased in a number of key agricultural counties between 1890 and 1900.

TABLE 9.11: Statistical Characteristics of Latifundia and Small-Farm Counties, 1890

County	# farms	Average farm size (acres)	% cultivated by owners	% 1,000 + acres rented & shared
State of California	52,894	405	82.2%	29.0%
Latifundia Counties				
Merced	798	1,101	70.8%	47.0%
Kern	730	976	89.7%	6.6%
Colusa	1,028	922	75.4%	35.6%
Small-Farm Counties				
Tuolumne	219	311	96.4%	0.0%
Santa Clara	2,117	205	83.7%	24.6%
San Bernardino	1,924	160	87.5%	25.0%
Amador	700	297	96.4%	8.3%
El Dorado	744	238	97.2%	4.8%
Sierra	107	417	95.3%	0.0%
Shasta	950	296	93.7%	15.4%
Calaveras	483	308	98.8%	0.0%
Alpine	31	315	96.8%	0.0%
Siskiyou	517	443	94.0%	8.8%
Mariposa	384	377	96.4%	8.0%

Source: Computed from US Census Bureau 1895d, 34)

CALIFORNIA'S POPULATION AND ECONOMY IN 1900: EVIDENCE FROM THE CENSUS

California's population was almost 1.5 million in 1900. There were only four general categories covered by the 1900 census. These were native white born of native parents, native white of foreign-born parents, foreign-born white, and "colored." A total of

644,428 (43.4 percent) were native whites; 441,794 (29.8 percent) were native foreign whites; 316,505 (21.3 percent) were foreign-born white, and 82,326 (5.5 percent) were classified as non-white or "colored," the great majority being Chinese Americans (US Census Bureau 1901, 575). An important change since 1880 was the drop, by over half, of the percentage of non-whites in the California population.

In terms of occupational structure, the state had 644,267 people employed, 556,345 male (86.4 percent of the total), and 87,922 female (13.7 percent of the total), a ratio of a little over 6 to 1. This again showed a gain for women workers, who only made up 7.5 percent of all workers in 1880. "Native white" workers dominated, making up 391,851 people (60.8 percent) of the total labor force. Foreign white was the next largest category in the records, at 192,794 (29.9 percent). The "colored" category, which included the Chinese, amounted to 59,622 (9.3 percent) (US Census Bureau 1904, 231, 234).

The female sector of the labor force continued to be concentrated in a few occupations, with domestic servants, dressmakers/seamstresses/tailors, farmers, teachers, laundresses, musicians, hotel and restaurant keepers and employees, boarding and lodging housekeepers, saleswomen, and nurses/midwives making up a big percentage of total female employment. There were also smaller numbers of female agricultural laborers, artists, general laborers, printers, physicians, hotelkeepers, bookkeepers, clerks, merchants, stenographers, typewriters, telegraph and telephone operators, boot and shoe makers, cotton and textile operatives, engravers, and bookbinders (US Census Bureau 1904, 234).

Again, the male labor force had a much more complex division of labor, but men also tended to be concentrated in certain occupations, with 51 percent working in only eight fields: agricultural laborers; farmers/planters; general laborers; miners; merchants/dealers; servants; carpenters; and draymen, hackmen, teamsters.

One key measure of how any capitalist system is functioning is how fast capital is accumulating. This rate of profit/return tends to fall over time, in spite of the attempts by capitalists to increase productivity through investment in automation, as well as wage and cost cutting, and speeding up the pace of work. This trend can be seen in table 9.12 below.

The falling rate of profit/return is true because, under capitalism, profit comes from the surplus value generated during the process of exploiting labor. As investment in improved machinery increases, the ratio of living labor to dead labor/capital changes, leaving a smaller ratio for living labor. With relatively less labor to exploit, the rate of return on capital declines, tending to create economic crisis. During the 1860 to 1900 period, capital used in manufacturing increased almost ten times, yet the rate of return on capital fell throughout the period. This is important background to the attempts by capitalists to increase the exploitation of labor during the 1880 to 1901 years, resulting in strikes and other rank-and-file rebellions, a topic covered in detail in the following two chapters.

TABLE 9.12: Increase in Manufacturing Capital,
Decline in Rate of Return, 1860–1900

Year	Capital	Rate of Profit/Return on Capital (value of production minus expenses divided by capital)
1860	$22,043,096	58.1%
1870	$39,728,202	45.6%
1880	$61,243,784	36.8%
1890	$146,797,102	26.6%
1900	$205,395,025	24.9%

Source: US Census Bureau 1895c, 67; 1902a, 41

In 1900, California manufacturing was an increasingly urban phenomenon; the state's top sixteen cities had 65.4 percent of total production and 72.7 percent of the workers in 1900. Although Los

Angeles was growing rapidly, San Francisco remained by far the leading manufacturing city, with 43.9 percent of production and 46.1 percent of California's workers. The comparative figures for second place Los Angeles were only 7 percent and 8.8 percent. However, San Francisco saw stagnation during the 1890–1900 decade. The number of manufacturing establishments in San Francisco declined by 1.4 percent, the value of its production declined by 1.9 percent, and total wages declined by 10.4 percent. On the other hand, capital investment increased by 7 percent and the number of workers was up by .5 percent during this decade (US Census Bureau 1902a, 39, 997–1003). The stagnation in the San Francisco economy and the ruling-class desire to reverse it by destroying unions was a key background factor in the explosion of struggle that took place in 1901, a conflict covered in chapter 11.

The 1900 census also provides figures on the makeup of two of the segments of the San Francisco workforce that went on strike in 1901. These were the draymen, hackmen, teamsters, and the boatmen and sailors. Census figures illustrate that, in both cases, one ethnic group made up an important part of the workforce. In the case of the draymen, hackmen, and teamsters, the Irish made up 36.4 percent of the total. In the case of the boatmen and sailors, Scandinavians made up 38.2 percent (US Census Bureau 1904, 720–721). Union leadership and decision making reflected the strong influence of these ethnic groups, which were able to unite a large part of the San Francisco working class to rebel and strike in 1901.

Key data from the census about California agriculture illustrates the continued dominance of the large farm in this key area of the state's economy. Both the big farms and the small farms often got bigger during the decade of 1890–1900. The average farm size in Merced County for example went up from 1,101 acres in 1890 to 1,705 acres in 1900. In Kern County, it went up from 976 acres (1890) to 1,431 acres (1900). Amador County went from 297 acres to 382, Calaveras from 308 to 370, and Alpine from 315 to 424 (table 9.11; US Census Bureau 1902b, 62–63).

Table 9.13 shows the statistic dominance of the large farms. Defined here as five hundred acres or larger, large farms made up only 13.9 percent of farms, but owned fully 75.5 percent of all farmland. Most of this land—over eighteen million acres, roughly the size of Scotland—was controlled by the one thousand-acre and larger farms. The large farms held almost half (46.6 percent) of the dollar value of farm property, employed about half of the farm labor, and produced nearly half (44.4 percent) of the dollar value of farm production in 1899.

This data also indicates that California's small, mainly family farms were more efficient. The under-a-hundred-acre-sized farms occupied only 3.8 percent of the state's farmland, yet produced 24.1 percent of the dollar value of farm products. Even though they controlled less than 4 percent of the land, these farms used 56.1 percent of all the fertilizer used in the state in 1899, indicating more intensive land use and the desire to increase the fertility of their land.

Table 9.13: The Dominance of the Large Farm in California Agriculture in 1900

Farm Size	State Total	1–99 Acres	100–499 Acres	500 Acres and Over
# of Farms	72,542	36,259	26,201	10,082
% of Total	100%	50%	36.1%	13.9%
Acres	28,828,951	1,108,385	5,943,879	21,776,687
% of Total	100%	3.8%	20.6%	75.5%
Value Farms (in millions)	$796.5	$198.1	$227.4	$371.1
% of Total	100%	24.9%	28.9%	46.6%
Labor Costs, 1899	$25,845,120	$5,486,070	$4,684,650	$12,245,190
% of Total	100%	21.2%	18.1%	47.4%
Value of Prod., 1899 (in millions)	$131.7	$31.8	$41.4	$58.5
% of Total	100%	24.1%	31.5%	44.4%

Source: US Census Bureau 1902b, 188–189

With the in-depth understanding of California's economy and ruling class during this era presented in this and the previous chapter, we can turn to examples of contemporaneous rebellions of the state's working people, the vast majority in the position of only having their labor power to sell.

10

Struggle—
The Pullman Strike in California
1894

The social and economic terrain of the 1890s into the first years of the new century was one of sharp class conflict, both from above and from below. Workers were joining together to demand their democratic rights, forming larger and more powerful unions and federated organizations. Sometimes these unions were public; other times they were secret to prevent retaliation by employers. By the early 1890s, these were sometimes linked together by organizations such as the Council of Federated Trades, which handled the task of coordinating San Francisco's unions. The bosses were also joining together; in 1891, they had organized the California Board of Manufacturers and Employers for the specific purpose of checking labor.

Conflict between these two opposing forces had become endemic. As the California Bureau of Labor Statistics stated in its 1891–1892 report, "At the present time the relations subsisting between capitalists and laborers are those of war, of intense conflict of interests ... claiming recognition with increasing intensity"

(California Bureau of Labor Statistics 1893, 29). An outstanding but little known event, the 1894 Pullman strike in California, led by the American Railway Union, is one illustration of the intense class struggle of this period.

BACKGROUND TO THE 1894 PULLMAN STRIKE

The largest and most intense mass strike that California had yet seen occurred in June and July of 1894. Well over ten thousand railroad workers and their supporters engaged in a titanic struggle for the empowerment of the working class, for the right to have an industrial union in the railroad industry. This rank-and-file mobilization was breathtaking in its scale and determination, illustrating both that another world was possible and that workers would fight to try to give it birth. The rank-and-file organized what was in effect an insurrection, took control of the rail lines, and showed that they had the capacity to organize society's productive apparatus. While they ultimately failed, due to both leadership shortcomings and repression by the federal government, this workers' struggle is instructive and inspirational about what could have been.

Prior to the early 1890s, the only railroad trade unions that existed were craft unions of skilled workers, unions that organized only small sections of the railroad workers. The most important of these was the Brotherhood of Locomotive Engineers, an openly class-collaborationist organization that combined elements of a fraternal order with those of a trade union. It and the other "brotherhoods" served the interests of the railroad corporations by dividing the workforce while making self-serving deals with the railroad owners. Their fellow workers in less-skilled jobs were left without a union or collective power and, therefore, at the mercy of ruthless, corporate ruling-class leaders like C. P. Huntington and George Pullman, who kept pay low and working conditions harsh in order to extract maximum surplus value in the form of large profits.

The labor leader Eugene V. Debs got his start in the union movement with the Brotherhood of Locomotive Firemen, but had concluded by the early 1890s that the brotherhoods had outlived their usefulness and that a larger, more powerful, industrial union was needed to unite all the workers in the industry together into one body. In Debs' view, only such a union could both adequately represent and protect working-class interests in the railroad industry and avoid strikes in the longer term. Such a union would be strong enough to make the corporate managers see the wisdom of treating workers and their union fairly and meeting them in a conciliatory spirit. Debs was thus a key founder and first president of the American Railway Union (ARU), which aimed at becoming the industrial union for the nation's most powerful industry.

This union, founded in mid-1893, became an almost instant success. It organized workers on the Great Northern Railroad, carried out a strike that same year, and achieved a victory. This gave thousands of workers hope—the belief that by self-organization, solidarity, and struggle they could alter the power equation between themselves and the corporate owners, begin to overcome alienation on the job, create a measure of economic democracy, and better their working conditions and wages.

Among the workers inspired by the vision of Debs and the ARU were the employees of Chicago's Pullman Palace Car Company, owned by George Pullman, a multimillionaire industrialist. Pullman operated a feudalistic company town and factory outside Chicago, manufacturing Pullman railroad sleeping cars to be used by railroad patrons desiring overnight accommodations on long-distance journeys. The depression of 1893–1894 decreased alternative employment opportunities for workers, giving Pullman his chance to further cut the wages of his workforce. The pay of the Pullman workers was then so low that many were at or near actual starvation in the company-owned town where they were required to live. Attempts to negotiate with Pullman were fruitless; he simply fired the workers' representatives who attempted to negotiate and refused to recognize any union and any rights of workers.

The workers were desperate. In the spring of 1894 their leaders went to Debs and the ARU, joined this new union, went on strike against Pullman, and were locked out. They then asked the ARU for help, specifically for a boycott of all Pullman cars to force Pullman to submit to arbitration so that there would be a chance to raise their wages at least back to 1893 levels. Debs and the rest of the union leadership were reluctant; they knew that the ARU was still a new and relatively weak union, though it had great long-run potential. Nevertheless, the request of suffering fellow workers could not be ignored, and Debs and the ARU leadership agreed to institute a boycott on Pullman cars and ordered all affiliates to do so.

In California, the boycott against Pullman cars meant actively taking on the largest employer and most powerful economic, political and social force in the state: the corrupt Southern Pacific Railroad (the SP), and its allied organizations, the larger Pacific Coast Ring. This ring controlled the state government, the courts, and the so-called "legitimate" use of imprisonment, force, and violence. Nationally, the boycott meant confronting the strongest force in American capitalism: powerful railroad corporations. It also meant resisting the United States government itself, a government that was under the control of these same corporate interests.

PHASE ONE: THE ARU UPSURGE OF LATE JUNE–EARLY JULY 1894

The ARU strike to enforce a boycott of Pullman cars was begun the night of June 26, when union leadership ordered their members to boycott Pullmans on the Illinois Central, the St. Paul and Kansas City, Wisconsin Central, Southern Pacific, and Santa Fe Railroads (*Los Angeles Times* June 27, 1894, 4). The ARU leadership were careful to explain that its fight was not against the railroad companies, only the Pullman Palace Car Company. ARU members would facilitate the passage of any train not pulling a Pullman car (*Sacramento Record Union* June 25, 1894, 1). Nevertheless, the General Managers Association, making up the united leadership of twenty-four railroad companies with 41,000 miles of track, met and decided that every train would go out with a Pullman car attached, setting up a power confrontation that it thought it could win (*Sacramento Record Union* June 26, 1894, 1). Within a few days, *The New York Times* had a front-page article calling the railroad strike the "greatest battle between labor and capital that has ever been inaugurated in the United States" (*The New York Times* June 29, 1894, 1).

SACRAMENTO: THE STRIKE HUB

In early summer of 1894, the city of Sacramento was at the center of the Southern Pacific Railroad's California transportation operations. Its rail lines ran north, south, east, and west from the large railroad depot located at California's state capital. Adjacent to this depot stood the railroad's giant "car shops," probably the single largest industrial facility in the western United States, with thousands of skilled and unskilled workers. The giant complex had a roundhouse, steel rolling mill, two foundries, a saw and planing mill, and various shops—car painting, car building, locomotive, machine, cabinet, hammer, copper, blacksmith, bolt, car machine, boiler, car repair, and a number of smaller shops and storage buildings. It was capable of taking raw materials and manufacturing not only a variety of railroad cars but also locomotives, the most powerful engines of the time, the symbol of the "railroad age."

The Southern Pacific's political machine also ran the state government, located in Sacramento. It was by far the richest of California's corporations and controlled politicians and government through outright bribery of many of the leaders of both the Republican and Democratic Parties. Members of the general public—including the farmers and merchants who shipped their goods on what was the only railroad in much of the state—knew that the system was grossly corrupt and exploitive. But they saw no way to do anything about it. They lacked unified organization, an alternative vision, and that crucial ingredient needed for revolutionary transformation—hope. The advent of the ARU gave them that hope, along with the belief that their own organized activity, their own agency, could transform their lives for the better.

The boycott of the Pullman cars and the reaction of the Southern Pacific Railroad, created a general railroad strike in Sacramento and throughout the state. The ARU was underground in California—secrecy necessary because a worker's union membership could get him fired. But the idea of unionization was so powerful—especially among less-skilled and therefore more-alienated workers—that many were secretly members and even more were sympathizers.

On June 28, ARU brakemen in Oakland refused to handle Pullman cars and were discharged by the SP, which announced a hard line: it would operate the line as it saw fit, with no compromise for the ARU or its members. The SP owned about three-fourths of the Pullman cars it used, and therefore argued that the boycott would harm the SP more than Pullman, but the workers did not see it that way. Once the Oakland brakemen were fired, Debs declared a general strike of the entire SP Railroad. Sacramento passenger trains were immediately shut down and about 1,500 shop men at the car shops went on strike as a result of the firing of the Oakland brakemen (*Los Angeles Times* June 30, 1894, 2; *Sacramento Record Union* June 28, 1894, 1; June 30, 1894, 3), completing the tie-up of the railroad in Sacramento. As the *Los Angeles Times* reported on June 30, "The west-bound overland, containing Pullmans, was stopped this morning by strikers throwing open the drawbridge across the Sacramento River. Strikers said they would allow mail coaches to go by, but not a pound of freight or a single passenger" (*Los Angeles Times* June 30, 1894, 2).

At the same time and adjacent to the same bridge, three men were hung in effigy. As the *Sacramento Record Union* (June 30, 1894, 3) reported, "Amid the shouts of a big crowd of strikers three effigies were hung from an arm of the switch-signal near the Yolo bridge. They bore placards as follows:

Henry Tremblay, *the Scab*
Swain, *the Friend of Scabs*
Wellington, *the Scab*

Also on June 30, the *Sacramento Record Union* newspaper interviewed SP Superintendent Wright, who declared that about three thousand men were on strike in the Sacramento area and that they could not do anything about it. "The men have called a general strike, and everything is at a standstill … The strike extends from Ashland in the north to El Paso in the south, and from San Francisco to the East. Not a train is running except a few locals that started this morning before the general strike was ordered. All traffic is paralyzed" (*Sacramento Record Union* June 30, 1894, 3).

On June 30, the *Los Angeles Times* reported that the strike tying up Sacramento and other points "is the greatest strike ever known on the Pacific Coast" (*Los Angeles Times* June 30, 1894, 2).

The Southern Pacific, led by C. P. Huntington, had decided that it would use its own power as well as its influence over the state and federal government to try to engineer the destruction of the ARU in its infancy by attaching Pullmans to all US Mail trains, whether they needed a Pullman or not. Furthermore, Huntington ordered that anyone who went on strike should be fired and blacklisted, never to be employed by the SP again, adding that he wanted a railroad line with no union men on it, and would employ more "colored people from the South" to further divide the workers and achieve this result (*Sacramento Record Union* June 29, 1894, 1; Deverell 1994, 83).

At Sacramento, the strikers in control of the depot and car shops had agreed that they would run US Mail trains without Pullmans. On July 3, they thought that they had the concurrence of Federal Marshall Barry Baldwin, who was on the scene, that a mail train would go out of Sacramento without an unnecessary Pullman sleeping car attached. Once the train was made up and began on its way, however, a Pullman was suddenly added by federal marshals and scabs under their protection, and strikers had to rush in and uncouple the Pullman. Marshall Baldwin then tried to take charge of the situation by ordering the striking workers to stand back so the Pullman could be reattached. When they refused, Baldwin drew the two revolvers he carried. If his intention was to point and shoot his weapons, he could not, because he was seized by the crowd, who disarmed him and bodily carried him to the stairs leading to the SP offices at the depot, which SP leaders were still allowed to control (*The San Francisco Call* July 4, 1894, 1).

Marshall Baldwin then sent a telegram to Governor Markham, who was out of town visiting Southern California, requesting a call up of the National Guard to break the strike. Markham, under the influence of the SP, readily agreed and mobilized troops from Sacramento, San Francisco, and Stockton, sending them to Sacramento to reclaim the depot, yards, and car shops for the SP, by force and violence if necessary. Meanwhile, Federal Marshall Baldwin, openly on the side of the SP, was busily swearing in over a hundred Sacramento businessmen as deputy marshals, men approved and paid by the SP. Even so, at least some of these men reportedly sympathized with the strikers, as the SP was widely unpopular (*The San Francisco Call* July 4, 1894, 1).

On July 3, the San Francisco National Guard's trip to Sacramento began on an ominous note, as it was jeered by hostile bystanders as they marched to the ferry that was taking them to Oakland. At least one guardsman was hit in the head and injured by a brick thrown by someone in the crowd. The troops carried a Gatling gun, as well as the usual assortment of rifles, tents, and other gear (*The San Francisco Call* July 4, 1894, 2). The guard was able to seize a train in Oakland and, pulling Pullman cars for emphasis, rushed to Sacramento.

On a hot Independence Day, about one thousand National Guard troops from San Francisco, Sacramento, and Stockton were ordered to clear the Sacramento depot, yard, and car shops of ARU strikers and their supporters, who numbered in the thousands. A newspaper reporter from *The San Francisco Call* described the drama of the class struggle as a "small revolution" that he observed from atop a railroad car at the Sacramento depot on that day, as workers overcame alienation with solidarity and collective action in their own interest:

> *In the general dark corridors the mob was packed in one enormous, seething mass: men hatless and coatless shouted and waved flags above the excited multitude. Rude eloquence was dispensed ... with telling vehemence. They talked of their rights, of their wrongs and of the injustice of the militia or civil interference. They yelled and they howled and yelled again. Strikers flocked in from every quarter and joined the mad crowd.*

> *Great engines and mail and passenger cars stood untended on dozens of tracks, and on the tops of these and on the buildings and trees and telegraph poles thousands of spectators as excited as the strikers were thickly thronged.*

> *Down the street which leads to the great massive depot building marched 1,000 militiamen in a formidable column of platoons ... It was not long before the troops arrived at the depot building and assembled around its eastern end among the silent engines and locked cars.*

The first platoon of militia, one of the Sacramento companies, executed a turn to the right and advanced with bayonets at a charge. The strikers never flinched ... Cries from the angry strikers warned the militiamen that persistence meant a beginning of hostilities ... so as the line advanced nearer, the bayonets gradually arose, and in an instant, the strikers were breast to breast with the militiamen.

Behind the first platoons of National Guardsmen was the Sacramento detachment, with the formidable Gatling gun limbered and ready for action. There were men beside it and around it who might have mowed down the whole mass of strikers in a few moments had orders been given.

In one of the rooms of the railroad office further in the depot building the generals and other authorities were in session. The serious aspect of the situation was apparent to all, and those in power had reason to act slowly and cautiously.

In the meantime the officers of the regiments engaged the strike leaders in discussion ... Time and again the great crowd were ordered to fall back and allow troops to pass into the depot building, but almost simultaneous with the command another leader yelled for a thicker assembly of the strikers ... The ardor of the strikers increased every moment and yells became louder and flags were more widely waved. The strikers pushed forward and mingled somewhat with the soldiers. The more magnetic of the talkers explained matters to the guardsmen and coaxed them and intimidated them.

Then the enthusiasm ran riot in another direction. The striking majority decided that if things were to come to the worst the spectators and whoever else gathered about the depot should share the flying lead. "If they're going to fire we must all be in it," they said ... There was no arguing with these men. The order of the mob was law just about then.

The unsuccessful attempt at arbitration with the strikers and the failure of those in authority to give extreme orders was easily calculated to weaken the spirit of the militiamen ... Finally, the matter resolved itself into a question of whether or not they could remain there under such conditions. Several of the companies, in fact all of those not from San Francisco, extracted the ball cartridges from their Springfields and marched off in the direction of the main portion of town. As company after company left the scene of intended action the strikers yelled like demons. They cheered the militia and threw hats and coats in the air. (The San Francisco Call *July 5, 1894, 1)*

The *Call* also reported, of the National Guard in Sacramento, that "several of the companies of this town openly announced, and still announce, that they will not fight the strikers. They are men in sympathy with the cause of the strikers ... Company A of the Second Infantry was dismissed from the service this afternoon, and will probably be disbanded" (*The San Francisco Call* July 5, 1894, 1).

Members of Company G, Third Infantry of San Francisco, were arrested and tried by a general court-martial for disobeying orders issued by the military authorities at the depot that day (*The San Francisco Call* July 7, 1894, 8).

Later reports on the confrontation at the depot added some key details. At the decisive moment of the initial National Guard bayonet charge on the strikers, the striking workers in the front ranks, strong believers in the justice of their cause, threw open their coats, yelling "go ahead." But the bayonets touched the shirts and stopped, as the guardsmen were unsure of the justice of killing their fellow workers for the SP and Pullman corporations. At the same time, the strikers and militia members began to talk, one striker later recounted that he spoke to an acquaintance on the front line of the guard at this key moment, "I went to school with you. It's a shame for you to come down here to kill your own people. You shouldn't kill working people" (*The* San *Francisco Call* July 7, 1894, 3).

The disintegration of elements of the California National Guard as an effective repressive force was a serious blow to the plans of the SP and state and federal authorities who aimed to break both the strike and the ARU. A revolutionary situation had suddenly developed, because of the failure of repression at the Sacramento depot; the ARU was in charge and the federal government feared that it had too few troops to control the situation. Meanwhile, the ARU and its supporters were building strength and moving from victory to victory. Union members and allies began to wear a white ARU ribbon to symbolize support for the struggle. In the words of *The San Francisco Call* (July 7, 1894, 3), "In Sacramento ... men, women, children, Negroes and even Chinamen are all wearing the ARU ribbon, and if it becomes necessary, the Sacramento ARU could turn out 40,000 people in the field."

Mass meetings to support the strike crowded venues in many cities. In San Francisco, a big strike benefit was held. The *Call* (July 7, 1894, 1) reported that, "The meeting is expected to be the largest gathering ever held by any labor organization in this city." Speeches at this event were militant, advocating government ownership of the railroads. The *Call*'s reporter described the meeting:

Metropolitan Hall was crowded from parquet to gallery last night with an enthusiastic gallery of men and women called together to listen to arguments in support of the position assumed by the American Railway Union in the great struggle now on between capital and labor, which has tied up nearly every railroad line in the country. Not only were all the seats in the house filled, but chairs were placed in front of the platform, so that every inch of available space might be occupied.

The crowd was a motley congregation from many points of view. First, there was the laborer, clad in rough garb, indicative of the path of life in which he walked. Next came the clerks, bookkeepers and others from the idle wholesale houses of the city, all intent upon showing their friendship for the strikers and their hatred for George M. Pullman and the officers of the Southern Pacific. Throughout the audience were well-dressed men, evidently merchants or professional men. They jostled against the rudest laborer in the hall, evidently temporarily forgetful of the social tie that separated them. Hatred for monopolies was the ruling spirit, and all joined in hissing the names of Pullman, Huntington and other well known railroad magnates whenever opportunity offered.

The tenor of the speeches was all in favor of turning over the ownership of the railroads to the Government. Huntington, Pullman and other railway magnates were characterized as brazen thieves and held up to public contempt as the legitimate products of the iniquitous custom of private ownership of railroads.

> *The present administration also came in for a large amount of denunciation. President Cleveland was accused of being the tool of Wall Street, and three members of his Cabinet were characterized as corporation lawyers, who have no interest in the welfare of the common people (*The San Francisco Call *July 7, 1894, 1).*

The highlights of the opening speech at the San Francisco meeting, given by the People's Party nominee for Superior Judge, A. W. Thompson, were as follows:

> *[T] he nation now faces the question, "Shall Americans, confessing themselves slaves, wear on their necks the iron collar of the corporations or on their breasts the silken colors of the American Railway Union and proclaim themselves freemen?" Beyond this, and to which the labor trouble is but an index finger, pointing, stands the real issue, "Shall the great Republic die and be succeeded by an oligarchy of capitalists with a nominal President, real Emperor, at its head?"*

> *We, the American people, must insist on remaining our own masters and the continuance of popular sovereignty, or abandon the glorious heritage of freedom bequeathed to us by our revolutionary sires and to all the world admit that governments of, by and for the people is a farce. Already the work of usurpation is well under way. Traitors in high places are turning over the National Government—its courts and army—to America's insidious foe, the few inordinately rich men, whose sole aim is self-aggrandizement, and who seek princely power. The open, actual war of money against manhood is upon us. The soldiers of the plutocrats stand ready*

*to kill the populace. Through accident, or fortuitous circumstances, the American Railway Union is the advance corps of our defensive army in the life and death struggle for the maintenance of American freedom ... We stand by the American Railway Union. (*The San Francisco Call *July 7, 1894, 2)*

Support for the Sacramento strikers was also strong in other Northern California cities. The small railroad town of Dunsmuir on the upper Sacramento River was a stronghold of the strike, and several hundred "well armed" ARU strikers seized a train and used it to rush to Sacramento to support the struggle there. At the same moment, about four hundred "heavily armed strikers" also seized a locomotive and cars and left Truckee, near the Nevada border, also bound for California's capital city. As these two special trains carrying hundreds of armed men traveled toward Sacramento, they passed through towns where the scent of revolutionary insurrection was in the air.

The *Call* reported the following scene at the Cottonwood Station in the upper Sacramento Valley: "There are a large number of American Railway Union men ... all armed to the teeth with Winchester rifles, knives and revolvers awaiting the special" (*The San Francisco Call* July 5, 1894, 2).

The developing situation, with the people beginning to act in an insurrectionary manner against the hated monopoly, frightened Southern Pacific leaders. Its agents at Chico and Marysville received orders to tear up the tracks and spike the switches to prevent the armed strikers on the Dunsmuir train from arriving in Sacramento. At Chico, the railroad workers sided with the ARU and refused to remove the tracks. Scabs were found to remove some track, but the order was soon countermanded and the rails replaced (*The San Francisco Call* July 5, 1894, 2).

In Fresno, the ARU was so popular that over two thousand new, white badges had to be struck off to keep up with the demand. An armed company was reportedly being organized to reinforce the Sacramento strikers, and scabs were captured by Fresno strikers and told not to work on any train carrying Pullmans. One scab had a rope put around his neck and walked out of town as a warning (*The San Francisco Call* July 4, 1894, 2; July 6, 1894, 1).

Farmers around Sacramento also had deep grievances against the SP, relating especially to overcharges on freight rates and, therefore, strongly supported the strike. The Farmers' Alliance, a populist group, offered all the free beef and potatoes the strikers wanted during the strike and a willingness to come to the aid of the Sacramento strikers if called upon (*San Francisco Call* July 6, 1894, 2; *Oakland Enquirer* July 5, 1894, 5).

In Red Bluff, where tracks had been greased, spikes pulled from the rails in the yard, and water emptied from water tanks to prevent trains from passing, the National Guard was so supportive of the ARU that their commander feared that they would turn their guns over to the strikers. So he ordered them all back to the armory, disarmed them, and sent them home (*Los Angeles Times* July 2, 1894, 4; *The San Francisco Call* July 6, 1894, 2). In Carson, Nevada, the citizens were reportedly for the strike, with "everyone wearing white ribbons" (*The San Francisco Call* July 6, 1894, 2).

Women's auxiliaries were also organized in many cities to support the strike. In Sacramento, the women there focused on forming a medical relief corps in case the struggle developed into open warfare (*The San Francisco Call* July 7, 1894, 8).

OAKLAND: THE NORTHERN SPOKE

While less central to the SP transportation network than Sacramento, the SP's West Oakland facilities were nevertheless very important. Oakland was a key terminal point for the transcontinental railroad. Its pier, a giant called the Oakland Mole, ran out into the bay to facilitate the ferrying of trains, freight, and passengers across the water to San Francisco. The terminal also had a depot, a roundhouse, a transfer table, train car shops, a Pullman Company storehouse, a car-cleaning shed, a car-cleaning storage building, a machine shop, a storage building for car repair parts, office, and a handcar house and yard.

On July 4, 1894, as the confrontation at the Sacramento depot was unfolding, no less radical actions were taking place in Oakland. As mentioned above, it was the June 28 refusal of ARU brakemen in Oakland to handle Pullmans that led to their firing and the walkout of all ARU members in California. However, it was enforcing the Pullman boycott that was the problem in Oakland, since scabs controlled the SP facilities there. To gain control of SP property, the strikers had to resort to drastic, non-violent tactics. A crowd of courageous volunteers and their supporters massed at the station, fifty or so blockading the railroad tracks outside the depot and a dozen lying down upon them, to stop an oncoming train. On July 5, a *Call* reporter who was present wrote about these dramatic events:

> *Rumors of what might occur on the mole yesterday were rife …while the American Railway Union was in session. They were so vague, however, and came from such no-nauthoritative sources that but little credence was placed in them and nobody expected that the scenes of yesterday would follow so quickly … every move … had been cleverly and carefully planned.*
>
> *The first move was on the Alameda broad gauge train into the mole, and showed at once that the men had tired of waiting for an opening, and were determined to move boldly on the company's inner works. A crowd of strikers had assembled at the Cedar Street crossing just a few minutes before 11:30 o'clock, when the Alameda train was due, bound for the sheds. In a short time the puffing of the engine was heard, and the American Railway Union volunteers were called for to stop the train. About fifty of them who were present in the crowd lined up across the*

track and waited. The engine steamed steadily on, the man in tower 2 gave the signal, "Track clear," and it began to look as if the big iron machine would mow through the human barricade if it remained where it was. On came the engine and firmly stood the fifty, not a man flinching. The grind of the wheels on the rails could be distinctly heard. The gap was closing up faster than the wind, and then a strange thing happened.

Down on their backs over the rails, stretched at full length, went half a dozen of the strikers, and the breaths of the spectators stopped for a moment … at the daring of the men. It was a most powerfully startling piece of planning, most wonderfully and realistically horrible … All was still save the whirr of the wheels and the puffing of steam for a second. The next instant the air went out on the brakes, the lever was reversed, and the train slowed within ten feet of the self-appointed victims of the Southern Pacific Juggernaut.

There was a sigh of relief from the crowd, a yell from the strikers as they saw their work accomplished and jumped for the engine, while the men who had dared so much to further the general plan rose slowly from their recumbent positions. There was an evident paleness in their faces.

Onto the engine clambered the men, from the rear and the sides, over the tender, and from both sides of the cab … The train … was allowed to proceed to the yard and discharge its passengers.

While all this was going on up above, another body of the strikers was busy at the roundhouse and in

> *the sheds. Stationed around the yards the company*
> *had about half of its 200 deputy Sheriffs, but when*
> *about 150 strikers appeared in a body … the deputies*
> *discreetly took the back tack, and the delegation of*
> *the ARU proceeded at once to the shops. The strikers*
> *entered by twos and threes and asked the men at*
> *work, some forty in number, to leave their work.*
> *Some few were a little slow about it, but the majority*
> *laid down their tools … and walked for the doors.*
> *They joined the strikers and shook hands all around.*
> *(San Francisco Call July 5, 1894, 3)*

Operating out of their West Oakland strike headquarters at Wood and Seventh Streets, the next day about a thousand strikers, working together in a disciplined, well-planned and executed action, shut down all locomotives and closed the Oakland Mole, the long pier where the transport ships that ferried trains across the bay docked. The Sheriff and his SP-chosen and paid for deputies were told by the SP not to use weapons against the strikers and to yield if the ARU men arrived in any numbers. The *Oakland Enquirer* (July 5, 1894, 5) reported what happened when the strikers arrived:

> *An army of nearly 1,000 strikers and others marched*
> *to the Oakland mole at 11 o'clock this morning and*
> *took possession. Forty deputy sheriffs stationed about*
> *200 yards from the pier formed a line across the*
> *tracks as if to intercept the strikers … Chief Deputy*
> *Kellogg … stood in front of his men and commanded*
> *the great throng to halt, but his order was lost in the*
> *shouts of "go on!" … There was no need for Kellogg*
> *to tell his deputies to fall back. The vast crowd had*
> *not paused an instant and the picket guards were*
> *pushed on ahead. Kellogg called out: "Let no deputy*
> *attempt to shoot until I give the order."*

411

> *It was unnecessary to caution the guards. They felt*
> *that they were between the devil and the deep sea.*
> *From three locomotives there was steam issuing, and*
> *it was toward these that the crowd moved. Engines*
> *1282 of the overland mail and 1242 of the Oakland*
> *local, and 1266 of the Berkeley local were uncoupled*
> *and "killed" and the water let out of switch engines*
> *1027 and 1034. The crowd was not boisterous.*
> *Hardly a word was said, but there was no indecision*
> *or confusion.*

Meanwhile, the SP superintendent argued that the railroad could and would do nothing until "properly protected" by the federal government. He added that the people of Oakland, many of whom supported the ARU, would demand an end to the strike when they realized how much they depended upon the SP. This would happen when they saw their mail cut off, no freight arrived, and they could no longer travel (*The San Francisco Call* July 6, 1894, 2–3).

As these events developed, a group of women met at Barlett's Hall at Seventh and Pine Streets in Oakland to form the ARU Sympathetic League to support the strikers and their families in whatever form necessary. They declared that they stood for the right of "action" and for "liberty." One supporter showed her class consciousness, stating, "Magnificent fortunes built up to the impoverishment of the working people will ultimately ruin republican principles. I would have every honest man, from the Atlantic to the Pacific, join the union organized for securing for labor a living wage" (*The San Francisco Call* July 6, 1894, 3).

By July 6, support in Oakland for the strike was very high, the membership of the ARU was up to 1,060 members just in Oakland, and there were meetings every day at Hansen's Hall in West Oakland. As the *Call* reported, "White badges are becoming the craze in Oakland. They are to be seen everywhere, even the women are wearing them. Judging from the number to be seen on the street, sympathy for the strikers must be very extensive" (*The San Francisco Call* July 7, 1894, 3).

Support for the Oakland strikers extended to San Francisco where it was reported that a meeting of working men was held on July 5 "for the purpose of forming a military company of 300 men for the purpose of helping the strikers in their fight in Oakland" (*Oakland Enquirer* July 6, 1894, 2).

LOS ANGELES: THE SOUTHERN SPOKE

Los Angeles railroad workers were also solidly with the strike and were able to shut down the rail service in and out of the city on that fateful Fourth of July. The *Call* reported on July 5:

> *Southern California is completely paralyzed by the great railroad strike, which extends into every branch of business more than in any other portion of the state. Not a train or a locomotive is moving south of Tehachapi Mountain. Railroad yards are deserted, provisions are running out in many interior towns, and taking the situation in a comprehensive view, it may be said the south is in a state of siege.*
>
> *As for Los Angeles, the ordinary routine of city life is upset so thoroughly that trade, excepting the absolutely necessary buying and selling, is at a standstill, and although order is maintained, the greatest excitement has taken hold of the people. The streets are thronged with men whose only thought seems to be about the strike. The newspaper, railroad and union bulletin-boards are surrounded by crowds such as are seen when the returns of national elections are announced.*
>
> *Sympathy is almost unanimously with the strikers ... Last evening the strikers adopted a white button or ribbon for their emblem and to-day nearly*

413

everyone here has a little white satin now on his or her breast. In many cases where ribbons could not be procured on the spur of the moment people cut slips of white paper and pinned them on their coats. Some fashionably dressed ladies who visited the depot displayed corners of elegant white lace handkerchiefs and others had white flowers or bunches of light silky material. The union men without exception wore tiny American flags above the badges. Over all they claim to be a patriotic body of men loyal to the flag, a feature which has won the southern capital entirely, for this is an out and out American city. (The San Francisco Call *July 5, 1894, 2)*

The SP tried to force strikers back to work with the threat of termination of employment, but the ARU men held firm:

An order was issued by the Southern Pacific Company yesterday to the strikers informing them that if they failed to report for duty at 10 A.M. to-day they would be discharged. This called the union together, and the men determined to tender their resignations in a body. Before 10 o'clock over 300 resignations were given Division Superintendent Burkhalter of the Mojave division. Some weak union men, it appears, were frightened at the order and reported for duty. The strikers did not know or would not divulge the number, and declined to discuss this first small break in the ranks. (The San Francisco Call *July 5, 1894, 2)*

Federal government marshals then arrested the Los Angeles leadership of the ARU, charging them with obstructing the carrying of the US mail. All of the witnesses who endorsed the indictments were officials of the SP and Santa Fe railroads (*The San Francisco Call* July 5, 1894, 2).

In Los Angeles, as in other California cities, the strike had rapidly become a bitter struggle, influencing the actions of the larger population with people choosing sides. As was the case in many parts of California, some strikers and their supporters were beginning to arm themselves, and the possibility of open warfare hung in the air. As the *Call* reported on July 5:

> *The strike has extended to the newsboys and a general boycott is on the* Times. *Newsboys refused to sell that paper to-day because "De Times" is against the strikers. Advertisements valued at $24,000 were withdrawn yesterday and 4,000 subscriptions were canceled to-day. The landlady of a Times reporter was visited by a stranger this morning and told she would have to have him leave her house. The reason for this bitter boycott is an editorial favoring the railroad side and attacking the union.*
>
> *The trades union held a meeting last night for the purpose of organizing a military body which shall carry arms and be to all intents an armed force. All labor organizations were invited to attend, and owing to the deep interest in all labor movements, the Council of Labor Hall was packed with ... workmen. A resolution as follows was adopted:*
>
> *Resolved, That we thoroughly sympathize with the struggles of the American Railroad Union with organized capital, and that we are organized for its support and assistance, and we believe in the maxim that an injury to one is the concern of all.*
>
> *At another meeting held to-night the body was given the name of the Los Angeles Independent Military Organization. About fifty men were enrolled previously, and as many more enlisted this evening.*

> *Members explain that the company is not organized*
> *for fighting unless forced to it, and also that it is not*
> *unlawful. (*The San Francisco Call *July 5, 1894,*
> *2)*

The Federal government rapidly rushed US troops from San Francisco to Los Angeles. These soldiers were largely unwelcome, however, and even the bakers went on strike and refused to bake bread for them. A boycott on the soldiers was declared and " … a feeling of indignation is everywhere manifested against the soldiers" (*The San Francisco Call* July 5, 1894, 2).

The soldiers were able to protect scabs, however, and the strike began to weaken. Still, the *Call* reported that local merchants had to deliver their goods by team as far north as Mojave (*The San Francisco Call* July 6, 1894, 1, 3). Breaking the strike in Los Angeles and getting the trains running again became the keystone tactic for the federal government in California. Once the situation was under control there, the troops could be sent north to break the strike in the two other key cities of Sacramento and Oakland (*The San Francisco Call* July 7, 1894, 1). This strategy began to succeed on July 8, when trains began to move out of Los Angeles with Pullmans attached, all well guarded by US troops ensuring that scabs could run the trains (*The San Francisco Call* July 9, 1894, 3).

PHASE TWO: REVERSAL OF FORTUNE

President Grover Cleveland's Democratic administration was determined to openly side with the railroad corporations and break the ARU strike by force if necessary. Cleveland's attorney general was none other than Richard Olney, who had been an attorney for the railroads prior to assuming his role as chief law-enforcement officer of the United States. Several other railroad attorneys also advised the president. The courts were also on the side of the corporations, and the judges of the time were typically propertied lawyers who had worked for or held interests in these same corporations. Using the argument that the constitutional right of interstate commerce was being violated, the attorneys for the railroads therefore had an easy time getting a series of court injunctions against the strikers, demanding that they cease and desist from shutting down the railroad lines (*The San Francisco Call* July 4, 1894, 2). The union and strikers ignored these court orders.

The Cleveland administration, seeing that the California National Guard was unreliable, decided that it had to declare martial law and intervene with US troops to crush the strike. Their strategy was clear by July 5: use US troops to protect scabs and allow trains to begin moving again, and arrest and jail strike leaders, destroying both the strike and the union. The potential power of an industrial union in the railroad industry was clearly too threatening to those in power, both in Washington and in corporate boardrooms. Working people had to be prevented, by violence if need be, from having any real voice in the operations of the railroad corporations, which were at the core of the US economy.

For their part, Debs and the California leader of the ARU, Harry Knox, had no answer for the corporate government offensive. The initial short-term strike demands of the California ARU were quite moderate: arbitration, a return to 1893 wage levels for the Pullman workers, severance of SP's relationship with the Pullman Company, and the restoration of all striking employees to their former positions. In exchange for these concessions, the ARU would transport all mail and express packages, but not freight and passengers (*The San Francisco Call* July 6, 1894, 2).

Recognition of the union and the rights to collective bargaining were left unmentioned, as was collective ownership and control, or even government ownership of the railroads. These had been mentioned in mass meetings and were on the minds of progressive thinkers, as well as the rank-and-file. There was apparently no way that the average worker or citizen could participate in a collective decision-making process and direct action that could have led to a different outcome. This was a serious leadership failure at a time when there was mass support for the class struggle from below.

As the strike got underway, the threat and promise of a nationwide general strike to support the ARU was widely discussed and both the American Federation of Labor's president, Samuel Gompers, and the Knights of Labor's leader, James Sovereign, were involved. Despite some early expressions of support for a general strike by all organized workers nationwide, nothing came of these discussions. On July 7, for example, the *Call* reported that the 25,000-strong Building and Trade Council of Chicago issued a call for such a national general strike and the Knights were also discussing it (*The San Francisco Call* July 7, 1894, 1). That same day, Debs stated that he was "assured" that in forty-eight hours every labor organization in the country would come to the rescue of the ARU.

Debs and Knox consistently opposed the use of any violence by strikers, arguing that it was counter-productive and that such tactics could not result in a victory for the workers. Debs' forty-eight hours came and went without a general strike, and then Cleveland proclaimed martial law in California and the western United States on July 9. At the same time, General Miles of the US Army, the military commander appointed to deal with the strike, stated that "rebellion and lawlessness" were rampant, and he vowed to "disperse, capture, or destroy" those who were in rebellion against the United States. The arrest of Debs, Knox, and other top ARU leaders was then ordered, and US troops went on the offensive (*The San Francisco Call* July 10, 1894, 1).

General Master Workman James Sovereign of the Knights of Labor, however, did declare a general strike on July 10. His call for a strike of all Knights, who then numbered almost one million workers, began as follows:

> *A crisis has been reached in the affairs of this nation*
> *that endangers the peace of the republic. Every fiber*
> *in our civil structure is strained to the breaking point.*

The shadows of factional hatred hover over our fair land with terrible forebodings. The arrogant lash of superiority is being applied by the corporations with relentless fury, and the chasm between the masses and the classes is growing deeper and wider with each succeeding day. If peace is restored and this nation saved from acts repulsive to the conscience of all Christian people, there must be wise action and that quickly. (The San Francisco Call *July 11, 1894, 2)*

But the Knights' strike failed; the workers were not willing to follow the call of their own leadership, thus effectively ending the existence of the Knights as an organization. Other attempts to spread the strike nationally were also unsuccessful. Gompers and the AFL refused to join the strikers, and the Chicago Trades Council also recalled its earlier strike order (*Oakland Enquirer* July 14, 1894, 1). The fate of the strikers and the strike were left to the mercy of the corporate bosses and their pawns, the US military.

On that same day, the elite Brotherhood of Locomotive Engineers carried out the final act of betrayal of the working class. Although a few of their locals did strike, throughout the early period this brotherhood had been mainly on the fence, meeting and debating amongst themselves about what to do (*The San Francisco Call* July 1, 1894, 1; July 3, 1894, 2; July 6, 1894, 3; July 7, 1894, 3). Then on July 11, *The San Francisco Call* reported that in an "*et tu* Brute" moment, a "large number" of brotherhood members had visited SP superintendent Fillmore and offered their services to the SP "whenever called upon." They stated that they had never gone on strike, had never affiliated with the ARU, and that they had no grievance with the Southern Pacific (*The San Francisco Call* July 11, 1894, 1).

THE FALL OF SACRAMENTO

On July 10, US troops were on their way to Sacramento, infantry in riverboats with cavalry traveling in conjunction along the riverbank. As the troops approached for a showdown, the armed strikers and their supporters at the Southern Pacific depot and vicinity were taking target practice with their Winchester rifles. Knox and other remaining ARU leaders instructed the men to disperse and not engage in violent combat, but they initially failed to obey. When the troops arrived in Sacramento, however, and with the remaining loyal National Guard units at the depot, most of the strikers dispersed. Some strikers and supporters were willing to engage in combat, however, and fired at the soldiers from across the river. At least fifty shots were reportedly exchanged.

In returning this fire, the soldiers shot and killed a Japanese American boy who was standing on the riverbank. Several days later, the federal troops also shot and killed two strike supporters on the streets of Sacramento (*The San Francisco Call* July 12, 1894, 1; July 18, 1894, 1; *Oakland Enquirer* July 13, 1894, 1). For their part, the strikers or supporters killed four soldiers and an engineer, injuring many others by derailing off a trestle the very first train that pulled out of Sacramento going west (*The San Francisco Call* July 12, 1894, 1).

The authorities then arrested Knox and other leaders of the California ARU, charging them with wrecking the train. Knox replied truthfully that he was innocent and had been keeping order and restraining the more militant elements of the ARU. There were also wholesale arrests for grand larceny of those men who had commandeered trains and used them to transport armed men to Sacramento (*The San Francisco Call* July 15, 1894, 1). With these arrests, the great majority of the Sacramento strikers gave up and quit the ARU, trying to save their jobs by declaring they were ready to return to work under conditions laid down by the corporation (*The San Francisco Call* July 17, 1894, 2). The SP was readying a comprehensive blacklist of all workers favorable to unionization, however, which was soon unmercifully implemented.

EVENTS IN OAKLAND

The Oakland strikers held out, even as the strike collapsed in Sacramento and Los Angeles. On July 14, Oakland strikers met and decided to shut down local trains. The tracks were obstructed with heavy timbers, forcing a local to stop, allowing the strikers to board the train and eject the scab fireman. Scab firemen on several other local trains were similarly ejected, and a call went out from SP for the military to disperse the strikers. A detachment of police and militia, the latter with Gatling guns, hurried to the scene and dispersed the strikers. *The New York Times*, which obviously favored the railroads, noted how successful troops with Gatling guns performed against unarmed strikers: "The efficiency of Gatling guns in dispersing rioters was demonstrated this afternoon, when a small mob, which attacked firemen on local trains, fled at the appearance of militia with the rapid fire ordinance" (*The New York Times* July 15, 1894, 5).

On July 16, the National Guard, with support from a US naval battalion, took over the West Oakland depot and began to try to run trains with scabs. Strikers had pickets up, however, and large supporting crowds along the First Street tracks. When the train to Mendota tried to pass by the crowds, strikers rushed in, uncoupled the cars, and released the air from the air brakes. The National Guard cavalry was nearby, however, and with sabers slashing at unarmed people, they attacked the crowd near Cedar and Sixth Streets sowing terror:

> *With sabers swinging in the air, slashing right and left and pistols clubbed, the cavalry came on at a swinging gallop, and men and women, little children, boys and girls gave way like sheep before a murrain.[3] Faster and faster they galloped, and ahead and on the sides the crowd gave way and fell back on the crowd further up, crowding them up Sixth Street*

3 Any of various highly infectious diseases of cattle and sheep, literally meaning "death"; plague.

and up and down Seventh and further on up Cedar on both sides of the engine. On and on after the horsemen came the infantry and Naval Battalion, and in the rear on the double quick the artillerymen with the Gatling and Hotchkiss guns. The infantry with guns clubbed, and the Naval Battalion with bayonets pointed, charged the crowds that had been swept to the side by the rush of the cavalry. Men were struck on the head and shoulders and fell and rose, and were clubbed and prodded again; women fled for their lives, shrieking in fear and trembling at the onslaught; little children were carried on in the general rush and panic, and their frightened screams could be heard even above the din of the charge, the shrieks of the women and the curses of the men.

Pell mell, this way and that, into every convenient doorway, in between houses and across lots, up and down the nearest crossways and on up Cedar and Seventh streets swept the crowd before the rush. And the soldiers dealt their blows right and left in a disorganized, indiscriminate way, men and women getting the benefit of their blows alike.

As Seventh Street was reached, a detachment of the cavalry soon followed infantry, each apparently without head or arm, charged on the sidewalks and up the middle of the street, after the fleeing, unresisting crowds. And on up Cedar Street the main body of the soldiery continued in its swoop. They charged and charged, cut this way and slashed that, with their bayonets thrusting and their clubbed guns swinging, the crowd moving in any way it could until Goss Street was reached.

The US Cavalry Attacks the Oakland Strikers

A drawing from *The San Francisco Call* depicts the military attack on the strikers, July 1894.

> *Cedar Street had been cleared and the crowds were*
> *still fleeing for their lives in any and every direction*
> *to get out of the way of what they considered certain*
> *death. There were any number with battered heads*
> *and bleeding faces and hands, with clothes torn by*
> *bayonet thrusts; but, despite rumors that a number*
> *of people had been killed, none were found on the*
> *field. (*The San Francisco Call *July 17, 1894, 3)*

It was a miracle that none were killed and only two seriously wounded. A number of strikers took refuge in a house at 1820 Goss Street where twenty-one were later arrested and taken to the city jail. Martial law was in effect in Oakland with troops constantly arresting strikers to destroy all resistance, ending the strike in Oakland. It is unclear exactly how many were arrested, but the *Oakland Enquirer* had an entire article about the event in its July 16 edition, entitled "Arrests Galore" (*The San Francisco Call* July 17, 1894, 3; *Oakland Enquirer* July 16, 1894, 1).

AFTERMATH

To investigate the facts surrounding the 1894 Pullman strike, President Cleveland appointed a Strike Commission. This commission called ARU President Eugene V. Debs as a witness. In his mid-August 1894 testimony about the origins of the strike, Debs pointed out that the railroad industry's General Managers' Association had been formed to destroy all railroad unions and set out to accomplish their aims. As Debs summed up:

> *The General Managers Association's ... evident*
> *aim was to drive organized labor from existence.*
> *No sooner had this association been formed than*
> *a systematic reduction in railroad wages all over*
> *the country began. The men were ready to strike*
> *and felt they had a cause: but the trouble would*
> *not have come when it did had it not been for the*

Pullman matter. The time was unpropitious. I did not order the strike. I had not the power. The men did that themselves. But I do not wish to shirk any responsibility and am willing to say that I heartily concurred in and approved of the action taken by the men. As to violence, I always condemned it. I have written and spoken against it, believing and knowing that a strike cannot be won by violence. (The San Francisco Call *August 21, 1894, 1)*

Debs also gave his opinion that the ARU had won the strike and the railroads were beaten when the state and federal governments intervened and used the courts, arrest power, and military violence to smash workers' power: "They were paralyzed ... but injunctions were soon broadcast, and shortly afterward the officials of the ARU were arrested for contempt of court. That beat us" (*The San Francisco Call* August 21, 1894, 1).

The following exchange ended the *Call*'s report on Debs testimony:

"What is your opinion as [to] the methods of preventing strikes?" asked Commissioner Worthington of Debs.

"My own idea, and it is the idea of the ARU, is to unify all the railroad men of the country. A power like that, prudently managed, would avoid strikes. The railroad managers would recognize the wisdom of treating it fairly and meeting it in a conciliatory spirit."

"Do you believe striking is justifiable that interferes with public convenience?"

"I believe striking is justifiable no matter what the result when it resists enslaving and degrading."

> *"Do you believe in Government ownership of railways?" asked Mr. Kernan. "Yes sir; I believe that Government ownership of railroads is decidedly better than railroad ownership of the Government"* (The San Francisco Call *August 21, 1894, 1).*

On the same day and on the same page, the *Call* reported both on the engagement of George Pullman's daughter to the German Prince of Isenburg-Birstein, a cousin of the Emperor of Austria, and the "near starvation" conditions of sixteen hundred families at the Pullman works near Chicago (*The San Francisco Call* August 21, 1894, 1).

The Southern Pacific and other railroads then organized a nationwide blacklist of anyone known to have participated in the strike in any way. This included the circulation of photos of the workers to be blacklisted. The result was privation for many workers, and some of them had to emigrate to other countries, because they could not find work in the United States. (*The San Francisco Call* August 18, 1894, 2; August 20, 1894: 1). The SP's severe blacklist lasted almost two years. Even when it was slightly modified in June of 1896, it still banned any worker who had committed any "overt act." A number of men were reportedly driven to suicide or starved to death due to lack of work as a result of this blacklist (*The San Francisco Call* June 4, 1896, 16).

One contemporary writer stated that the great Pullman strike in California "should never be forgotten" since it gave the Golden State "an especial title to honor and fame" (Swinton 1894, 133). Nevertheless, the strike was a disastrous setback for the California and US working class. From being potentially the most powerful union in the state and nation, the ARU had been totally destroyed in less than a month, and an industrial union in the railroad industry never existed again. Many thousands of workers who wanted freedom from alienated labor and the rights, protections, and solidarity of union membership had been denied.

11

THE 1901 GENERAL STRIKE
ON THE SAN FRANCISCO WATERFRONT

Intense struggles by California workers for their freedom did not end with the Pullman strike. Only seven years after the defeat of the American Railway Union, a massive, three-month-long strike on the San Francisco waterfront resulted in a triumph for the rank-and-file and a strengthening of the labor movement. The strike began on July 30, 1901, when the City Front Federation, representing over fifteen thousand men from fourteen San Francisco waterfront unions, led by the teamsters, the Sailors' Union of the Pacific, and four different longshoremen's unions, walked off the job. This strike was the largest and most significant in the history of California to this point in time.

Although the great waterfront strike of 1901 developed out of a complex set of circumstances unique to its time and place, at the heart of the struggle was the continuing story that new unions were claiming freedoms and asserting their human rights, while at the same time, most of the leaders of the ruling class of San Francisco were refusing to accept any role for the working class in economic decision making.

THE SEPTEMBER 1900 TEAMSTERS' UPSURGE

The strike's immediate origins can be traced to the formation of the Teamsters' Union in August of 1900. This event was to be of special importance for both the 1901 waterfront strike and the future of the San Francisco labor movement. Led by Michael Casey, the union was initially small, less than fifty members, but the men who drove the horse teams often worked more than twelve hours a day—some even eighteen hours a day—seven days a week, at low wages ($3.50 to $16 a week) and under very competitive conditions; virtually all of them were ready to assert their humanity and respond to the union call (Cronin 1943, 40).

On Labor Day 1900, McNab & Smith, one of the leading draying firms, in an employers' tactic typical for the time, tried to break the new union by firing drivers who refused to quit the union. Casey and the union men called upon the remaining drivers to strike the offending firm, and when, to the shock of McNab and Smith, almost one hundred men went out, the employer settled after only one day, immediately reinstating the discharged unionists. In the wake of this quick victory, San Francisco saw one of its fastest single union expansions ever. In the space of only a few weeks, about twelve hundred men joined the Teamsters' Union, and in mid-September, Casey and his membership demanded improved hours and working conditions.

The employers' group, the Draymen's Association, wanted a stabilization of the all-out cutthroat competition characteristic of the industry, so it was open to an agreement that would prevent new competitors from entering the field except as members of the association. The association was therefore willing to recognize the union, and on October 1, 1900, a detailed formal agreement was signed. The workers got a regular twelve-hour day, with overtime pay for over twelve hours and for work on Sundays, as well as the union shop designation and an agreement that no assistance would be given to public drayage firms employing nonunion men.

In return, the union agreed not to work for any firm that refused to join the association or for a wage lower than set forth in the contract, thus helping to stabilize employer costs and assisting employers in forcing other firms to join the Drayage Association. This agreement tied the workers' union and owners' association together in a mutually convenient effort to stabilize competition within the industry (Knight 1960, 58–60).

FOUNDING OF THE CITY FRONT FEDERATION, EARLY 1901

Waterfront workers in San Francisco had often been divided, with various jurisdictional disputes causing conflict, especially between the Sailors' Union of the Pacific and the several longshoremen's unions. Recognizing that disunity among workers handed a powerful weapon to the bosses, in the fall of 1900, the sailors and longshoremen signed an agreement that not only delineated lines of jurisdiction in cargo handling, but also established a policy of mutual assistance by specifying that members of these unions would not cooperate with nonunion workers in receiving and discharging cargo. This led to an even stronger alliance, when, in early 1901, a federation of all onshore and offshore waterfront unions, including the teamsters, was formed. Called the City Front Federation, it was a labor body with formal, centralized authority. Its constitution authorized its president to order a strike vote of all member-unions if an employer offensive made it "necessary to order a general strike" (Knight 1960, 61).

By the summer of 1901, the City Front Federation included fourteen unions, between 13,000 and 16,350 members, and had a treasury of $250,000 (Knight 1960, 61; *The San Francisco Examiner* July 21, 1901, 18). The Federation was anchored by the sailors, the teamsters, and four locals of the Longshoremen's union, but also included a number of smaller unions, such as the marine firemen, porters, packers and warehousemen, ship repair craftsmen, and harbor workers. Together they could largely control the transportation and commerce of San Francisco and therefore had formidable power to choke off the city's economic life and force employers to recognize and negotiate with their unions.

THE FOUNDING OF THE EMPLOYERS' ASSOCIATION, APRIL 1901

Employer organizations of various types had existed in previous decades in San Francisco, but had become inactive. With unions growing more powerful in 1900 and 1901, the key capitalist businessmen of San Francisco concluded that they should organize a counteroffensive to roll back and destroy the growing democratic power that the unions represented. In April of 1901, fifty militant employers formed a secretive organization known as the Employers' Association. The organization was to serve as the guiding anti-union body for the San Francisco ruling class during this period. To make sure that ample funds existed to carry out their policies, each pledged one thousand dollars to the organization. As other employers joined, they were also required to post bonds as guarantees of their observance of the association's policies. In this way, the anti-union strikebreaking fund of the bosses grew to an estimated five hundred thousand dollars (Knight 1960, 67).

Although a semi-secret organization, the Employers' Association is estimated to have had a membership of over three hundred firms, with influence over many more. The association exercised centralized control over its member firms, forbidding any member from granting a union demand or settling any labor dispute without the express consent of the association's executive committee. The members of this executive committee, along with their key corporate connections are listed in table 11.1 below.

TABLE 11.1: Executive Committee of the Employers' Association, Summer, 1901

Committee Member	Corporate Connection
Frederick W. Dohrmann Jr	Secretary, Nathan, Dohrmann Company
A. A. Watkins	Vice President, Montague & Company; president San Francisco Board of Trade
Charles Holbrook	President, Holbrook, Merrill & Stetson; a director of United Railroads San Francisco, Union Trust Company, and the Mutual Savings Bank
Harvey D. Loveland	Vice President, Tillmann & Bendel
F. W. von Sicklen	Dodge, Sweeney and Company
Percy T. Morgan	President, California Wine Association; a director of California Fruit Canners Association
Isaac Upham	Payot, Upham and Company
Frank J. Symmes	President, Day Company, president of the Merchants' Association; a director of Spring Valley Water Company and Central Trust Company
Edward M. Herrick	President, Pacific Pine Company and Grey's Harbor Commercial Company
Akin H. Vail	Sanborn, Vail and Company
Joseph D. Grant	Murphy, Grant & Company, a director of Donohoe-Kelly Banking Company, Mercantile National Bank, Mercantile Trust Company, and Natomas Consolidated
Jacob Stern	First Vice President of Levi Strauss & Company, a director of the Bank of California, Union Trust Company, and North Alaska Salmon
S. Nickelsburg	President, Cohn, Nickelsburg & Company
Adolph Mack	Mack & Company; also a director of City Electric Company

Committee Member	Corporate Connection
Andrew Carrigan	Vice President, Denham, Carrigan & Hayden Company
Henry D. Morton	Morton Brothers
J. S. Dinkelspiel	J. S. Dinkelspiel & Company
George D. Cooper	W. and J. Sloane & Company

Source: *The San Francisco Examiner* July 30, 1901, 2; August 7, 1901, 3

The Employers' Association was representative of the highest economic circles of San Francisco, with close ties to the Board of Trade, Merchants' Association, and many of the biggest and most important firms of the city. The presence of direct connections to United Railroads, the Spring Valley Water Company, and the Bank of California, as well as several other leading banks is especially telling, for these were among the largest and most powerful corporations in the state. Its one weakness was that it had no direct ties to what was by far the single largest and most powerful corporation of the time, the Southern Pacific Railroad.

Based in San Francisco, the railroad would be affected by the developing class struggle and also had the most influence with Governor Henry T. Gage, who had served as one of its attorneys. Despite the absence of the SP, the Employers' Association was nevertheless an organization by and for leading ruling-class circles of San Francisco. It could also be confident in the support of the mayor and city administration, due both to the natural tendency of capitalist government—Democratic or Republican—to side with big vested interests and because the Democratic mayor, James D. Phelan, was also a leading capitalist and had served on the same corporate boards of directors as some of the executive committee members.

THE LABOR COUNCIL AND INDUSTRIAL DISPUTES IN OTHER TRADES

The San Francisco Labor Council had been founded in late 1892 with thirty-four affiliates. Although it had been on the decline during the next few years due to employer attacks and internal conflict, it revived after mid-1897. From then on, with business conditions improving, it grew rapidly (Knight 1960, 31, 36). By early 1901, the Labor Council, led by Ed Rosenberg and W. H. Goff, had become a real force in San Francisco. Its efforts to organize all workers, regardless of skill level, made San Francisco preeminent among major American cities in the degree of unionization among less-skilled workers. Unfortunately, this positive effort resulted in a division in labor's ranks when the craft union–oriented Building Trades Council, led by P. H. McCarthy, broke with the Labor Council, openly scorning its efforts to organize unskilled, more easily replaced workers (Knight 1960, 63–64). Some of the individual unions that made up the Building Trades Council later supported the City Front Federation in its conflict with the Employers' Association, but most did not, violating a key labor principle held by the more advanced elements of the labor movement: the need for solidarity and unity among workers and their organizations.

Other unions were also on the move. In May of 1901, conflicts broke out in both the restaurant and metal trades industry. More than a thousand restaurant workers struck for the ten-hour day and four to five thousand workers in the metal trades struck for the nine-hour day. Other unions supported both strikes, but the Employers' Association intervened in these conflicts, strengthening the will and the resources of the employers involved. Both strikes eventually fell well short of their goals, even though the strike in the metal trades went on for about ten months (Knight 1960, 67–71, 90–91).

THE TEAMSTERS LOCKED OUT, MID-JULY 1901

With the lines of battle between organized capital and organized labor more and more sharply drawn, and neither side willing to budge from basic principles, it did not take much to set off a new and more explosive conflict. The spark was a seemingly small and unimportant dispute over handling the baggage of a religious group arriving in San Francisco to hold a convention. The Morton Special Delivery Company, a nonunion firm, which did not belong to the Draymen's Association, was to handle the baggage. It had, however, subcontracted part of the job to a firm that was part of the Draymen's Association and that had union workers. Moreover, the Morton firm's owner, Henry Morton, was a vigorous opponent of the Teamsters' Union (*The San Francisco Examiner* July 21, 1901, 8; Knight 1960, 72).

The Teamsters' Union, therefore, decided not to handle the baggage, which was justified by their contract with the Draymen's Association that said that union drivers were to reject employment by nonunion firms. The union not only wanted to foster the union shop in transportation, but also to push back against the strongly anti-union attitude of Morton Special Delivery. As Michael Casey put it, "We stand by the proposition not to work for or with those who have shown an unfriendly spirit toward union men. We stand by that resolution" (*The San Francisco Examiner* July 20, 1901, 7).

Despite the contract they had with the union, the Draymen's Association (and behind it the Employers' Association) felt the Teamsters' Union had to be challenged and crushed, and now they had an excuse. It said its agreement with the Teamsters would be rendered null and void if the teamster members did not handle what Casey had labeled "hot cargo." They began to dismiss and lockout all teamsters who refused to obey the orders of their respective bosses to handle the baggage for Morton Special Delivery. The Draymen's Association began to hire scabs to take the places of ousted workers and took a stand amounting to an ultimatum to the teamsters: "quit the union or lose your job." The Draymen were pressured to take this stand by the Employers' Association, which reportedly met with the Draymen specifically on this issue (*The San Francisco Examiner* July 21, 1901, 18). Within a few days, almost a thousand teamsters Union men had been dismissed from their jobs, locked out because they refused to handle the "hot cargo" (*The San Francisco Examiner* July 23, 1901, 1).

During the first few days, the teamsters played a waiting game to see how things would develop and to put the responsibility for a wider strike upon the shoulders of the employers, while commencing with notifications and discussions with their allies in the City Front Federation. Jefferson D. Pierce, Pacific Coast organizer for the American Federation of Labor, visited Teamster headquarters and, after appraising the situation, telegraphed President Samuel Gompers about the lockout. Meetings were held with the Sailors' Union of the Pacific and representatives of the City Front Federation, but no decisions were made. Union pickets were sent to various key locations to watch and intercept any nonunion drivers, explain the situation to them, and try to influence them to join the union. This tactic was successful in at least one instance, when nonunion drivers, reportedly imported from Benicia, gave in and returned their teams to the stables (*The San Francisco Examiner* July 22, 1901, 2; July 23, 1901, 2).

At this point in the developing situation, the *Coast Seamen's Journal,* the organ of the Sailors' Union of the Pacific, published a powerful editorial in support of the teamsters, warning the entire labor community of the likely result of the actions of the employers:

> *There was but one thing left for the Teamsters to do, and that they promptly did; they refused to do the work of the non-union concern. At this juncture the Employers' Association showed its hand in the matter. The Draymen's Association, against its will,*

as it appears, had been forced into the secret order of industrial assassins, and acting upon the mandate of that body the Draymen notified their employees that they must either "quit the union or quit their jobs." This was a deliberate challenge of the Teamsters' right to maintain their organization; it was a challenge dictated in the spirit that has all along characterized the Employers' Association and its predecessors—the spirit of war and destruction to trade-unionism ... Should the trouble spread, as it undoubtedly will if the Employers' Association has its will ... the result to this city and port may be better imagined than described.

The Brotherhood of Teamsters may be depended upon to make the fight interesting for its opponents. Behind the Teamsters stand a large number of fellow trade-unionists who may also be depended upon to make a good run. It looks as though the crucial point in the conflict between the Employers' Association and Organized Labor has been reached. There is but one way that we can see at present in which an upshot of far-reaching effect upon the city can be forestalled, and that is by a counter organization, tacit or formal, of press and public to offset the inequitable and desperate policy of the Employers' Association. The only question at issue is as to whether or not men have the right to organize for their own protection and to hold their employers to the agreement made with them. The press and public can settle this question quickly and effectually. Unless they do, they will be responsible for whatever may happen as a consequence of leaving it to settlement by physical demonstration (July 24, 1901, 6).

POLICE AND CITY GOVERNMENT
SIDE WITH THE EMPLOYERS

Late July saw a new development, the decisive intervention of Mayor James Phelan's administration on the side of capital by detailing large numbers of police to help strikebreaking scabs destroy the union. Already by late July of 1901, over one-half of the city's police force, 300 out of 588 men, was detailed to protect the strikebreakers (*The San Francisco Examiner* July 27, 1901, 3; September 26, 1901, 12). This was initially done at the behest of the Draymen and not due to any need to protect law and order. On July 24, George Renner, the manager of the Draymen's Association, was quoted in *The San Francisco Examiner*: "We have had mounted police and patrolmen detailed to accompany the teamsters who are at work, not because of any overt act, but because prevention is better than cure. It will take some time ... to fill the places of all of the men who have refused to obey orders; but it will be accomplished in time" (*The San Francisco Examiner* July 24, 1901, 4).

City police were stationed on wagons (called "trucks"), driven by scabs, to act as guides and even drivers for those strikebreakers who did not know the city and to try to prevent union pickets from convincing them to join the union. Police not only acted as escorts for scabs, they sometimes even called for them in the morning at their homes and accompanied them home at night (*The San Francisco Examiner* July 28, 1901, 19). This intervention almost immediately led to conflict, with police squads attacking and beating union men in union-dominated neighborhoods in the south of the Market area, which led to retaliatory violence against the strikebreakers by angry members of the local working-class community. *The San Francisco Examiner* vividly described several incidents on July 25:

> *In the morning at 8 o'clock three non-union drivers*
> *were leaving C. B. Rode & Co.'s barn on Bryant*

Street, near Fifth, with trucks, and the police requested the union pickets to leave the teamsters alone. The pickets argued the matter and in the meantime a crowd of union sympathizers, numbering about 300, collected. The manager of Rode & Co. telephoned to police headquarters, and Captain Wittman, with a score of policemen, hurried to the scene. Wittman ordered his men to charge the crowd with clubs. The union men say the crowd was orderly and that the pickets were conducting themselves within the law. Four or five men were badly clubbed by Wittman and his squad. The crowd quickly dispersed. One of the drivers decided to join the union; the other two drove on with policemen on the trucks to protect them while going for loads.

In the afternoon about 4 o'clock the union sympathizers gathered in large numbers at Sixth and Folsom streets. A truck owned by McNab & Smith came along Sixth street ... The crowd closing around the truck forced the horses ... into the depression on one side of the street ... The crowd hooted and tried to persuade the driver to leave his seat. Someone threw a stone, which hit him on the back of the head. That decided him, and he made a break through the crowd to get away ... Two more teams, belonging to the same firm, came along and the crowd speedily persuaded their drivers to join the strike ... A policeman drove the dray down to the depot ... The crowd soon gathered again and Sergeant Campbell and eighteen men were sent to disperse the gathering, which they did with some display of force. (The San Francisco Examiner *July 25, 1901, 3*)

These events apparently led Teamsters' Union leaders Michael Casey and John McLaughlin to call out on strike almost all of the remaining union teamsters. By the next morning, a total of fifteen hundred men were on strike (*The San Francisco Examiner* July 25, 1901, 3).

With even more angry teamsters on strike, the confrontations between the local community of unionists and their supporters and scabs imported by employers from as far away as Bakersfield and Los Angeles quickly grew larger and more threatening. Police, who actively supported the bosses by protecting scabs and attacking workers, also were even more involved. *The San Francisco Examiner* reported on July 26:

> *About 6 o'clock last night a crowd of union sympathizers attacked a non-union driver on one of McNab & Smith's trucks at Bryant and Third streets. There were about thirty boys and a number of men; Policeman Porter was on the truck. Rocks were thrown and an effort was made to pull the non-union driver from his seat. A crowd quickly collected and in a couple of minutes, there were fully 500 people about the truck.*

> *Policeman Porter drew his club, but he could do little with it, because the crowd closed in on him. Policemen Harrison, Eastman and half a dozen others from the Southern station who were in the district, learned of the trouble and charged on the crowd with clubs. The crowd kept increasing until there were more than 1,000 people on the street. Rocks and other missiles were hurled at the truck. Policeman Porter was struck on the left leg and injured. A rock also struck Policeman Harrison. The patrolmen cracked a number of the more aggressive men with their clubs.*

> *As fast as the policemen cleared a way more men closed in on them. Fully twenty men were struck*

*with the clubs of the officers before the truck was
again started for the stables.*

*The crowd followed at a distance and continued to
hurl stones at the policemen, and the non-union driver
finally got his load to the barn at Eighth and Brannan
streets. Policeman Porter will be incapacitated for
duty by reason of the injury to his leg …*

*In the same neighborhood one of the trucks of
McNab and Smith that are used to carry fruit for
the California Cannery Company was disabled. A
nut had been removed from one of the front wheels,
and, without any warning, it came off, scattering
fruit all over the street. Cannery hands were called
out to carry the fruit into the sheds. The crowd
became large and troublesome and began hooting
the cannery employees. Sergeant Christensen, assisted
by Policemen Hook and Burdette, charged the
onlookers, who soon dispersed. (*The San Francisco
Examiner *July 26, 1901, 3)*

More incidents illustrating that a growing community
rebellion against the injustice of scabs and police trying to destroy
the Teamsters' Union was underway followed on the next day:

*Thomas Bryan, a Petaluma teamster, hired … by
McNab & Smith, was seriously injured while on his
way to supper by strike sympathizers on Thursday
night. Bryan had both arms broken and was otherwise
hurt … Policemen Peshon and P. L. Smith drew their
revolvers and dispersed a crowd of men at Second
and Folsom streets who had attacked the driver of
a team … In a clash which occurred between the
police and a crowd at Sixth and Folsom, John Ely, a
teamster … received a severe laceration of the scalp*

*from a club in the hands of Policeman Max Fenner ...
In a disturbance which occurred at Fifth and Bryant
streets last evening, Adolph Thiler, a cabinetmaker ...
was badly beaten by Policeman Peter J. Burdette ...
Over 300 policemen are at present engaged in
protecting the interests of the draying firms against
their striking employees. All available men have been
called to do actual police duty and are detailed either
as convoys to trucks and teams or are patrolling the
districts where trouble is most likely to arise. (*The San
Francisco Examiner *July 27, 1901, 3)*

THE EMPLOYERS' ASSOCIATION'S ULTIMATUM

The situation was still developing at the end of July when the
Employers' Association pressured various San Francisco capitalists
to force their workers to choose between their union and their jobs.
As *the San Francisco Examiner* (July 28, 1901, 19) reported:

*In many business houses yesterday the proprietors
summoned their employees and put the question
squarely to each one: "Will you take orders from
us, or from your union?" On the answer hung the
option of further employment. Those who elected to
stand by their labor organization were "given their
time"—that is to say, were paid off and dismissed.
Those who chose to remain at work were required to
write out their resignations from the union.*

The workers at the various San Francisco beer-bottling
establishments were presented with this ultimatum, as were
workers at local box-manufacturing factories and many members
of the porters and packers union. Most of the affected workers
stayed with the union and went on strike. It was clear to all that
the Employers' Association was behind this demand:

> *Inquiry among the employers at the different beer-bottling establishments led conclusively to the decision that their action had been prompted by the Employers' Association and foreshadowed the steps taken by other employers yesterday in asking men to choose between their labor organizations and their employment ... The employers made no secret of the fact that their action was concerted and the result of an understanding had in the Employers' Association.*
> (The San Francisco Examiner *July 28, 1901, 19)*

SAN FRANCISCO AND BAY AREA
UNIONS PREPARE TO FIGHT

With the situation reaching a crisis point, the San Francisco Labor Council gave its executive committee power to take any necessary defensive or offensive steps against the "arbitrary action of the Employers' Association." It also adopted a resolution that read in part:

> *Whereas, Organized labor of San Francisco and vicinity now finds itself menaced from every quarter by a secret body known as the Employers' Association, with the purpose of destroying the trades unions, thus denying the members thereof the right to combine for their own protection ... and*

> *Whereas, The trades unions have now and at all times in the past executed every possible means to insure amicable relations between employer and employee, and in event of dispute to bring about a restoration of harmony by conference, conciliation and concession, and*

> *Whereas, The Employers' Association has persistently rejected these steps and now seems determined to pursue its policy of strife and destruction ... and*

442

Whereas, The dangerous and unlawful motives of the Employers' Association are proved by its actions in forcing, by threats of retaliation and ruin, employers who are well disposed toward their employees ...

Resolved, That, until said Employers' Association makes formal declaration of its purposes and official personnel, it shall be regarded as having no legal right to exist and as having no claim to recognition ...

Resolved, That the San Francisco Labor Council pledges itself, and urges a like declaration by each of its constituent bodies, to stand firm to the principles upon which we are organized, the first of which is the right of the workers in all callings to combine for mutual help as individuals and as organizations ...

Resolved, That we reaffirm our position as favoring the adjustment of all existing and future disputes by means of conference between the parties involved ... failing acquiescence in this proposal by the employers concerned, the responsibility for the continuance or expansion of the present strikes, lockouts and boycotts must be laid upon that party which has proved itself unapproachable to reason and...to the appeals of common humanity. (The San Francisco Examiner *July 27, 1901, 3)*

FINAL ATTEMPTS TO CONCILIATE FAIL

True to their principles and word, the highest-level representatives of San Francisco's organized working class—the Labor Council, the City Front Federation, and the teamsters—were ready to meet and discuss the adjustment of any and all disputes with all appropriate parties. On the afternoon of July 29, even in the face of the blatant and continuous police aid given to the employers, they conferred with Mayor Phelan, the Municipal League's "Conciliation Committee," and some business representatives at the mayor's office to try to reach a compromise.

True to form, the Employers' Association refused to attend and meet with labor; the mayor had to take labor's proposals to the headquarters of the Employers' Association in the Mills Building. After meeting with the leaders of the Employers' Association, the mayor came away without an agreement even to start negotiations, only a response in the form of a letter from M. F. Michael, the association's attorney. The essence of this letter reprinted in full in the *Examiner*, was contained in the following paragraph:

> *I am instructed by the Executive Committee of the Employers' Association to advise you that the proposition thus submitted appears to the association not to present a satisfactory solution of the present difficulties; furthermore, that the association is of the opinion that an agreement in the shape proposed could not be adequately maintained or enforced. (July 30, 1901, 2)*

It was clear that the organized employers wanted total power over the workers. The exercise of such power was a main cause of the alienation that the workers had felt and were rebelling against. Collective power in a union gave the workers a feeling of wholeness and freedom they could gain no other way. As Sailors' Union of the Pacific's leader Andrew Furuseth commented to the press after the meeting,

> *It is not the unions that are bringing this upon the city. The employers ignore us entirely ... [T]hey will not recognize our committees or delegates or agents. They are willing to give the individual employment, but they are determined to crush the unions. They had no representatives at this afternoon's meeting in*

*the Mayor's Office, and of course there could be no
results. (*The San Francisco Call *July 30, 1901, 1)*

The lines were now drawn in the sand; it was up to working
people and their leaders to act.

JULY 30, 1901: GENERAL STRIKE
ON THE WATERFRONT

Immediately following the conciliation talks, the leaders of the
City Front Federation called a meeting for that same evening,
July 29. All the issues involved were carefully and thoroughly
discussed, and it was not until about midnight that the following
decision in favor of a general strike of all member unions was
made:

> *Resolved, That the full membership of the City
> Front Federation refuses to work on the docks of
> San Francisco, Oakland, Port Costa and Mission
> Rock and in the city of San Francisco, but that
> the steamships Bonita and Walla Walla, which
> sail tomorrow morning, and which have booked
> passengers, be allowed to go to sea with the union
> men of their crews. (*The San Francisco Examiner
> July 30, 1901, 1)*

While the leaders were deliberating, mass gatherings of rank-
and-file members were organized all over San Francisco, and, as
the night wore on, these union members were anxious for news.
About six hundred members of the Brotherhood of Teamsters were
assembled at the hall of the San Francisco Athletic Club at the
corner of Sixth and Shipley Streets. When Michael Casey arrived
after midnight and announced that the City Front Federation was
calling a general strike on the waterfront:

> *[A] scene of the wildest enthusiasm ensued. Cheer
> after cheer was given. Since the inception of the*

strike the teamsters have been compelled to fight the merchants and bosses single-handed, and it was generally admitted that the strikers would be ignominiously defeated unless other unions rendered immediate assistance. Thus the men had come to look on the City Front Federation, embracing the strongest combination of united labor on the Pacific Coast, as their most desirable ally.

After Business Manager Casey announced the decision of the City Front Federation, the Brotherhood of Teamsters decided by a unanimous vote to fight the strike out to the bitter end without regard to the cost or consequences. The brotherhood has in all almost 2,000 men now on strike. (The San Francisco Call *July 30, 1901, 1)*

The scene at California Hall, where the members of the Porters, Packers, and Warehousemen waited for word, was no less dramatic. The two thousand members of this union were ...

unanimous in wishing that a general strike would be ordered and could not understand why the men of the city front could not come to the same conclusion without the necessity of a lengthy session ... The guard at the door of the union's meeting place was the first man to receive the news. When he opened the door and announced to the anxiously waiting laboring men that their wishes had been granted and that on the morrow 16,000 men would quit work and enter the ranks of the strikers and the locked-out men the cheers were deafening. The men yelled themselves hoarse, for the announcement of the general strike meant that their fight was to be made the fight of every laboring man in this city. (The San Francisco Call *July 30, 1901, 7)*

Similar "tumultuous cheering" took place once the decision to strike was announced at the mass meetings of the sailors, the four longshoremen's locals, and other interested unions (*Coast Seamen's Journal* July 31, 1901, 11). Speaking before hundreds of sailors at their headquarters, Andrew Furuseth said that the "employers are determined to wipe out labor unions one after another ... There is no other way of having peace except by fighting for it" (Knight 1960, 77). The organized workers of San Francisco were practically unanimous on the need for a general strike on the waterfront to counter the attempt to crush their unions (*The San Francisco Call* July 30, 1901, 1).

There were ten striking unions with an approximate membership of sixteen thousand (see table 11.2).

TABLE 11.2: Membership Strength of Striking Unions July 30, 1901

Unions	Number of Members
Sailors' Union of the Pacific	4,500
International Longshoremen's Association (four branches)	4,500
Brotherhood of Teamsters	2,000
Porters, Packers, and Warehousemen	2,000
Pacific Coast Marine Firemen	1,500
Marine Cooks and Stewards	700
Piledrivers and Bridge Builders	300
Ship and Steamboat Joiners	300
Coal Cart Teamsters	200
Hoisting Engineers	75
Total	**16,075**

Source: *San Francisco Examiner*, July 30, 1901, 1

On July 30, these unions, organized as the City Front Federation, issued a statement on the causes of the strike, asserting the rights of the working class against "arrogant capital":

Having closely watched the trend of affairs throughout the country and being cognizant of the policy of the employers, which is to disrupt labor organizations … the Federation claims the right for its members to organize for their mutual benefit and improvement … We further claim the right to say how much our labor is worth and the conditions under which we will work. The Employers' Association, composed of the principal importing and jobbing concerns of this city … have tried with more or less success to destroy some of the smaller organizations, and as their minor successes gave them confidence, they reached out further with the idea that ultimately their plan would be successful …

In view of the fact that the teamsters were locked out the Federation found it absolutely necessary to take action … The Federation has exhausted all honorable means to have the difficulty adjusted … and finds that there is nothing left but to appeal to its membership to be true to the cause for which organized labor stands … We are satisfied that we have done everything we could to avert this crisis, but arrogant and designing capital willed it otherwise. Those individuals in society who would use their industrial power to rob us of our right of organization … must bear the responsibility for whatever may now take place. (The San Francisco Call *July 30, 1901, 1)*

The strike's aim was to economically punish the employers in order to put irresistible pressure on the Employers' Association to agree to negotiate a fair settlement that preserved and enhanced union power. Andrew Furuseth, secretary of the Sailors' Union of the Pacific, was elected chairman of the strike committee. He said at the outset that "We have dallied long enough with the Employers' Association … our action will teach them that we mean business. Every man is determined and the sooner the association appreciates this the better it will be for them and the business interests of this city and vicinity. All the talk has been done—this is action" (*The San Francisco Call* July 30, 1901, 7).

The all-out battle for the union rights of working people and against the Employers' Association was underway.

THE STRIKE LEADERS: FURUSETH AND CASEY

The top leadership for the strike was lodged in the persons of two men: Andrew Furuseth of the Sailors' Union of the Pacific, who was chairman of the Strike Committee, and Michael Casey of the Brotherhood of Teamsters, who was president of the City Front Federation. Furuseth had been a leader of the Sailors' Union almost from the founding of this union in a torch-lit meeting on the Folsom Street wharf on March 6, 1885. The militant unionism of Furuseth and the sailors' had developed out of the exceptionally abusive system developed by the shipping companies, boardinghouse owners, and ship captains, who had long worked together to keep the individual sailor in a state of perpetual indebtedness and semi-slavery. The strong feelings of injustice, the constant conflict with the bosses, and the rough-and-tumble brotherhood of the sea led to a special commitment to worker solidarity and class struggle on the part of the sailors.

It was the visionary unionist and utopian socialist Burnett G. Haskell who had pleaded the sailors' cause on the Folsom Street dock in 1885, but it was the two thousand militant sailors who immediately joined that made up the solid foundation of what already, by 1901, was a union steeped in struggle. The sailors had to constantly be ready to battle, because the capitalists, the captains, and the boardinghouse owners never gave them a rest. On August 7, 1901, the *Coast Seamen's Journal* published its call to battle in an editorial entitled "The Old Guard in Front," recalling the many bitter fights for the survival of their union:

> *Fortunately or unfortunately ... the Sailors have*
> *never had peace enough with their masters to allow*

of their growing fat and lazy. The present generation of the Union has been born to a heritage of trials and hardships, not so severe perhaps as those encountered by the men who founded the organization, but yet severe enough to call forth the best energies of every member. It should be in every man's care to see that he lacks in nothing to uphold the prestige of the Sailors' Union and to honor the memory of the men who fought to establish it on its present firm foundation.

The unanimity and enthusiasm shown by the seamen at the call of duty is proof of a spirit that counts no sacrifice too great in defense of principle. At the same time, it is well to reflect that it was only by such sacrifices in the past that the Union was rooted deep in the soil, and thus enabled to withstand the desperate assaults made upon it from time to time. Of the old Union boys who met on Folsom Street Dock in San Francisco on March 6, 1885, and dedicated the organization to everlasting life and glory, who carried its banner so high through all the dark days and years that followed, that its folds caught the light of heaven through mist and murk—of those men, some are with us still, others are scattered throughout the world spreading the fame and lesson of the Union they helped to form, while still others have passed into line with the undying dead whose memory inspires the world's greatest deeds for humanity. No member of the Sailors' Union, standing to-day upon the verge of a conflict that, no matter what comes, will mark the greatest epoch in the history of the Union, but must feel … as men always feel when they go into a clean fight for a good cause—that victory cannot fail us except by chance … In this fight … the line is *clearly drawn between the two great forces, the labor movement and the Employers' Association.*

Every man, then, may feel that when he strikes, his blow will tell in the right spot.

Comrades, remember the past of our grand old Union and be true to its traditions!

The labor movement and the lovers of humanity on the Pacific Coast, throughout the United States and the world, are watching and waiting upon us. The Union is our shield in peace and war. Let us take it up and say, as did the Spartan mother to her boy: "With it or upon it!" (Coast Seamen's Journal *August 7, 1901, 7)*

Like many of his fellow union members, Andrew Furuseth was an immigrant and was both completely devoted to his union and stoically uncompromising toward its enemies. Unlike many of his mates, he was intellectual and solitary. When threatened with a jail sentence for strike activity, he told an interviewer that he was not afraid of a jail cell, since, "They can't put me in a smaller room than I've always lived in, they can't give me plainer food than I've always eaten, and they can't make me lonelier than I've always been" (Chiles 1981, 5).

Furuseth expressed his philosophy about the labor movement—how it was a freedom movement for the workers—and the requirements of his time in his own words:

The labor union of to-day is really a powerful bulwark of liberty and a mighty aid to the advancement of civilization. This sounds large, I know, but the claim is none too large. It encourages the workingmen to a feeling of oneness with their fellows—a feeling that promotes gentleness in their relations with one another, both in sickness and in health. It teaches men to study their condition in the world ... and it leads them to struggle the harder to move upward. It has a strong influence toward counteracting dangerous tendencies toward political and industrial absolutism. And finally, it is a preventative of that degree of competition which makes for social regression. Without labor organizations, the competition of laborer with laborer would have full play, and full play would be ruinous with capital selfish as capital always has been and always will be. Unchecked competition in the labor world means a gradually sinking standard of wages, causing a gradually sinking standard of living—less of comfort, less of leisure, less of light, less of sweetness, more of barbarism.

Andrew Furuseth (1854–1938)
Leader of the Sailors' Union of the Pacific, chairman of the Strike Committee for the 1901 General Strike on the San Francisco waterfront. [Courtesy of the Bancroft Library, University of California, Berkeley.]

Combinations of capital must be met by combinations of labor, or there will be an increase of servility, an increase of poverty among the masses, and diminishing manhood and womanhood. (The San Francisco Examiner *August 1, 1901, 1, 8)*

In 1901, Michael Casey of the Teamsters' Union was a no less impressive figure, as *The San Francisco Examiner* reported:

Mr. Casey is thoroughly representative of the great class of which he is a leader. He is a toiler, and has been one since childhood. His tall, muscular form says work: his determined blue eyes and his bronzed seamed face say work: his manner of carrying himself says work. He is forty years of age and looks older; he is a native of Ireland, but has spent all save the few opening years of life in the United States, and most of his boyhood and all since then in California; and gained an education in the public schools and a private business college of this city. He has a wife and six children, and is dependent on his personal earnings for a livelihood.

You couldn't help feeling friendly to Casey, no matter what your interest might dictate; for there are honesty and kindliness in his deep-set blue eyes, and there's earnestness in every line of his rugged countenance.

He feels that the present strike is a symptom of a widespread condition, and that it is very much more significant and vastly more important than is generally believed. He does not merely talk this way, understand—he FEELS it; and when he speaks on the subject his voice vibrates with sincerity,

"It has seemed to us recently that a considerable number of the heavy employers in San Francisco have determined

453

to crush the labor unions. Indeed in some cases within the last two weeks there have been open declarations obliging men to choose between membership in the unions and retention of their employment. Under the circumstances the only rational course open to us has been to stand for the principle attacked, even at the cost of an extensive strike ... "

He interprets the attitude of California capitalists as sympathetic with the attitude of capitalists in the greater money centers ... "There is a tremendous change in process," he said, looking thoughtful and serious. "A man can't consider the recent centralization of capital in the other States without something of a shiver, if he is a breadwinner. Every day narrows the freedom of individual capitalists and substitutes a new centralization of power. The formation of the Billion-Dollar Steel Trust is really one of the most threatening signs of modern times—and only a sign, mark you, a sign of a sweeping tendency."

Against the steadily centralizing sway of capital, he feels that labor must offer a steadily unifying front. The labor unions he regards as a necessity for the preservation of freedom as we now understand freedom ... he has a pretty definite notion that capital as capital is "void and empty from any dram of mercy." His own strength and the co-operation of men in his own walk of life are THEIR safeguards he concludes.

"The working classes must stick together," he observed. "When their unions are assailed they must resist. Unless they do, there will be a gradual sinking backward into the conditions out of which we have struggled." (The San Francisco Examiner *August 1, 1901, 1, 8)*

As immigrants from Scandinavia and Ireland respectively, Furuseth and Casey were representative of the unions they led, and this fostered group solidarity. In 1900, boatmen and sailors made up the fifth-largest male occupation in the port city of San Francisco, and by far the largest group of boatmen and sailors (38.2 percent) were from Scandinavia. United States-born workers made up only 12.1 percent of San Francisco's boatmen and sailors; the rest were immigrants, with the Scandinavians dominant. In 1900, draymen, hackmen, and teamsters made up the seventh-largest male occupation in San Francisco, and immigrants from Ireland were by far the largest group, making up 36.4 percent. United States-born workers made up only 20.6 percent of San Francisco's draymen, hackmen, and teamsters in 1900; the remainder were immigrants (computed from data in US Census Bureau 1904, 720–723).

Scabs and Conflicts

The core strategy of the capitalists was to break the strike through the massive use of scab labor. But on the day before the general strike on the waterfront was declared, *The San Francisco Call* announced that seventy-two nonunion teamsters, whom the Draymen's Association had recruited from Bakersfield to help break the Teamsters' Union, had left the city to return to their homes. They had been convinced of the justice of the union cause, no longer wanted to be scabs, and had even become union men! As the *Call* (July 30, 1901, 7) reported, "Before departure most of them had been won over to the side of the brotherhood and had been made honorary members. Although they had come in passenger cars at the expense of the Draymen's Association, they were shipped back in a freight car attached to a Santa Fe freight train."

The loss of these men, and no doubt many more who left individually or in smaller groups not reported by the press, put the bosses in a bind. The unions were successful in convincing large numbers of men not to scab on the strike, threatening the rapid defeat of the Employers' Association. It therefore began to send out employment agents to recruit strikebreakers from groups among the population who had fewer reasons to be in solidarity with unions: men and boys from farms and smaller, interior towns; soldiers returning from the Philippines; students from University of California, Berkeley, and Stanford University; Chinese, Filipinos, and African Americans from as far away as the Midwest. The use of people of color as strikebreakers had long been a common and reprehensible tactic of the capitalists to divide the workers, break their solidarity, and get them fighting amongst themselves. Unfortunately, workers too-often fell into the trap of supporting white supremacy and established discriminatory, all-white unions. Banned from membership by almost all AFL unions, African Americans and other people of color often had very little incentive to refrain from strikebreaking against those who refused to welcome them into the American labor movement (Knight 1960, 79).

The use of African American strikebreakers led, on the very first day of the general strike, to the first of what were to be many shootings, most of them by nonunion men who were carrying guns. The employers also had well-connected attorneys ready to defend scabs who engaged in violence. *The Examiner* reported on the incident:

> *Roscoe Horn and William Ferguson, non-union teamsters, fired eight shots into a crowd of strikers yesterday at Eleventh and Harrison streets. They are colored men employed by G. W. Emmons & Co. draymen. Patrick Lynch, a union teamster, residing at 351 Eleventh Street, was wounded in the hip by one of the shots ... In telling the story of the affray Ferguson said: "Horn and I were on our way to work when at the corner of Eleventh and Harrison streets we were met by a gang of teamsters who yelled at us*

and then began throwing stones. I drew my revolver and fired a shot in the air to scare them. A crowd that was at Eleventh and Bryant streets was attracted by the report and came towards us. We were between two mobs and they began throwing stones. We then fired directly at them and they scattered. I fired five shots and Horn three. We then made our way to the stables."

Sergeant Campbell stated that the crowd was threatening in its attitude and a non-union teamster had been beaten only a few moments before. Lynch, the wounded man, stated that he had no intention of molesting the men, but was walking across the street when he was struck.

Both Horn and Ferguson were released from custody on $100 cash bail. Bond Clerk Greeley says he fixed the bail at that small sum on the assurance of Attorney Joseph Coffey that it was an unimportant affair ... Attorney Coffey has been retained to defend non-union teamsters who get into trouble. Lawyer Coffey is the attorney for Chief of Police William P. Sullivan and the Chinese gamblers. (The San Francisco Examiner *July 31, 1901, 2*)

Over the next few weeks, numerous similar incidents were reported in the newspapers. Below is a sample of events that illustrate a number of characteristics of the strike, including: several shootings and near-shootings, the strong support that the workers had among the mass of the people, rank-and-file outrage at the scabs and the police who helped them; and the public's developing engagement in what was becoming a community rebellion for the freedom to organize and defend collective working class rights:

*For twenty minutes yesterday, between 4 and 5 o'clock,
traffic was blocked on Market Street at the crossing of
Third by a truck belonging to Farnsworth & Ruggles,
draymen, and driven by a non-union teamster.*

*The truck was heavily loaded with boxes and the day
was hot. The asphalt pavement in spots had assumed
the consistency of mucilage and in front of Lotta's
fountain one wheel settled and stuck fast. The truck
was anchored and the driver did not seem to know
enough to get out of the hole. The other wheels of the
truck rested on the car tracks …*

The crowd was not complimentary.

*"Get him out, officer," they shouted as the policeman,
who was acting as escort, took the lines. It was evident
that the horses were badly frightened by the shouting
and surging crowd.*

*"Them's union horses," remarked a bystander, "and
they won't be driven by any but a union man."*

*There were women in the crowd and it was evident that
their sympathies were all against the non-union driver.*

*"Go for him, Jimmy," shouted one of them, as a young
man stepped up close to the driver. "He's taking the bread
and butter out of our mouths, Jimmy, go for him."*

*It began to look like a fight … but the police came in
with drawn clubs and quelled the fighting instinct. The
woman, who had urged on "Jimmy" turned away and,
in a disgusted manner, said to a little girl by her side:*

*"Come along Maggie, let's go home and make your
father's supper."* (The San Francisco Examiner
August 1, 1901, 2)

C. F. Blair, a non-union teamster, was beaten at Buchanan Street and Golden Gate Avenue yesterday morning ... As a group of men moved toward him in a threatening manner, Blair drew a revolver from his pocket and began to back away from them. They approached closer, whereupon he pulled the trigger. The cartridge did not explode, and he snapped the trigger repeatedly, but without firing a single bullet at his pursuers. Seeing that Blair's pistol and cartridges were harmless, they closed in upon him and beat him over the head and shoulders. (The San Francisco Examiner *August 1, 1901, 2)*

John Telford, a non-union teamster in the employ of McNab & Smith, who resides at 100 Park Hill avenue, was ambushed Saturday night ... by a gang of unknown men. As he passed a clump of bushes on his way home they made known their presence by firing a volley of stones. Facing his assailants, he drew a revolver ... and ... fled to the house of Robert Ewing ... The stone throwers followed to the door, several displaying revolvers ... The situation was critical. Revolvers were flourished in the crowd, stones were thrown and threats were freely made ... The approach ... of two policemen ... was the signal for the dispersal of the crowd. (The San Francisco Examiner *August 5, 1901, 4)*

Attacked by a crowd of strike sympathizers, yesterday morning Henry Davies, a non-union teamster, used a revolver with probably fatal effect. He fired one shot, which struck and seriously wounded Samuel Cole, a teamster who resides at 57 Clara Street. Davies is eighteen years of age ... While going to work he was set upon by six men at the corner of Howard street and New Montgomery, nearly opposite his home.

He was knocked down and kicked. Upon regaining his feet Davies drew his revolver and fired one shot at his assailants, who ran in every direction. Cole, who was struck, was removed subsequently by his comrades ... The bullet entered his left side and penetrated his lungs. He will probably die. (The San Francisco Examiner *August 7, 1901, 3)*

Wilfred Horton, a non-union colored stevedore, was attacked by strike sympathizers while on his way to work yesterday morning and, after firing his own revolver, was severely wounded in the shoulder. (The San Francisco Examiner *August 8, 1901, 1)*

The union leadership counseled against such violence, recognizing that it could backfire, lose the support of public opinion and even bring in the state militia, something the Employers' Association wanted. Strike Chairman Furuseth stated in a speech on August 8 for example: "If you want us to win this struggle for human liberty you must make a solemn promise to yourself not to allow any one to induce you in any way to break the peace." (The San Francisco Examiner *August 9, 1901, 2)*

On August 21, the *Coast Seamen's Journal*, in its review of the situation up to that point in time, made the following comments:

There never was a cleaner and juster fight than that now being made by the trade-unions of San Francisco in defense of a principle dear to every man of intelligence and ambition; if public opinion amounts to anything, as we believe it does; there never was a better chance of victory for labor. If the fight is lost it will be because of the forfeiture of public support, and that can only be caused by an overt act on the part of the strikers, or attributable to them. The conduct of the latter up to the present time is a fair assurance that no such act will be committed in the future except upon provocation beyond ordinary human endurance to withstand. In such event the persons in authority responsible for it will be convicted of a terrible, an indescribable, crime. (Coast Seamen's Journal *August 21, 1901, 7)*

Davies Shoots Cole

During an August 6, 1901 altercation, scab driver Henry Davies shot striking teamster Sam Cole in the chest. [Drawing from *The San Francisco Call*, August 7, 1901.]

The employers' importation of scabs, often by railroad from distant locations, continued throughout the strike, but the unions were able to effectively counter the technique by stationing pickets along the railroad to talk to potential scabs and get most of them to defect to the union even before they got to San Francisco. The unions were aided by the fact that the employers lied to potential scabs about conditions in San Francisco. As a result, many men were recruited into the union cause. African Americans recruited to be scabs were often successfully invited to join the union cause, and at least one of them, George Smith, became a picket for the City Front Federation, acting as a union delegate to talk to other African Americans to induce them to join the unions and not to scab (*The San Francisco Examiner* September 23, 1901, 4). *The Examiner* reported:

> *Seven men of forty-seven recruited at Cincinnati to take the places of the strikers in San Francisco reached the city yesterday and were stowed away on the steamer Colon at the Pacific Mail Dock. Forty men, who said they were induced by misrepresentations to come here, left the overland train at Sacramento. They had listened to the statements of union men who went up the road and, learning the condition of affairs, they refused to take the places of the striking stevedores and teamsters.*

> *The seven men who decided to go to work, one of whom is colored, were brought ... to the Long Wharf at Oakland by a special train, guarded by railroad police. From the wharf they were taken to the mail dock by a tug, on which were Sergeant Wolf and a policeman of the San Francisco force ...*

> *Agents of the City Front Federation met the Eastern laborers at Reno, and when the train reached Sacramento nearly all the men had determined*

not to proceed to San Francisco. The gang which left Cincinnati was composed of thirty-two whites and fifteen colored men ... The colored men were gathered at the levees at Cincinnati ...

*Curt Hall, President, Presley T. Johnson, Secretary, D. D. Sullivan, Treasurer, and George Ward of the Sacramento Council of Federated Trades, were at the depot on the arrival of the train. They took the laborers to eating houses, where at the expense of the council they were given the only warm meal they had since they left Cincinnati ... After their hunger was appeased each man was given a dollar. They were destitute. They were taken to an employment office, where all were furnished employment in Sacramento and on nearby ranches (*The San Francisco Examiner *September 21, 1901, 7)*

As stated above, strikebreakers were also recruited from local universities. To try to cut off this source for scabs, W. H. Goff, president, and Ed Rosenberg, secretary of the Labor Council, addressed a letter to Benjamin Ide Wheeler, president of the University of California, requesting him to prevent strikebreaking activities by members of the university community. Wheeler refused, stating that, "The university is the most important instrument that we possess for preventing the crystallization of society into fixed strata. Let us do nothing to hamper it in the fullest exercise of this, its work" (*Coast Seamen's Journal* September 11, 1901, 2).

In their response to Wheeler's justification of the use of students as scabs, Goff and Rosenberg defended the working peoples cause with wit and sarcasm:

Do you think that a university can prevent the process of crystallization in society? We are only plain workingmen, but we venture to express our opinion that your university education is as powerless to prevent the crystallization of society as it is to prevent the crystallization of primary molecules. This, however, is little to our present purposes. We have a more serious matter than crystallization to consider. We are only anxious to prevent the pulverization of the workingmen, and we ask you if the University of California exists for the prevention of "the crystallization of society into fixed strata," or is its business to help club the workingmen, who support it, into fixed slaves? We ask for a plain answer, Dr. Wheeler. Please crystallize your verbiage into yes or no.

A last word and a plain one: The University is supported by the people of California. It exists by their will, and ought to reflect their ideas ... as the people control the revenues we shall have something to say as to what those revenues shall amount to. Be perfectly assured that so long as the University remains what it ought to be, the school of the people, it will have the support of the people. When it becomes an instrument in the hands of the rich to grind the faces of the poor, something is going to happen. What, in your opinion, would be the result if the revenues of the University were to undergo a process of crystallization? (Coast Seamen's Journal *September 11, 1901, 3)*

POLICE AND SPECIAL DEPUTY VIOLENCE

The workers fighting for their rights were up against not only scabs and employers, the forces of the state in the form of city authorities were also always on the side of the employers. Chief of Police Sullivan and head of the Police Commission Newhall, a member of a wealthy landowning family, were completely against unions and the strike. The police chief secretly instructed his men to use force to unconstitutionally prevent free association and drive union men off the streets. An *Examiner* reporter was able to acquire a copy of an extraordinary speech Chief Sullivan made to members of the various police watches on September 5:

> *I am dissatisfied with the conduct of you men toward the strikers. I have gone about the city and seen my police chatting with strikers. You have neglected your duty by being too lenient with the strikers. I warn you that by so doing you are not carrying out your instructions.*
>
> *The strikers must be driven from the streets. You must see that this is done. Keep them from congregating on the street corners. Drive them to their homes and see that they are kept there. The strikers must not be allowed on the streets ...*
>
> *If any of you men do not feel disposed to carry out these orders you can send in your resignations and go and join the strikers. I am going to have policemen who obey me ...*
>
> *I do not want you men to speak to any one of what I have said.* (The San Francisco Examiner *September 6, 1901, 1)*

Acting on the spirit of the chief's instructions, members of the police force also went out disguised as longshoremen to provoke trouble with union men on the waterfront, acting as provocateurs to try to incite violence. As *The Examiner* reported on September 10:

> *Lieutenant of Police William Price ... has been making efforts to obey Chief Sullivan's order to drive*

union men "off the earth." Saturday night Sullivan's
subordinate sent Policeman P. N. Herlihy out in
disguise to provoke trouble with union pickets along
the water front. Price is in command of the harbor
police in the absence of Captain Dunlevy. Without
the knowledge or consent of his commanding officer,
Price took it upon himself to incite union men to
commit offenses ... Following out this scheme Price
and four policemen arrested twenty-four union men
and charged all but one with the heinous offense
of being drunk. (The San Francisco Examiner
September 10, 1901, 5)

Later that month, Lieutenant Price ordered wholesale arrests
of union men, without cause, again charging them as drunks.
In three days in mid-September, at least 104 union men were
reportedly arrested in this way (*The San Francisco Examiner*
September 24, 1901, 4).

The Employers' Association had a problem: there were not
enough police available to guard every truck and dray and carry
out the chief's instructions to drive the union men off the streets.
Already by July 31, there were four hundred police detailed to ride
on and guard trucks all day. This was over two-thirds of the total
police force and the maximum number the police department
could spare for such work. Dozens of teams and drivers were ready
to go out, but could not due to lack of police protection, adding
to the tie-up of the waterfront area (*The Examiner* August 1, 1901,
2). This led to the city authorities, at the behest of the Employers'
Association, to adopt the policy of hiring and deputizing large
numbers of "Special Policemen," questionable characters who
could then engage in violence under the cloak of authority. There
were already 125 "specials" by August 12, when two hundred
more were sworn in. These paid guards were armed with pistols
and clubs (*The San Francisco Examiner* August 12, 1901, 1).

The Police Commission, at the request of the Employers' Association, eventually appointed 685 special policemen, giving the employers a greater number of policemen than were on the regular force. Even though some of the appointments were later revoked, the very large number of "specials" was nevertheless remarkable.

The Examiner (August 28, 1901, 1) pointed out that the commission rushed through the appointments without a full inquiry into the character of the applicants. Teamsters' Union men also noted "that many of the policemen on duty have been receiving little presents and other favors for their service," and complained that the policemen should be strictly nonpartisan, but clearly were not (*The San Francisco Examiner* August 2, 1901, 2).

Given these facts, it is remarkable that only a few men were killed and several hundred injured during the strike. There could have easily been many more casualties. That there were not is a tribute to the overall restraint shown by the strikers, who were given great provocation. There were many newspaper reports of police and special deputies attacking strikers, including these from *The San Francisco Examiner*:

> *While thus employed Harris ordered Griffith to move on. A fight followed, and Griffith took Harris' cane from him. Another man took the Special Policeman's revolver. Feld then arrested Griffith, clubbing him so severely that he was sent to the receiving Hospital. (August 4, 1901, 29)*

> *Two non-union teamsters, who imagined that they were to be attacked by some men who were chatting on the sidewalk at the southwest corner of Sutter street and Grant avenue last night, drew revolvers and fired across the street. The knot of men scattered ... Women screamed and dodged into doorways to escape the flying bullets. When the revolvers of the non-union men were empty they scurried away and took refuge in an opium den on Bush street, leaving one wounded man*

*behind them on the sidewalk and another nursing his
side, which was grazed by a bullet that went through
his coat ... The Police Commission at its last meeting
gave them permission to carry the revolvers they used
last night. (August 18, 1901, 1)*

*Policeman Orman H. Knight was found guilty of
battery yesterday for having clubbed James Madison,
a marine engineer, in front of the Oceanic dock
about a week ago. (August 22, 1901, 4)*

*Peter Callahan, a marine fireman, living at 542
Harrison street, who was doing duty as a picket in
the ranks of the strikers, was shot and perhaps fatally
wounded early last night by Edward Furey, a special
policeman, who was recently appointed by Chief of
Police Sullivan, given a star and permitted to carry
a revolver. Witnesses of the shooting state that Furey
was the aggressor. (August 22, 1901, 2)*

*Otto C. Colby, a recent arrival in the city, carrying
a club and revolver provided by the Curtin Detective
Agency, used that club yesterday on John Lavin, a
marine fireman, beating him within an inch of his
life. The assault occurred at the coal bunkers of the
Pacific Coast Company on Beale street, where Colby
claimed to be on duty as a special policeman, although
he was without a star, had never been sworn in and
could show no warrant of authority. Lavin received
two long and deep cuts on his scalp. His right ear was
almost torn off and behind it was another cut on his
scalp. On his right arm were many bruises inflicted
with the club. (August 24, 1901, 2).*

*C. Falkner, one of Chief Sullivan's recent appointees
as a special policeman, fired five shots last night into*

*a crowd of young men at Turk and Jones streets ...
Falkner is one of John Curtin's force. For several days
he has been riding around on a truck with a non-
union teamster. He was walking up Turk street ...
when ... one of the men in a crowd standing there
made some remark. Falkner resented it, and some
blows were exchanged. The special then ran into the
middle of the street and drew his revolver ... fired
five times at the young men. (August 28, 1901, 5)*

HIGH MORALE, MILITANT STRUGGLE: MASS MEETINGS, DEMONSTRATIONS, AND LABOR SOLIDARITY

To keep morale high during what was a long and difficult strike, a number of mass meetings and at least two major organized union demonstrations took place. The first demonstration, on August 24, was a "parade for unionism." About nine thousand people took part, with the biggest contingents coming from the longshoremen, teamsters, sailors, machinists, and associated trade unions, the packers, porters, and warehousemen, and the marine firemen (*The San Francisco Examiner* August 25, 1901, 17).

A much bigger event took place on Labor Day, September 2, 1901. Under headings like "Army of Labor Marches Twenty Thousand Strong" and "Workers Furnish An Object Lesson," *The Examiner* described what it called "the largest outpouring in the annals of San Francisco," adding, "It was more than a mere display bent on holiday observance. The men in the ranks were there for a loftier purpose" (September 3, 1901, 1).

The *Coast Seamen's Journal* (September 4, 1901, 7) described the parade in detail: "A close estimate places the numbers in the parade at 20,601. In addition there were one hundred and fifty carriages and several wagonettes occupied by the women unionists, eight floats and a dozen bands."

The approximately twenty thousand marchers were divided into five union divisions, the largest contingents being three thousand Longshoremen, twelve hundred sailors, eleven hundred boilermakers and boilermakers' helpers, one thousand teamsters, one thousand machinists and one thousand packers, porters and warehousemen. The fifth division was made up of the City Front Federation:

> *[I]t was so large that it had to be divided into three sections. Marshall Ed Anderson wore a uniform and the longshoremen of four unions followed him, marching eight abreast and in close order ... The warehousemen from Crockett and Port Costa came down to join in this part of the display, and there was also a representative body of machinists from Vallejo. "In Union There is Strength" and "United We Stand" were conspicuous mottoes.*

> *The shipjoiners, calkers, riggers and hoisting engineers were followed by the attractive float of the marine painters, a sloop decorated in red, white and blue and filled with merry children. The piledrivers and trestle builders took out a donkey engine and piledriver. The engine tooted clamorously and the piledriver was worked with vigor ...*

> *The Brotherhood of Teamsters and the sand teamsters headed the second section of the Fifth Division and were cheered everywhere. The brotherhood showed a new silk flag and a banner announcing the union's organization on August 18, 1900 ...*

> *Then, making up the last section of the Fifth Division and bringing the procession to a close, came the Marine Firemen, the Sailors of the Seamen's Union, many of whom were in their natty uniforms of white*

*and blue, and the marine cooks and stewards. The
marching of this section was noticeably fine. (*The
San Francisco Examiner *September 3, 1901, 2)*

At the rally after the march, several speakers, including strike
leader Andrew Furuseth, addressed the workers. Furuseth said
the workers were winning the strike, that the employers had tried
starvation, scabs, and dividing the labor force, but had failed to
break the strike. Their final tactic, he correctly predicted, would be
to try to bring in soldiers and cause rioting. He urged the assembled
to defeat this tactic by turning "yourselves into martyrs. Suffer any
indignity. But don't let them draw you into any violence. I was told
three months ago that we would be forced into a strike, incited to
violence, and then soldiers would be called in. This was to break
the organization of labor. If you don't know what to do, find out
what your enemies want you to do and then—don't do it." (*The San
Francisco Examiner* September 3, 1901, 4).

Another way to unite and inspire the people was through
mass rallies. Several were held, but probably the most important
was held on September 21, at the Metropolitan Temple, because
it highlighted the powerful oration of Father Peter C. Yorke, a
local Catholic priest.

Father Yorke had gathered a following. He became a key
player in the strike because of his ability to speak clearly about
the key issues in the struggle. Yorke had been reluctant to get
involved, but he was at last convinced. He said,

*We were face to face with a most serious condition
of affairs, that the labor unions of California were
threatened with extinction and that a cavalcade ...
on horseback was formed for the charge to ride
roughshod over the wage-earners of this city and the
State. Being so convinced, my duty was plain, and
all my powers were at the disposition of the men who
were battling so nobly for the elementary rights of
American citizenship.*

*It will be seen, therefore, that I did not push myself
into this controversy. I held back as long as I could ...
But when I was asked by those who had a right to ask
me, whose need gave them a claim upon me, from
whose ranks I am sprung, who are bone of my bone
and flesh of my flesh, mine own people, who am I
that I should refuse them what is theirs? (*The San
Francisco Examiner *September 25, 1901, 4)*

Speaking to the workers at an evening meeting, Yorke argued
that as a Catholic priest he was ...

*Sent out from that little home in Nazareth where
Jesus and Joseph worked for their daily bread. And
if being such, if I were not found on the side of the
poor, when I go back to my Master he would say to
me, "I never knew you."*

*I owe no apology to anybody to speak in behalf of
labor, but I should owe an apology to the past, to the
great men of the past, and to those who founded my
church, if I were to be found in any place except the
place I am to-night. (*The San Francisco Examiner
September 22, 1901, 19)*

Yorke then went on to discuss his view of the real meaning of
the current struggle for freedom and the duty of working people:

*I believe that you are engaged in a struggle that goes
down to the very foundation of things ... You are
fighting for a principle, and it is principle that makes
life worth living, ... It is principle that gives dignity
to everything that men do ... Between the people
who were locked out and the Employers' Association,
there was a difference of principle and that difference
of principle cannot be compromised ...*

The principle of the Employers' Association ... practically all the capital in the city of San Francisco engaged in wholesale and manufacturing business, and I am afraid, the banks also—is that unionism must be destroyed ... there must be no compromise with unionism; unionism must be torn up by the roots, cut up and thrown in the fire ... That is their principle.

I believe that the principle of the workingmen, not the teamsters alone, not of the City Front Federation, but of all the other unions of workingmen in the city is, that unionism must be preserved ...

All the rich men and hangers-on of the rich men of the city got together—against what? Against the teamsters? Not much. Against the longshoremen? By no means. Against every man and every women who is earning wages in the city of San Francisco, in the State of California ...

If the rich men are all sticking together ... what is the duty of the people who earn wages? Is it not their duty to stick together as close, if not closer, than the rich men? The poor have nobody to defend them but themselves, let me tell you again and again. You have nobody but yourselves ... The rich men unite against you, and it is necessary for them to be united, it is ten thousand times more necessary for every man and woman of you to stand shoulder to shoulder, and to be knit together with bands of steel ...

So I say to you that the man who tries to put division between union men and union men is an emissary of the devil ... if you are a man who is earning wages, a union man committed to union principles, you

Laurence H. Shoup

> *are a brother to every other union man. (*The San
> Francisco Examiner *September 22, 1901, 20)*

Father Yorke subsequently wrote several articles for *The Examiner*, and two of these are worth briefly quoting as well. One dealt with the question of violence and nonviolence:

> *Before I close let me say one word on the general question of violence. I have warned the men against it, but I am beginning to cast in my mind if there be not worse things than violence. Violence is to be reprobated when the law protects you, but if the law is perverted, what then? The action of the police in this city, especially within the past few days, has been intolerable. I have seen an old man with gray hair and of venerable aspect ridden down and clubbed by one of Sullivan's Bashi Bazouks⁴. Every hour peaceable citizens are held up, searched, robbed, assaulted and there appears to be no remedy. Never in Russia did the police act as they are acting to-day on the water front of San Francisco and in our streets.*
>
> *People of California, what is done to-day to the longshoremen may be done to you tomorrow.*
>
> *Wage earners of San Francisco, will you stand by and see your brethren clubbed into submission to the Employers' Association? The object of this violence is not to keep the peace, but to compel the men to return to service. When the strike leaders protested to Mayor Phelan, what was the answer? Listen to it, ye freemen: "If they don't want to be clubbed ...go to work."*
>
> *As of old the refractory slaves were lashed into obedience, so now American citizens in San Francisco*

---

4   A metaphor referring to irregular soldiers of the Ottoman Empire known for their "lack of discipline"; literally, damaged head (Turkish).

are to be clubbed into slavery. How long will ye stand it, ye wage earners of San Francisco?

*It is your fight. The police that terrorize the sailors to-day will terrorize the clerks, the mechanics, to-morrow. It is time for you to think! And as for me, if the responsibility of giving advice should again be put upon me, I should consider long and earnestly if there are not worse things than violence, and if the American Constitution does not call us to preserve our liberties even at a sacrifice. (*The San Francisco Examiner *September 26, 1901, 3)

Father Yorke Addresses the Working Class
During August and September of 1901, Catholic priest Peter C. Yorke spoke before audiences of San Francisco, encouraging them to unify and continue to struggle until victory, because "gold has no mercy." [Drawing from *The San Francisco Call* August 9, 1901.]

In a different article, Father Yorke also put what he saw as the real issue squarely before the people:

> *Again and again let me insist upon it, the real*
> *question at issue is not between the Employers'*
> *Association and a few leaders of the Teamsters. The*
> *real question is, shall one union, a rich men's union,*
> *destroy the other unions, the poor men's unions.*
> *There is no wage earner in California who is not*
> *affected ... It is a fight between the rich and the*
> *poor. The rich refuse the poor their rights, especially*
> *their right to organize. This is the issue, the whole*
> *issue, and there is none other. Oh, that the wage*
> *earners of California would realize it ... God help*
> *them if the rich win. Gold has no mercy. In past*
> *centuries it has ground the faces of the poor, to-day*
> *its power is ten thousand times increased.* (The San
> Francisco Examiner *September 27, 1901, 3)*

Workers and their unions around the country agreed with Father Yorke and recognized the great importance of this struggle for freedom, and came to the aid of the San Francisco strikers. In early August, for example, workers in Portland, Oregon, began organizing their own City Front Federation to help their California brothers and sisters, and workers in both that city and Astoria, Oregon, used pickets to prevent scabs from being recruited and sent to San Francisco (*The San Francisco Examiner* August 8, 1901, 2).

Twenty-three unions and their members, making up the Western Labor Union in Butte, Montana, organized a boycott of goods imported from companies connected to the Employers' Association:

> *To-day a large delegation of the union men of the*
> *city, representing the various unions ... paid a*
> *visit to the firms complained of and informed the*

*managers that the union men of Butte were standing
by the San Francisco men and warned them at once
to cease handling the goods that are under ban. No
threats were made, none were needed ... "We have
been asked to aid our brethren on the Coast," said
Mr. McDonald ... "and you can rest assured that we
will do it. An injury to one is an injury to all, and
it seems to me that the trouble in San Francisco is a
direct blow at organized labor in the West. We will
do our share in aiding the Coast men to win." (*The
San Francisco Examiner *August 14, 1901, 2)*

Solidarity also came in the form of strike-fund donations
from all across the United States and even from the Canadian
provinces of Ontario and British Columbia. A total of $38,400.05
was raised, nothing like the funds available to the Employers'
Association, which reportedly commanded well over ten times
this amount, but still a large fund for the time, and especially
impressive because it overwhelmingly came in small donations
from fellow workers and their unions. Union supporters in twenty
different California cities sent funds, as did workers in twenty-
seven other states and the District of Columbia. Sailors in Boston
sent donations, as did Western Federation of Miners locals in ten
states and Canada (Goff and Rosenberg 1901). They all recognized
the dire implications of their own struggles for fair wages, hours,
and conditions should this strike be lost and capital succeed in
breaking the San Francisco unions.

The fact that *The Examiner*, one of the city's main newspapers,
fairly covered the workers' side of the strike and even editorialized
in favor of unions was also a morale booster for workers. One of
these editorials was printed under the title "Unions Have Come
To Stay" on August 10:

*Once more "The Examiner" respectfully advises the
Employers' Association to arrange its difference with
the Brotherhood of Teamsters. Sentiment in San*

Francisco is almost unanimous. On one side are about 350 employers and their immediate relatives, on the other are 400,000 people, who realize that unionism is all right and has come to stay ... It is quite easy to understand why the Employers' Association does not wish to deal with the union. The old European idea of the relations of master and servant is very strong in the minds of some of the reactionists of Sansome street and Front street ... Now that they have grown rich and powerful, their money seems almost to be useless to them if they cannot enact the role of master with a capital M and bluster and bully their servants with a capital S, as they were bullied when they were boys. It is so hard to get some people to realize that they have not the right to do as they please ...

It is so difficult for some men to understand that they cannot do all the dictating ... When the Employers' Association says it will not be dictated to, it means that it will not forego the privilege of dictating to everybody else. One of the greatest difficulties ... is the fact that many members of the Employers' Association really believe that they are entitled to do as they like. Having had this idea kicked and cuffed into them when they were boys, it has become almost a part of their nature, and it will probably take as much kicking to get the idea out of their heads as it took to put it in. But it will have to come out sooner or later.

Unionism is a good thing. The Teamsters' Union of San Francisco is a good union ... The attempt of the Employers' Association to destroy the Teamsters' Union is a piece of criminal viciousness that has had no parallel in San Francisco. Furthermore, many

members of the Employers' Association are ashamed
of themselves. This they show by trying to keep their
membership secret and by attempting to bring all
sorts of influence to bear on the newspapers not to
publish the facts about the strike.

CONFLICTS WITHIN THE RANKS OF CAPITAL

As the strike wore on, more and more economic interests began
to be affected by the tie-up of trade and the consumer boycotts
created by the ongoing struggle. Divisions within the ruling class
increased. The standstill at the port was indeed nearly complete.
On August 10, the *Examiner* reported that 181 vessels were idled
because of the strike, and since August 1 only ten ships had
cleared the port, compared to forty-four during the same period
the year before (August 10, 1901, 2).

Agriculture was one area of economic life that was, in
important respects, dependent on sea-borne commerce. As the
strike wore on both farmers and shippers of cereals, fruit, and other
crops became concerned that their interests would be seriously
affected. Consequently, some business leaders in this field began
to meet with and put pressure on the Employers' Association to
compromise and settle with the workers and their unions. At one
such meeting, George W. McNear, a large shipper of California
cereals, made the following points in a discussion with Frank J.
Symmes, president of the Merchants' Association, and chairman
of the executive committee of the Employers' Association:

> *At present vast quantities of grain are lying in the*
> *fields and along the navigable rivers of the State,*
> *awaiting transportation to deep water ... until the*
> *congested warehouses can be cleared by shipments of*
> *grain in ocean going vessels, the waiting crops cannot*
> *be moved ... numerous ships and steamers of the*
> *grain fleet are rocking idly at anchor in our waters,*

> *unable to take in cargoes while the strike continues unmodified ... the time remaining before the fall rains ... is barely sufficient to move the crops with every usual facility utilized to the full ... Unless some concession is made that will enable us to move the grain crop promptly, much of it will be caught in the open by the autumn rains, and it will rot where it lies.* (The San Francisco Examiner *August 8, 1901, 1)*

Symmes was not moved by McNear's argument and reportedly made the following response:

> *The fight the merchants are making is one of principle; and we cannot and will not recede from the position we have taken. We are not going to have labor unions run our houses for us. The farmers will have to stand their share of the unfortunate consequences of intemperate unionism. If, by reason of a struggle we are making on principle and in defense of individual liberty of action, the grain crop can't be moved without a surrender of our position,* LET IT ROT. (The San Francisco Examiner *August 8, 1901, 1)*

Symmes' comments created an uproar, and two days later the *Call* published a statement from Symmes stating that he never made such a statement (*The San Francisco Call* August 10, 1901, 2). The truth is unknown, but the conflict had reached a stage that many believed that he could have and had made such a statement.

By late August, some of the smaller firms that were members of the Employers' Association began to rebel against their own executive committee and the coercive methods it was using not only against labor but also against other employers. The Employers' Association ordered its members to refuse to sell to firms that employed union men. Some companies, however, refused to follow orders, and others began to request a conference to settle the strike. It became public knowledge that the Employers' Association forced some firms to join and threatened others with ruin if they did not. As *The San Francisco Examiner* (August 16, 1901, 1) reported:

> *It is now a well-known fact that the Draymen's Association would not have taken the stand it did against the Brotherhood of Teamsters had they not been forced to do so by the Employers' Association. The threat which was held out to the draymen was that if they did not stand firm against the Brotherhood the wholesalers would form a drayage company of their own that would practically drive the draymen … out of business … That this was no idle threat is proved by the fact that a number of wholesalers, none of whom is engaged in the drayage business, formed a corporation for the purpose of conducting a warehouse and drayage business … On the next day after the articles of incorporation were filed, the Draymen's Association for the first time took a firm stand toward the Brotherhood of Teamsters.*

Thomas Roberts, carriage-maker and dealer in wood and coal, told *The San Francisco Examiner* (September 1, 1901, 1), "I was forced to join the Employers' Association. I had no alternative … It is rule or ruin with them … They would have ruined my business if I had attempted to fight them."

This conflict and the consistent favorable coverage the *Examiner* gave to unions and the strike led the main business organizations of San Francisco to accuse it of "fomenting … strikes," encouraging " … the depraved and lawless" … and inciting " … class against class, thus sowing seeds of discord among our people, tending … to create discontent, disorders, riots …" (*The San Francisco Call* September 27, 1901, 1).

This coverage led business leaders to organize a boycott against the *Examiner*. As the *San Francisco Call* reported,

> *The commercial bodies adopting the scathing resolutions in condemnation of the Examiner represent the entire vast commercial, industrial and shipping interests of this city and port, together with the allied lumber industry of the forest counties ... Collectively they represent about all the active invested capital in San Francisco. (September 27, 1901, 1)*

By mid-September, another factor began to enter the calculations of the political authorities and all parties to the strike. The strike was gradually causing a paralysis of the Southern Pacific Railroad system due to the strike's success in slowing down the unloading of incoming freight. Nor was there space to store everything that was unloaded but could not be delivered. As the backup grew, a shortage of freight cars was created. On September 13, 1901, there were reportedly already 2,850 Southern Pacific cars, containing fifty-seven thousand tons of freight held up by the strike. Farmers all over the state who depended upon the railroad to haul their products to market were unable to ship, and as summer turned to fall, they became increasingly nervous about losing their crop, the result of many months' hard work and expense (*The San Francisco Examiner* September 13, 1901, 8).

The Southern Pacific and its owners were by far the most powerful economic and political actors on the state level. While generally anti-union, so far they had not acted decisively for or against either party, but their interests were now increasingly involved; they would have to act soon if they were to prevent the complete blockage of their railroad line.

INCREASING VIOLENCE

At this critical moment, sustained gun battles between union supporters and Employers' Association supporters took place in the streets of San Francisco. On September 29, 1901, the *Examiner* carried a major article reporting on a Sunday morning gunfight between special police and a crowd at Market and Kearny Streets:

> *There was a pitched battle in the heart of the city at about 1 o'clock this morning ... Men were dropping in all directions. The shots came in volleys and could not be counted.*
>
> *A crowd had followed some special policemen and non-union men from the Thalia dive, at Market and Turk streets. They came down Market Street and turned into Kearny Street. Between Market and Kearny streets the shooting became general all along the block.*
>
> *First a man opened from in front of the "Chronicle" office. The next flash came from in front of Gruenhagen's candy store. Then it was flash, flash from both sides of Kearny street, the men firing guns at will.*
>
> *People not interested in the scrimmage scattered in all directions. Some of the injured men tried to get away and dropped as they ran. One fell on Grant Avenue between Geary and Post. Another came down with a thud on Geary Street, near Brook Alley. A third tumbled in front of the Vionna bakery at Post and Kearny streets, and said he fell where he had been shooting and had downed the man who downed him. (The San Francisco Examiner September 29, 1901, 18)*

A follow-up article quoting eyewitnesses said that the special police had fired about 80 percent of the shots that evening (*The San Francisco Examiner* October 1, 1901). This and other less spectacular incidents involving special police at about the same time indicated that a new stage of the strike was underway, a stage which was unpredictable in its outcome, as union men, scabs, and the special police, were increasingly armed. And the special police were particularly ready to use their weapons with little or no provocation. (*The San Francisco Examiner* September 28, 1901, 4; October 2, 1901, 8).

GOVERNOR GAGE INTERVENES TO FORCE A SETTLEMENT

California Governor Henry T. Gage had kept a careful eye on the situation in San Francisco during the entire course of the strike and had even visited the city for a period of several weeks to personally observe conditions. His impression was that there was no cause for the state to resort to military intervention. Thus, in mid-September, when the State Board of Trade requested the National Guard be called out to break the strike to assure that the agricultural harvest would be successfully transported, the governor was not convinced. Gage responded that there was no clear need to substitute military for civil power, the laws were being executed, and there was no insurrection or foreign invasion to deal with (*The San Francisco Examiner* September 15, 1901, 27; *Coast Seamen's Journal* September 18, 1901, 1).

As governor, Gage was nevertheless acutely interested in a settlement of the strike and a return to normal conditions. He was in close touch with parties to the conflict, including Father Yorke. Gage was also doubtless in touch with the Southern Pacific Railroad. He had been a Southern Pacific attorney prior to being elected governor, and Thomas Bard, a state leader of the period, even labeled him a "tool" of the Southern Pacific (Olin 1981, 51).

The railroad's interests were being harmed by the strike and it had long had its own conflicts with the merchants and manufacturers of San Francisco. The increasing struggle in the streets of San Francisco, while not enough to justify military intervention, nonetheless gave the governor additional reason to become directly involved. It is unlikely that what happened at the end of September was a mere coincidence. First, the Southern Pacific put pressure on the merchants and draymen by telling them that demurrage[5] rates would be charged against them for the freight cars being tied up because of the strike. Second, the SP said it would stop all incoming freight until all loaded cars had been unloaded (Cronin 1943, 84). Finally, with the draymen and merchants under further pressure, Gage stepped in with an ultimatum, one reportedly suggested by none other than Father Peter C. Yorke, who was advising the governor. Gage threatened to put San Francisco under martial law, something that would certainly have hurt business interests and could also have harmed the unions.

The governor and his assistants then organized negotiations. The leaders of the Draymen's Association, Brotherhood of Teamsters, and Civic Front Federation all discussed and agreed to a settlement with the governor directly. R. P. Schwerin, representing the governor, met several times with the executive committee of the Employers' Association, gaining their acceptance of the agreement. The formally ratified agreement basically returned to the status quo before the strike (*The San Francisco Call* October 3, 1901, 1).

On October 2, 1901, Governor Gage announced that the strike was over. The news was greeted with cheer after cheer by the workers,

> *[A]nd there were tears in the eyes of some of the older members as they passed quickly down the steep stairs to carry the good news home to those to whom "strike" means "suffering" …*

---

5   Compensation for loading or unloading delay.

> *For the first time in quite a while men gathered along the waterfront in groups. Everybody was in good humor and there was never a "Move on" from the members of Chief Sullivan's waterfront squad ... It was peace, from Meiggs wharf to the Mail dock.*
> (The San Francisco Call *October 3, 1901, 2*)

It is clear that in many ways the agreement represented a compromise, reflecting what was, in many respects, a stalemate between the contending parties. But the Employers' Association's goal of the destruction of union power had not only come up short, but unions in San Francisco and the greater Bay Area emerged from the struggle stronger than ever.

In 1902, the Draymen's Association recognized and entered into a formal contract with the teamsters, and that same year the ship owners recognized and entered into a formal contract with the Sailors' Union of the Pacific. During the strike, the San Francisco Labor Council had grown from ninety to ninety-eight affiliated unions. The unions had successfully stood their ground, and only a month after the end of the strike, the Union Labor Party won the mayor's office in San Francisco.

The Employers' Association, on the other hand, was defunct less than two years after the end of the strike (Knight 1960, 88–90). The ruling-class attempt to achieve unlimited exploitation, dispossession, and oppression—with no checks on their power—had failed. Conversely, the victory of the San Francisco working class was a victory for freedom, solidarity, and all working-class rebels, locally and nationally.

The new century which lay ahead would see a number of new offensives by both the ruling class and the working class. But the 1901 workers' victory represented a key milestone for California, a landmark in the long human struggle for freedom, to overcome alienation and achieve a more just socioeconomic order.

POSTSCRIPT—

FROM HISTORICAL NARRATIVE TO HISTORIC TRANSFORMATION

Rulers and Rebels has presented historic examples of both ruling-class control and "dangerous" uprisings. The examples of resistance and rebellion were instances of propertyless working people taking direct action for themselves to overcome the types of disempowering alienation that they were subject to by a powerful ruling class. The rank-and-file acted as if another world was possible and struggled to assert their humanity in all its aspects: equality, solidarity, community, full democracy, empowerment, and protagonism, the idea that all people should be the subjects of their destiny and not mere objects. They fought to change the content and meaning of labor and life in an effort to become whole and full human beings.

Knowing and understanding this history allows us to overcome the historical amnesia so common in our country and begin to recover aspects of our own vernacular revolutionary traditions. As we have seen from the narrative history of this book, key aspects of this past included, first and foremost, domination from the top of society and periodic rebellions—both successful and unsuccessful—by those who were excluded from power.

Direct action of a segment of the people in solidarity with each other was always the means to change the policies and actions of the powerful, not elections. Another important fact was the racialization of some people; the frequent use of racial differences by the powerful and by white workers themselves to facilitate the exploitation and dispossession of those at the bottom of society. Finally, understanding class as well as the mutually exclusive processes of alienation and self-actualization is a way to bring all of these different aspects together in an integrated way.

CLASS AND RACE IN EARLY CALIFORNIA

The question of class is mainly ignored in mainstream culture, our rulers pretend that we live in a classless society with one common interest, and history is not seen in class terms. *Rulers and Rebels* tries to show how class analysis systematically applied to California history can both illuminate and inspire. The concept of class is complex, and how it is defined and used can be controversial, but it is fundamental to all social analysis. Class shapes all social relations and identities; it has great potency as an explanatory concept, both for society and individuals. The concept of class as expressed in this book attempts to be comprehensive and all-inclusive, having to do with the entire socioeconomic and political system, how society is organized, and how large-scale social power is used. This can only be fully understood historically, focusing, as this book has, on the actions of people in contradictory situations, a process that produces class consciousness, class organization, and class struggle.

Class, as the term has been used in this book is a concept both dynamic and dialectical, focusing on relationships between people. Class is both a top-down and a bottom-up relationship. From the top of the social structure—occupied by the *owners* of the means of production—class is an alienating relationship of exploitation, dispossession, and domination. From the bottom of the society—occupied by those who *do* the work—class is typically a relationship aiming at self-actualization in daily life through refusal, resistance, and rebellion in relation to the owners and in solidarity with fellow workers.

Class struggle from above involves an increase in the power of the powerful, and, therefore, an increase in alienation: the ruling class tries to increase its profits through the extraction of more surplus value from those who do the work. Class struggle from below involves measures by the rank-and-file and their communities to become aware of themselves and their collective power by refusing, resisting, and rebelling against the alienation of exploitation, dispossession, and domination. Class is thus the collective social expression of the existence of alienation and exploitation, of rebellion and attempts to achieve self-actualization, as expressed by the varied organizations and actions of both the ruling class and the working class.

This view of class comes from the belief that understanding class involves knowledge of the basic historical structures and processes (including strikes and other forms of rebellion, as well as the activities and offensives of the corporate capitalist and other types of ruling classes), which constantly mobilize and demobilize classes over time, making history, and defining the fate of large groupings of people. A class exists only in relations to another class, and class boundaries—as well as benefits or oppressions—are a product of historical processes of mobilization and struggle.

Fundamental to this perspective is the view that situations produce class, and class cannot be defined except in terms of relationships with other classes over time. A system of social differences creates sets of people who become aware of their common interests and position in the social structure, join together, and enter into conflict—class struggles—with another group who has a different position and different agenda. Classes are the organized groupings produced when these processes occur. The actions of real people produce class, so class is as class does.

Class consciousness and class memory, then, are how these experiences are handled in cultural terms, the realm of ideas, ethics, value systems, folklore, and traditions. Class is thus an emergent structure in an ongoing historical process of conflict between alienation and self-actualization. It is important to understand that the domination by a well organized, mobilized, and authoritative owning/ruling class over a less-organized, less-mobilized, and subordinate working class is never permanent. The all consuming logic of the market, which works in favor of the capitalist class, can only be overcome through rank-and-file solidarity and class struggle for self-realization by and for those at the bottom of society.

As we have seen in this book, issues of race and ethnicity are also central to the understanding of class and power in the history of California and the United States. Since its early development as a colony of white settlers, America has had a white supremacist class system, a sociopolitical construction based on the racialization of groups of people developing side by side with class hierarchies. At the beginning, the European Americans ("whites") seized power as rulers over everyone else. Those who were racialized, including Asian, African, indigenous, and the Spanish-Native hybrid, now known as the Latin peoples, all had a different skin tone and culture than whites. The whites defined these other people as inferior, and denigrated, ostracized, excluded, and grossly exploited them. People of color were forced to become part of a kind of internal colony, outside the community and deprived of full social, economic, and political rights. Furthermore, the whites were socialized to feel and act superior, to control, and even to terrorize non-white individuals and groups. One result was the rapid development after 1848 of a kind of double race/class structure in California.

Racialization created and reinforced an inner social cohesion and consensus in white society and often opened the door to uncontrolled violence and terrorism against any person of color. Violence in effect became law and the racialized victims had no recourse since they were often excluded both from the white community and full social, political, and economic rights. The ruling class created this system, perpetuated it, and benefited greatly from the super exploitation and dispossession that was possible due to it. The process of ruling-class divide-and-conquer, using people of color and racialization, led much of the working class to follow a policy of exclusion toward other races. Fewer resources and less effort was required to exclude a visible and vulnerable minority group than to challenge a dominant ruling class. So it is that the often-fractured working class, characteristic of capitalist society in California and elsewhere, arises not only through racism and false consciousness, but also as a rational short-term response of workers trying to protect their jobs and incomes from the threat posed by any group of people willing to work for less. This is similar to the way many workers today fear the impact immigrant workers will have on a depressed job market.

However, such race-based exclusivity was (and is) also exploitation, making the white working class a central part of the white supremacist system which helped to destroy their own attempts to achieve full, collective self-realization. The exception to this was the 1901 general strike on the San Francisco waterfront, when ruling-class attempts to bring in people of color as scabs to destroy the strike largely failed due to the union's strategy of accepting and working for the equal rights of people of color.

The multi-class alliance of European Americans, held together by white supremacy and based on ruling-class divide-and-conquer policies, has been one of the main guarantors of ruling-class domination of social life in California and the United States and has prevented even greater mass rebellions. The injustice and shortsightedness of putting white supremacy ahead of class solidarity created massive divisions within the working class and seriously deformed it, altering its development, something that is still ongoing today. The unity needed to win class struggles from below has often been lost due to the relations of competition and exclusion created as part of the racialization of important sectors within the working class. Gender exclusion works in a similar way;

male supremacy puts women in positions of inferiority, further dividing working people.

The divisions characteristic of racialization, white supremacy, and sexism are thus created through complex processes involving competition for jobs, nationalism, opportunism, actions of the ruling class, the lack of a working class political party, and the divisions and false consciousness created by ruling-class propaganda. Racism and sexism are therefore best understood as relationships of exclusion—an identifiable group is said to be different and inferior, and popular hostility is developed against this group, leading to open violence against them and exclusion.

If relationships of exploitation between the ruling class and working class are a class struggle, then relationships of exclusion between white supremacists and people of color are more like a war, where some people are considered to be completely outside the law and community and at the mercy of the dominant whites who make alliances only on the basis of shared whiteness. In this way, racialization became fundamental to the historical and current organization of class, and a key framing feature of working class historical development. Race even became a language through which America's class contradictions were, and still are, commonly expressed.

ALIENATION AND HUMAN SELF-ACTUALIZATION

Generalizing from the early California experience at a higher level of abstraction, we can conclude that two great historical processes in conflict have shaped California's (and by extension) humanity's past during recent centuries. These are the processes of alienation and its opposite, the process of human self-actualization or self-realization. Alienation is caused by the oppressive power and control of the ruling class over people living in a given economy and society, and self-realization is fostered by the struggle of the rank-and-file workers to create a more just social order, one more conducive to the unfolding of their full humanity. These two great processes form dialectical opposites, operating in the realm of contradiction and struggle.

While alienation and self-actualization are opposed to each other, in their modern forms they develop out of the same capitalist system. In this system, the capitalist class monopolizes productive property, and a division of labor is established in needed production and related political and social structures. Alienation originates in the life of workers who do not own any means of production, when their labor and their products are taken over and controlled by the owner, and the workers' creativity and free, active participation are not included in the work process. The worker's spontaneous human activity is lost, he or she is no longer a free, active agent, but rather a passive object, existing for the process of production rather than the process of production existing for the worker. Human beings become commodities, bought and sold on a labor market controlled by capital.

Inadequate pay results in material deprivation, but the psychological results of alienation are also serious. Alienation causes work to cease to be a social, pleasurable, and creative joy, instead becoming a dull, repetitive, slave-like compulsion. The power of the worker to influence the work is taken away, and the worker is commodified under a regime of discipline that he or she has no control over. Mass unemployment is even worse, since people's livelihoods are taken away, and they are made superfluous—resulting in materially deprived human beings without any higher collective or community purpose. The results are seen in the reports of mass mental illness we hear about everyday: neurosis, addiction, suicide, violence, child abuse, cults, and feelings of anomie, helplessness, meaninglessness, despair, and depression. Alienation also carries over from the socioeconomic into the political world. We live in an era when private, neo-liberal corporate ruling-class rule is continuing to strip rank-and-file working people and their communities of their agency and power, the ability to affect the trajectory of the future.

This aspect of powerless alienation is achieved in several ways, one key one being keeping "dangerous" but inspiring memories of the past hidden and unknown. Such historical amnesia helps keep our minds shut to the possibilities raised by past freedom struggles, such as the ones recounted here in these pages. Another important way is making everything, including politics, subordinate to the capitalist market. This creates a formalistic politics without any substantive revolutionary or even reformist content, a "low-intensity democracy" that is run by and for corporations and the ruling class and has no transformative capacity. Such a "democracy" is usually reduced to appeals to factions of the ruling class and their lowest common denominator: who controls and can spend the most dollars on advertising, advisers, and staff.

The end result of the alienation process is a separation of people from key aspects of their potential humanity, their species-essence as conscious, social, community-creating, empathetic, and altruistic beings. The fostering of self-actualization through the promotion of equality, solidarity, protagonism, and participation can overcome the pervasive alienation characteristic of our world. With an active role in directing his or her own work and other activities within a collective, cooperative setting, individuals can become subjects rather than objects; they can flower and fully develop their humanity individually, and in free, social, cooperative labor organized by and for the people. As Marx expressed it: "the free development of each becomes the condition for the free development of all."

This book is thus a record of ruling-class domination, but also of historical events announcing when alienation and the everyday class exploitation and racial oppression characteristic of both pre-capitalist and capitalist-class rule were recognized as unjust and illegitimate by the exploited and sometimes successfully resisted in various ways, including organized strikes and rebellions aimed at achieving a solidarity society and human freedom.

Rulers and Rebels, while striving to discover and tell the truth about the California past holistically, is also supportive of a transformative socioeconomic political project. This project is one where, through continuous development of the human person—the new human being—the working class overcomes alienation and is self-realized by being reunited with the means of production, each other, and nature. People become protagonists in their own future, constructing their own vision of an alternative world based on their own experience, values, interests, and worldview. In this way, a self-emancipated working class develops its human power as its own end, and overcomes the commodification of its labor power and the exploitation, dispossession, and alienation of its spirit, characteristic of both current life at work and daily life.

Thus, in this book, history is seen not only as a chronology of the past, but also as a challenge to us all to develop an alternative future. Consciousness, together with class-wide solidarity, organization, direct democracy, and concrete struggle has made and can make another, more human world of freely associated labor by and for the producers and their communities possible. Great advances can come when people begin to think and act collectively. The point is maximum democracy, overcoming the alienation-producing dictatorship of a tiny minority of wealthy people over us all, expanding the capacities of people, overcoming the barriers that separate what we are from what we might become.

Those who resisted and rebelled in the past have thus made an inestimable contribution to humanity; they have shown us the way forward, building class consciousness and memory, never letting people forget that there is always an alternative—collective resistance leading to freedom. It is up to us in the present moment to resume the task of radical transformation of ourselves as individuals and our society, for we are not here to tinker with the world; we are here to change it, to free our species from alienation, to promote and achieve full human liberation. Such liberation aims for the full and free development of every individual as a part of the free community of associated producers living in harmony with each other and nature. Understanding our history in this way helps us move theoretically from historical narrative toward historic transformation.

REFERENCES

Ainsworth, Brig. Gen. Fred C., and Joseph W. Kirkley. 1902. *The War of the Rebellion: A Compilation of the Official Records of the Union and Condederate Armies*. Additions and Corrections to Series I, Vol. L. Government Printing Office, Washington DC.

Almaguer, Tomas. 1994. *Racial Fault Lines: The Historical Origins of White Supremacy in California*. University of California Press, Berkeley.

American Gas-Light Journal. 1863 (June 1).

Anonymous. 1884. *A Social Manual for San Francisco and Oakland …* The City Publishing Company, San Francisco.

Appleton and Company. 1870. *Annual Cyclopaedia and Register of Important Events*. D. Appleton and Company, New York.

_____. 1873. *Annual Cyclopaedia and Register of Important Events*. D. Appleton and Company, New York.

Archibald, Robert. 1978. "Indian Labor at the California Missions: Slavery or Salvation." *Journal of San Diego History* 24(2):172–182.

Argonaut Publishing Company, The. 1879. *The Elite Directory for San Francisco and Oakland.* The Argonaut Publishing Co., San Francisco.

Atherton, Gertrude. 1914. *California, an Intimate History.* Harper and Brothers, New York.

Ayres, W. O. 1886. "Personal Recollections of the Vigilance Committee." *Overland Monthly,* 2nd Series, Vol. 8:166.

Baggett, Joseph & Company. 1856. *San Francisco Business Directory* … Joseph Baggett and Company, San Francisco.

Bancroft, H. H. 1886. *History of California,* Vol. 1. The History Company, San Francisco.

———. 1886. *History of California,* Vol. 2. The History Company, San Francisco.

———. 1886. *History of California,* Vol. 4. The History Company, San Francisco.

———. 1887. *The Works of Hubert Howe Bancroft,* Vol. 37, *Popular Tribunals,* 2. The History Company, San Francisco.

———. 1890. *History of California,* Vol. 7. The History Company, San Francisco.

———. 1891. *History of the Life of William T. Coleman: A Character Study.* The History Company, San Francisco.

———. n.d., *Brief Account of the Safety Committee of 1877* … On file, F870 C5 B18, Bancroft Library, University of California, Berkeley.

Bancroft Scraps. 1877. Set W, Vols. 6, 24, 30. On file, Bancroft Library, University of California, Berkeley.

Bailey, Lynn R. 1996. *Supplying the Mining World: The Mining Equipment Manufacturers of San Francisco 1850–1900.* Westerlore Press, Tucson, Arizona.

Bannon, John F., ed. 1964. *Bolton and the Spanish Borderlands.* University of Oklahoma Press, Norman.

Barth, Gunther. 1964. *Bitter Strength: A History of Chinese in the United States.* Harvard University Press, Cambridge.

Bean, Walton. 1973. *California: An Interpretive History.* McGraw-Hill Book Company, New York.

Beck, Warren A., and Ynez D. Haase. 1974. *Historical Atlas of California.* University of Oklahoma Press, Norman.

Becker, George F. 1882. *Geology of the Comstock Lode and the Washoe District.* United States Geological Survey, Washington DC.

Beebe, Rose Marie, and Robert M. Senkewicz, eds. 2001. *Lands of Promise and Dispair: Chronicles of Early California, 1535–1846.* Santa Clara University, Santa Clara, and Hayday Books, Berkeley.

Bell, Horace. 1881. *Reminiscences of a Ranger ...* Yarnell, Caystile & Mather, Los Angeles.

Bowles, Samuel. 1869. *Our New West: Records of Travel.* Hartford Publishing Company, Hartford, Conn.

Boyer, Richard O., and Herbert M. Morais. 1955. *Labor's Untold Story.* United Electrical, Radio and Machine Workers of America, Pittsburgh.

Brechin, Grey. 1999. *Imperial San Francisco: Urban Power, Earthly Ruin.* University of California Press, Berkeley.

Brewer, William H. 1966. *Up and Down California in 1860–1864: The Journal of William H. Brewer.* University of California Press, Berkeley.

Brown, Richard Maxwell. 1994. "Violence." In Milner II, O'Connor, and Sandweiss, *The Oxford History of the American West.* Oxford University Press, New York.

Browne, J. Ross, and James W. Taylor. 1867 *Reports Upon the Mineral Resources of the United States.* United States Treasury Department, Washington DC.

California Bureau of Labor Statistics. 1887. *Second Biennial Report ... for the Years 1885–1886.* State Printing Office, Sacramento.

————. 1888. *Third Biennial Report ... for the Years 1887–1888.* State Printing Office, Sacramento.

————. 1893. *Fifth Biennial Report ... for the Years 1891–1892.* State Printing Office, Sacramento.

California Immigrant Union. 1870. *Statement of Objectives, Purpose and Plan of Operation.* On file, xF866.C192, Bancroft Library, University of California, Berkeley.

California Labor and Employment Exchange, San Francisco. 1869. Articles of Association and By Laws ... On file, xF862.6C52, Bancroft Library, University of California, Berkeley.

California Weekly, The. 1909. (January 26).

Commercial and Financial Chronicle, The. 1875. (September 11). 1883 (January 20). 1890 (May 10). 1891 (May 19).

Carlson, Helen Swisher. 1955. "Names of Mines on the Comstock." MA thesis (English), University of Nevada, Reno.

Carlson, Wallin John. 1941. "A History of the San Francisco Mining Exchange." MA thesis (Economics), University of California, Berkeley.

Castillo, Edward. 1978. "The Impact of Euro-American Exploration and Settlement." In *California, Vol. 8 of Handbook of North American Indians.* Ed. Robert F. Heizer. Smithsonian Institution, Washington DC.

————. 1989. "The Native Response to the Colonization of Alta California." In David H. Thomas (ed). *Columbian Consequences.* Smithsonian Institution Press, Washington DC.

Caughey, John. 1940. *California.* Prentice -Hall, New York.

Caughey, John, and Laree Caughey. 1976. *Los Angeles: Biography of a City.* University of California Press, Berkeley.

Chiles, Frederick C. 1981. *War on the Waterfront: The Struggles of the San Francisco Longshoremen, 1851–1934.* University Microfilms, Ann Arbor, Michigan.

Chinn, Thomas W., H. Mark Lai, and Philip P. Choy. 1969. *A History of the Chinese in California: A Syllabus.* Chinese Historical Society of America. San Francisco.

Chiu, Ping. 1967. *Chinese Labor in California, 1850–1880, an Economic Study.* State Historical Society of Wisconsin, Madison.

Coast Seamen's Journal. 1901 (July 24, 31; August 7, 21; September 4, 11, 18).

Cole, Cornelius. 1908. *Memoirs of Cornelius Cole.* McLoughlin Bros, N.Y.

Coleman, Charles M. 1952. *PG&E of California.* McGraw-Hill Book Company, New York.

Colton, Walter. 1850. *Three Years in California.* A. S. Barnes & Company, New York.

Colville, Samuel. 1856. *San Francisco City Directory for the Year Commencing October, 1856.* San Francisco.

Commercial and Financial Chronicle. 1875 (September 11). 1883 (January 20). 1890 (May 10). 1891 (May 19).

Conise, Titus. 1868. *The Natural Wealth of California.* H. H. Bancroft & Company, San Francisco.

Conlogue, William. 1999. "Farmers' Rhetoric or Defense: California Settlers verses the Southern Pacific Railroad." *California History* 78(1): 40–55.

Cook, Sherburne F. 1976. *The Conflict Between the California Indian and White Civilization.* University of California Press, Berkeley.

Cornford, Daniel. 1998/1999 "We All Live More like Brutes than Humans: Labor and Capital in the Gold Rush." *A Golden State: Mining and Economic Development in Gold Rush California.* Eds. James J. Rawls, and Richard J. Orsi. University of California Press, Berkeley.

Cowan, Robert G. 1956. *Ranchos of California.* Academy Library Guild, Fresno.

Crane, Lauren E. 1894. *Newton Booth of California: His Speeches and Addresses.* G. P. Putnam's Sons, New York.

Cronin, Bernard C. 1943. "Father Yorke and the Labor Movement in San Francisco 1900–1910." Doctoral dissertation (Social Science), Catholic University of America, Washington DC.

Cross, Ira. 1927. *Financing an Empire; History of Banking in California.* The S. J. Clarke Publishing Company, Chicago.

———. 1935. *A History of the Labor Movement in California.* University of California Press, Berkeley.

Cutter, Charles H. 1963. "Michael Reese: Parsimonious Patron of the University of California." *California Historical Society Quarterly* 42:127–144.

Daily Alta California (San Francisco). 1853 (June 26; July 22; August 2; October 15). 1855 (June 16; August 11, 13). 1856 (May 1). 1859 (November 2, 13). 1860 (August 17; November 17). 1863 (March 3; August 3). 1864 (April 3, 8). 1867 (July 1, 3). 1868 (March 16; May 8, 9, 13, 15). 1869 (January 4, 5). 1870 (July 8, 17; August 19). 1871 (June 2, 22, 23, 25, 26, 27; July 7, 16, 22, 26, 27, 28, 30; August 1, 2). 1875 (October 3). 1876 (April 15). 1877 (July 25). 1879 (October 9). 1880 (February 26).

Daily Evening Call (San Francisco). 1877 (July 25).

Daily Evening Post (San Francisco). 1878 (August 6, 10).

Davis, Winfield J. 1893. *History of Political Conventions in California 1849–1892.* California State Library, Sacramento.

Decker, Peter R. 1978. *Fortunes and Failures: White Collar Mobility in Nineteenth Century San Francisco.* Harvard University Press, Cambridge.

Derks, Scott. 2000. *Working Americans 1880–1999, Vol 1: The Working Class.* Grey House Publishing, Lakeville, CT.

Deverell, William. 1994. *Railroad Crossing: Californians and the Railroad 1850–1910.* University of California, Berkeley.

Dillon, Richard H. 1962. *The Hatchet Men: The Story of the Tong Wars in San Francisco's Chinatown.* Coward-McCann, New York.

———. 1984. *Iron Men: California's Industrial Pioneers, Peter, James and Michael Donahue.* Candela Press, Point Richmond, California.

Donahue, Peter. n.d. Manuscript C-D 231:3 On file, Bancroft Library, University of California, Berkeley.

Drummond, Herbert W. Jr. 1952. "Squatter Activity in San Francisco, 1847–1854." MA thesis (History), University of California, Berkeley.

Dunlap, Carol. 1982. *California People.* Peregrine Smith Books, Salt Lake City.

Dumas, Malone, ed. 1936. *Dictionary of American Biography,* Vol. 18. Charles Scribner's Sons, New York.

Eargle, Dolan H. 2000. *Native California Guide: Weaving Past and Present.* Trees Company Press, San Francisco.

Eaves, Lucile. 1910. *A History of California Labor Legislation …* University of California Press, Berkeley.

Egenhoff, Elisabeth L. 1953. "De Argento Vivo: Historic Documents on Quicksilver and its Recovery in California Prior to 1860." *California Journal of Mines and Geology* 49(4): 3–142.

Ellison, William Henry. 1950. *A Self-Governing Dominion: California 1849–1860*. University of California, Berkeley.

Elsasser, Albert B. 1978. "Development of Regional Prehistoric Cultures." In *California, Vol. 8 of Handbook of North American Indians*. Ed. Robert F. Heizer. Smithsonian Institution, Washington DC.

Emmons, S. F., and G. F. Becker. 1885. *Statistics and Technology of the Precious Metals*. US Census Office, Washington DC.

Engelhardt, Zephyrin. 1912. *The Missions and Missionaries of California*, Vol. 2. The James H. Barry Company, San Francisco.

_____. 1913 *The Missions and Missionaries of California*, Vol. 3. The James H. Barry Company, San Francisco

ERM-West, Inc. 1991. *Overall Site Remedial Investigation/Feasibility Study … Sacramento Rail Yard Sacramento, California*. ERM-West, Inc., Walnut Creek CA.

Finkelman, Paul, ed. 1995. *His Soul Goes Marching On: Responses to John Brown and the Harper's Ferry Raid*. University of Virginia Press, Charlottesville.

Florcken, Herbert G. 1936. "The Law and Order View of the San Francisco Vigilance Committee of 1856." *California Historical Society Quarterly* XV(1): 70–87.

Forbes, Jack. 1982. *Native Americans of California and Nevada* (Revised Edition). Naturegraph Publishers, Happy Camp CA.

Ford, Paul L, ed. 1904. *The Works of Thomas Jefferson in Twelve Volumes*. G. P. Putnam's Sons, New York.

Galloway, John D. 1950. *The First Transcontinental Railroad*. Simmons-Boardman, New York.

Goerke, Betty. 2007. *Chief Marin: Leader, Rebel, and Legend*. Heyday Books, Berkeley.

Goff, W. H., and Edward Rosenberg. 1901. San Francisco Labor Council Strike Fund, April 23, 1901 to November 30, 1901. On file, F869 S3.7 S1378x, Bancroft Library, University of California, Berkeley.

Gonzalez, Michael J. 1998. "The Child of the Wilderness Weeps for the Father of Our Country': The Indian and the Politics of Church and State in Provincial California." In *Contested Eden: California Before the Gold Rush.* Eds. Ramon A. Gutierrez and Richard J. Orsi. University of California Press, Berkeley.

Gordan, John D. 1987. *Authorized by No Law: The San Francisco Committee of Vigilance of 1856.* Ninth Judicial Circuit Historical Society, Pasadena.

Gottesman, Ronald (ed). 1999. *Violence in America,* Vol. 1. Charles Scribner's Sons, New York.

Gould and Curry Silver Mining Company. 1862. Annual Report. On file, F845.3 G 65x, Bancroft Library, University of California, Berkeley.

Grant, Campbell. 1978. "Chumash: Introduction." In *California, Vol. 8 of Handbook of North American Indians.* Ed. Robert F. Heizer. Smithsonian Institution, Washington DC.

Hackel, Steven W. 1998. "Land, Labor and Production: The Colonial Economy of Spanish and Mexican California.". In *Contested Eden: California Before the Gold Rush.* Eds. Ramon A. Gutierrez and Richard J. Orsi. University of California Press, Berkeley.

Hall, Henry. 1884. *Report on the Shipbuilding Industry of the United States.* Government Printing Office, Washington DC.

Harlow, Neal. 1982. *California Conquered: The Annexation of a Mexican Province.* University of California Press, Berkeley.

Heizer, Robert, ed. 1978. "California." *Handbook of North American Indians, Vol. 8.* Smithsonian Institution, Washington DC.

Heizer, Robert F., and Alan F. Almquist. 1971. *The Other Californians: Prejudice and Discrimination Under Spain, Mexico and the United States to 1920.* University of California Press, Berkeley.

Helper, Hinton. 1855/1949. *Land of Gold: Reality versus Fiction.* H. Taylor, Baltimore.

Hittell, John S. 1869 *The Resources of California ...* A. Roman and Company, San Francisco.

_____.1878. *History of the City of San Francisco ...* A. L. Bancroft, San Francisco.

————. 1882. *The Commerce and Industries of the Pacific Coast.*

————. 1883. "Chronology of Events in California." On file, Mss. C-E 138, Bancroft Library, University of California, Berkeley.

————. n.d. *Hittell Scraps,* Vol. 1, Vol 4. On file, F851 H5, Bancroft Library, University of California, Berkeley.

Hittell, Theodore H. 1885. *History of California,* Vol. 2. Pacific Press Publishing House and Occidental Publishing Company, San Francisco.

————. 1898. *History of California,* Vol. 3. N. J. Stone & Co., San Francisco.

————. 1898. *History of California,* Vol. 4. N. J. Stone & Co., San Francisco.

Hobsbawm, Eric. 1959. *Primitive Rebels: Studies in Archaic Forms of Social Movement in the 19th and 20th Centuries.* Manchester University Press, Manchester, England.

Hornbeck, David. 1983. *California Patterns: A Geographical and Historical Atlas.* Mayfield Publishing Company, Palo Alto.

Hoy, William. 1942. *Chinese Six Companies.* Chinese Consolidated Benevolent Association, San Francisco.

Hudson, Millard F. n.d. *The Last Indian Campaign in the Southwest.* On file, XF786 C635 v.7, Bancroft Library, University of California, Berkeley.

Hungerford, Edward. 1949. *Wells Fargo: Advancing the American Frontier.* Random House, New York.

Hurtado, Albert L. 1988. *Indian Survival on the California Frontier.* Yale University Press, New Haven.

Igler, David. 2001. *Industrial Cowboys: Miller & Lux and the Transformation of the Far West, 1850–1920.* University of California Press, Berkeley.

Ignaliev, Noel. 1995. *How the Irish Became White.* Roulledge, New York.

Issel, William, and Robert W. Cherny. 1986. *San Francisco, 1865–1932: Politics, Power, and Urban Development.* University of California Press, Berkeley.

Jackson, Donald Dale. 1980. *Gold Dust.* University of Nebraska Press, Lincoln.

Jackson, Robert H. 1994. *Indian Population Decline: The Missions of Northwestern New Spain, 1687–1840.* University of New Mexico Press, Albuquerque.

Jackson, Robert H., and Edward Castillo. 1995. *Indians, Franciscans, and Spanish Colonization.* University of New Mexico Press, Albuquerque.

Jelinek, Lawrence James. 1998–1999. "'Property of Every Kind': Ranching and Farming during the Gold Rush Era." In *A Golden State: Mining and Economic Development in Gold Rush California.* Eds. James J. Rawls and Richard J. Orsi. University of California Press, Berkeley.

Judson Pacific-Murphy Corporation. 1946. *A Romance of Steel in California.* Judson Pacific-Murphy Corporation, San Francisco.

Kelley, Robert. 1959. *Gold vs. Grain: The Hydraulic Mining Controversy in California's Sacramento Valley.* Arthur H. Clark Co., Glendale CA.

Kelly, J. Wells. [1862] 1962. *First Directory of Nevada Territory.* The Talisman Press. Los Gatos, California.

Klein, Julius. 1908. "The Development of the Manufacturing Industry in California Up to 1870." MA thesis (history). University of California, Berkeley.

Knight, Robert Edward Lee. 1960. *Industrial Relations in the San Francisco Bay Area, 1900–1918.* University of California Press, Berkeley.

Koford, Henning. 1938. *Dr. Samuel Merritt: His Life and Achievements.* The Kennedy Co., Oakland.

Kowalewski, Michael. 1997. *Gold Rush: A Literary Exploration.* Heyday Books, Berkeley.

Kroeber, Alfred L. 1925. *Handbook of the Indians of California.* Smithsonian Institution, Washington DC.

Langley, Henry G. 1858a. *The California State Register and Year Book of Facts.* Henry G. Langley, San Francisco.

———. 1859a. *The California State Register and Year Book of Facts.* Henry G. Langley, San Francisco.

——— 1862. *The California State Register and Year Book of Facts.* Henry G. Langley, San Francisco.

———. 1867. *The Pacific Coast Business Directory for 1867.* Henry G. Langley, San Francisco.

———. 1871. *The Pacific Coast Business Directory.* Henry G. Langley, San Francisco.

———. 1858b. *The San Francisco Directory. Commercial Steam Presses*, San Francisco.

———. 1859b. *The San Francisco Directory. Commercial Steam Presses*, San Francisco.

————. 1863. *The San Francisco Directory. Commercial Steam Presses*, San Francisco.

————. 1869. *The San Francisco Directory. Commercial Steam Presses*, San Francisco.

————. 1879. *The San Francisco Directory. Commercial Steam Presses*, San Francisco.

Langley, Henry G., and Mathews. 1857. *San Francisco Directory.* Henry G. Langley, San Francisco.

La Perouse, Jean-Francois de. 1786/1989. *Monterey in 1786: The Journal of Jean-Francois de La Perouse.* Heyday Books, Berkeley.

Larkin, Thomas O. 1846/1863. "The Prominent Men of California in 1846." *The Pacific Monthly* 10 (4) August, 1863.

Lavender, David. 1975. *Nothing Seemed Impossible: William C. Ralston and Early San Francisco.* American West Publishing Co., Palo Alto.

Lawson, Kristan, and Anneli Rufus. 2000. *California Babylon.* St. Martin's Griffin, New York.

Leach, Frank A. 1917. *Recollections of a Newspaperman.* Samuel Levinson, San Francisco.

Levy, Richard. 1978. "Costanoan." *Handbook of North American Indians, Vol. 8: California.* Ed. Robert F. Heizer. Smithsonian Institution, Washington DC.

Lewis, Oscar. 1947. *Silver Kings.* Alfred A. Knopf, New York.

Loomis, Noel M. 1868. *Wells Fargo.* Clarkson N. Potter, Inc., New York.

Lord, Eliot. 1883. "Comstock Mining and Miners." *United States Geological Survey,* Washington DC.

Los Angeles Times, The. 1894 (June 27, 30; July 2).

Lugo, Jose del Carmen. [1877] 1950. "Life of a Rancher." *The Historical Society of Southern California Quarterly* 32(3): 185–236.

Luomala, Katharine. 1978. "Tipai and Ipai." *California, Vol. 8: Handbook of North American Indians*, Ed. Robert F. Heizer. Smithsonian Institution, Washington DC.

Lyman, George D. 1937. *Ralston's Ring: California Plunders the Comstock Lode.* Charles Scribner's Sons, New York.

Mann, Ralph. 1982. *After the Gold Rush: Society in Grass Valley and Nevada City, California, 1849–1870.* Stanford University Press, Stanford.

Mariposa Gazette. 1881 (November 5).

Marks, Bernhard. 1854. "Letter to Cousin Jacob." Reprinted in Michael Kowalewski. 1997. *Gold Rush: A Literary Exploration.* Heyday Books, Berkeley.

Marshall, James. 1891. "Marshall's Own Account of the Gold Discovery." Reprinted in Michael Kowalewski. 1997. *Gold Rush: A Literary Exploration.* Heyday Books, Berkeley.

Martinot, Steve. 2003. *The Rule of Racialization: Class, Identity, Governance.* Temple University Press, Philadelphia.

McCarthy, F. C. 1958. *The History of Mission San Jose, California 1797–1835.* Academy Library Guild, Fresno.

McLeod, Alexander. 1948. *Pigtails and Gold Dust.* The Caxton Printers, Caldwell ID.

McWilliams, Cary. 1949. *California: The Great Exception.* Current Books, New York.

———. 1968. *The California Revolution.* Grossman Publishers, New York.

Mechanics' State Council of California. 1868. "Communication in Relation to Chinese Immigration, March 12, 1868." On file, xF870 C5C51 V. 1:6 BANC Bancroft Library, University of California, Berkeley.

Mercantile Gazette and Prices Current. 1864 (June 22).

Milliken, Randall. 1995. *A Time of Little Choice: The Disintegration of Tribal Culture in the San Francisco Bay Area 1769–1810.* Ballena Press, Menlo Park.

Mills, D. O. 1881. Deposition, Case No. 3050. Superior Court, City and County of San Francisco, State of California. On file, F869.S3.72 R2R3x, Bancroft Library, University of California, Berkeley.

Mining Magazine, The. 1853 (November); 1854 (January); 1857 (November).

Mining and Scientific Press. 1862 (May 23; November 29). 1863 (August 17; May 18). 1864 (January 2; February 6, 27; May 21). 1865 (August 12; September 2, 9, 23, 30). 1866 (December 15). 1867 (March 16). 1871 (April 8; June 17; July 1, 15, 22, 29). 1877 (February 24).

Mining and Statistic Magazine, The. 1854 (August). 1858 (February, March). 1860 (April, May, June, July).

Minturn, William. 1877. *Travels West.* Samuel Tinsley, London.

Miranda, Gloria E. 1981. "Gente de Razon Marriage Patterns in Spanish and Mexican California: A Case Study of Santa Barbara and Los Angeles." *Southern California Quarterly* 63 1):1–21.

Moffat, Frances. 1977. *Dancing on the Brink of the World: The Rise and Fall of San Francisco Society.* G. P. Putnam's Sons, New York.

Monroy, Douglas. 1998. "The Creation and Re-creation of Californio Society." *Contested Eden: California Before the Gold Rush.* Eds. Ramon A. Gutierrez and Richard J. Orsi. University of California Press, Berkeley.

Moratto, Michael J., David A. Fredrickson, Christopher Raven, and Claude N. Warren. 1984. *California Archaeology.* Academic Press, New York.

Muscatine, Doris. 1975. *Old San Francisco: The Biography of a City.* G. P. Putnam's Sons, New York.

Nevada. 1866a. *State Minerologist Report.* On file, F846.7 M4N4 1866x, Bancroft Library, University of California, Berkeley.

————. 1866b. *Annual Report of the Surveyor-General.* State of Nevada, Virginia City.

Nevada City Daily Transcript, The. 1877 (September 18).

New York Times, The. 1870 (July 13), 1876 (November 26, December 3, 11, 15), 1877 (September 19), 1878 (June 22). 1880 (May 19, 20, 21, 22), 1881 (April 24), 1886 (November 23), 1887 (January 19), 1890 (September 26, November 4, 17, 25, 27), 1892 (September 4), 1894 (June 29; July 15).

Norris, William. 1887. "The California Steam Navigation Company." On file, Mss. C-D 767, Bancroft Library, University of California, Berkeley.

Northrop, Marie E. 1976. *Spanish-Mexican Families of Early California: 1769–1850,* Vol. 1. Southern California Genealogical Society, Burbank.

————. 1984. *Spanish-Mexican Families of Early California: 1769–1850,* Vol. 2. Southern California Genealogical Society, Burbank.

Oakland Enquirer. 1894. (July 5, 6, 13, 16).

Olin, Jr., Spencer C. 1981. *California Politics, 1846 -1920: The Emerging Corporate State.* Boyd & Fraser, San Francisco.

Olson, James S., and Susan Wladover. 1992. *Dictionary of United States Economic History.* Greenwood Press, Westport CN.

Orsi, Richard J. 2005. *Sunset Limited: The Southern Pacific Railroad and the Development of the American West 1850–1930.* University of California Press, Berkeley.

Osio, Antonio Maria. [1851] 1996. *The History of Alta California: A Memoir of Mexican California.* The University of Wisconsin Press, Madison.

Ostrander, Gilman M. 1966. *Nevada: The Great Rotten Borough, 1859–1964.* Alfred A. Knopf, New York.

Pacific Rolling Company. 1866. Articles of Incorporation. On file, No. 7313, California State Archives, Sacramento.

Paul, Rodman. 1947. *California Gold: The Beginnings of Mining in the Far West.* University of Nebraska Press, Lincoln.

Perlot, Jean-Nicolas. [1897] 1985. *Gold Seeker: Adventures of a Belgian Argonaut during the Gold Rush Years.* Yale University Press, New Haven.

Phelps, Alonzo. 1881. *Contempory Biography of California's Representative Men, Vol.* I. A. L. Bancroft and Company, San Francisco.

———. 1882. *Contemporary Biography of California's ...* Vol. 2.

Phillips, Catherine Coffin. 1929. *Cornelius Cole: California Pioneer and United States Senator ...* John Henry Nash, San Francisco.

Phillips, George Harwood. 1993. *Indians and Intruders in Central California 1769–1849.* University of Oklahoma Press, Norman.

Pitt, Leonard. 1966. *The Decline of the Californios: A Social History of the Spanish-Speaking Californians, 1846–1890.* University of California Press, Berkeley.

Placerville Mountain Democrat, The. 1877 (September 22).

Pomeroy, Earl. 1965. *The Pacific Slope: A History of California, Oregon, Washington, Idaho, Utah and Nevada.* Alfred A. Knopf, New York.

Poor, Henry V. 1870. *Poor's Manual of the Railroads of the United States.* Poor and Company, New York.

———. 1880. *Poor's Manual* ... Poor and Company, New York.

Porter, Robert P. 1884. *Report on Valuation, Taxation and Public Indebtedness in the United States.* Government Printing Office, Washington DC.

Quinn, Arthur. 1997. *The Rivals: William Gwin, David Broderick, and the Birth of California.* University of Nebraska Press, Lincoln.

Ralston, Andrew Jackson. n.d., "Statement on William C. Ralston." On file, Mss C-D 346:1–7. Bancroft Library, University of California, Berkeley.

Rawls, James J., and Richard J. Orsi. 1998–1999 *A Golden State: Mining and Economic Development in Gold Rush California.* University of California Press, Berkeley.

Rice, Richard B., William A. Bullough, and Richard J. Orsi. 1988. *The Elusive Eden: A New History of California.* Alfred A. Knopf, New York.

Rodriguez, Junius P. 1997. *The Historical Encyclopedia of World Slavery,* Vol. 2. ABC-Clio, Santa Barbara CA.

Rosenus, Alan. 1995. *General M. G. Vallejo and the Advent of the Americans: A Biography.* University of New Mexico Press, Albuquerque.

Ross, Robert J. S. and Kent C. Trachte. 1990. *Global Capitalism: The New Leviathan.* State University of New York Press, Albany.

Royce, Josiah. [1886] 1970. *California from the Conquest in 1846 to the Second Vigilance Committee in San Francisco* ... Houghton Mifflin, Boston.

Russell, Charles Edward. 1912. *Stories of the Great Railroads.* Charles H. Kerr & Company, Chicago.

Sacramento Daily Union. 1855 (November 14). 1861 (April 12). 1867 (February 22, March 7, July 1, 3). 1869 (April 3, November 27). 1870 (January 1, July 4, 11, November 4). 1871 (July 22, October 26). 1872 (April 18). 1873 (June 21, December 22). 1877 (June 23). 1879 (August 2, November 17).

Sacramento Record Union. 1883 (January 1, June 26, 27, 28, 29; July 2, 13, 17, 24). 1894 (June 25, 26, 28, 29, 30).

Sacramento Settlers' League. 1853. *Address, Preamble and Constitution of the Settlers' League of Sacramento County.* On file, xF862.1.S42, Bancroft Library, University of California, Berkeley.

St. Clair, David J. 1998–1999. "The Gold Rush and the Beginnings of California Industry." *A Golden State: Mining and Economic Development in Gold Rush California.* Eds. James J. Rawls and Richard J. Orsi. University of California Press, Berkeley.

Sanborn Map Company. 1886. *Sanborn Map of San Francisco.* On file Earth Sciences Library, University of California, Berkeley.

San Francisco Call, The. 1868 (February 23). 1871 (August 6, 8). 1873 (December 20, 21). 1877 (July 25, 27). 1878 (September 29). 1879 (October 22). 1880 (March 14). 1882 (January 10, 24; February 7; September 12). 1885 (February 10, 13, 17, 18, 20; October 24, 25, 27, 29, 30, 31; November 1). 1894 (July 4, 5, 6, 7, 10, 11, 12, 15, 17, 18; August 21). 1896 (June 4). 1901 (July 30; August 10; September 27; October 3). 1909 (June 5).

San Francisco Chronicle. 1869 (December 5). 1870 (July 12). 1871 (August 20; September 10; October 5). 1873 (December 21, 22, 23, 24). 1877 (July 24, 25, 26, 27).

San Francisco Herald. 1856 (August 19, 26). 1857 (August 6).

San Francisco Evening Bulletin. 1855 (November 19, 20). 1856 (January 17; March 12; May 14, 15, 19, 23; August 23, 27, 29; November 8). 1860 (January 24; April 19, 23, 25; June 12). 1861 (January 9). 1867 (February 12). 1868 (February 24). 1870 (May 13). 1875 (August 30).

San Francisco Examiner, The. 1877 (July 24, 25). 1892 (July 15). 1901 (July 20–28, 30–31; August 1, 2, 4 ,5, 7, 8, 10, 14, 16, 18, 22, 24, 25, 28; September 3, 6, 10, 13, 15, 22–29; October 1, 2).

Sandos, James A. 2004. *Converting California: Indians and Franciscans in the Missions.* Yale University Press, New Haven.

Saxton, Alexander P. 1971. *The Indispensable Enemy: Labor and the Anti-Chinese Movement in California.* University of California Press, Berkeley.

———. 1990. *The Rise and Fall of the White Republic: Class Politics and Mass Culture in Nineteenth Century America.* Verso, London.

Scherer, James A. B. 1939. "The Lion of the Vigilantes." *William T. Coleman and the Life of Old San Francisco.* The Bobbs-Merrill Co., New York.

Senkewicz, Robert M. 1985. *Vigilantes in Gold Rush San Francisco.* Stanford University Press, Stanford.

Severson, Thor. 1973. *Sacramento; An Illustrated History: 1839 to 1874.* California Historical Society, Sacramento.

Shaffer, Ralph E. 1952. "Radicalism in California 1869–1929." Doctoral dissertation. (History Department), University of California, Berkeley.

Sherman, William T. [1875] 1890. *Memoirs,* Vol. 1:D. Appleton and Company, New York.

_____. 1875. "Memoirs of William T. Sherman." Reprinted in Michael Kowalewski. 1997. *Gold Rush: A Literary Exploration.* Heyday Books, Berkeley.

Shinn, Charles H. 1896. *The Story of the Mine.* Appleton & Company, New York.

Shoup, Laurence H., and Randall T. Milliken. 1999. *Inigo of Rancho Posolmi: The Life and Times of a Mission Indian.* Ballena Press, Novato CA.

Shumsky, Neil L. 1972. "Tar Flat and Nob Hill: A Social History of Industrial San Francisco during the 1870s." Doctoral dissertation (History), University of California, Berkeley.

Silliman, Steven W. 2004. *Lost Laborers in Colonial California: Native Americans and the Archaeology of Rancho Petaluma.* The University of Arizona Press, Tucson.

Silverstein, Michael. 1978. "Yokuts: Introduction." In *Handbook of North American Indians, Vol. 8: California.* Ed. Robert F. Heizer. Smithsonian Institution, Washington DC.

Smith, Grant H. 1943. "The History of the Comstock Lode 1850–1920." *Geology and Mining Series,* University of Nevada Bulletin Vol. 37 (3).

Social Manual for San Francisco and Oakland ..., A. 1884. The City Publishing Company, San Francisco.

Stone, Irving. 1956. *Men to Match My Mountains.* Doubleday & Co., New York.

Street, Richard S. 2004. *Beasts of the Field: A Narrative History of California Farmworkers, 1769–1913.* Stanford University Press, Stanford.

Streeter, William A. [1878] 1939. "Recollections of Historical Events in California, 1843–1878." *California Historical Society Quarterly* 18(2):157–179.

Sullivan, Maurice S. 1936 *Jedediah Smith: Trader and Trail Breaker.* Press of the Pioneers, New York.

Swinton, John. 1894. *Striking for Life: Labor's Side of the Labor Question.* Keller, Phildelphia.

Tays, George. 1936. *Fort Gunnybags, Registered Landmark #90.* California Department of Natural Resources, Berkeley.

Tevis, Lloyd. 1881. *California: An Address of Mr. Lloyd Tevis ... Before the American Bankers' Association ...* On File, Bancroft Library, University of California, Berkeley.

Thompson and West. 1876. *Historical Atlas of Santa Clara County, California.* Thompson and West, San Jose.

Tibesar, Antonine, ed. 1955. *Writings of Junipero Serra,* Vol. 1. Academy of American Franciscan History, Washington, D.C.

Tilton, Cecil G. 1935. *William Chapman Ralston, Courageous Builder.* Christopher Publishing House, Boston.

Treadwell, Edward F. 1931. *The Cattle King.* The MacMillan Company. New York.

Trusk, Robert J. 1960. "Sources of Capital of Early California Manufacturers, 1850–1880." Doctoral dissertation (Economics), University of Illinois, Champaign.

Tutorow, Norman E. 1971. *Leland Stanford: Man of Many Careers.* Pacific Coast Publishers. Menlo Park.

Twain, Mark. 1872. "Roughing It." In Michael Kowalewski, 1997. *Gold Rush : A Literary Exploration.* Heyday Books, Berkeley.

United States Census Bureau. 1860. *Manuscript Population Census for San Francisco,* on file, Bancroft Library, University of California, Berkeley.

————. 1864. *Population of the United States in 1860 ...* Government Printing Office, Washington DC.

————. 1865. *Census of Manufacturers ... 1860* Government Printing Office, Washington DC.

————. 1870. *Population Census for San Francisco.* Manuscript on file, Bancroft Library, University of California, Berkeley.

————. 1872a. *The Statistics of Wealth and Industry of the United States ... 1870.* Vol. 3 Government Printing Office, Washington DC.

————. 1872b. *The Statistics of the Population of the United States ... 1870.* Vol. 1. Government Printing Office, Washington DC.

————. 1883a. *Statistics of the Population of the United States ... 1880.* Vol. 1. Government Printing Office, Washington DC.

————. 1883b. *Census of Manufacturers,* Vol. 2. Government Printing Office, Washington DC.

————. 1883c. *Report on Agencies of Transportation.* Government Printing Office, Washington DC.

————. 1883d. *Report on the Productions of Agriculture.* Government Printing Office, Washington DC.

————. 1886. *Report on the Statistics of Wages in Manufacturing Industries ...* Government Printing Office, Washington DC.

————. 1895a. *Report on Population of the United States ... 1890 Part I.* Government Printing Office, Washington DC.

————. 1895b. *Report on Population of the United States ... 1890 Part II.* Government Printing Office, Washington DC.

————. 1895c. *Report on Manufacturing Industries of the United States ... 1890 Part I.* Government Printing Office, Washington DC.

————. 1895d. *Report on the Statistics of Agriculture of the United States ... 1890.* Government Printing Office, Washington DC.

————. 1901. *Census Reports: Population ... 1900 Part I.* Government Printing Office, Washington DC.

————. 1902a. *Census Reports: Manufactures ... 1900 Part II.* Government Printing Office, Washington DC.

————. 1902b. *Census Reports: Agriculture ... 1900 Part I.* Government Printing Office, Washington DC.

————. 1904. *Special Reports: Occupations at the Twelfth Census.* Government Printing Office, Washington DC.

Walker, H.D. 1910. *Walker's Manual of California Securities and Directory of Directors.* H. D. Walker, San Francisco.

Wallace, William J. 1978. "Northern Valley Yokuts." In *California, Vol. 8 of Handbook of North American Indians.* Ed. Robert F. Heizer. Smithsonian Institution, Washington DC.

Webb, Edith B. 1952. *Indian Life at the Old Missions.* University of Nebraska Press, Lincoln.

Weeks, Jos. D. 1884. *Report on Trades Societies in the United States.* U.S. Census Bureau, Washington DC.

Wegars, Priscilla, ed. 1993. *Hidden Heritage: Historical Archaeology of the Overseas Chinese.* Baywood Publishing Company, Amityville, New York.

Wilson, Neill C. 1964. *400 California Street: The Story of the Bank of California.* Bank of California, San Francisco.

Wright, Doris Marion. 1941. "The Making of Cosmopolitan California: An Analysis of Immigration 1848–1870." *California Historical Society Quarterly* 20:65–79.

INDEX

Astoria, OR 476
Atwood, Melville 144
Auction Lunch Saloon 233, 238

B

Babcock, William F. 146, 149, 333, 343
Baker, Col. E. D. 111
Bakersfield, CA 439, 455
Baldwin, Barry 400
Baldwin, E. J. ("Lucky") 236, 239, 241, 243, 252
Baltimore 308
Bancroft, George 66
Bancroft, Hubert Howe 82, 95, 302
Bandini, Juan 49
Bank Crowd 184, 211, 230
Banker, E. P. 156
bank failure 97, 238
Bank of California 172, 175, 177, 179, 180, 181, 182, 183, 184, 188, 189, 190, 193, 208, 209, 210, 211, 212, 217, 220, 222, 230, 234, 235, 241, 243, 244, 252, 253, 296, 297, 299, 333, 335, 336, 344, 345, 352, 353, 354, 432
bankruptcy 172, 257
Bard, Thomas 484
Baring Brothers 244
Barrollet, Henry 338
Barron and Forbes 139
Barron & Company 180
Barron, J. 338
Barron, William E. 180
Barth, Gunther 267
Bear Flag Revolt 66

Beaumont, Lord 346, 348
Belcher Mine 234
Bell, Horace 84
Bell, Thomas 146, 179, 239, 297, 338
Belmont, CA 336
Bennett, H. C. 271
Bennett, J.W. 300
Bensley Water Company 170
Berger, Henry 356
Big Four 118, 192, 211, 216, 221, 225, 238, 239, 240, 241, 242, 286, 289, 321, 342, 343, 367, 375
Billion Dollar Steel Trust 454
blacklist 399, 420, 426
Blair, C. F. 459
Blanding, Mrs. Gordon 347
Blanding, William 146
Bluxome, Isaac, Jr. 115, 333
Bolton, Jas. R. 157
Booth, Newton 221, 301
Borel, Alfred 210, 211
Boston 477
Bowie, Augustus J. 157
boycott 476, 479
  newspaper 415, 482
Breckenridge, John C. 343
Brewer, William H. 263
Brittan, J. W. 116
Broderick, David 89, 106, 107, 121, 150
Brotherhood of Locomotive Engineers 394, 419
Brotherhood of Locomotive Firemen 395
Brown, John 152
Buchanan, James 66, 127

Buckley, Christopher 368
Building and Trade Council of
   Chicago 418
Building Trades Council 433
Bull, Alpheus 146
Burlingame Treaty 258, 266,
   291
Business Man's Revolution 119
Butte County 134
Butte, Montana 476
Butterworth, Samuel 181, 193
Byrne, James 299

C

Calaveras County 134, 380,
   387, 390
California Board of
   Manufacturers and Employers
   393
California Dry Dock Company
   243, 245
California Fruit Canners
   Association 431
California Labor and
   Employment Exchange 281
California Metallurgical Works
   140
California Miners' Association
   338
California Mutual Life Insurance
   Company 181
California Mutual Marine
   Insurance Company 180, 181,
   210
California Redwood Company
   354
California State Telegraph
   Company 175, 178, 182, 189

California Steam Navigation
   Company 115, 117, 121, 142,
   169, 175, 178, 179, 180, 181,
   182, 185, 190, 212, 338
California Street Railroad 243
California Telegraph Company
   178
California Trust Company 338
California Wine Association 431
Californios 59, 68, 75, 197, 292
   as ruling class 42, 95
   discrimination against 87, 90,
      93
   expropriation of mission
      properties 38, 46, 49
   rebellion of 48
Callahan, Peter 468
capitalism
   development of 40, 72, 98,
      129, 139, 143, 192, 207,
      215
   racial equality and 154, 188
   transition from merchant to
      industrial 103, 106, 129,
      157
Capitol Gas Company 243
Carpentier, Horace W. 182,
   189, 244
Carquinez Strait 22, 28
Carrigan, Andrew 432
Carrillo, Carlos 43, 44
Carrillo, Don Jose' Antonio 41
Carrillo, Jose Antonio 42, 46
Carr, William B. 226, 381
Carson, NV 147, 408
Casey, James P. 112, 120
Casey, Michael 428, 434, 438,
   445, 449, 453

524